Democracy and Post-Communism

The collapse of communism was widely heralded as the dawn of democracy across Eastern Europe and the former Soviet Union. However, the political outcome has been much less uniform. The post-communist states have developed political systems ranging from democracy to dictatorship.

Using examples and empirical data collected from twenty-six former communist states, Graeme Gill provides a detailed comparative analysis of the core issues of regime change, the creation of civil society, economic reform and the changing nature of post-communism. Within these individual cases, it becomes clear that political outcomes have not been arbitrary, but directly reflect the circumstances surrounding the birth of independence.

Students of comparative politics, international relations, and Russian and post-Soviet studies will find this book compelling reading.

Graeme Gill is Professor of Government and Public Administration at the University of Sydney, Australia. He has held visiting positions in Moscow, St Petersburg, London, Oxford, Washington, Honolulu and Florence. He has published widely on Soviet and Russian politics, titles including *Stalinism* (1990, 1998), *Peasants and Government in the Russian Revolution* (1979), *The Rules of the Communist Party of the Soviet Union* (1988), *The Origins of the Stalinist Political System* (1990), *Russia's Stillborn Democracy?: From Gorbachev to Yeltsin* (with Roger Markwick, 2000) and *The Dynamics of Democratization: Elites, Civil Society and the Transition Process* (2000).

Routledge Research in Comparative Politics

1 Democracy and Post-Communism
Political change in the post-communist world
Graeme Gill

Democracy and Post-Communism

Political change in the post-communist world

Graeme Gill

London and New York

First published 2002
by Routledge
11 New Fetter Lane, London EC4P 4EE

Simultaneously published in the USA and Canada
by Routledge
29 West 35th Street, New York, NY 10001

Transferred to Digital Printing 2003

Routledge is an imprint of the Taylor & Francis Group

© 2002 Graeme Gill

Typeset in Times by
HWA Text and Data Management, Tunbridge Wells
Printed and bound in Great Britain by
Intype London Ltd

All rights reserved. No part of this book may be reprinted or reproduced
or utilised in any form or by any electronic, mechanical, or other means,
now known or hereafter invented, including photocopying and recording,
or in any information storage or retrieval system, without permission in
writing from the publishers.

British Library Cataloguing in Publication Data
A catalogue record for this book is available from the British Library

Library of Congress Cataloging in Publication Data
Gill, Graeme J.
    Democracy and post-communism: political change in the post-
communist world / Graeme Gill
    p. cm.
    Includes bibliographical references and index.
        1. Europe, Eastern–Politics and government–1989– 2. Former
Soviet republics–Politics and government   3. Post-communism–
Europe, Eastern.   4. Post-communism–Former Soviet
republics.   5. Democracy, Europe, Eastern.   6. Democracy–
Former Soviet republics.   I. Title.

JN96.A58 G54 2002
320.947–dc21   2001049227

ISBN 0–415–27205–X

Contents

List of tables vii
Preface ix
List of abbreviations xi

1 A democratic post-communism? 1
2 Negotiating regime change 15
3 Civil society and the onset of negotiations 83
4 Creating civil society? 111
5 Paths to democracy? 174
6 Conclusion: democracy and post-communism 194

Notes 204
Bibliography 244
Index 264

Tables

1.1	Elections: democracies	7
1.2	Protection of rights: democracies	7
1.3	Elections: façade democracies	8
1.4	Protection of rights: façade democracies	9
1.5	Elections: non-democracies.	10
1.6	Protection of rights: non-democracies	10
2.1	Patterns of development and regime types	82
4.1	Freedom of the media	114
4.2	Non-government organisations	115
4.3	Levels of participation in post-communist national elections	117
4.4	Communist system of government, positive rating	119
4.5	Communist system of government, negative rating	119
4.6	Present system of government, positive rating	119
4.7	Present system of government, negative rating	119
4.8	Future system of government, positive rating	120
4.9	Future system of government, negative rating	120
4.10	Trust in institutions	121
4.11	Dates of commencement of privatisation programs	124
4.12	Private sector output of GDP, in %	125
4.13	Privatisation of large enterprises	126
4.14	Privatisation of small enterprises	126
4.15	Beneficiaries of primary mode of privatisation of large enterprises	127
4.16	Party system data for Poland and Hungary	134
4.17	Party system data for Bulgaria and Albania	138
4.18	Shares of votes for BSP/UDF	140
4.19	Shares of votes for SPA/DPA	140
4.20	Party system data for the Czech Republic and Slovakia	141
4.21	Share of votes in Slovakia	144
4.22	Party system data for Latvia, Lithuania, Estonia, Moldova, Georgia, Armenia and Croatia	145
4.23	Party system data for Russia, Ukraine, Slovenia and Macedonia	153
4.24	Party system data for Romania, Serbia and Montenegro	157
4.25	Ethnic composition in % in 1989	162

4.26 Political orientations in Estonia 166
4.27 Political orientations in Latvia 166
5.1 First year of economic growth (when change in the GDP ceased to be in the negative) 176
5.2 Price rises of consumer goods: year they dropped to double figures 176
5.3 Institutional forms and types of political systems 180

Preface

This book looks at the most momentous political change in the international community since the end of the second world war. The transformation of what formerly had been called the communist bloc brought about a wholesale restructuring not just of the lives of many of the citizens of the countries undergoing it, but of the structure and processes of world politics. But this transformation has not been a simple process, nor has it taken the same form in all states. Some are entering the twenty-first century as democracies while others, the majority, have adopted political forms which fail the democratic test. With a broadly similar time of starting and, at least in terms of formal political institutions, point of departure, the diversity of political outcomes has been a surprise for many. This book attempts to explain this divergence of political trajectory. The substantive analysis goes up until the end of 2000, although in one case the analysis has been extended into 2001.

Many debts, both institutional and personal, have been incurred whilst working on this book. I was fortunate in enjoying visiting attachments in the Robert Schuman Centre for Advanced Studies in the European University Institute in Florence, St Antony's College, Oxford, and the Institute of World Economy and International Relations, Moscow. In Sydney, the former Department of Government and Public Administration, now part of the School of Economics and Political Science, has been a stimulating place to work. In particular, I would like to single out Rod Tiffen, Roger Markwick, Linda Weiss and Tim Rowse, all of whom made comments at various times which dissuaded me from barren paths. For research assistance, I would like to thank especially John Brookfield who ferreted out much of use for the argument, and Aleksei Popyrin. And finally, to Heather, without whom this book could never have been completed.

Abbreviations

11OC	11 October Bloc (Georgia)
ADP	Agrarian Democratic Party (Romania)
ADP	Authentic Democratic Party (also known as Saimnieks) (Latvia)
AFD	Alliance of Free Democrats (Hungary)
AGUR	All-Georgian Union of Revival
AP	Agrarian Party (Russia)
APF	Azeri Popular Front
AR	Association for the Republic (Czech Republic)
ARF	Alliance of Reform Forces (Macedonia)
ARF	Armenian Revolutionary Federation
AWS	Association of Workers of Slovakia
AWS	Solidarity Electoral Alliance (Poland)
AYD	Alliance of Young Democrats (Fidesz) (Hungary)
BANU	Bulgarian Agrarian National Union
BBB	Bulgarian Business Bloc
BCP	Bulgarian Communist Party
BDPM	Bloc for a Democratic and Prosperous Moldova
BE	Better Estonia
BEAB	Electoral Bloc Braghis Alliance (Moldova)
BSP	Bulgarian Socialist Party
CA	Centre Alliance (Poland)
CC	Common Choice (Slovakia)
CDA	Civic Democratic Alliance (Czech Republic)
CDC	Croatian Democratic Community
CDM	Christian Democratic Movement (Slovakia)
CDP	Christian Democratic Party (Lithuania)
CDP	Christian Democratic Party (Slovenia)
CDP	Civic Democratic Party (Czech Republic)
CDPFA	Christian Democratic Popular Front Alliance (Moldova)
CDPP	Christian Democratic Peoples Party (Hungary)
CDU	Christian Democratic Union (Czech Republic)
CDU-PP	Christian Democratic Union-People's Party (Czech Republic)
CF	Civic Forum (Czech Republic)

xii *Abbreviations*

CFP	Croatian Farmers' Party
CIP	Confederation for Independent Poland
CIS	Commonwealth of Independent States
CL	Country of Law (Armenia)
CM	Centre Movement (Lithuania)
CP	Communist Party (Armenia)
CPBM	Communist Party of Bohemia and Moravia
CPM	Communist Party of Moldova
CPP	Country People's Party (Estonia)
CPP	Croatian People's Party
CPR	Croatian Party of Rights
CPRF	Communist Party of the Russian Federation
CPRU	Coalition Party and Rural Union (Estonia)
CPSU	Communist Party of the Soviet Union
CPU	Communist Party of Ukraine
CSLP	Croatian Social Liberal Party
CUG	Citizens Union of Georgia
DA	Democratic Alternative (Macedonia)
DAA	Democratic Alliance of Albanians (Montenegro)
DAPM	Democratic Agrarian Party of Moldova
DC	Democratic Convention (Romania)
DCM	Democratic Convention of Moldova (an alliance of five groups including CDPFA)
Demos	Democratic Opposition of Slovenia
Depos	Democratic Movement for Serbia
DF	Democratic Forum (Hungary)
DLA	Democratic Left Alliance (Poland)
DNSF	Democratic National Salvation Front (Romania)
DOS	Democratic Opposition of Serbia
DP	Democratic Party (also known as Saimnieks) (Latvia)
DP	Democratic Party (former NSF) (Romania)
DP	Democratic Party (Georgia)
DP	Democratic Party (Serbia)
DP	Democratic Party (Slovakia)
DPA	Democratic Party of Albania
DPMS	Democratic Party of Montenegrin Socialists
DPP	Democratic Party of Pensioners (Slovenia)
DPR	Democratic Party of Russia
DPS	Democratic Party of Slovenia
DSP	Democratic Social Pole of Romania
DUA	Democratic Union of Albanians (Montenegro)
DUS	Democratic Union of Slovakia
ECP	Estonian Centre Party (Estonia)
ENIP	Estonian National Independence Party
ERM	Equal Rights Movement (Latvia)

ERP	Estonian Reform Party
ERU	Estonian Rural Union
FBL	For a Better Life (Montenegro)
FFF	For Fatherland and Freedom (Latvia)
Fidesz	Alliance of Young Democrats (Hungary)
FP	Fourth Power (Estonia)
FRY	Federal Republic of Yugoslavia
FSU	Former Soviet Union
FU	Fatherland Union (Estonia)
FU	Farmer's Union (Latvia)
FU	Freedom Union (Poland)
G	Greens (Ukraine)
GDP	gross domestic product
GDR	German Democratic Republic
GNA	Grand National Assembly (Bulgaria)
GP	Green Party (Georgia)
GPS	Green Party in Slovakia
GRP	Greater Romania Party
GS	Greens of Slovenia
H	Homeland (began as Christian National Union)(Poland)
H	Hromada (All-Union Association) (Ukraine)
HC	Hungarian Coalition
HDF	Hungarian Democratic Forum
HDU	Hungarian Democratic Union
HJL	Hungarian Justice and Life
HSP	Hungarian Socialist Party
HU	Homeland Union (Lithuania)
HU-LCT	Homeland Union-Lithuanian Conservative Party
IMRO	Internal Macedonian Revolutionary Organisation
IS	Independent Smallholders (Hungary)
ISP	Independent Smallholders Party (Hungary)
KOR	Workers' Defence Committee (Poland)
LAM	Liberal Alliance of Montenegro
LCC	League of Communists of Croatia (which became the Party of Democratic Change)
LCD	Latvian Christian Democratic Party
LCM-PDR	League of Communists of Macedonia-Party of Democratic Reform
LD	Liberal Democracy (Slovenia)
LDC	Liberal Democratic Congress (Poland)
LDLP	Lithuanian Democratic Labour Party
LDP	Liberal Democratic Party (Macedonia)
LDPR	Liberal Democratic Party of Russia
LFU	Latvian Farmers' Union
LNC	Latvian National Conservative
LP	Liberal Party (Macedonia)

LSP	Latvian Socialist Party
LSU	Liberal Social Union (Czech Republic)
LU	Liberal Union (Lithuania)
LUP	Latvian Unity Party
LWA	Latvia's Way Alliance
M	Miasnutian (formerly RB) (Armenia)
M	Moderates (Estonia)
MDS	Movement for a Democratic Slovakia
MPF	Moldavian Popular Front
MRF	Movement for Rights and Freedoms (Bulgaria)
MRP	Movement for the Reconstruction of Poland
MSM	Moravian Silesian Movement
Musavat	Moslem Democratic Party (Azerbaijan)
ND	New Democracy
NDPG	National Democratic Party of Georgia
NDU	National Democratic Union (Armenia)
NEP	New Economic Policy
NF	National Front (Albania)
NGO	Non-Government Organisation
NHP	National Harmony Party (Latvia)
NLP	National Liberal Party (Romania)
NML	National Movement for Latvia
NP	New Party (Latvia)
NPRB	Non-Party Reform Bloc
NSCPP	New Slovenia Christian People's Party
NSF	National Salvation Front (Romania)
NUC	National Unity Coalition (Montenegro)
NU-SL	New Union-Social Liberal Party (Lithuania)
OEA	Opposition Electoral Alliance (Croatia)
OHE	Our Home is Estonia
OHR	Our Home is Russia
OSCE	Organisation for Security and Cooperation in Europe
OVR	Fatherland-All Russia
PA	Peasant Alliance (Poland)
PANM	Pan-Armenian National Movement
PAV	Public against Violence (Slovakia)
PB	Peace Bloc (Georgia)
PCU	Party of Civic Understanding (Slovakia)
PDF	Party of Democratic Forces (Moldova)
PDL	Party of the Democratic Left (Slovakia)
PDP	Party for Democratic Prosperity (Macedonia)
PDP	People's Democratic Party (Ukraine)
PDP	People's Democratic Party (Uzbekistan)
PDR	Party of Democratic Revival (Slovenia)
PFB	Popular Front of Belarus

PFE	Popular Front of Estonia
PFL	Popular Front of Latvia
P-IB	Peasants and Intellectuals Bloc (Moldova)
PLA	Albanian Party of Labour
PP	People's Party (Latvia)
PPCD	Christian Democratic People's Party (Moldova)
PPM	Peoples Party of Montenegro
PPP	Polish Peasants' Party
PPT	People's Party of Tajikistan
PPU	Peasants Party of Ukraine
PRES	Party of Russian Unity and Accord
PSP	Progressive Socialist Party (Ukraine)
PSU	Party of Serbian Unity
PSY	Party of Slovenian Youth
PUU	People's Unity Union (Kazakhstan)
PUWP	Polish United Workers Party
R	Rukh (Ukraine)
RB	Republican Bloc (Armenia)
RC	Russia's Choice
RNUP	Romanian National Unity Party
RPA	Republican Party of Albania
RU	Rights and Unity (Armenia)
Rukh	Peoples Movement of Ukraine
RWP	Right Wingers' Party (the Republican and Conservative People's Party) (Estonia)
S	Solidarity (Poland)
SD	Social Democratic Party (Albania)
SD	Social Democratic Party (Czech Republic)
SDA	Social Democratic Alliance (Latvia)
SDC	Slovak Democratic Coalition
SDC	Social Democratic Coalition (Lithuania)
SDP	Social Democratic Party (Croatia)
SDP	Social Democratic Party (Lithuania)
SDP	Social Democratic Party (Slovenia)
SDP	Social Democratic Party (Ukraine)
SDPR	Social Democracy Party of Romania (formerly DNSF)
SDPR	Social Democrats of the Polish Republic
SDU	Social Democratic Union (Romania)
SDUM	Social Democratic Union of Macedonia
SLP	Socialist Labour Party (Romania)
SNP	Slovak National Party
SNP	Slovenian National Party
SP	Socialist Party (Moldova)
SPA	Socialist Party of Albania
SPM	Socialist Party of Macedonia

SPP	Serbian People's Party
SPP	Slovenian People's Party
SPP	Socialist People's Party (Montenegro)
SPPB	Socialist and Peasant Parties Bloc (Ukraine)
SPS	Socialist Party of Serbia
SPS	Socialist Party of Slovenia
SPU	Socialist Party of Ukraine
SRM	Serbian Renewal Movement
SRP	Serbian Radical Party
SWP	Shamiram Women's Party (Armenia)
U	Unity (Russia)
UB	Unity Bloc (Georgia)
UDF	Union of Democratic Forces (Bulgaria)
UL	Union of Labour (Poland)
UL	United List (Latvia)
ULSD	United List of Social Democrats (Slovenia)
UNS	Union for National Salvation (Bulgaria)
UNSD	Union for National Self-Determinaton (Armenia)
UPHR	Unity Party of Human Rights (Albania)
UPP	United People's Party (formerly part of OHE)(Estonia)
URF	Union of Rightist Forces (Russia)
USSR	Union of Soviet Socialist Republics
UTO	United Tajik Opposition
VONS	Committee for the Defence of the Unjustly Prosecuted (Czechoslovakia)
WR	Women of Russia
Yab	Yabloko
Zhir	Zhirinovsky Bloc (Russia)

1 A democratic post-communism?

The fall of the Berlin wall in November 1989, a metaphor for the collapse of communism throughout Eastern Europe and the former Soviet Union (FSU) between 1989 and 1991, ushered in a new era in world politics. It removed the chief structural basis upon which post-war politics had rested, thereby transforming the nature of international relations. But as well as changing the geopolitical map and the dynamics of international politics, it also fundamentally transformed the conceptual map that had long underpinned our understanding of the world. With the collapse of communism, the major conceptual challenger to Western liberal democracy seemingly disappeared. This does not mean that all states now had political and economic systems like those in the capitalist West, but throughout most of the globe where such systems did not exist, the sets of politico-economic arrangements which were in place were not generally presented as viable long term alternatives to Western liberal democratic capitalism, or intent on creating societies different from those of the West. The range of dictatorial and authoritarian regimes still to be found in various parts of the world hardly represented the onset of a new civilisation. A partial exception to this generalisation can be found in parts of the Islamic world, where some states profess to rest upon religious principles and to be building a society based upon fundamentals very different to those of Western liberal capitalist democracy. But even here the aspiration to underpin society by strict observance of religious principles has generally been muted or, where it has been sought vigorously as in Iran, of relatively short-term duration. Secularism and industrialism have tended to impose their own logics. But in any case, given that the construction of a society based upon Islamic principles would require commitment to that religion generally within the populace, this has not appeared to be a realistic conceptual threat to Western liberal democracy, at least in the short term. Unlike communism, Islam does not rely upon the processes of Western capitalism to predict the fall of that civilisation and its own dominance.

An important part of the fall of communism and the perception that this removed a major challenge from Western liberal democratic capitalism has been the assumption that communist regimes would be replaced by democratic polities. This assumption, widely shared by scholars and public figures alike, has been reflected in the inclusion of the former communist regimes in the so-called 'third wave' of democratisation,[1] a sweep of political change across the globe beginning in southern Europe in the early–mid 1970s, extending into Latin America in the 1970s and 1980s, east Asia in the 1980s and the communist world in the 1980s and 1990s. The imagery of this metaphor of a wave suggested something that could not be stopped, a force that overwhelmed opposition and left in its wake a thriving democratic polity. But as a close analysis of virtually any of the cases of democratisation shows, the reality was far from this simple. Even when democracy was created, it was not on a basis like the scoured sand left by the retreating waves, but on the political institutions and cultural patterns that were the legacy of the old regime. Furthermore, not all cases of regime change resulted in a democratic outcome. In some cases, the regimes emerging from this process of political change have not been democracies, despite in many cases the outward appearance of democratic forms. This is particularly true of many of the former communist countries. In the mid-1980s, there were nine states in the Eastern Europe-Soviet Union region; ten years later, there were 27. Four had disappeared: the GDR had been swallowed up by West Germany while the Soviet Union, Yugoslavia and Czechoslovakia had broken up and their constituent republics had become independent states. Only Poland, Hungary, Bulgaria, Romania and Albania remained in the geographical shape they had in the mid-1980s. Of the 26 countries that are the subject of this study,[2] by the end of the 1990s some had achieved stable democratic political systems, others had not. This book seeks to explain these different political trajectories.

An important issue is the basis upon which judgements about the democratic nature or otherwise of the post-communist states may rest. Two principal criteria are used to evaluate the democratic nature of the political system:[3]

1 The system must meet the minimal procedural criteria for democracy. These criteria revolve around free and fair regular contested elections. This means that elections through which the most important political offices in the land are filled are held on a regular basis and in such a way that all who wish to compete for office are able to do so on an equal basis,[4] and all who wish to participate may do so equally and without fear. Hence there must be a secret ballot and voters must face a realistic choice. This latter requirement implies the existence of political parties that oppose the government and are able to compete effectively in the political sphere. The votes must be counted fairly, and the outcome of the election must be reflected in the identity of the government. Furthermore, it is important that the rules whereby politics are played out are followed by political actors in between the elections, so that the government put into power by the voters is able to carry out the policies for which it has gained a mandate.
2 There must be widespread observance of political and civil rights. The basic rights of free speech, association, belief and (within limits) action, must be observed within society and without prescriptive exclusion. Access to these rights must not be denied to individuals or groups on a systematic basis, but must be enjoyed by all who dwell within the state's borders. Clearly there are times when some such rights may have to be restricted temporarily, such as

during times of national security, but these must be extraordinary circumstances. Generally the observance of rights, and the restriction of government by such rights, is central to a democratic polity.

These two criteria, procedural minima and observance of rights,[5] are both essential to the characterisation of a political system as democratic. A system cannot be adjudged to be democratic if only one of these criteria is present; both must exist for democracy to apply.

Two principal objections may be advanced to this way of proceeding. First, it takes no account of the way in which a procedural definition of democracy misses the way in which the structure of economic power in the society undercuts the formal political institutions by delivering greater power to those with economic resources than those without. This view, often presented in terms of the class analysis of society, has considerable merit. Clearly, the distribution of economic resources shapes access to effective power in any society, and the exercise of those resources can ensure that regardless of what form the political institutions take, democracy can be undercut. Although governments can moderate it, in any society based upon the private ownership of property, inequality of resources is inevitable. And so too, therefore, is inequality of potential power and access. In this sense it is taken as axiomatic that there will be inequality stemming from economic position and power in all democracies, including those newly emergent from communism. If we were seeking to establish how closely the post-communist states approached an ideal form of democracy, this question of private economic resources would be relevant. However we are interested in the extent to which the new systems approach democracy as it is realised elsewhere rather than as an ideal type. With Western states being recognised as liberal democracies regardless of the unequal distribution of wealth within them, it is legitimate to exclude this dimension of the question from our analysis.

Second, it involves an excessively narrow conception of democracy by excluding from it all notion of social or welfarist rights. In this sense, it is ideological. It is true that the conception of democracy being used here excludes such social rights from the analysis, but it is not particularly useful to criticise it for being ideological. Just as a conception of democracy which omits social rights may be called ideological, so too can the conception which includes such rights. The question is not whether a particular conception is ideological or not (because in a very real sense, all conceptions are ideological), but how useful it is. And in studying the post-communist states, a conception which included social rights (such as rights to employment, housing and a range of welfare benefits) is not particularly useful. This is mainly because the post-communist states have not had economies which have been performing in such a way as to make the realisation of these social rights realistic. Governments have not been able to sustain an effective social welfare net, with the result that if such considerations were included in the conception of democracy, all of these states would be ruled out by definition. This would not be a useful outcome. Moreover, even in the Western liberal democracies social rights have been wound back over the last two decades, so that inclusion of such rights in the conception of democracy being applied to the post-communist states would mean applying criteria that are not evident in the comparators to the West.

Analysis of the post-communist states on the basis of the two criteria outlined above shows that those states fall into three broad categories:

1 *Democracies*. These are states which exhibit both the procedural minima for democracy and widespread observance of civil and political rights.
2 *Façade democracies*.[6] These are states which usually exhibit at least some of the procedural minima for democracy and there is some observance of political and civil rights, but this latter is usually denied to a section of the population, or sometimes more generally for a brief period of time, or there are limits to the rights the state observes.
3 *Non-democracies*. These are states in which the procedural minima are lacking and there is at best limited observance of civil and political rights.

These categories need to be further refined into regime types. The term 'democracy' is widely recognised as a regime type in itself, and therefore will not be further qualified. However the other two categories, 'façade democracy' and 'non-democracy', are umbrella designations under which a number of regime types may shelter. Categorisations of authoritarian regimes are legion,[7] but in order to provide a parsimonious schema of explanation, only four types will be identified.[8]

a *Ethnic democracy*, where the institutional forms of democracy are present and there is widespread observance of civil and political rights, but a group in the society is excluded from full involvement on the grounds of their ethnic identity.
b *Plebiscitary democracy*, where the institutional forms of democracy are present, and both president and parliament claim a popular mandate and a share of power. The president uses the power of the office and a direct appeal to the populace to sideline and marginalise the parliament and any opposition forces, and thereby expand his personal power. The parliament retains a political role and some power but is significantly diminished. There may be some respect for the observance of rights.
c *Sultanism*, where the president is virtually unconstrained by opposition forces or the parliament, and elections and the parliament are a figleaf covering personal rule. Such rule may extend to a form of patrimonialism whereby the president uses the state and its resources as his own property. There are serious deficiencies in the protection of rights.[9]
d *Oligarchy*, where power is usually shared between groups in a balance that is not stable. The formal apparatus of electoral democracy may be in place and it may be the means of bringing about changes of leadership, but it is often subject to manipulation and opposition may be intimidated. There is little popular control, except perhaps at elections, and the observance of rights is deficient. Oligarchies may in turn be divided into open and closed oligarchies.

In the former, changes in the identity of state leaders (president or government) has been brought about through the electoral process, thereby building in a sense of at least episodic accountability even if this is not realised between elections. In the latter, changes in personnel are engineered within the oligarchy itself with elections having little effect upon the identity or structure of the rulers.

Of these four regime types, sultanist regimes and closed oligarchies are clearly non-democratic while open oligarchies and ethnic democracies are façade democracies. Plebiscitary democracies may be either façade democracies or non-democracies depending upon the details of their *modus operandi*.

It is important to recognise that the borders between these categories are neither firm nor clearly defined, and that this is not a static schema. The post-communist countries are following political trajectories, which means that they are developing and over a period of time could, in principle, move between these different categories. Indeed, there have clearly been movements in both a democratic and a non-democratic direction since the fall of the communist regimes. Recognition of this is a matter of judgement; whether an election is free and fair or is flawed cannot always be measured with any precision. Nevertheless we can make judgements about it. Similarly, the placement of a country in one or other of the categories is also a matter of judgement. The central criterion here for recognition as a democracy is that the two criteria noted above (procedural minima and respect for rights) are present over the course of at least two election cycles. The principle of two elections has been widely used as a yardstick for establishing the consolidation of democracy,[10] and although it is a rough measure, it seems to have gained general assent.

Characterisation of a country as a democracy, a façade democracy or a non-democracy therefore rests upon judgements about the procedural minima for democracy and the respect for political rights and civil liberties. While the former clearly embraces all of the institutional structures of the political system, a focus upon the nature of elections will provide a useful way of getting at this issue without being overwhelmed by the details of institutional complexity in the range of countries under review. The presence of free and fair elections will not ensure that other institutional structures function in a democratic fashion, but such structures are unlikely to be democratic if elections are not free and fair. Consequently if elections are considered free and fair by independent observers, this is a good indication that the procedural minima for democracy are being met. The second criterion, respect for political rights and civil liberties, is more difficult to evaluate, both because of the range of activity that must be embraced and because of the nature of rights and liberties themselves. Nevertheless over the years, Freedom House has developed a set of indices of the observance of rights and liberties which have been applied internationally to produce a ranking of countries in terms of their freedom. Such rankings are based upon judgements about the degree to which a defined list of rights and freedoms are enjoyed in the countries under review.[11] Although such surveys are vulnerable to some variance resulting from their reliance upon subjective judgements of individual country observers and may present a sense of false precision owing to the allocation of numbers to countries' performance, these surveys (and this methodology) have attained considerable respect and authority among those interested in such issues. They are reliable indicators of the state of political rights and civil liberties, and have been used by scholars to distinguish between political systems in the post-communist world.[12] Using these two criteria, the nature of elections and the state of political rights and civil liberties, we can distinguish between the three broad categories of post-communist regime types. To break this distinction down further into the narrower regime types noted above (ethnic democracy, plebiscitary democracy, sultanism and oligarchy), we will need to look further than these criteria, at the way the systems actually function. This will be done in Chapter Two. The categorisation of regime types which follows relates to the location of each country throughout much of the 1990s. Changes which occur in the category to which a country belongs during the 1990s will be discussed later in the book.

Democracies

Six of the post-communist countries qualify as democracies under the provisions outlined above. Table 1.1 provides details of the evaluations given by observers of the elections held in each of the countries that have been classified as democracies. The evaluations are of legislative and, where relevant, presidential elections.

Turning to the protection of political rights and civil liberties, according to Freedom House,[19] on a scale of 1–7 with 1 the highest level of achievement and 7 the lowest,[20] the countries classed as democracies performed as shown in Table 1.2.

In the democracies, the electoral system has consistently met the criteria of fairness and freedom applied by independent observers, while the recognition of rights and liberties has been at a high level, even if in some cases it took a year or so to eliminate the communist legacy.

Façade democracies

A different pattern from that of the democracies is evident in the table on protection of rights (Table 1.3 and Table 1.4), where the levels of achievement are generally lower than in the democracies. While Estonia and Latvia appear as anomalies because of their good ratings in terms both of electoral performance and rights protection, their location is explained below.

Most of the façade democracies combine a record of elections in which there have been major irregularities with deficiencies in the protection of rights. The scale of electoral irregularities has ranged considerably. Instances have included intimidation of opposition candidates and local electoral officials, invalidation of votes for opposition candidates, multiple voting and open ballot boxes, manipulation of electoral boundaries and eligibility criteria, and biased media (details are to be found in the following chapter). Even when elections were deemed to be free and fair, there were often minor irregularities. In all of these countries,

Table 1.1 Elections: democracies

	1989	1990	1991	1992	1993	1994	1995	1996	1997	1998	1999	2000
Bulgaria[13]		F	F	F		F		F	F			
Czech Republic[14]		F		F				F				
Hungary[15]		F				F				F		
Lithuania[16]				F	F			F	F			F
Poland[17]	F	F			F		F		F			F
Slovenia[18]		F		F				F	F			F

Note: F denotes free and fair, N not free and fair

Table 1.2 Protection of rights: democracies

	1989–90	1990–1	1991–2	1992–3	1993–4	1994–5	1995–6	1996–7
Bulgaria								
Political	7	3	2	2	2	2	2	2
Civil	7	4	3	3	2	2	2	3
Czech Republic								
Political	6	2	2	2	1	1	1	1
Civil	6	2	2	2	2	2	2	2
Hungary								
Political	4	2	2	2	1	1	1	1
Civil	3	2	2	2	2	2	2	2
Lithuania								
Political			2	2	1	1	1	1
Civil			3	3	3	3	2	2
Poland								
Political	4	2	2	2	2	2	1	1
Civil	3	2	2	2	2	2	2	2
Slovenia								
Political			2	2	1	1	1	1
Civil			3	2	2	2	1	2

the apparatus of democratic elections was present, but some of the characteristics of the way in which it was made to function called into question its democratic credentials. Similarly with regard to the protection of rights and liberties, a legal structure formally guaranteed political rights and civil liberties, but these were infringed on a consistent and systematic basis, at least for a time.

Two further points should be made about these façade democracies. First, Estonia, Latvia and Slovakia may be considered marginal in the sense that all elections in these countries were considered to be free and fair, and the levels of infringement of rights and liberties, at least as measured by Freedom House, have been lower than in the other countries. However the citizenship policies of Estonia and Latvia, which consistently discriminated against non-indigenes, makes these countries ethnic democracies, while in Slovakia the policies pursued by the Meciar

8 A democractic post-communism?

Table 1.3 Elections: façade democracies

	1989	1990	1991	1992	1993	1994	1995	1996	1997	1998	1999	2000
Albania[21]		F	F					N	N			
Croatia[22]		F		F			N		N		F	F
												F
Estonia[23]				F			F			F		
Georgia[24]		N	F				F				N	F
Latvia[25]					F		F			F		
Macedonia.		F				N				F	N	
Moldova[26]		N				F	F		F			
Romania[27]	N		F					F				F
												F
Russia[28]					N		N	N			N	N
Slovakia[29]		F	F	F		F				F		
Ukraine[30]			F			F				F	N	

Note: F denotes free and fair, N not free and fair

regime, especially in the late 1990s, made that country an open oligarchy with discrimination directed toward its Hungarian minority. Second, if the post-communist history of these countries is seen in terms of a trajectory, both Romania and Moldova have become more democratic, with improvements in protection of rights and liberties and elections becoming free and fair, while Ukraine has gone in the opposite direction.

So in the façade democracies, a formal democratic structure has been undermined by patterns of practice which are at odds with democratic principles.

Non-democracies

In the non-democracies, the scale of electoral irregularities is even greater than in the façade democracies (see Table 1.5). In some cases, the situation is better seen as one in which the anti-democratic elements are structural and systemic rather than a function of the manipulation of political actors.

The record of the non-democracies on the recognition and protection of political rights and civil liberties is even worse than that of the façade democracies, as Table 1.6 shows.

It is clear that the non-democracies are deficient with regard to democracy in terms both of the procedural principles whereby they function and the protection they give to political rights and civil liberties. Although these countries may have competitive elections, and some like Turkmenistan do not, that competition is conducted on anything but a fair and equal footing. If opposition is not illegal, it is either effectively rendered non-existent or is encumbered by significant obstacles imposed by the regime. This may, as in Belarus, Kazakhstan, Turkmenistan and Uzbekistan, be at the behest of a single dominant leader or, as in Armenia, Azerbaijan, Montenegro in FRY and Tajikistan, by a ruling elite whose composition is determined autonomously from society as a whole. Opposition is suppressed, the constitution is used as a weapon, and extra-constitutional forces may be

Table 1.4 Protection of rights: façade democracies

	1989–90	1990–1	1991–2	1992–3	1993–4	1994–5	1995–6	1996–7
Albania								
Political			5	4	3	3	3	4
Civil			5	3	4	4	4	4
Croatia								
Political			3	4	4	4	4	4
Civil			4	4	4	4	4	4
Estonia								
Political			2	3	3	3	2	1
Civil			3	3	2	2	2	2
Georgia								
Political			6	4	5	5	4	4
Civil			5	5	5	5	5	4
Latvia								
Political			2	3	3	3	2	2
Civil			2	3	3	2	2	2
Macedonia								
Political				3	3	4	4	4
Civil				4	3	3	3	3
Moldova								
Political			5	5	5	4	4	3
Civil			4	5	5	4	4	4
Romania								
Political	7	6	5	4	4	4	4	2
Civil	7	5	5	4	4	3	3	3
Russia								
Political			3	3	3	3	3	3
Civil			3	4	4	4	4	4
Slovakia								
Political	6	2	2	2	3	2	2	2
Civil	6	2	2	2	4	3	3	4
Ukraine								
Political			3	3	4	3	3	3
Civil			3	3	4	4	4	4

mobilised to aid the cause of the rulers. Political rights and civil liberties may be expressed in the formal documents of the regime, but they are little observed. There has also been some evidence of movement along a trajectory among the non-democracies. Both Azerbaijan and Belarus have become less democratic during their decade of independence, while within the FRY, Montenegro moved in the opposite direction.

Post-communism, therefore, has been characterised by a variety of political forms. This not only raises the issue of what we mean by post-communism and whether this is a useful label to use when discussing these countries (this is discussed in the Conclusion), but how we are to explain these divergent trajectories. After all, these countries seemingly began from a common starting point. They all emerged from the Soviet regime or regimes which had been modelled upon the

10 A democractic post-communism?

Table 1.5 Elections: non-democracies

	1989	1990	1991	1992	1993	1994	1995	1996	1997	1998	1999	2000
Armenia[31]							N	N		N		
Azerb.[32]			F	N			N					N
Belarus[33]						F	N					N
FRY												F
Serbia[34]		N		N	N				N			F
Montenegro[35]	N		N					N	F	F		
Kazakhstan[36]		N				N	N				N	
Kyrgyz Republic[37]			N	N			N F*					N
Tajikistan[38]						N	N					N
Turkmenistan	N		N									
Uzbekistan		N				N				N		

Note: *In 1995 in the Kyrgyz Republic, international observers adjudged the legislative election to be subject to a variety of abuses, including ballot box stuffing, exaggeration of turnout figures, bribery, intimidation and interference with local officials, while the presidential election of the same year was said to be free and fair.

Table 1.6 Protection of rights: non-democracies

	1989–90	1990–1	1991–2	1992–3	1993–4	1994–5	1995–6	1996–7
Armenia								
Political			5	4	3	3	4	5
Civil			5	3	4	4	4	4
Azerbaijan								
Political			5	5	6	6	6	6
Civil			5	5	6	6	6	5
Belarus								
Political			4	4	5	4	5	6
Civil			4	3	4	4	5	6
FRY								
Political								
Civil								
Kazakhstan								
Political			5	5	6	6	6	6
Civil			4	5	4	5	5	5
Kyrgyz Republic								
Political			3	4	5	4	4	4
Civil			4	2	3	3	4	4
Tajikistan								
Political			5	6	7	7	7	7
Civil			5	7	7	7	7	7
Turkmenistan								
Political			6	7	7	7	7	7
Civil			5	6	7	7	7	7
Uzbekistan								
Political			6	6	7	7	7	7
Civil			5	6	7	7	7	6

Soviet prototype and which shared a number of important political characteristics. These include a highly penetrative political system, a totalist conception of politics and of public life which left no room for opposition or dissent, an economy which in structural terms was mobilisational and geared toward the achievement of the aims of the political leadership, and a culture impregnated by an ideology which sought to standardise both thought and action. In addition to this common legacy, the post-communist countries emerged at roughly the same time and were therefore subject to the same intellectual influences sweeping the world, in particular the hegemonic status of notions of democracy and liberal economics, and were to be found geographically contiguous to each other. These commonalities seemed to presage a common path into the future. But this has not been the reality.

Why different trajectories?

The divergent trajectories pursued by the post-communist countries also seem to fall into broad patterns. Geographically, the north-west is the general home of democracies, the south-east of non-democracies, and the zone in the middle of the façade democracies. Culturally, democracies seem to have occurred in Western Christian lands, façade democracies in Orthodox Christian countries, and non-democracies in Muslim lands. In terms of industrial development, the higher the level of such development, the greater the likelihood of democracy; the lower that level, the more likely non-democracy. Politically, democracy appears much less likely within the former Soviet Union than in Eastern Europe. Of course these patterns are not exact. For example, Latvia, Estonia and Belarus do not fit geographically or culturally, but the broad coincidence of political forms and these sorts of distinctions is striking. The question this raises is why the post-communist countries have followed different political trajectories.

This question has been addressed by scholars. Most studies of the region have been single country studies, lacking any comparative dimension. An exception to this has been Valerie Bunce. In a stimulating discussion, Bunce argues that there is a correlation between the political and economic trajectories taken by the post-communist states: democracy and capitalism coexist in supportive harmony producing stable politics and sustained economic growth following an initial decline, authoritarian politics coexists with a semi-socialist economy producing stable politics and reasonable economic performance, and a middle path followed by most states results in unstable politics and poor economic performance.[39] These trajectories are to be explained, for Bunce, by 'the socialist past and whether that past produced a rough consensus about the political and economic successor regimes to state socialism'.[40] Where such consensus existed, the result was equilibrium, of either the democratic capitalist or authoritarian semi-socialist type. Where such consensus was absent and there was 'a relatively equal distribution of economic and political resources among preference "camps"', the result was political instability and poor economic performance. Important here was the founding election. Where this led to the clear victory of the opposition (perhaps in alliance with reform communists), democratisation and the transition to capitalism

12   *A democractic post-communism?*

occurred together as a package. Where the election led to the victory of the ex-communists because of the weakness of the opposition, there was a rejection of democracy and economic reform. Where there was no clear victory in the election, democratisation and economic reform became unbundled, with some regimes pursuing one but not the other or compromising on both.[41] Bunce's analysis highlights a crucial element in the explanation of the different political trajectories, but as it stands it is a blunt instrument.

Bunce's analysis has a number of shortcomings.

1 The central explanatory variable in Bunce's analysis is consensus. The presence or absence of consensus and the type of consensus (pro-democratic capitalist or anti-democratic capitalist) is determined by the outcome of the first election. But this outcome, which is clearly crucial to her analysis, is not explained. Such explanation would require looking at the constellation of political actors that was emerging at the time of the fall of communism. The identity of these political actors and their outlooks is what both determines whether consensus emerges or not and shapes the initial electoral contest, and is therefore the primary causal factor. Their emergence must be explained.
2 The notion of consensus as Bunce uses it is problematic.[42] If consensus is simply taken to mean a preference for moving the country in a democratic direction or retaining as much of the old structure as possible, this distinction is clearly relevant. But it is not clear that to talk in terms of consensus is particularly useful. The politics of these countries has often been characterised by anything but consensus, even when there has been general agreement about the broad direction in which the country should go. For example, the Polish case, is usually identified as the exemplar of the democracy-capitalism nexus. However immediately following the 1989 election, political elites were divided over the path to the future, and even when the communists were removed from the scene there was considerable conflict among the remaining Solidarity-based elite over the forms the political structure should take, and more specifically over the powers of the presidency *vis-à-vis* the legislature. Given that this distinction between presidential and parliamentary democracy is considered important for a democratic outcome,[43] differences over this within the elite must call into question the view of the existence of broad consensus. The presence of similar debates elsewhere, including in Hungary and the then Czechoslovakia, suggests that care must be taken in accepting the argument cast in terms of consensus.
3 Significant emphasis is placed upon the first competitive, 'foundation', election. The problem is, how do we identify the foundation election? Were the republican elections that took place in the Soviet republics in 1990 the foundation elections, or were they the first elections after the collapse of Soviet power? Or in Romania, was the election of 1990 or that of 1996 (when the communist successors were thrown out) the foundation election? And in any case, what was crucial to the structuring of the first post-communist election was the constellation of forces that produced that election. The election was

not something that emerged of its own accord. It was constructed and shaped by the dominant political forces at the time of the communist regime's fall, and it cannot be understood in isolation from those forces. Bunce's identification of the pattern and content of public protest under socialism as the key determinant of the elections[44] is not a sufficient explanation because, as will be shown below, such protest was not the only force shaping the identity of important political actors at the time of the fall of communism.

4 The close association Bunce draws between political form and economic reform obscures the distinction between democratic transition and consolidation. While economic reform may help in the long-term consolidation of democracy, it cannot explain that which Bunce sees as fundamental to the future trajectory, the outcome of the first competitive election.

Bunce's analysis thus needs to explain the initial disposition of political forces at the time of the fall of communism[45] if it is to tell us why countries embarked upon (as opposed to remained on) particular political trajectories.

Bunce's analysis is linked to that of M. Steven Fish by the emphasis upon founding elections and economic reform.[46] Fish seeks to explain the different political trajectories of the post-communist regimes in terms of three core explanatory variables.

a) The development of autonomous societal organisation, seen in terms of the strength, density and differentiation of political parties and the organisation of civil society more generally. The highest achievers in democratisation have the best developed party systems and civil society infrastructures. Fish is adamant that this is a cause, not an effect, of democratisation.[47]

b) The extent to which the constitution concentrates power: the greater the concentration, the less democratisation. This is not a distinction between presidentialism and parliamentarism, but rather the presence or absence of 'super-executivism'. The presence of a very powerful executive figure, be that president or prime minister, who can sideline the legislature, will thereby aid the concentration of power and the marginalisation of political parties, and thereby weaken democratisation.[48]

c) The extent of economic reform: the greater the economic reform, the greater the democratisation. Fish argues that the direction of causality between these two factors is unclear, but that the chief determinant of the extent of economic reform is 'the outcome of the initial election held at the beginning of transitions', 'the early postcommunist elections – that shaped the composition of the governments that set the course of economic policy change'.[49]

Like Bunce, Fish's analysis is a cogent explanation of some of the factors which have led to the consolidation of democracy and its absence in the post-communist countries, but it does not provide an explanation of the transition to democratic political forms in the first place. All three of the factors Fish discusses are raised in the context of the period following the fall of communism. Both constitutional centralisation and economic reform are conceived explicitly in terms of post-communist phenomena, respectively the constitution and the first post-communist election (although there is ambiguity in this – see below), while the development of societal organisation is discussed with reference to the post-communist period. But as with Bunce, what is important but omitted is the constellation of political forces which pushes the country onto the democratic path in the first place, which shapes the initial election and which makes decisions about the disposition of power. These forces can only be understood in terms of the circumstances of the fall of the old regime, and although such an analysis must take into account the development of autonomous societal forces of the sort Fish recognises (see Chapters 2 and 3), their development prior to the fall of communism is crucial to an understanding of their role at the time of communism's fall.

Fish's analysis also highlights the ambiguity of the notion of a founding election. He sees economic reform as related to the outcome of this election, describing this as 'the initial election held at the beginning of transitions' and 'the early post-communist elections'. The problem is that these two are not always the same. In the former Soviet Union, the identity of the republican governments that emerged from the elections of 1990 was crucial for shaping early post-communist developments, but it does not seem particularly sensible to see these as 'post-communist elections', even if the power of the party had been changed fundamentally by this time, especially in some parts of the country. Furthermore if one were looking for 'the initial election held at the beginning of [the Soviet transition]', it is to that of March 1989 for the Soviet Congress of Peoples' Deputies that we should look. This was clearly crucial for the later development and ultimate fall of the USSR, but it had little direct or immediate effect upon the shaping of power or the likelihood of economic reform in the post-communist republics. Elections are important, but they cannot be understood outside the context within which they take place, and this means the circumstances of the initial transition from communist rule.[50]

It is clear that the post-communist states have not all followed the same trajectory. Some seem well established as liberal democracies, others as authoritarian systems. Yet others fall between these poles. The question that we must answer is why these trajectories have been followed. In doing so, it is to the mode of transition that we must look in the first place because this shapes the political actors which in turn determine the trajectory upon which the country embarks. But a word of qualification is necessary. There is no assumption that any of these states have reached any sort of final resting point. Just because, for example, Poland is democratic, Russia a façade democracy, and Turkmenistan a non-democracy does not mean that they are destined to remain in that situation. All political systems can change, and although future development is linked with the former path of development, it is not predetermined.

2 Negotiating regime change

Questions of regime change rarely arise in the absence of a regime crisis or, at least, a major challenge to the status quo. Ruling political elites rarely look to bring about fundamental change to the sets of political arrangements whereby they rule unless they are forced to do so. It may be that the regime is faced with a legitimation crisis brought on by performance failures, a succession crisis may paralyse the regime and prevent it from handling its daily administrative chores, popular mobilisation may engender a crisis of confidence among the rulers and a rejection of prevailing political forms, or the regime may be confronted with another development which it cannot easily handle. The sorts of things which can throw a regime into crisis are legion but, if the record of regime change tells us anything, it will usually involve perceived performance failure of some sort.[1] When a regime is faced with such a crisis, political elites must decide how to respond. They can dig in, reaffirm existing institutional arrangements, and seek to ride out the difficulties with perhaps only minor changes to the regime's structure. Or they can seek to implement a program of liberalisation, of strictly limited change, which will involve greater inclusiveness of the population in the political process without allowing any real power to slip out of their hands. Or they can opt for a process of regime change. Whatever they decide will be important in structuring the political outcome and thereby the shape of the future regime. The decisions they make regarding both the broad strategy to be adopted in dealing with the problems and, maybe, the more specific issues of what sorts of institutional forms to adopt, will be crucial in determining whether the response to regime crisis is democratic government or a restabilisation of authoritarian rule. This is clearly evident in the former communist states.

In the case of the former communist states, when the crisis of 1989/91 hit, political elites recognised that any response they might make had to involve at least some rejigging of the institutional structure.[2] With the communist system widely seen as bankrupt, its continuation unchanged was not seen as a viable option; some sort of institutional change was necessary, although views differed over the extent of it. This was particularly the case throughout most of East Central Europe given that during the process of regime change there was no revolutionary transformative elite nor a counter-elite with a clear conception of what they wanted to put in place instead of the discredited communist institutions.[3] Furthermore the internationally hegemonic status of the ideology of democracy following the end of the cold war mandated that any changes brought about had to be justified in democratic terms. Even if the institutional changes that were made were minor, their legitimation had now to be based on democratic rhetoric. Indeed, throughout the post-communist world, the rhetoric of democracy was taken as given. But the institutional forms adopted varied considerably, and it is in the detail of these that the validity of a regime's democratic credentials rests.

Institutional engineering

There were a number of different areas of institutional design which were central to elite negotiation (on what negotiation means, see p. 20–1) and to the democratic credentials of a regime.

1 *The Constitution.* In most cases of the shift from authoritarian rule, there is significant pressure to replace the former regime's constitution. Often this will be essential to introduce institutions that are compatible with democracy, but in the case of the former communist countries, this imperative has been less in evidence. This is because in these countries, in a formal sense, the constitutions have often been very democratic. The institutional structures and relationships formally spelled out have been quite consistent with democratic principles, even if there were elements which were contrary to such a vision; the provision enshrining the communist party's leading role is a clear example of this. In practice, such elements could be removed from the constitutional document through a simple process of amendment, leaving the democratic shell into which the real substance which had been missing in the communist period could be poured. In this way, the purely formal democratism of the communist period could be transformed into a more practical and real democracy. However this ignores the importance of symbolism, and the fact that, in principle, post-communist democratic regimes saw it as necessary to reject the legacy of the past by replacing the former set of rules of the political game by a new set untainted by communist associations and openly linked to the new avowedly democratic regime. But of course what is important is not just the introduction of a new constitution, but the structure of institutions which it creates.[4]

2 *Type of system: presidential vs parliamentary.*[5] In principle, there are two pure types of democratic system, a presidential and a parliamentary model, with a range of mixed types in between. The essential difference between the two relates to the relative power of the head of state compared with the parliament: a parliamentary system exists when the parliament is sovereign, the government is located in the parliament and the head of state possesses only symbolic power, while a presidential system sees the head of state with a preponderance of power, the government answerable to him, and the parliament in a subordinate position. Although the essential difference is one of the powers of these actors and the power each possesses is not inevitably

related to the means of selection of the head of state, a pure presidential system usually sees the president chosen by popular vote while the pure parliamentary system usually has the head of state chosen by the parliament or it is a hereditary post. There has been considerable debate over which of these two systems is more conducive to democratic politics,[6] and the balance of the argument favours the parliamentary form. Studies have suggested that the historical record shows that a parliamentary system is more likely to facilitate the long-term survival of a democracy than a presidential system.[7] This is said to be due to a number of factors. First, a parliamentary system offers a number of channels of access into the political system, in the sense that the parliamentary chamber will comprise a number of different elements (usually in the form of parties) which thereby provide scope for the institutional representation of a diversity of interests. In this way, the parliament provides a diversity of possible points of access into the system on the part of social interests, and thereby a means of satisfying those interests within the political structure. In contrast, in a presidential system the chief organ of government is unitary and thereby provides no scope for the representation of different interests. The parliamentary system is thereby held to be both more amenable to the existence of the diversity of interests which is at the heart of democracy and more sensitive to the social forces of which society consists than a presidential system. Second, a parliamentary system has as its essence the notion of debate and compromise, while the presidential system is associated with decisiveness and firm leadership. This is why it has often been seen as the answer in times of uncertainty and difficulty. Third, it has been argued that in a parliamentary system, power is shared because of the way in which different parties gain representation; politics is therefore not a zero sum game in which one actor wins and all of the others lose. In contrast, in a presidential system there is no such sharing of power; only one actor wins the presidency, and all of the others gain nothing. Politics is thus a zero sum game, with the stakes accordingly significantly higher than in a parliamentary system. It is for these sorts of reasons that the choice between parliamentary and presidential system has been considered to be of significant import for the political outcome of regime change.

3 *Electoral system.* The type of electoral system adopted is significant because it structures a major means of popular access to the political system, shapes the type of party competition that emerges, and, especially important in the initial post-communist elections, can influence which types of parties gain electoral success and which do not. Two aspects of the electoral system are relevant: its inclusiveness, and its dynamics. In terms of inclusiveness, the fewer restrictions on participation in the election, the more democratic the system will be. No electoral system permits universal participation; all have at least a minimum age qualification, and many disbar those in penitentiary and psychiatric institutions. Some also impose citizenship or residential qualifications, and it is in the detail of these that their democratic/undemocratic nature is to be found. More clearly anti-democratic are restrictions based on ascribed criteria: gender, ethnicity, religion and regional identity. Decisions

on who may participate and who may not are therefore central to the issue of the structuring of popular access. Turning to the dynamics of the electoral system, there is a wide diversity of types of system whose diverse dynamics have different impacts on the playing out of political life. The basic distinction of most relevance to this discussion is that between a system of proportional representation (PR) and one of single member constituency (SMC). Although there will be differences of detail between different variants of both these systems (and these differences of detail can have significant effects), the basic logic behind each remains intact. PR involves multi-member constituencies (often a single national constituency) and the return to the parliament of party members in accord with the proportion of votes gained by the party.[8] SMC involves a series of electoral contests in territorially defined electorates, with the parties' seats in the parliament being the sum of the number of individual constituency contests which their representatives win. These different systems encourage different sorts of developments within the party structures. The PR system encourages the development of strong central party organs (or, if there is a series of large constituencies, regional party organisations) and weak local party organisations; what is important is drawing up the list of party candidates from whom those to enter the parliament will be drawn and mounting a national campaign to attract votes from right across that national constituency.[9] Under these circumstances, local party organisations are of secondary importance. In contrast, the SMC system promotes the development of local party organs because it is on the local level that candidates must be found and the campaign mounted; while central organs may be significant in financing and coordination, it is the local organs which are central to the mounting of the local campaigns. Thus PR promotes strongly centralised parties while SMC encourages parties with a weaker centre and stronger lower level organisations. The reverse effect of this also applies: PR rewards those parties with a strong national organisation and penalises those which lack it, while SMC rewards those with an effective organisation soundly rooted in the localities and penalises those without such a structure. PR may produce a parliament with fewer parties than SMC if there is an electoral threshold in place, but it should also ensure that all major groups gain representation, thereby reducing the chances of extra-constitutional clashes occasioned by exclusion from the political process. The introduction of a threshold in the PR system will eliminate small party representation and thereby strengthen the more powerful parties. In SMC a first-past-the-post system of balloting will strengthen major parties at the expense of smaller parties. While the question of which of these systems is the more democratic remains open (e.g. PR produces a closer approximation between voter support and party representation while SMC emphasises the link between representative and voter), it is clear that they have a significant impact on the shape of political life and especially party competition.

4 *Conditions for effective competition.* The essence of a democratic system is competition, but this needs both to be structured (and thereby kept within

bounds) and constructed in such a way that there is approximate equality of opportunity for all. The development of political parties is crucial for this process, since these are the vehicles through which popular control may be exercised in a mass society. The effects of the choice of electoral system have been noted above, but also important are regulations relating to party formation: how difficult is the process of party registration? how much popular support is required for registration? are any types of parties (e.g. ethnic or religious parties) not permitted? Also relevant are regulations relating to popular involvement more broadly, in particular rights of organisation in defence of interest and rights of free assembly, demonstration and speech. The issue of free speech also has relevance in terms of the access available to all political forces to the media. An important aspect of this is the independence of the media from the government. Finally, there is the creation of a system of political administration that is widely seen as having integrity and is not subject to corruption by political forces, including the government. One way in which this is often conceived is in terms of the incorruptibility of the electoral system; if elections are conducted without widespread well-founded complaints of fraud and manipulation, the system of political administration is likely to be seen as possessing the sort of integrity which encourages both popular belief in it and commitment to it.

The importance of decisions on institutional matters like these for the political outcome is evident if we look at the shape of the different post-communist systems. By the end of 1999, all of the countries had new, post-communist constitutions, with the exception of Latvia which had re-introduced its 1922 constitution and Hungary which had changed its constitution through substantial amendments; an attempt to draft a new one late in the 1990s stalled. Of the nine countries that had elections that were really competitive, seven had a parliamentary system (Bulgaria, Czech Republic, Estonia, Hungary, Latvia, Slovakia and Slovenia) and Poland and Lithuania had a mixed presidential-parliamentary system. The other two countries having parliamentary systems (Albania and Macedonia) had queries over the fairness of some of their elections. All cases of clearly non-competitive elections occurred in countries which had presidential systems (Armenia, Azerbaijan, Belarus, Kazakhstan, the Kyrgyz Republic, Tajikistan, Turkmenistan and Uzbekistan). Seven of the eight countries with queries over the nature of the elections had mixed parliamentary-presidential systems (FRY/Serbia, Georgia, Moldova, Romania, Russia, Ukraine, Croatia; Macedonia was parliamentary). Turning to the type of electoral system, of the eight countries with a pure PR system, six had a record of competitive elections (Czech Republic, Estonia, Latvia, Poland, Slovakia and Slovenia) while in the other two (Moldova and Romania) there were queries over the nature of the elections. Of the eight countries having a pure SMC election type, in six the elections were non-competitive (Belarus, Kazakhstan, the Kyrgyz Republic, Tajikistan, Turkmenistan and Uzbekistan) while in Macedonia and Ukraine there was a query over their nature. Of those ten countries with a mixed PR-SMC system, in four the elections were truly competitive

(Albania except in 1996, Bulgaria, Hungary and Lithuania), in two they were non-competitive (Armenia and Azerbaijan), and in four there were queries over their nature (Croatia, Georgia, Russia and FRY/Serbia and Montenegro). It is clear from the above that certain combinations of institutions seem to be associated with certain sorts of outcomes. If democracy is defined purely in terms of competitive elections, then the achievement of democracy is best facilitated through a combination of parliamentary system with PR voting and authoritarian rule through a presidential system with SMC voting. Although the fit is not exact, the trends are clear. But of course pointing to trends does not provide an explanation of dynamics. Of itself, it does not tell us whether the institutions produced the outcome, or the desires of political actors to produce such an outcome led to the creation of the particular institutions. To answer this question, we need to look at the dynamics of elite relations at the time of the shift from communist to post-communist rule.

The institutional contours adopted by each regime has in part been a function of the process of negotiation that attended the fall of the old regime.[10] The notion of negotiation refers to the process of interaction between regime elites and non-regime elites chiefly about the contours the political system should take. Negotiation could take a number of forms. The clearest form was when formal talks were instituted between regime elites and non-regime elites (these collective actors will be discussed see p. 21–2), usually in Eastern Europe in the form of round tables.[11] These gatherings could extend over many months, and usually sought to end with a pact or agreement involving a timetable for the shift to democracy and some idea of the institutional forms that were to be set in place, at least in the interim. But it would be wrong to limit our notion of negotiation to such formal meetings. One feature of the shift towards democracy is both the opening of the political agenda up to public discussion and the mobilisation of non-regime forces into political life. Such public discussion, with the vigorous putting of diverse views and usually extensive criticism of the regime, itself constituted a form of negotiation with regime forces. It made clear what different political actors were willing to accept and gave regime elites the opportunity both to spell out the limits of what they would be willing to accept and to alter their stance in the face of opposition positions. This was a much more informal process, but the course of public debate was nevertheless a crucial aspect of negotiations. Election campaigns could also feed into the negotiations, providing a structured forum for the expression of negotiating positions and, through the electoral outcome itself, shifting the balance of power between the various sides (on 'founding' elections, see p. 23–4). Defined in this way, the course of negotiations could extend for a considerable period of time; they did not always end when an election ushered a new regime into power. Nor were negotiations always peaceful. The use of force could be a potent weapon used by either side, with the arrest of oppositionists and the mobilisation of popular demonstrations being established tactics by regime and opposition respectively. This means that the use of force does not necessarily signal the end of negotiations, although in some cases it clearly does mean that; in other cases it is merely the conduct of negotiations by other means.

The unrolling of negotiations assumes the existence of at least two sides, the regime elite and the opposition. The regime elite is that group of people who are the leaders of the regime at the time negotiations begin. They are not restricted to official office-holders, but usually the individuals concerned will be the incumbents of the most important political offices in the system. It is a characteristic of the breakdown of authoritarian regimes that during this process the ruling elite splits,[12] usually on the question of whether and how far to liberalise, and thereby to compromise with the opposition. Opinion within the regime elite may span the spectrum from those who refuse to accept any changes and support the coercive suppression of opposition, through those who support limited change that will not alter the basic division of power but will give a sense of participation to the opposition and thereby blunt their more radical demands, to those who are willing to forsake the old regime and support the introduction of democratic political forms. At the beginning of the process of change, there are generally few of this third category in the upper reaches of the regimes, but as the process continues and the agenda is radicalised, it is not unusual for individuals to move to this position. Such a shift in opinion within the regime elite during the negotiation process can be highly significant.

In cases of democratic transition the regime elite's chief negotiating partner comes from outside the regime itself, although the crossing of individuals from the regime into the ranks of the opposition has been a common occurrence. Given that meaningful negotiations cannot be conducted directly with the mass of the populace (even though that populace may play a crucial part in shaping the course of regime change), the chief interlocutors with the regime will be opposition elites. The immediate question is that given that the communist regime made no provision for opposition, how are such opposition elites chosen? In terms of those who were involved in the early stages of negotiations with the regime, there were two basic sources of such elites. First, those who had gained a position of moral leadership and authority by virtue of their history of public opposition to the regime. These were the dissidents, people like Vaclav Havel in Czechoslovakia and Andrei Sakharov in the USSR whose moral authority rested on enormous personal integrity and a history of suffering for their beliefs. But significant though these people may have been in the early stages of negotiation, they were usually soon superseded by the second type of elite, that emanating from leadership of a mass organisation. One of the characteristics of regime change from authoritarian rule is that it is usually accompanied by the blossoming of large numbers of organisations independent of regime control.[13] With the previous restrictions on political organisation eroding, bodies seeking to have some say in the unrolling of political life usually proliferate. It is from among these that opposition elites usually emerge.[14]

The problem for regime elites may be deciding with whom negotiations should be conducted. Sometimes, as in Poland, it is clear where leadership of the opposition lies. But in cases where independent organisation is slow to emerge, it may not be easy to discern who the leading figures in the opposition are going to be. Similarly even when large numbers of independent organisations do burst onto the public stage, the difference between those that will be ephemeral and those of more substance may not always be easy to see. What is important here is the relationship between these new organisations and the mass of the populace. Those organisations which either are thrown up by or are able to establish their roots within the broad mass populace, and thereby may be seen to represent some popular constituency, possess a more stable basis for enduring political activity than bodies which lack such roots. Their constituency gives them potential power, even if only in the form of the ability to mobilise their supporters onto the streets. In this sense, they are forces which should be included in the negotiations because to exclude them threatens potential disruption. Furthermore given that regime elites will want to get from the negotiations the best possible outcome for themselves, including very often exit guarantees in the form of promises of immunity from arrest, it makes no sense to negotiate with organisations which can not exercise any control over the populace. Any agreements that are made must be made to stick, and therefore they must be made with organisations that can commit their followers to abide by the agreements their leaders make.

This sense of connectedness between political organisation and mass constituency is important for another reason also. The closer the link between political organisation and mass constituency, the greater the likelihood that the former will be sensitive to the views and interests of the latter. Where political elites are isolated from the populace because the structures they head lack a basis within the population, they may have greater room for manoeuvre, but the likelihood that they can adequately represent the views of the populace is reduced. Elites left to themselves are more likely to reach agreements among themselves at the expense of the broader populace than elites whose very standing is dependent upon the mass support upon which their organisations rely. To the extent that there are significant constituencies within the population at large that will favour an opening up of the political process and its consequent transformation in a democratic direction, these will constitute an important source of pressure for democratisation exerted through the mass-based political organisations. These mass-based organisations which represent popularly-based constituencies may be called civil society forces; they give form to the sorts of interests which constitute a civil society[15] and both represent and are influenced by those interests during the process of regime change negotiations. The most common form of such organisation is the political party.

The course of negotiations will be shaped by a number of different considerations. The unity of both sides will be crucial. Within the regime elite, the balance of opinion among the three positions noted above and how that potential for conflict is resolved will greatly affect the flexibility of the regime during the course of negotiations. Among the opposition, the degree of fragmentation, the capacity of leaders to develop and sustain a coalition, and the unity of purpose will have significant consequences for the conduct and outcome of negotiations. But having said that, at a higher level of generality, the fundamental political factor in shaping the outcome of the process of regime change in the post-communist world has been the degree of involvement of civil society forces in the negotiations. Where those forces became directly involved at an early stage and exercised an important influence, a democratic outcome eventuated. Where they became involved in a significant fashion at a later stage, the initial authoritarian/quasi-authoritarian outcome of the collapse of communism could be superseded by more democratic forms. Where civil society forces were largely excluded from the process, despite the presence of democratic forms, the substance of the regime has tended to be undemocratic. These simple distinctions can be demonstrated through a survey of the regime change experiences of the respective post-communist states.

Before turning to this, the issue of 'founding' elections, touched on in Chapter One, should be addressed. Some theorists of democratic transition have seen 'founding' elections as being of primary importance in structuring the outcome of this process.[16] Such elections are seen as important mechanisms for transferring power away from the old rulers into the hands of the new, which thereby enables the consolidation of a new set of structures and processes. Some students of post-communism have also seen initial elections in this way.[17] Such elections can be very important in defining the elite which will construct a new polity. This was certainly the case with regard to the republican legislative elections in the USSR in 1990.[18] As the following analysis will demonstrate, the outcome of those elections, held while the Soviet authorities were still in power, defined the political elite which guided the republics into independence. In some countries of Eastern Europe, specifically Poland, Yugoslavia, Albania and Bulgaria, similar elections occurred while the old regime was in power. In Hungary[19] and Czechoslovakia, such elections followed the toppling of the old regime. These elections were important because they gave a legitimacy and a political power base from which the elite could direct the affairs of the state. But the elections themselves should be seen within the context of the developing situation in each of these countries. The elections did not independently restructure the political situation. Rather what they did was to embed in the political system the changing balance of political forces that was already underway in each country. This was most clearly the case in Poland, Hungary, Czechoslovakia, Bulgaria and Slovenia where round table talks between opposition and regime preceding the elections set out the broad parameters of future development. But in all of the other states too, the elections were preceded by a changing balance of political forces. The election registered (and to some degree froze) this change; it did not bring it about. The political elite whose position was confirmed by the election then led the country into the post-communist future. In many cases the elite was not clearly distinct from that which had ruled in the dying days of communism,[20] but they were no less important for shaping the future of their countries than were those whose ascendancy marked a significant break with the past. If we are to talk of founding elections in relation to post-communism, it is therefore not particularly useful to include only those which constitute a real break from the past.[21] It is much better to see these elections as part of the continuing process of negotiation between regime elites and opposition elites than as having a significance of their own.

There have been six basic patterns of regime change and the subsequent shaping of a new set of institutional contours in the post-communist world, with a number of different paths within some of these patterns. The nub upon which these patterns turned was control of the state and the position of civil society forces.

Pattern One

Civil society forces emerge and become sufficiently strong that, when the perception of crisis takes hold within the regime and the regime splits, the more liberal side of the regime elite sees those society-based forces as appropriate partners for meaningful negotiations. Early negotiations/pacting occurs, leading to elections, which remove the old regime from power and ensure that the subsequent negotiations about the form the regime will take are dominated by civil society forces. It is those forces which overwhelmingly shape the political outcome, a stable democracy. The former ruling communist party transforms itself into a social democratic party as part of this process. There are two examples of this pattern, Poland and Hungry.

In **Poland** the chief interlocutor with the communist regime was Solidarity, the social movement that was based in the shipyards and that had emerged out of the industrial unrest in 1980–81. Although it had been outlawed in 1981, Solidarity's ability to transcend its trade union origins and to adopt the mantle of Polish nationalism had given it a constituency much wider than the industrial workforce. The moral authority it possessed meant that when elements within the regime sought partners from within society with which to negotiate in the face of the continuing crisis, it was the obvious one. Despite considerable opposition within the old regime elite, elements led by the president General Jaruzelski approached Solidarity leader Lech Walesa with a view to opening Round Table negotiations with that organisation and a range of other bodies in an attempt to gain a consensus approach to the solution of the economic problems and to the relegalisation of Solidarity.[22] Such negotiations began in February 1989. As elsewhere in the region, the commitment by both sides to Round Table discussions constituted an agreement to evolutionary change by lawful means and through the existing institutional structures. It also implied no retrospective legislation or punishment of the servants of the old regime.[23]

The agreements that emanated from these negotiations in April 1989 were designed to establish a period of power-sharing between the regime and the opposition. This reflected a willingness on the part of the opposition to compromise and to accept some regime prerogatives, a view which probably stemmed from an over-estimation of the power of the regime relative to that of the opposition.[24] Provision was made for multi-party elections in the June, but for the lower house (Sejm) these were to be semi-competitive, with Solidarity forbidden to run candidates in 65% of Sejm constituencies; however the Senate was to be freely elected. Provision was made for a strong presidency[25] elected by the parliament, for the legalisation of Solidarity, the strengthening of the position of the Church, and for a series of economic measures. This agreement was meant to provide some limited access into the political system for Solidarity while guaranteeing that the ruling Polish United Workers' Party would retain its dominant position; not only was the PUWP and its allies guaranteed 65% of the seats in the Sejm, but it was also understood that party leader Jaruzelski would be elected president. In four years time, completely free elections would be held. However the June elections were a disaster for the communists. They won only the seats set aside for them, while

Solidarity won all the seats in which it competed in the lower house and 99 of the 100 seats in the Senate. This result robbed the PUWP of any political authority at all, and with the defection of some of its allies in the Sejm, it also soon lost its numerical majority. But Solidarity was initially reluctant to form a new government. As a social movement, it lacked the structures to be able easily to slip into a governing role, and its leaders also realised the possible political consequences of the harsh economic measures which were deemed necessary. Nevertheless ultimately it had little choice, and formed a coalition government led by Tadeusz Mazowiecki with some communist participation. In October, a policy of economic shock therapy was announced, to take effect from 1 January 1990.

By the summer of 1990, the PUWP had restructured itself into Social Democracy of the Polish Republic (SDPR) while its former allies the United Peasants' Party had become the Polish Peasants' Party and the Democratic Party had died, the communist ministers had left the government, and Jaruzelski had resigned the presidency. The old regime was no longer a part of the power structure. On the other side of politics, there were also significant developments. The dominating position Solidarity occupied in the opposition effectively prevented the emergence of independent opposition forces when the system had been freed in 1989.[26] However that dominance was soon shaken as the social movement itself began to fragment. Conflict emerged between the Mazowiecki government, the Solidarity representatives in the parliament, and the trade union wing led by Lech Walesa. The most important axis of this was the Mazowiecki–Walesa conflict, which was sharpened considerably when Walesa ran for the presidency in November/December 1990, beating Mazowiecki (who failed to reach the second round) in the election.[27] But this breaking apart of Solidarity did not accelerate the development of independent programmatic parties. Instead the intensely personal nature of the conflict and the fact that the election was for the presidency rather than the parliament fuelled the development of personalised parties.[28] In addition, Solidarity refused to transform itself into a political party, instead allowing a number of parties to co-exist under its umbrella, which undermined its coherence as well as inhibiting general party development.[29]

The election of Walesa and resignation of Mazowiecki did not end the conflict within the Polish polity. Walesa had an expansive and interventionist view of the role of the president but he lacked a clear policy programme. Not only did he expand the presidential apparatus to give himself greater capacity for playing an activist political role,[30] but he continually sought to interfere in the running of successive governments. The government also had difficulty in achieving stable support within the parliament. These problems and the perception that the parliament that had emanated from the Round Table agreements was compromised by its mode of selection fuelled the view that new elections were necessary. But there was widespread disagreement about the rules under which such elections should be conducted. A Law on Political Parties had been adopted in July 1990, but this provided for the establishment of a party on the signature of only fifteen people. As a result, a multitude of small parties had emerged. These parties favoured a system of PR which promised them some prospect of gaining representation in the Sejm; so too did the communist successor party. Walesa and those around him favoured a more restricted majoritarian system or a threshold which would favour large parties. The result was different systems for the two houses: PR for the Sejm[31] and a plurality system in multi-member districts for the Senate. When the election was held in October 1991, the result was fragmentation of the political system: 29 groupings gained representation in the new parliament with no party receiving more than 12.3% of the vote.[32] This made effective parliamentary functioning impossible and, along with continual intervention by the president, ensured weak governments.

The low hurdle to the establishment of parties did promote the emergence of a very large number of such groups, but many were little more than a name on a piece of paper.[33] Effective, programmatic parties with their roots in a popular constituency were slow to emerge. But the low barrier to political participation also ensured that there were many people and groups who had some interest in the drawing up of the rules for the new political system. The clear evidence of the way in which disputes between the three branches of the state, president, government and parliament, had led to deadlock gave a sense of urgency to this question of new political rules. Although the differing conceptions of what was desirable prevented agreement on a completely new constitution,[34] the main political actors were able to agree on a so-called 'Little Constitution' which was introduced on 17 October 1992. A constitutional statute on relations between the parliamentary and executive authorities,[35] the Little Constitution formalised presidential primacy in matters of internal and external security and spelled out more clearly the conditions under which the president could dissolve the parliament. The position of the government *vis-à-vis* both president and parliament was strengthened: the president could remove ministers only at the prime minister's request and he was not allowed to request the resignation of the government as a whole; the parliament's ability to pass a vote of no confidence was restricted (the Sejm could dismiss the prime minister only when it had named a replacement), it was to have less say in reorganising the composition of a government, the government could set priorities in the parliament's dealing with bills, and it could request extraordinary powers to deal with particular issues. This did not end the 'war of institutions' at the top of the Polish state, but it did bring some rationalisation and institutionalisation to it[36] by effectively embedding a mixed parliamentary-presidential system.

This stabilisation of institutional relationships was matched by an attempt to eliminate the excessive fragmentation in the parliament and to facilitate the growth of large parties at the expense of small through changes to the electoral laws. New thresholds were introduced: individual parties had to obtain 5% and coalitions 8% of the national vote to obtain seats on a PR basis in the constituencies, and 7% to receive any of the 69 national list seats. The September 1993 election saw these rules working, with only six parties gaining representation in the Sejm, although this was at the expense of representation. The communist successor Democratic Left Alliance (an alliance formed in 1991 between Social Democracy of the Polish Republic and the communist-led All-Poland Trade Unions Federation)-Peasant

Party alliance won 65.9% of the seats with 35.9% of the votes; 33% of votes were wasted on parties that did not cross the electoral threshold,[37] a statistic which called into question the representativeness of the parliament and, therefore, its authority. The election of the communist successors to government was the source of tension with President Walesa, especially when the latter sought to flex his political muscles in the lead up to the presidential election in 1995,[38] while the coalition partners in the government also had significant policy differences. In addition, the leader of SDPR, Aleksandr Kwasniewski, was attempting to position himself for a run for the presidency. When the election was held in November 1995, Kwasniewski defeated Walesa (51.7% of the vote to 48.3%), thereby ensuring that both government and president were of the same political complexion. The implication was clear. The people had rejected a combative president whose concerns seemed excessively rooted in refighting old battles in an attempt to expand his own power in favour of someone who promised both a more forward-looking approach and a more amicable relationship with the government. This seemed to be realised with the introduction in June 1996 of a draft constitution, which was subsequently adopted by popular referendum in May 1997 (and took effect on 17 October), despite opposition from both Solidarity and the Church. In September 1997 in a parliamentary election, the DLA was thrown out of government with the victory of the Electoral Action Solidarity coalition, a new coalition of 40 Solidarity successor parties. This balance between leftist president and Solidarity successor government was reinforced in the October 2000 presidential election. Kwasniewski was re-elected on the first ballot, receiving 53.9% of the vote while the Electoral Action Solidarity candidate came in third with only 15.6% of the vote.

In Poland the pattern is clear: the old regime fell away following the electoral setback in June 1989, leaving the political arena and consequent negotiation about future political forms to civil society forces. But what is striking is that the breakup of the umbrella organisation which had spearheaded opposition to the regime, Solidarity, seems to have destroyed the possibility of consensus on the rules of politics among those emerging from its shell. That agreement on the rules was obtained only when the communist successors held both presidency and government. The election of the communist successors and their subsequent expulsion from office suggests that the rules have become embedded and the system is clearly democratic, with changes in government coming as a result of free and fair electoral contests.

Discussion about the shape of a post-communist **Hungary** had begun long before the regime fell. The liberalisation of Hungarian society that had been part of the regime's effort to rebuild its domestic base following the 1956 uprising had involved a significant shift away from the traditional communist model. In this sense, the inertial effect of the continuation of the Hungarian 'model' itself, including the liberalising direction in which social forces were driving it, effectively constituted a debate about the future form of Hungarian society even before the regime entered what was to be its terminal crisis. And given that a real sense of civil society had developed, at least in Hungarian cities, this debate was not restricted to political elites but had its roots in society more generally among that range of groups that had emerged in the more liberal atmosphere.[39] Thus even though when parties emerged towards the end of the 1980s (Hungarian Democratic Forum [HDF], September 1987; Alliance of Young Democrats [Fidesz], March 1988; Alliance of Free Democrats [AFD], November 1988; Independent Smallholders Party [ISP], February 1988; and the Christian Democratic Peoples Party [CDPP], April 1989)[40] they were primarily small groups of intellectuals with few links into the populace at large,[41] the intellectual environment they were in encouraged them to keep the debate open to society as a whole rather than to close it off among political elites.

Discussion had also begun within the regime where a reformist wing focused on Imre Poszgay had developed in the late 1980s as the economy declined and the regime's legitimation problems grew. This wing was crucial for the opening to society that enabled the form of regime change that occurred to take place. As early as September 1987 Poszgay sought to forge a link between reformists in the party and those favouring change outside, and it was in part due to the strength of those reformists within the regime that the old party leadership was overthrown in May 1988. The new leadership moved in November of that year to legalise political parties, something achieved in January 1989. Taking advantage of this opening, in March nine opposition groups formed an opposition Round Table to discuss how to go about dismantling the regime.[42] This strengthening of opposition to the regime and hardening of the line against compromise (which reflected the opposition's growing strength and confidence) was the precursor to the formal Round Table with the regime that lasted from June until September 1989.

These negotiations[43] assumed from the outset a multi-party system and the need for early fully competitive elections, thereby avoiding the power-sharing model that had been the outcome of the Polish negotiations. This outcome may reflect the strength of the opposition relative to the government as well as the latter's willingness to compromise, perhaps in the belief that, in the presence of a fragmented opposition, it would be able to prevail at the polls. The elections were set for March 1990[44] with a mixed voting system: 45.6% (176) of the seats were to be elected by SMC and 54.4% (210) by PR. There was a 4% threshold. Reflecting the early strength of opposition parties, there was a consensus for a parliamentary system with a weak president, but there was no consensus over how that president was to be chosen. The reform wing of the ruling party favoured the direct popular election of the president, in the belief that this would favour Poszgay. They were supported in this by the HDF, which was at this time considering an alliance with reformists in the ruling party.[45] The AFD and Fidesz believed that the president should be elected by parliament, and accordingly refused to sign the Round Table agreement. They were able to bring on a popular referendum on this question in November, at which 50.14% on a turnout of 58% supported a president chosen by the parliament following parliamentary elections.[46] Despite the disagreement over the mode of election of the president, the Round Table produced the outline of the new system, which was enshrined in amendments to the constitution in October

1989. Although officially a process of constitutional amendment (the opposition parties argued that the communist era parliament lacked the authority to adopt a new constitution), in fact the document was almost completely new. The Round Table thus produced the basic rules for the new political system. However these were to be changed following the first election.

The electoral system worked out in the Round Table was designed to assist large parties and increase the margin of the winners: in order to gain seats through PR, parties were required to present candidates in a certain number of SMC constituencies, and there was a 4% threshold with residual votes distributed to national party lists. As a result of this system, only six parties gained representation in the parliament, the five established opposition parties (HDF, AFD, Fidesz/AYD, ISP and CDPP) and the reform communists who had split off from the ruling party to form the Hungarian Socialist Party (HSP). A non-communist HDF-ISP-CDPP coalition government was formed, thereby creating a clear ideological divide within the parliament: a populist/nationalist/Christian government based principally on the countryside and provincial towns faced an opposition of urban liberals and reform communists.[47] But the government lacked the two-thirds majority needed to amend the constitution. For this, the HDF needed the support of the AFD (together they had 66% of the seats), and HDF leader Jozsef Antall went about securing this. Antall was concerned about the strength accorded to the parliament compared with the government by the Round Table negotiations. Accordingly he approached the head of the writers union, Arpad Goncz who had been elected to the parliament as a member of the AFD and promised to support the election of the president by the parliament and the election of Goncz as president if Goncz would persuade the AFD to support measures to circumvent the two-thirds rule and strengthen the government. Goncz agreed, and this was then presented to the major party leaders as a *fait accompli*. The result was the adoption by parliament of a series of measures which rounded out and significantly qualified the constitutional settlement of 1989. The pact confirmed the principle of parliamentary election of the president, significantly reduced the number of laws to which the two-thirds rule applied, and introduced the notion of the 'constructive no confidence' vote; i.e. a no confidence motion could be moved only against the prime minister (and therefore the whole government) rather than individual ministers, and had to include the name of a replacement prime minister. This clearly strengthened both the government and the prime minister; ministers were now directly responsible to the prime minister rather than the parliament.[48]

There was widespread criticism of these changes and the way they were brought about, and many now looked for a balance to the increased power of the government. Although for many the Constitutional Court was the most likely body for this, in fact it was the presidency which emerged to play this role. Goncz took literally his constitutional responsibility to safeguard the democratic working of the institutions of the state. Accordingly he refused to approve government appointments to a series of posts which he believed would compromise the independence of the media, referred a number of laws to the Constitutional Court for a judgement as to their constitutionality, and publicly opposed government plans to use force to break strike activity in October 1990.[49] But despite these actions, the presidency remains constitutionally limited in the power it can wield.

The formal rules of the new political game were therefore settled reasonably quickly, and principally as a result of the involvement of the major parties in debate and discussion about them. There also emerged some stability in the structuring of party competition. The parties have sought to moderate their initial highly ideological positions in favour of programmatic policies directed at solving contemporary problems rather than achieving idealised visions of what the future might be like. With this has gone the attempt to build up mass constituencies, and although only some 2% of the populace belonged to parties in the middle of the decade,[50] there is some evidence that they have been able to do this. This lies chiefly in the fact that in all three post-communist elections (1990, 1994 and 1998) five of the six original major parties were by far the largest parties in the parliament. But this is the result not only of the development of popular bases of support. It also reflects the way they were able to take advantage of the privileged position they acquired as a result of their early establishment and the corresponding dominance they gained in 1990. The electoral system has helped them to maintain their dominance, but as their individual changing fortunes show, it has not protected a party which was deemed to have performed badly from retribution by the voters. The initial HDF-led government was thrown out after one term, as was its successor the HSP, despite in the case of the latter its vote holding up almost intact; it was defeated by the mobilisation of new electoral support for Fidesz/AYD.[51]

The consolidation of the party system through the electoral process also saw the return to power of the former reform communists in the HSP in 1994. The party played by the new rules, surrendering power when defeated in 1998. As in Poland, its election did not bring about any questioning of the new political arrangements, suggesting that the settlement of 1990 had been accepted by all major actors in Hungarian politics. Only in Hungary in East Central Europe have all parliaments and governments run their full terms, and the prime minister was replaced only due to election defeat or, in the case of Antall, death. Politics has been largely compromise-based. This is clearly reflected in the way in which in 1996, when the coalition government sought procedural agreement on the drafting of a new constitution, it said it would not seek a two-thirds majority as required in the constitution, but a four-fifths majority of MPs or all parties minus one.[52]

There is a clear common pattern here with Poland: initial agreements on the form of political life reached with the old regime elite were modified substantially once that elite lost power at an election. The difference is that in Poland, the main interlocutor with the regime was a social movement which, once the communists had lost power, broke up causing significant instability among civil society forces. In Hungary from the outset there was a variety of political parties with independent roots which both negotiated with the regime and, when that regime fell, among themselves, to produce a new structure. Civil society forces in Hungary appeared weaker than in Poland, but the reformist wing of the regime was stronger. But in both it was a case of a weakly organised society versus a weak state. In both, popular involvement through the ballot box was significant.

Pattern Two

When the old regime elite perceives the onset of crisis, civil society forces are not sufficiently developed to be a powerful negotiating partner and are not immediately able to displace that elite. The old regime elite is able to transform itself, and in the new guise as a successor regime, engages in negotiation with society-based forces and wins the first election. There are two instances of this pattern, Bulgaria and Albania, with each constituting a separate path of development. In one path, the Bulgarian, political actors accepted the initial set of agreements and set in place a democratic system, while in the second, Albania, one side (that stemming from society rather than the regime) refused to accept the institutional structure established at the outset of the post-communist period. Open oligarchy was the result.

A number of opposition groups had emerged during the last years of communist rule in **Bulgaria**. The most important of these were human rights organisations, environmental groups, a few quasi-parties and an independent trade union organisation (Podkrepa).[53] Against a background of popular protest and strike activity, in November 1989 15 of them came together to form an umbrella organisation that was to play a significant role in structuring the political outcome in Bulgaria, the Union of Democratic Forces (UDF).[54] It was this body which entered the Round Table discussions with the reformed leadership of the ruling Bulgarian Communist Party (BCP) in the first months of 1990. At this same time significant changes were occurring in the ruling circles of the BCP. In November 1989 the party leader since 1954, Todor Zhivkov, was replaced by the more reformist Petur Mladenov, and decisions were made on a series of constitutional amendments, including dropping the term 'socialist' from the country's name, removal of the party's leading role, the granting of some minority rights, and provision for the establishment of opposition parties. Round Table discussions between regime and opposition opened in January and lasted until May, and resulted in agreement on a number of constitutional amendments including the separation of powers and a popularly elected president responsible to parliament, a range of freedoms, a law on political parties, and the rules under which an election would be held in June 1990.[55] The electoral system adopted was a compromise between the UDF's preference for PR in order to overcome potential manipulation by local communist electoral officials and the BCP's (which in April became the Bulgarian Socialist Party – BSP) preference for first past the post; half were to be elected by PR with a 4% threshold, and half by SMC with provision for a run off if no candidate received an absolute majority. The negotiations also produced agreement forbidding parties based on ethnic or religious grounds. This was important because moves in the last years of communist rule to assimilate the Turkish population had led to significant tension and unrest and to the emergence of a party to represent Turkish interests, the Movement for Rights and Freedoms (MRF). The election was to be for a Grand National Assembly which was to sit for eighteen months to prepare a new constitution.

When the election was held in June, only four parties exceeded the 4% threshold. The two largest were the BSP which won 47.2% of the votes and 52.8% of the seats and thereby formed the government, and the UDF which won 36.2% of the votes and 36% of the seats. In sharp contrast to Poland and Hungary, the communist successor party emerged victorious from the poll.[56] It benefited from its role in moving toward change, albeit belatedly compared with some other parties in the region, which enabled it to present itself as a body which could usher in the required changes. In contrast, the UDF was unable to show itself as having played a major role in the shift from communism and its umbrella nature meant that it could be portrayed as merely a coalition of ill-fitting parts.[57]

The first government, led by leading BSP figure Andrei Lukanov, was unable to stabilise its rule. It was confronted with student protest at the refusal of the electoral commission to publish what they believed to be details of electoral irregularities, opposition figures refused to join the government or support many reform initiatives, and it was rent by conflict within the ranks of the left, particularly between Lukanov and party leader Lilov. Towards the end of 1990 as economic difficulties mounted and popular unrest escalated, the government appeared to be vacillatory and indecisive, and lost public support. In November Lukanov was driven from office by popular protest, to be replaced by a coalition government of all parties in the Grand National Assembly (GNA) (the parliament elected in June) except the MRF. This was headed by the non-party Dimitar Popov.[58]

This sort of political instability was also present in regard to the presidency. During the Round Table negotiations, the two sides had disagreed on how the president should be chosen. Both assumed that Mladenov would be elected, and the BCP therefore favoured direct election for a five-six year term, while the UDF favoured election by the parliament for a one year term. Ultimately it was agreed that the existing, communist era, parliament would nominate a candidate and, once elected, the new Grand National Assembly would then formally elect the president. In April, the parliament nominated Mladenov, but he was never confirmed by the GNA.[59] However agreeing on a replacement was a major difficulty. It took six votes in the GNA for the election of UDF leader Zheliu Zhelev in August 1990. With the current government ineffective and with the support of the UDF, Zhelev was able to expand the capacities of the presidency, especially through the establishment of the Political Consultative Council whose offices he used effectively to defuse a number of crises[60] and to structure the work of the GNA.

With a new president and government, attempts were now made to stabilise the political situation. On 20 December 1990, all major parties signed an 'Agreement Among the Political Forces Represented in the GNA on Guaranteeing the Peaceful Transition to a Democratic Society'. In this agreement, the parties confirmed their commitment to parliamentary democracy and individual liberty, and agreed on a timetable for political and economic reform. This was followed on 8 January 1991 by a tripartite government-trade unions-employers agreement whereby a promise of no strikes for 200 days was offset against a government commitment to provide a safety net for those affected by reform and managerial promises of sensitivity to workers when implementing change. These political and social pacts were the precursor to price deregulation and the more vigorous pursuit of economic reform. They also led to the formal adoption of a new constitution by the GNA on 12 July 1991. This document, which was drafted mainly by the BSP and was opposed by part of the UDF, confirmed Bulgaria as a republic and introduced the separation of powers, a constitutional court, and a directly-elected presidency with limited powers, and banned parties based on ethnic, racial or religious lines. Having completed the task envisaged for it in the Round Table agreements as a constituent assembly, the GNA now dissolved itself in preparation for new elections in October 1991.

The election was held under changed electoral rules compared with the mixed system used in June 1990. A straight PR system with a 4% threshold ensured that, of the 38 parties competing, only three gained representation in the new parliament: the UDF, BSP and MRF.[61] This time despite some fragmentation and splitting,[62] the UDF was the largest party (34.4% of votes, 45.8% of seats) and formed a minority government supported in the parliament by the MRF. The BSP was the opposition (33.1% of votes, 44.2% of seats). A presidential election in January 1992 returned Zhelev to office.[63]

With the stabilisation stemming from the political and social pacts and the new constitution, and with president and government both coming from the UDF (although Zhelev had more sympathy for the positions of some of those who had left the UDF than for those who remained), the conditions seemed propitious for a stabilisation of the political system as a whole. But the government was unable to provide stable and effective administration. The need to make hard decisions and the lack of a parliamentary majority brought the coalition within the UDF[64] and the relationship with the MRF under strain. The UDF government fell in November 1992 and was replaced by an expert, non-party government resting on a support coalition comprising the BSP, MRF and some dissident UDF members, but bitterly opposed by the UDF. This government lasted until September 1994 when new elections returned the BSP to office with a parliamentary majority. The re-election of the BSP to government after a period of rule by others is different from the return of successor parties in Poland and Hungary because the Bulgarian party had not transformed itself to anything like the same degree as its counterparts elsewhere.[65] When the economy deteriorated again in 1996, the BSP had no answers, and in the subsequent election in April 1997, the UDF was returned to power with a majority of both votes and seats. In the presidential election of October-November 1996, UDF candidate Petar Stoyanov, defeated his BSP rival.

So the Bulgarian experience was one in which negotiations early in the post-communist period led to the resolution of most political issues and established a system which produced a change in government at each election. It was a system in which government oscillated between two parties which, together, never failed to win at least two-thirds of the popular vote. Importantly, one of those parties was the successor communists, which meant that these lineal descendants of the old regime elite were able through their initial majority in the GNA and the fact that they formed the government in 1990 and 1994, to have a decisive influence in shaping the contours of the new system. Their continuing prominence reflects their much stronger position compared with independent civil society forces than their counterparts in Poland and Hungary.

The ruling **Albanian** Party of Labour (PLA) had been the last to respond to the wave of change sweeping across the region. During 1990 under the leadership of Ramiz Alia who had been its head since 1985, and with changes in July and December in the personnel of the party and government leadership to bring in more reformist figures, the regime tried to institute moderate reform from above in the face of mounting mass protest. Finally at the end of 1990 it was forced to concede a multi-party system. But the opposition had no real leader and no stable organisation to give structure to its activities, so its effect was diffused; there was no one who could present him/herself as a viable negotiating partner with the regime. A potential candidate emerged with the formation of the Democratic Party of Albania (DPA) led by Sali Berisha in December 1990. In an attempt to dampen down the rolling mass protest and to catch the opposition before it had time to organise properly, the authorities called an election for March-April 1991.[66] Seven parties participated, with the PLA gaining 56.2% of the vote and 169 of the 250 seats; the DPA got 38.7% of the vote and 75 seats, thereby making it a viable political actor. The opposition claimed electoral fraud (claims not supported by international observers), refused to cooperate with the government, and objected to a draft constitution presented to the parliament in April 1991. Instead the parliament adopted interim constitutional amendments, which introduced an executive presidency elected by a two-thirds majority of the parliament. Alia was elected to the post. However no stability in government could be obtained. The first, all-PLA, government of Fatos Nano fell in June 1991 in the face of continuing popular direct action, the coalition government of Ylli Bafi fell when the DPA walked out in December 1991, while a government of non-party experts led by Vilson Ahmeti took the country to a new election in March 1992.

The parliamentary election to a new smaller assembly was to be conducted by a mixed SMC (100 seats)/PR (40 seats) system with a 4% threshold. The PLA, which had become the Socialist Party of Albania (SPA) was soundly defeated by the DPA, which won 62.1% of the votes and 92 of the 140 seats; they won 90 of the 100 SMC seats. The DPA's Berisha was elected to a presidency with expanded powers. The DPA used its position in the parliament to consolidate Berisha's position and effectively establish a form of personal rule, but it was unable to get the population to support the introduction of a new constitution which would have formalised his personal control.[67] Criticism of his increasingly authoritarian style was growing; the population rejected a referendum which would have replaced the parliamentary by a presidential system, and as elections approached in 1996 Berisha took a number of measures designed to improve his party's prospects. In September 1995 he introduced lustration laws banning former communists and informers (and therefore many in the SPA) from running, and he reduced the PR component of those to be elected from 40 to 25. When the election was held in

May-June 1996, the successor party opposition SPA boycotted the second round in protest at the fraud and intimidation and violence directed against it,[68] with the result that the DPA won 122 of the 140 seats. But Berisha's victory was shortlived. The festering popular resentment was ignited by the collapse of a pyramid investment scheme in February 1997. Popular protest escalated into low intensity civil war as the country split along regional and tribal lines. Western intervention was needed to stabilise the situation and prepare for new elections in June 1997. These elections resulted in sweeping victory for the SPA. Soon after the election, a number of figures who had been prominent in the former administration were arrested, leading to DPA-sponsored public protests. A DPA leader (Azem Hajdari) was assassinated on 12 September, leading to violent protest, invasion of prime minister Nano's office, and an attempted coup by Berisha supporters. Although the government was able to re-establish its control, Nano stepped down and was replaced by SPA general secretary Pandeli Majko. Despite Berisha's calls for a boycott, the population ratified a new constitution (which the DPA had refused to help draft) by referendum on 22 November. The DPA also continued to boycott parliament. This was reflective of the conflictual nature of Albanian politics and the way in which leading political actors did not feel themselves bound by the rules of a functioning democratic system.

In both paths of this pattern we see the alternation of the successor party with another party in power and the writing of constitutional provisions principally by that successor party. The successor party was therefore a major determinant of regime contours. But the paths diverge considerably in terms of the basic dynamic for change. In path 1 (Bulgaria) early agreement set the rules which the main political actors followed, while the mass of the populace exercised influence principally through the ballot box. In path 2 (Albania), major elements in the initial opposition did not support the emerging rules of the game, instead attempting to restructure those rules to their own advantage. That this failed is largely due to the fact that popular involvement in this path was not only through the ballot box, but through direct popular mobilisation. The system as it emerged in Albania was openly oligarchic rather than democratic with the failure to agree on the rules of the democratic political game moulding elite political struggle into an oligarchic rather than a democratic form.

Pattern Three

The old regime collapses without any substantive negotiation with civil society forces. Those emergent forces then negotiate among themselves about the future outlines of the political process. There is only one case of this pattern, Czechoslovakia, although the outcome in both republics has been quite different: in the Czech Republic, a stable democracy emerged, but Slovakia was for much of the 1990s an open oligarchy.

The collapse of the **Czechoslovak** regime was quick and unique in the region. Growing popular demonstrations in the second half of 1989 grew in intensity in November-December and seemed to be acquiring an organisational form with the emergence in November of two umbrella organisations, Civic Forum (CF) in the Czech Republic and Public Against Violence (PAV) in Slovakia. Round Table talks were held in November-December, which created the conditions for the transition from communist rule, but in contrast to Hungary and Poland, they did not broach the institutional structures that might replace communism; they dealt purely with changes in leadership and position.[69] In the face of this, the regime just withered away. On 3 December the government was reconstructed, but four days later it resigned, and on 10 December the president resigned. A new 'government of national understanding' with a non-communist majority was put into office, and at the end of the month the Federal Assembly elected former dissident playwright Vaclav Havel president. In January the communist party withdrew 100 of its deputies from the Federal Assembly, allowing them to be replaced by representatives of the opposition groups, with the result that the parliament no longer had a communist majority. By early 1990, those who had run the state in communist times were no longer in office and unable to play any meaningful part in building the new system.

The absence of old regime representatives from the discussions about the shape of the new system meant that the sorts of compromises evident in Poland did not have to be made in Czechoslovakia, but there was a major complicating factor: the national question. This was to overshadow political life until the break up of the country at the end of 1992. The first step of the former opposition was to convene a Round Table discussion of the major parties, groups and movements in January-February 1990. The aim was to organise competitive elections in order to create a parliament with a mandate to introduce a new constitution. The parliament's term was set at two years, which it was believed would be ample time to draft a new constitution. A law on parties, requiring 10,000 members or supporters for registration, and an interim electoral law were agreed. The electoral law involved a proportional multi-member list system with a 5% threshold.[70] In the election, voters were to vote for two houses of the federal parliament and for the republican parliaments, the Czech and Slovak National Councils.

The election in June 1990 saw CF and PAV as the largest groups in the respective republics,[71] the former movement party led mainly by communist-era dissidents, the latter by technocrats and middle-level managers.[72] At the federal level, CF gained 45.3% and PAV 12.7% of seats in the lower house. Significantly the only party to win seats in both republics was the communist party, and yet because of its role as the ruling party prior to 1989, it was effectively discredited in the eyes of the political elites and was largely sidelined in the discussions that followed. The discussions about the future form the country should take were complicated by two factors. First, the parliamentary structure of the republic.[73] The lower house of the Federal Assembly, the House of the People, was meant to represent the country as a whole and had 101 seats in the Czech lands and 49 in Slovakia. The upper house, the House of Nations, had a section for each nationality, each with 75 deputies. These two sections were to meet separately to vote on major issues. In order to be adopted, decisions on major issues required a 60% majority in the House of the People and in both sections of the House of Nations, a provision which effectively gave a blocking power to 31 deputies in either section. And in the course of constitutional discussion, most issues were classified as major and therefore triggered this provision. Moreover a vote of no confidence in a government required only a simple majority of those deputies present in any of the three constituencies, a provision which ensured weak government. The result was that little progress could be expected on constitutional issues from the parliament.

Second, the development of the party system and the implications that had for the respective republican governments. In both republics the governments issuing from the 1990 elections were broad coalitions, with only the Slovak nationalists, Hungarian coalition and communists excluded.[74] The coalitions were headed by CF and PAV. But like umbrella organisations elsewhere, these were reluctant to transform themselves into political parties; there remained within them strong anti-organisational, anti-hierarchical sentiments, a lack of discipline, coherence, communication and accountability.[75] But social movements cannot function effectively as governments, and under the pressure of having to make and implement decisions of national importance, these organisations began to fray. During 1991 CF spawned a number of parties including the Civic Democratic Party, the Civic Democratic Alliance[76], and the Club of Active Non-Partisans.[77] PAV gave birth to three: Movement for a Democratic Slovakia (MDS), Civic Democratic Union, and Hungarian Civic Party. The splitting of CF had little immediate impact on Czech politics, with the same prime minister and government remaining in office until the election in June 1992. However it did generate increased competition, in the sense that each of the parties (including those like the social democrats and the communists which did not stem from CF) now had to define positions on issues in ways which distinguished them from their former partners. The relationship with Slovakia was significant in this regard. In Slovakia, the splitting of PAV[78] led to the ousting of the prime minister Vladimir Meciar, who now tried to create a constituency for himself and the MDS by taking an increasingly hard line on the relationship with the Czechs and on economic reform. Importantly, no major new federal party, well-represented in both republics, emerged.

These factors meant that there could be no agreement on the basic question of the type of relationship between the two parts of the country.[79] As a result, by the time the mandate of the parliament ran out in mid-1992, no new constitution had been adopted. The election in June 1992 brought the issue to a head. In the Czech Republic, Vaclav Klaus' Civic Democratic Party (CDP) won 38% of the seats (its closest competitor was the communists with 17.5%) and became the major party in a coalition government. In Slovakia the MDS won 49.3% of the seats (with the communist successor Party of the Democratic Left next with 19.3%) and proceeded to form the government. Klaus' main priority was economic reform while Meciar continued to emphasise the issue of Slovak separateness and equality and the costs of radical economic reform. Constitutional reform at the federal level continued to founder, and was effectively killed off when in September 1992 a new Slovak constitution was adopted which declared the supremacy of Slovak laws over federal legislation in a number of areas. With a lack of political will on the part of Klaus to stand in the way of Meciar's drive towards Slovak independence,[80] the two leaders reached an agreement whereby the two parts of the country would split at the end of 1992. Neither had a popular mandate for this[81] and no popular referendum was undertaken. It was a result purely of elite agreement.

In the **Czech Republic** political elites sought legitimacy in the appropriation of much of the symbolism of the old Czechoslovakia, including the person of the president himself. The Klaus government, with the economy performing well, emphasised economic performance, and although there were arguments over the status of the former communist regime (should it be declared to have been illegitimate?) and the restitution of church property,[82] its period in office was relatively untroubled. The forceful leadership of Klaus, the disorganisation of the opposition and the fact that Havel sought to play a constructive role (in contrast to the part played by Walesa) were mainly responsible for this.[83] A new constitution was introduced in 1992 and consolidated the new political rules, although there was controversy on a number of issues: the need for provision for a popular referendum[84] and the mode of electing the president (Havel had wanted the president to be directly elected, at least in the first instance, but was overruled[85]) excited some debate, while the Senate provided for in the constitution was not finally established until 1996.[86] Klaus and his party were the main influence on the form of the constitution. In the party arena, the most important development was the growth in strength of the Social Democratic Party, the only such party in the region to become a major force that was not a successor party to the communists; it was a so-called 'historical' party, which had existed before the communist period and was refounded after the fall of the regime.[87] The Social Democrats won 30.5% of the seats in the June 1996 election, second only to the Civic Democratic Party's 34%, which was able to form a minority government on the back of a series of agreements with the Social Democrats.[88] The stability of the system is suggested by the fact that this government was able to ride out the economic downturn and introduction of austerity measures in 1997. New elections were called in June 1998 which were inconclusive, with the Social Democrats gaining the largest number of seats and forming a minority government. An attempt to stabilise the situation was made through an agreement with Klaus' CDP, but this did little to secure the government's future. This situation encouraged the leading parties to explore ways in which smaller parties might be weakened and larger ones strengthened, with little immediate result.[89] Throughout the post-communist period, the main political actors have abided by the emergent rules of a democratic system, with issues of substance never leading to the questioning of the basis of those rules.

In **Slovakia** the situation was less stable. The sliding threshold introduced for the June 1992 election (5% for parties, 7% for coalitions of 2–3 parties, and 10% for coalitions of four or more) meant that five groups gained representation in the parliament.[90] The MDS was initially two deputies short of a majority, and so had to rely on support to get its measures passed, but with the separation from the Czech Republic, much of the cement holding it together disappeared. During 1993 the movement splintered, and Meciar was able to consolidate his personal position.

In March 1994 the Meciar government fell to a vote of no confidence. A minority coalition government (with Party of the Democratic Left (PDL) participation) lasted until a new election in September 1994. This election, in which all parties participated through electoral alliances,[91] returned Meciar's MDS as the largest party with 40.7% of the seats (its nearest rival was a leftist coalition with 12.7%), and after extended negotiations, a coalition was formed with the Slovak National Party and a splinter from the PDL, the Workers' Association of Slovakia.[92] The opposition was weakened by disunity, and Meciar set about consolidating power into his own hands. Cronies were appointed to a large range of positions, the government took charge of parliamentary committees, supervisory boards for the media and the body overseeing privatisation, and attempts were made to exclude one party, the Democratic Union, from the parliament.[93] Meciar's opponents were harassed and intimidated and the position of the opposition within parliament weakened. In addition, there was significant conflict with the president. Meciar's relations had been strained with president Michal Kovac during his first period in office,[94] and in 1995 the relationship broke down. Meciar prevented the holding of a referendum on whether the president should be directly elected by the people, as supported by Kovac. The Supreme Court declared Meciar's action illegal, but Meciar ignored the judgement. When Kovac's term ran out, Meciar took over as acting president. Meciar's government also introduced a more restrictive language law and a new criminal law which seemed to make illegal the spreading of untruths about Slovakia, and promoted the nationalist scapegoating of the ethnic Hungarian population. Meciar clearly used his position to reshape the political rules that had been agreed in 1992 in order to strengthen that position by creating a form of 'super prime ministerialism'[95], and to weaken that of the opposition. Changes to the electoral rules for the September 1998 parliamentary poll were part of this. These required each party in a coalition to gain 5% of the votes to win parliamentary seats, thereby undercutting the rationale for coalition formation and striking at Meciar's main opponents in the SDC and the Hungarian Coalition.[96] In the September 1998 election, Meciar's party was again returned as the largest party in the parliament, but now it was hard pressed by the Slovak Democratic Coalition (SDC); the MDS gained 43 seats (28.6%) compared with the SDC's 42. The latter formed a new coalition government, which proceeded to remove many Meciar appointments to the bureaucratic and judicial apparatuses. The new government was also able to amend the constitution to introduce a directly-elected president[97] and thereby avoid the deadlock which had so allowed Meciar to expand his power. In May 1999, Meciar was defeated in a presidential poll by Rudolf Schuster, the candidate of the SDC.[98] In the following period, Slovak politics became more democratic and open in both its tone and processes, although the MDS continued to maintain pressure on the government; in November 2000 it sponsored a referendum calling for new parliamentary elections two years ahead of schedule. This failed because the required 50% level of participation was not achieved; only some 20% of voters participated. In contrast to the Czech Republic, Slovakia has thus seen significant levels of elite conflict, although this has been accompanied by general acceptance of most of the formal constitutional rules, if not always the human rights of all. There was also substantial intolerance by the Meciar government towards the opposition and the Hungarian minority.

Thus Czechoslovakia is a case where the collapse of the old regime left the shaping of the future in the hands of oppositionist politicians,[99] but where the trajectories of the two republics diverged sharply. In the Czech Republic the rules agreed upon in 1992 laid the basis for the growth of a stable party system, and one which all major actors respected. In Slovakia, principally through the drive of one man and his party, the rules agreed in 1992 were continually being challenged by support for the emergence of a more personalised style of politics, albeit one with a democratic form of legitimation through the ballot box. Politics was a type of open oligarchy, with general adherence to electoral principles accompanied by significant pressure on the rights of the Hungarian and Roma minorities.

Pattern Four

This pattern can only occur in a formal federation. The government of a republic is in the hands of civil society forces in the form of a nationalist popular movement when the regime in the federal capital falls. Prior to the collapse of communism, a process of negotiation occurs, albeit desultorily, between republican and federal authorities. When the federal government falls, the republican government inherits power and oversees the negotiations which culminate in the formation of a new system. There are four paths in this pattern.

1. The opposition group in power disintegrates, with the result that government is by weak coalitions. A party based system emerges, but it is one that rests on an ethnically exclusionary basis. Two countries followed the path to ethnic democracy, Estonia and Latvia.
2. The opposition group in power is replaced through the ballot box by the communist successor party. In Lithuania this was not a function of the splitting of the initial governing group, and the successor party was thrown out of office at the subsequent election. A democratic system emerged in Lithuania. In Moldova, the initial opposition split, chiefly over the definition of the polity as part of the development of an ethnic democracy.
3. The opposition in power self-destructs. Power eventually is stabilised in the hands of a former prominent Soviet official. A plebiscitary democracy emerged in Georgia.
4. The initial opposition group is able to stabilise its position in power, in part through undue pressure on other opposition groups. The result, reflecting the strength of particular political leaders, was a closed oligarchy in Armenia and plebiscitary democracy in Croatia.

In **Estonia**, political forces had been becoming increasingly radicalised in the last years of the 1980s. Following the foundation of the Popular Front of Estonia (PFE) in April 1988, the widespread popular desire for independence had become increasingly pointed and more open. This was reflected in the way in which the PFE had to contend with radical nationalists who rejected the authority of Soviet institutions and sought to establish an alternative parliament, the Congress of Estonia. The dynamic of this relationship on the nationalist side of politics was bound to radicalise the respective political forces and increase the pressure to shift from demands for better treatment by Moscow to calls for independence; in October 1989 the PFE endorsed full Estonian independence. The local authorities were unprepared for the strength of this sentiment.[100] The local communist party had in 1988 replaced the conservative leadership by the more reformist Valyas and, in November 1988, the government it dominated adopted the first declaration of republican sovereignty in the USSR. In March 1990 the party formally announced itself independent of the CPSU. This precipitated a split within the party, leading to the presence of two communist parties, one loyal to Moscow, the other supporting independence. Following the republican election held in March 1990,[101] the distribution of forces in the parliament was as follows: PFE 49, Free Estonia (reformist communists) 29, and Joint Council of Workers' Deputies (pro-Soviet) 27. Although aggregated under the PFE, the 49 deputies actually represented an array of smaller political organisations loosely united under the front umbrella organisation. A minority government based on the PFE and supported by Free Estonia was established, with Edgar Savisaar as prime minister. The government repudiated Soviet sovereignty on 30 March 1990 and, its popular support bolstered by the violence in the Baltics in January 1991,[102] sponsored a popular referendum on 3 March 1991 in which 77.7% of an estimated turnout of 83% supported independence; almost all ethnic Estonians and more than 25% of non-Estonian residents supported this.[103] Until the August 1991 coup in Moscow, the Estonian authorities made some efforts to engage the Soviet leadership in negotiations that might lead to independence, but to no avail. The Estonians refused to participate in the negotiations Gorbachev mounted to devise a new union treaty for a revised federation. As the coup destroyed the Soviet centre, the Estonians declared their full independence on 20 August, a claim recognised by the Soviet authorities on 6 September. The course of the struggle for independence and the Moscow coup completely discredited the conservative, pro-Soviet anti-independence side of politics, and thereby left the field clear for those associated with the PFE to turn to the building of an independent Estonia.

One of the earliest, and most difficult, issues facing the government was the definition of Estonian citizenship and determination of who had the right to vote. Estonia had a Russian minority constituting 30% of the population at the time of independence, most of whom had migrated into the country after its incorporation into the USSR in 1940. By a decision in November 1991, confirmed by the parliament in February 1992, the 1938 citizenship law was reintroduced, effectively denying citizenship and the vote to those (mostly Russians) post-1940 migrants. Descendants of post-1940 migrants had to pass a language test and undergo a waiting period (there was a two-year residency requirement dating from 30 March 1990 and an additional one-year waiting period) before they could gain citizenship, a provision which effectively excluded them from the constitutional referendum and election held in 1992. This not only enflamed the Russian population of Estonia and was opposed by Russian-based political organisations in the country, but strained relations with Russia. This situation was exacerbated in 1993. Measures were adopted on a language standard that would-be citizens had to achieve, and in May non-citizens were prevented from standing in local elections. In June 1993 the parliament adopted a Law on Aliens which would have enabled the government to refuse residency permits to non-citizens, but it was sent back for reconsideration by the president. The following month a law was passed giving Soviet-era citizens the right to a residency permit,[104] and in October 1993 all permanent resident adults were able to vote in the local elections (although only citizens could be candidates). In January the Riigikogu (the parliament) extended the period of residence required to attain citizenship from two to five years. This issue of citizenship and voting rights was important because it was about defining who was a member of the polity and who was not, and its effect was to disfranchise over a quarter of the population.

The PFE-supported government fell in January 1992, with a caretaker prime minister (Tiit Vahi) being installed to remain in office until a new constitution was introduced and elections held. A new constitution was drafted and put to the voters in a referendum on 28 June 1992;[105] it was approved by 91.3% of voters on a 66.8% turnout,[106] the first post-Soviet constitution approved in the FSU. This provided for a parliamentary system with a four-year single chamber parliament (the Riigikogu) and a president to be elected by the parliament except for the first instance in 1992 when the parliament would choose between two candidates only if neither got an absolute majority in a direct popular vote. The election (the first in the FSU) was held for the parliament and presidency on 20 September 1992. In the election to the parliament, which was by PR with a 5% threshold, seven of the 12 party lists competing exceeded the threshold. The PFE had decided to remain a social movement rather than transform itself into a party,[107] and so did not contest the election. The government was a coalition headed by the Christian Democratic Fatherland Union (FU) and including the Moderates (representing the social democrats and the rural centre) and the Estonian National Independence Party. This coalition constituted a new political generation compared with those (including former communist officials) who had dominated the first PFE administration.[108] These groups together had 51 of the 101 seats in the Riigikogu, which because of the citizenship provisions noted above was mono-ethnic in composition.[109] In the presidential election, no candidate received an absolute majority so the election went to the Riigikogu where the FU's Lennart Meri was preferred over former communist politician Arnold Ruutel despite the latter polling more votes than Meri in the popular election. Thus the government was led by the FU and a member of that organisation was president. The relationship was not conflictual, although there were issues of tension; Meri did moderate the government's anti-Russian thrust, vetoing the Law on Aliens noted above.[110] The coalition came under significant strain in 1994,[111] falling in September to be replaced by another coalition arrangement. Following the elections of March 1995[112] and 1999, a succession of weak coalition governments has succeeded one another. This was exacerbated by the banning of coalitions in November 1998, a measure which forced parties to go it alone[113] but which in 1999 meant that there were only 12 party lists for voters to choose from (compared with 16 in 1995). Meri was re-elected president in September 1996, and given the continuing fragmentation in the parliament, was able to expand the competence of the presidency.

So in Estonia from the 1990 election of a PFE-supported government, old regime forces were minor actors, and following the Moscow coup, had no part to play at all in structuring Estonian politics. None of the main political forces stemmed from the old regime. But nor could the PFE continue to exercise a unifying influence, with the result that successive governments were weak coalitions. But on the major issue for negotiation, that of the definition of the membership of the polity, there was more unity among Estonian political forces, and this was reflected in the substantial exclusion of the Russian section of the population from the political process and the establishment of an ethnic democracy.

Unlike Estonia, in **Latvia** the emergence of a more liberal leader (Vagris) in the ruling communist party in October 1988 did not lead to the displacement of the conservatives, with the result that until the party split in April 1990, its leadership remained a battleground for opposing forces. This clearly handicapped it in its attempt to respond to the challenge from the opposition. On the opposition side, again in contrast to Estonia, the Popular Front of Latvia (PFL) worked in cooperation with more radical nationalists to present a more consistent and united voice ultimately in favour of Latvian independence.[114] This pressure increased with the approach of the republican election in March 1990 and escalated substantially after it. The election resulted in an even stronger pro-independence vote than in Estonia, with the PFL and its allies winning 131 seats, anti-independence candidates 55 (with most going to the Interfront movement set up by the authorities), and 15 affiliated to neither group.[115] The new prime minister, Ivars Godmanis, against a background of opposition from the local communist party (since April 1990 led by the more conservative Rubiks) attempted to open negotiations on autonomy/independence with the Moscow authorities, but was rebuffed. Nevertheless the popular pressure leading to independence was maintained, sustained by the Soviet-inspired violence in Riga in January 1991, a solid 73.7% (on a turnout of 87.6%) vote for independence in the March 1991 referendum, and the May Latvian declaration of independence. Godmanis refused to participate in Gorbachev's negotiations for a new union treaty. However Latvian aspirations were not accepted in Moscow until the August coup destroyed the power of the centre. As in Estonia, the collapse of Moscow's authority left the opposition in power in Latvia and the former rulers irrelevant.

In power, the PFL began to fragment under the pressure of having to make hard decisions and without the unifying effect of the communists. This disintegration was exacerbated by the approach of elections in June 1993 as different groups within the Front sought to manoeuvre to improve their position for the coming poll. The creation of alliances was important for small groups because it had been decided that the election would be held on the basis of PR with a 4% threshold. An important factor in this was also the citizenship/nationality question. According to the 1989 census, Latvians accounted for only 52% of the population, the remainder being minority groups including many immigrants from during the Soviet period. Most of these were Russians.[116] The government's initial position was to accord citizenship only to those who were citizens prior to 1940 and to their descendants, with the question of naturalisation to be deferred.[117] This effectively disbarred more than a third of the population, mainly Russians, from full membership of the polity. This not only meant that parties based in the Russian population were neutered, but so too was any possible questioning of the independent status of Latvia.

The election resulted in a coalition government of the moderate rightist Latvia's Way Alliance (36% of seats) and Farmers' Union (FU – 12% of seats) supported on individual issues by other of the eight party groups which had exceeded the threshold (of 23 which stood). The Saiema, or parliament, introduced an amended version of the 1922 Constitution rather than design a new one,[118] and elected the FU's Guntis Ulmanis president. This government, led by Valdis Birkavs, largely continued the economic policies of its predecessor, but it also sought to be more restrictive with regard to non-Latvians. The government attempted to restrict the number of non-Latvians who could be naturalised each year, but Ulmanis refused to sign the law. A new law on naturalisation was passed in July 1994 with residence, language and age requirements; under 20s could apply from 1 January 1995, 20–25 year olds from 1 January 1996 and so on.[119] In effect, this was the sort of quota the government had been unable to get earlier.

Owing chiefly to policy differences and to the poor performance of Latvia's Way in the May 1994 local elections, the government collapsed in July 1994. It was replaced by another coalition led by Latvia's Way which lasted until new elections in September-October 1995. Nine parties[120] crossed the, increased, 5% threshold, but only four of these gained more than 10%, with a range from 12% to 15.2% of votes and 14 to 18 seats. This fragmentation of party support and the different policy priorities of the groups made the formation of a narrow coalition government impossible. As a result, when the government was formed after three months of negotiations,[121] it comprised six parties, excluding only the extreme nationalist National Movement for Latvia (Siegerists), the successor Socialist Party led by Rubiks, and the National Harmony Party which championed the rights of non-Latvians. The coalition was inherently unstable, and finally gave way to fresh elections in October 1998 which produced a similar spread of votes and therefore the same problem of a weak coalition government.[122]

So as in Estonia, an oppositionist government inherited power at the time of the Soviet collapse and entrenched a party-based electoral system that was ethnically exclusionary. But the fragmentation of political forces made for weak coalition governments in the Latvian ethnic democracy.

In **Lithuania** the reform movement Sajudis (the Lithuanian Movement for Perestroika) emerged in 1988 and soon took up the most hard line stance of any of the Baltic fronts on the question of independence; pro-independence Sajudis candidates won 36 of the 42 seats to the Soviet Congress of People's Deputies in the March 1989 election.[123] The strength of this sentiment generally resulted in a split in the local communist party in 1989, with a section splitting from the Moscow loyalists to form the Lithuanian Democratic Labour Party (LDLP). The terms of early negotiations with Moscow were much more uncompromising here than in any other of the Soviet republics. The February 1990 republican election produced a parliament that was solidly, uncompromisingly, in favour of Lithuanian independence. Sajudis won 99 seats in the 141 seat parliament while the LDLP which had supported the Sajudis-led thrust for independence won 22 seats. The pro-Soviet communists won only seven and were effectively sidelined. The parliament elected a leading figure in Sajudis, Vytautus Landsbergis, chair of the parliament and head of state, and in March 1990 adopted a declaration of independence. Moscow refused to recognise this, even though Gorbachev's visit to Vilnius in January 1990 seemed to give him a greater appreciation of the inevitability of change in the relationship between Moscow and at least this republic. The Lithuanian leadership pressed on, sustained by the violence in Vilnius in January 1991, a vote of 90.5% support (turnout 84.7%) for independence in the February 1991 referendum, and Soviet economic pressure against the republic. But its independence was not recognised until the Moscow coup undermined the power of the Soviet centre.

At independence, Lithuania had the sort of political spectrum that existed in no other post-Soviet state: a strong right in the form of Sajudis faced a substantial left in the form of the LDLP, both within the political arena defined by Soviet collapse and acceptance of Lithuanian independence. Furthermore Lithuania did not have the sort of substantial Russian minority that was present in the other Baltic states, so the question of definition of the polity did not arise with the same clarity; from the outset, everyone living and working in Lithuania in 1989 was eligible for citizenship. But the institutional problems were similar: the Soviet structure had to be replaced by institutions with a Lithuanian pedigree, at least symbolically, and this was not without conflict. Upon gaining independence, the Lithuanian parliament reinstated the 1938 constitution for one hour in an attempt to emphasise continuity with the non-Soviet past, suspended it, and then adopted a Supreme Law, which was effectively the body of laws adopted before independence. This was to act as a *de facto* constitution until a new one was drafted.

The constitutional issue raised the question of the relationship between president and parliament. Landsbergis and much of the social movement Sajudis favoured a strengthened presidency, but most of the Sajudis deputies in the parliament favoured enhanced parliamentary supremacy.[124] Urged on by his supporters, Landsbergis mounted a popular referendum in May 1992 in which the people were asked to back a strengthened presidency, and although a majority supported the proposal, not enough voted to render the result valid. Landsbergis now scheduled parliamentary elections in the belief that he would be able to build on the majority support in the referendum to extend his control over the new body. The elections were schduled for October and were to take place under a mixed SMC-PR system for a new unicameral 141 seat parliament called the Seimas. Seventy one seats were to be filled from single member districts and 70 from national lists by PR with a 4% threshold.

The election result stunned Sajudis. The LDLP won 44% of the votes and 51% of the seats compared with the main political representative of Landsbergis and Sajudis Homeland Union (Conservatives of Lithuania) 21.2% of the votes and 19.9% of the seats.[125] The communist successor party could rule in its own right. At the same time in a popular referendum on a constitutional draft, the populace supported (75.8% on a 74.9% turnout) a constitution establishing a parliamentary system of government. In December 1992 the Seimas elected LDLP leader Algirdas Brazauskas acting president, a position confirmed in the presidential election of February 1993 in which Brazauskas received 61.1% of the vote. The LDLP now clearly controlled the political agenda and the parliamentary system, and although one LDLP government collapsed in February 1996 (principally as a result of a bank scandal in December 1995 that involved the prime minister) there was no challenge to this dominance by the opposition before the next election. But the support for the LDLP eroded in the face of economic difficulties and a range of other policies, with the result that when the new election was held in October 1996, the party received only 10% of the votes and 8.8% of the seats. With 51.1% of the seats (on 31.3% of the votes), the Homeland Union was able to form the government. The parliament was both more conservative and more fragmented than its predecessor. When the presidential election was held, no party candidate got past the first round, with two independents running off in the second round. The fragmentation of the Seimas was sustained following the election in October 2000. Following this election, the LDLP successor the Social Democratic Coalition emerged as the biggest group in parliament with 31.1% of the votes and 34.75% of the seats, but the government was formed by a four-party coalition (Liberal Union, New Union-Social Liberal, Centre Union, and Christian Democratic Union) supported by two minor parties. The former leading governing party, the Homeland Union, received only 6% of the votes, reflecting a decisive rejection of the more conservative elements in politics. But with 16 parties in the Seimas and the government composed of a broad coalition, politics remained fragmented.

So in Lithuania although the opposition was in office at the time of the collapse of the USSR, the communist successor party gained government at the first post-Soviet election and then lost it at the second, and although it did not regain government at the third, it was the largest party. The rules of the game were defined by a combination of those forces which had opposed Soviet rule and some whose roots were clearly in the old regime; it was under the latter that the basic rules of the game, the constitution, was adopted. Lithuania has fulfilled the criteria of a democracy.

In **Moldova**, as the republican election of February 1990 approached and the Moldavian Popular Front (MPF) appeared to pose a challenge to continuing party rule, the communist party, led since November 1989 by Petru Lucinschi, attempted to shift in a more nationalist direction. But this was to little avail, as in the election the MPF in alliance with a number of other groups won more than two thirds of the seats in the Supreme Soviet. MPF-supported communist party member Mircea Snegur was elected Chair of the Supreme Soviet[126], a new government was sworn in, and in June 1990 Moldovan sovereignty was proclaimed and the communist party forbidden from organising in the workplace. The government refused to participate in Gorbachev's negotiations for a new union treaty and in his March 1991 referendum on the future of the USSR. However this attitude and an increasingly nationalist Moldovan stance (although already there was a distinction between those who favoured complete independence and those who wanted to re-unite with Romania) generated opposition among ethnic Russians in the Transdnestr district, many of whom refused to recognise the authority of the MPF-dominated Supreme Soviet, and the minority Gagauz region.[127] This alienation increased following the declaration of Moldovan independence after the Moscow coup; both regions had supported the coup and the maintenance of the USSR.

In December 1991 Snegur was elected president unopposed in a direct popular election, a result which liberated him from dependence on the MPF. However the election was boycotted in the Transdnestr and Gagauz regions and by the MPF, which rendered Snegur's authority somewhat problematic. The boycotts reflected the considerable disagreement within Moldova over the future of the country. The Russian population in Transdnestr favoured a continued link with Russia and feared the other two alternatives currently under review, full independence or unification with Romania. The MPF boycotted the election, and cut its links with Snegur, for three reasons: in 1990–91 it had become more radical than Snegur in exploring the full independence/unification with Romania options, Snegur had removed the radical nationalist MPF prime minister Mircea Druc from office, and Snegur favoured a presidential system of government while the MPF leaders favoured a parliamentary system. Snegur further alienated the MPF (from early 1992 the Christian Democratic Popular Front of Moldova) when, following the failure of his attempt to resolve the Transdnestr question by force in March-August 1992, he moved closer to Russia and sought her help on this question. This not only drove a wedge between Snegur and his former PF support base, but also helped to split the PF along nationalist lines: support for Romanian unification compared with going it alone within the CIS.[128] This split was to be a significant barrier to future electoral success.

Domestically Snegur sought to strengthen his position by building bridges to the former communist party bureaucrats in the parliament. In June 1992 he forced the resignation of the Muravschi government for failure to make headway on economic reform, leading to a 'government of national consensus' led by Andrei Sangheli (a former communist party official). Later in the year there was also a change in the chairmanship of the Supreme Soviet, with the MPF's Alexandru Moghanu being replaced by former communist party leader Lucinschi. In the eyes of the MPF, the government under Snegur had tilted dangerously in favour of people who looked for inspiration to the former regime. And indeed, the three leading positions (president, prime minister, and chair of the parliament) were held by former members of the communist party Politburo. In March 1993 the Supreme Soviet under Lucinschi's guidance ratified a new constitution declaring Moldova an independent state. This seemed definitively to close off the MPF option of reunification with Romania and thereby remove from the political agenda one of the key questions of this early period, the identity of the state. Four months later Snegur brought on a parliamentary crisis by calling on the parliament to ratify the CIS agreement on membership. This failed, owing to MPF opposition and a walk out by enough deputies to render the meeting inquorate. Most returned in October to adopt a new electoral law and set parliamentary elections for February 1994.

The elections were held on the basis of PR with a 4% threshold, and they returned to government the party that had been the basis of the Sangheli government since mid-1992, the Democratic Agrarian Party of Moldova (DAPM – it won 56 of 104 seats).[129] The basis of this communist successor party was the leaderships of the state and collective farms. This victory confirmed both Sangheli and Lucinschi in office. The agreement on CIS membership was now ratified, and a popular referendum rejected unification with Romania by a vote of 95% (turnout 75%). In July another constitution was adopted, containing guarantees of ethnic minorities' rights and autonomy for the Transdnestr and Gagauz regions, although separatist sentiment within the former remained; although it was granted republican status within Moldova in mid-1996, its leaders continued to press for confederation rather than simply autonomy within Moldova. As the next presidential election approached in late 1996, leading figures in the DAPM began to manoeuvre for advantage. In August 1995 Snegur left the DAPM and formed his own party, Rebirth and Consolidation, Sangheli consolidated his position within the DAPM, while Lucinschi looked for support to the newly-formed (January 1995) leftist Party of Social Progress. The heads of the three main institutions of state, the presidency, government and parliament, were preparing to run for the presidency. However when the election was held in December, Sangheli was discredited by a corruption scandal. The second round saw Lucinschi come from behind to defeat Snegur 56%:44%. All three main institutions of government were now headed by figures from the left, the lineal successor of the former communist party. At the following election in 1998, a right centrist coalition achieved power, even though the Communist Party of Moldova gained almost a third of the votes and 40 of the 101 seats. In June 1999, some Christian Democratic Popular Front MPs supported amending the Constitution to introduce a parliamentary form of government, but this sentiment was opposed by Lucinschi who continued throughout the year to press for constitutional change to expand presidential powers at the expense of the parliament. The tension between president and parliament, which was instrumental in the collapse of the government in November 1999 and its replacement by one led by former communist youth leader Dumitru Braghis, lasted throughout the year, but in the struggle both sides were content generally to appeal to and abide by the Constitutional Court. However during this struggle, in July 2000, the Constitution was amended to provide for the parliament to elect the president. At the end of 2000 another political crisis erupted with the failure of the parliament on four occasions to elect a new president. This failure was due to the split between the left, which supported the Communist Party candidate Voronin and the centre-right which supported former Constitutional Court judge Barbalet. Failure to resolve this impasse led Lucinschi to dissolve parliament and call new elections. In the February

2001 elections, the Communist Party won 70% of the seats with just under 50% of the vote, sufficient to elect their preferred candidate as president.

Thus the course of negotiations in Moldova saw an initial oppositionist elite fragment, principally over the question of definition of the Moldovan polity, and power coming into the hands of communist successor forces, which retained power until 1998. However the failure of those in the Transdnestr and Gagauz regions to participate fully in the polity renders Moldova an ethnic democracy.

Georgian opposition forces had come together principally in the Round Table Free Georgia movement in April 1990 (although Round Table was originally part of the Committee for National Salvation formed in October 1989). In the republican election in October-November 1990 it humbled the regime, winning 54% of the vote and 155 seats to the communist party's 29.6% of the vote and 64 seats in the 250 seat parliament. The dominance of the nationalist movement was capped when its representative, former dissident and chair of the Supreme Soviet since October 1990 Zviad Gamsakhurdia, won the presidency against five opponents in May 1991 with 86.5% of the votes. Sustained by a 99.1% support for independence in a referendum in March 1991, this administration sought to realise this aim in its interactions with the Moscow authorities, but this was not achieved until the Moscow coup destroyed the Soviet centre. But in the meantime, the opposition umbrella organisation began to fracture, chiefly under the impact of the increasingly authoritarian policies and style of the president.[130] He sought to concentrate power in his own hands and to project a form of plebiscitarian authority, something which generated increased opposition to him both inside and outside the parliament. Important here was the growth, initially in 1990, of privately-organised armed formations and Gamsakhurdia's attempt to bring them under control.[131] This culminated in armed clashes in Tbilisi in December 1991–January 1992 and Gamsakhurdia's flight into hiding. Representatives of opposition parties and groups met and declared the creation of a Military Council which would take over power, remove the president and suspend parliament. A provisional government was established under former prime minister Tengiz Sigua, and attempts made to coordinate its work through the creation of a consultative council involving representatives of the major political forces and the Military Council.

In March power was passed to a newly-formed State Council headed by the recently returned former Soviet foreign minister, Eduard Shevardnadze. The Council comprised the main anti-Gamsakhurdia opposition leaders, and was meant to restore the parliamentary dominance over the executive that had been lost under Gamsakhurdia. Its attempts to stabilise the situation were complicated by military activity; forces seeking the independence of South Ossetia and Abkhazia were active in both regions,[132] with fighting breaking out in March and October 1992, respectively, while fighting with pro-Gamsakhurdia forces also began in March. The continuing activity of the armed militias in several parts of the country contributed to the clear loss of central capacity to project its control throughout the republic. There was an effective 'collapse of central power'.[133] This sort of tension and conflict was to be the backdrop for Georgian politics for much of the decade. In October 1992, elections were to be held in an attempt to give the administration an acceptable form of mandate.[134] The leaders adopted an electoral system based on a single transferable vote without a threshold in order to maximise the number of parties that gained representation and hinder the prospects of a party led by a prominent individual from gaining a majority, measures clearly reflecting their concern that Gamsakhurdia could still attract significant electoral support.[135] As fear of Gamsakhurdia declined, in August 1992 a new electoral law was introduced with a combination of SMC and PR. Shevardnadze was elected as chair of the parliament (effective president) with 95% of the vote, although he was the only candidate standing and pro-Gamsakhurdia forces boycotted the poll. The parliament that issued from the election was highly fragmented, with 23 parties winning seats but none being close to a majority.[136] This made the parliament ineffective, although in November it did pass a decree on state power which was to serve as a constitution until one could be introduced properly. This gave Shevardnadze ultimate executive power in conjunction with the government, with parliament designated as the supreme executive body. The head of state was to be elected by the parliament, could be removed by a two-thirds majority vote, and lacked the power to dissolve parliament or appoint officials without parliamentary approval.

However because of its fragmentation, and the threatening military situation in the country with conflict in Abkhazia and South Ossetia and the continuing struggle with pro-Gamsakhurdia forces, the parliament was unable to translate this supremacy into actuality. In June 1993 Shevardnadze began to call for expanded powers so he could provide the country with the strong leadership it needed, and in July the parliament granted him extra powers, including the right to introduce decrees without parliamentary approval and to dismiss any official except the prime minister. In September, with the defeat of Georgian forces leading to the *de facto* independence of Abkhazia, Shevardnadze introduced a state of emergency, but was able to gain parliamentary agreement only after threatening to resign, public support by the Patriarch of the Georgian Orthodox Church, and demonstrations in the streets. He also sought to build a political base with the formal establishment in August 1993 of the Citizens Union of Georgia (CUG), which, in the following November, elected him its leader. Throughout 1994 the military situation remained critical but this, added to widespread popular support, sustained Shevardnadze against criticism of his leadership by opposition groups.

A new constitution was introduced on 24 August 1995.[137] This provided for a presidential republic with a directly-elected president for a maximum of two five-year terms, and a unicameral parliament with a four-year term, with 150 seats to be filled by PR on a 5% threshold and 85 by first past the post. Elections were scheduled for October. In the lead up to the elections, the campaign being waged by Shevardnadze against irregular militias was seen to have a political edge, when, in the wake of an unsuccessful assassination attempt on Shevardnadze in August, he cracked down on a powerful para-military group (the Mkhedrioni) associated with a leading figure, Dzhaba Iosseliani. In July Iosseliani declared that this had been transformed into a political society and that it would contest the elections, but at the beginning of October it was disbanded, just after Iosseliani withdrew his nomination for the presidential election, declaring Georgia to be a 'police state'. In the presidential election, Shevardnadze received 74.9% of the vote, with only one other candidate receiving more than 2%.[138] In the parliamentary election,[139] only three parties of the 53 registered to participate (compared with 35 in 1992) crossed the 5% threshold. Shevardnadze's CUG was the largest party in the parliament, with 107 seats of a total of 231; there was no voting in Abkhazia and South Ossetia, and some PR seats remained unfilled. The election clearly strengthened Shevardnadze's position with almost all deputies loyal to him,[140] and ten days after the voting Iosseliani was arrested. He was accused of involvement in the August 1995 attempt to assassinate Shevardnadze. Despite Shevardnadze's win, the situation in the country remained unstable; fighting continued in some regions, secessionist forces had not been subdued (Abkhazia retained its stance of seeking independence), assassination attempts continued against leading figures including Shevardnadze,[141] and armed militias had not been eliminated. Against this background there was continuing pressure for a strengthening of Shevardnadze's position. This seemed to be achieved with the parliamentary election in October-November 1999. Of the 33 parties and blocs competing in the election, only two cleared the 7% threshold, with Shevardnadze's CUG gaining a majority. There was some international criticism, with OSCE observers refusing to endorse it as free and fair because of some interference with the opposition, some irregularities of procedures, and serious violations including intimidation of electoral officials in some constituencies. Shevardnadze's dominance was consolidated when he was victorious in the presidential poll in April 2000. He won 80.4% of the vote, compared with his nearest challenger communist leader Patiashvili who won 16.6%.

Thus while an oppositionist regime was in power at the time of the Soviet collapse, the administration self-destructed with a coup against the elected president. Within the context of bitter armed conflict, debate between executive and parliament resulted in the strengthening of the position of president, a former high official in the USSR who, in part also because of the weakness of organised political forces, was able to exercise plebiscitarian authority.

Politics in **Armenia** was overshadowed by the conflict with Azerbaijan over Nagorno-Karabakh and by the dire economic conditions that this conflict brought.[142] Armenia embarked on independent statehood with a government dominated by the popular front movement, the Pan-Armenian National Movement (PANM), which held 110 of the 245 seats in the Supreme Soviet. In the October 1991 presidential election, its representative Levon Ter-Petrossian won 87% of the votes against five candidates. Throughout 1992, despite the substantial economic difficulties, some tension between government and parliament over reform, and opposition calls for a new constitution, political life was relatively uneventful. However during 1993-94 popular demonstrations against the government and its handling of the economy unrolled in the capital Yerevan, and these soon became associated with calls for the resignation of the president and the parliament and the convening of a constituent assembly to oversee the holding of elections and the adoption of a new constitution. At the end of 1994 Ter-Petrossian moved against the main opposition party, the Armenian Revolutionary Federation (ARF), suspending its activities on the basis of charges of its involvement in terrorist activity. During this initial period the PANM had splintered, with a number of political parties emerging from it, although the principal differences between them were personality rather than policy-based.[143]

Parliamentary elections were scheduled for July 1995, and the regulations for these were introduced in April. These provided for a mixed SMC (150 seats)/PR party list (40 seats) system with a 5% threshold. A number of opposition parties as well as the ARF were barred (National Progress Party and the bloc of 10 parties called the Constitutional Assembly) from involvement in the election. Following the voting, the electoral coalition used by Ter-Petrossian's PANM, the Republican bloc, emerged as the largest entity, with 119 of the 190 seats (on 42.7% of the votes). The opposition protested about voting irregularities and the prevention of some parties from participating, while OSCE observers suggested that the ban on the ARF could have influenced the result and that the election had not been conducted fairly.[144] In a simultaneous constitutional referendum, just over two-thirds of voters supported the draft, although there were claims that the result had been fabricated.[145] The new constitution, which was drafted by those around Ter-Petrossian, centralised power in Yerevan at the expense of the regions and greatly strengthened the president in comparison with the parliament.

Pressure was maintained on the opposition, with 31 members of the ARF being put on trial in March 1996, charged with planning a coup soon after the election. Presidential elections had been scheduled for September 1996, and when these were held Ter-Petrossian scored an easy victory in the first round, gaining 51.8% of the vote compared with his nearest rival Vazgen Manukian's 41.3%. The opposition claimed that the results had been rigged to give Ter-Petrossian more than 50% and thereby avoid a second round, a charge supported by OSCE observers.[146] Large demonstrations by Manukian's supporters broke out and were met by considerable force; many opposition activists were arrested and the headquarters of the main opposition parties closed down. Ter-Petrossian was thus able to use force to stabilise his rule. However his position was not invulnerable. In early 1998 conflict broke out between him and his prime minister, Robert Kocharian, chiefly over the latter's proposals for bringing peace to Nagorno-Karabakh. In February the Republican bloc split over this issue and Ter-Petrossian resigned. Kocharian became acting president pending elections in March. Kocharian relegalised the ARF and released many of its activists from gaol. When the election was held, Kocharian won 59.5% in the second round against former communist party leader Karen Demirchian. Opposition figures protested about vote rigging and about Kocharian using the advantages of incumbency to assist his candidacy. OSCE observers reported violations of electoral procedures, including falsification of voting and intimidation of voters, and declared that the election fell below the standards required for fairness. In May 1998 Kocharian announced the establishment of a commission to draft constitutional amendments reducing presidential prerogatives and increasing the powers of government. In May 1999, in an election widely criticised by international observers, the reworked Republican bloc now called Miasnutian was returned to power, although it had to rely upon communist support to govern. However the potential instability of Armenian politics was again demonstrated in October 1999 when armed gunmen burst into the parliament and assassinated the prime minister and a number of other MPs, a development which enabled the president again to assert his authority.

Thus in Armenia the same opposition organisation that had found itself in power when the Soviet centre collapsed retained power throughout this period, although this was not without change of personnel at the top or unfair pressure upon other opposition groups. A closed oligarchy was the result.

By 1989 the communist regime in **Croatia** was largely bereft of new ideas, in part because of the purging of independent thought that had occurred following the 'Croatian Spring' of 1971, and faced a growing crisis as a result of the disintegration of the established principles of the Yugoslav polity, fuelled especially by the mounting Serb nationalism fanned by Milosevic. The political scene was soon dominated by new parties and groups,[147] and when elections were held in 1990, the communist party was swept from power. In the parliamentary election in April-May 1990, the umbrella organisation of six parties called the Croatian Democratic Communty (CDC) won 42% of the votes and 66% of the seats. Its leader, Franjo Tudjman, was then elected president. Tudjman pursued a Croatian nationalist course,[148] which exacerbated the growing problem of the Serbs within Croatia (especially their feelings of being under threat) and led ultimately to armed conflict between Serbs and Croats in Croatia beginning in late 1990 and Croatian involvement in the wars of the Yugoslav succession. This involvement, and after it ended the shadow cast by the continuing conflict in Bosnia-Herzegovina, helped to shape Croatian politics and to reinforce the apparent appeal of Tudjman's nationalism. Tudjman used his dominating position in the political sphere to drive his agenda; there were no negotiations with other parties about democratisation or any sharing of power with them, freedom of the press was curtailed, and pressure placed on opposition forces. Power was increasingly concentrated in presidential hands.[149] A new constitution was introduced in December 1990 which brought in a powerful, directly-elected president and which asserted Croatia's sovereignty and its right to secede from Yugoslavia. Despite both political and military pressure from Belgrade, Croatia (and Slovenia) pressed for the dissolution of the federal republic.[150] In May 1991 a referendum in Croatia produced a 94% majority (on an 83% turnout) favouring independence, after which Croatia formally declared its sovereignty and, on 25 June 1991, its independence. However this was soured by the way in which following armed conflict, in the second half of the year the Krajina Serbs, supported by the Serb-controlled Yugoslav National Army, were able to establish a form of independence from Zagreb's rule.

Domestically the dominance of Tudjman and the CDC was reaffirmed at the 1992 and 1995 elections. Despite some evidence of internal disunity,[151] the CDC was able to consolidate its hold on power, in both elections winning more than half the seats in the parliament. In 1992 the CDC won more than twice the number of votes of its nearest rival, while Tudjman was elected president with 57% of the vote in a field of eight. Although there was no interference in voting and opposition parties could campaign freely, the CDC enjoyed special access to the media. Its nearest rival in 1995, a coalition of seven parties called the Croatian Electoral Alliance, received 18.3% of the vote, less than half that of the CDC. The 1995 victory was assisted by the manipulation of the legal framework of administration of the election (gerrymandering, supporters in embassies responsible for absentee/ diaspora voting) and a compliant media with pressure on those which were not.[152] Despite gaining a foothold in local government and the outbreak of widespread popular demonstrations in 1996 when Tudjman tried to consolidate his power by closing down the last independent broadcaster in Croatia, the opposition was able to make few inroads into the position of the CDC and its president.[153] Tudjman used nationalism to buttress his rule, a ploy strengthened by the successful offensive launched in August 1995 to retake the Krajina. This nationalist theme was important in establishing his personal dominance over the Croatian political scene,[154] a dominance confirmed by his election victory in June 1997 (he gained 61.4% of the vote to his nearest rival's 21.0%) in an election that was deemed to be free but not fair, principally because of media bias. Tudjman's personal dominance slipped only when he became very ill in late 1999. His death in December 1999 stimulated a shake up in the political system. In the legislative election in January 2000, the CDC vote fell to less than a third, while a majority of seats was gained by the opposition Social Democrat-Social Liberal coalition in alliance with the United List.[155] A more open, less ideological politics has ensued, reflecting the importance of the person of Tudjman in the shaping of the initial contours of Croatian politics. This is also clear in the decision taken on 9 November 2000 by the parliament to alter the Constitution to reduce presidential powers, to make the government responsible only to the parliament, and thereby institute a parliamentary democracy.

So in Croatia the old regime was removed at the first election which brought to power a section of the former opposition. This then consolidated itself domestically within Croatia while negotiating independence from the federal government. It then used nationalism to consolidate its control over the domestic political scene while its leader used a personalist appeal to consolidate plebiscitary democracy.

Pattern Five

This pattern can only occur in a federation. When the centre collapses, power is in the hands of a republican political elite which consists of an amalgam of oppositionist and old regime forces. The balance between these may be uneasy and can change over time. This balance differed in different countries: in Russia, Ukraine and Macedonia an old regime (albeit reformist) president faced a mixed parliament, in Slovenia an old regime (reformist) president faced a predominantly oppositionist parliament, and in the Kyrgyz Republic a new president faced an old regime parliament. The new structure was shaped in the dynamic between these elements.

In **Russia** the republican election had returned a parliament which was divided between those who owed their positions to their membership of the Soviet communist party and those whose loyalties had shifted to one of the weak society-based groups and proto-parties that had emerged under Gorbachev in Russia. The Russian leader soon became Boris Yeltsin, a former high party official who had been officially disgraced in 1987–88 but who had managed to fight his way back to political prominence by mobilising popular support and appealing to emergent democratic groups in Russian society in the March 1989 Soviet and March 1990 republican elections. In May 1990 Yeltsin was elected Chairman of the Russian Supreme Soviet and in June 1991 he was popularly elected president from a field of six. From May 1990 onward, Yeltsin conducted a vigorous campaign of negotiation and confrontation with Soviet leader Mikhail Gorbachev to increase the republic's autonomy from Moscow.[156] Following the August coup, this accelerated, and it was Yeltsin along with Ukraine's Kravchuk and Belarus' Shushkevich who effectively killed off the USSR.

When an independent Russia emerged, it had a government that had its origins in the Soviet period but whose tone was set by younger radical reformers, a parliamentary structure with a nominal communist majority but also with a substantial number of reformist deputies who were looking for effective leadership, a president with an exaggerated view of his rights and duties (and who was building up his presidential apparatus, initially with many old regime functionaries but also a sprinkling of radical reformers[157]), and a Soviet-era constitution. During the confrontation between Russia and the Soviet centre in the first half of 1991, parliament and president had stood substantially together, with the differences between them being submerged in the interests of seizing power from the centre. However when independence had been achieved, the unifying effect of the common enemy disappeared, and with this differences over structure and policy emerged. On structure, both president and parliament had expansive views of their own rights and perogatives and differed over whether Russia needed a presidential or a parliamentary system. On policy, the chief difference turned on the attitude to economic reform and how it was to be managed. Through 1992 and 1993 this conflict escalated.

The conflict was played out by the elite with no effective input from outside. Although Yeltsin had relied upon Democratic Russia for his election as president,[158] once in that office he made no attempt either to mobilise that organisation or to build up his own political party, with the result that his main channel into the populace was the media. Throughout his time in office he used the media to project his appeal directly to the people, seeking to create a charismatic tie between himself and the populace and thereby to marginalise other political institutions. The parties in the parliament were only weakly developed and therefore not in a position to mobilise the populace widely on this question. This was essentially an elite argument in which the actors were located in the regime's power structures and stemmed overwhelmingly from the Soviet era.[159] The dispute took the form of debate over economic policy and constitutional form, with the two sides arguing for a parliamentary system or a presidential system. During the course of the stand off, seven constitutional drafts (two presidential and five parliamentary) were presented and dismissed. But despite the increasingly bitter rhetoric and threats, until autumn 1993 both sides generally obeyed the emergent rules of the game. The dispute was resolved in autumn 1993, when Yeltsin suspended the parliament. When the parliamentary leaders objected, and encouraged violence by their supporters, Yeltsin mobilised a reluctant military against them. His opponents were killed, arrested, or cowed into silence. At the same time Yeltsin called new parliamentary elections (by a mixed PR party list/SMC system, with 225 deputies elected by each method and a 5% threshold) and a constitutional referendum for December, but he also banned some parties from participating, closed some media outlets, and placed restrictions on what could be discussed. Furthermore the constitutional draft, worked out by Yeltsin's advisers and rejecting much of what the parliament had wanted, was presented to the electorate only a couple of weeks before they were to vote and therefore gave them very limited time for analysis and discussion.

When the poll results came in, they were not the ringing endorsement Yeltsin had sought. Parties that were critical of Yeltsin did much better than those which were popularly seen as being associated with him, even though the largest party in the lower house (the State Duma) was Russia's Choice which was led by Yeltsin's former prime minister Egor Gaidar and which got 70 seats. The successor Communist Party of the Russian Federation (CPRF) got 48 seats, while the nationalist Liberal Democratic Party (LDPR) got 64. The communists, who had been Yeltsin's fiercest critics, had done much better than anticipated. In the constitutional referendum, a majority of 58.4% on a turnout of 54.8% was reported to have approved of the draft. This ushered in a presidential republic in which the powers of president and parliament were decisively weighted in favour of the former.[160] However it has been claimed, and never disproved, that not only was there significant fraudulent behaviour in the counting of votes in the election, but that the participation rate was overstated and that only 46.1% participated in the ballot. If this was the case, formally the constitution had not been approved. However the Russian political elite has turned a deaf ear to such claims; it is not in their interest to undercut the rules of the political game which had gained some legitimacy, no matter how questionable, through the voting.

Although the membership of the parliament elected in December 1993 seemed to spell danger for the president, there was little subsequent conflict between these two parts of the state. In part this was because of the new political rules which had cleared up some of the ambiguity that surrounded the respective powers of president and parliament. But it was also because both sides had been chastened by the eruption of violence in autumn 1993 and ensured that they did not provoke the other. In addition, with Victor Chernomyrdin as prime minister, there was someone who because of his background and disposition was better able to deal with the legislators than his predecessor (Gaidar) had been, and he was also more cautious in the policies he had pursued. Consequently the system functioned with greater predictability as political actors acted in accord with the rules arising out of 1993.

The parliamentary election of December 1995 saw further gains by the CPRF, which now became the largest party in the parliament with just over one-third of the seats. Yeltsin's chief critic had substantially improved its parliamentary position while those parties which sought to project the President's message (especially Our Home is Russia) had done relatively badly. Six months later in the presidential election, with the aid of a heavily biased media and almost unlimited funds,[161] Yeltsin defeated his communist rival Gennady Ziuganov. In the view of many Yeltsin stole the election because of his wealthy connections. Despite this, the rules adopted in 1993 seem to have held. Even though this is a highly presidential system, it has continued to function despite Yeltsin's prolonged absences through illness. This has given increased power to the succession of prime ministers that Yeltsin has appointed and then sacked, a clear reflection of the way the tenor of this system is shaped by the personality of its central actor, the president.[162]

An even more substantial indication of the power of the presidency and those immediately surrounding that office is to be found in the circumstances of the December 1999 parliamentary election. In August Yeltsin sacked his prime minister, Sergei Stepashin, and replaced him with the relatively unknown Vladimir Putin, whom he also publicly acknowledged as his preferred successor as president. Through an extensive media campaign associated with the revival of the Chechen war, Putin became the most popular political figure in Russia. As the election approached, those around Yeltsin in the Kremlin created a new political movement, Unity, designed to contest the election as a stalking horse for Putin. Unity had no clear policy or program, and its main appeal came to be its association with Putin. In the election, Unity officially received almost a quarter of the vote, just less than the CPRF (although there were rumours about the count having been manipulated to diminish CPRF support and inflate that of Unity). Thus this body with no clear policies and formed only weeks before the election but with the powerful backing of the presidency (although Yeltsin did not personally play a public role), emerged as a major political force. Its success also significantly boosted the perception that Putin was certain to win the forthcoming presidential election. This impression was strengthened by Yeltsin's resignation on 31 December 1999 and the appointment of Putin as acting president pending the election in March 2000. These events were a clear illustration of the way in which a plebiscitary president sought to use the rules of the game to pass personal power on to his chosen successor. Putin was elected president in March 2000 with 52.9% of the vote in the first round; his nearest challenger, CPRF leader Ziuganov, won 29.2%. Putin was now in a dominant position and proceeded to exercise strong leadership.

Thus in Russia conflict between reformist and old regime forces generated a political crisis which resulted in the establishment of a plebiscitarian democracy in which the president used his power and authority to, in some degree, marginalise the parliament, and thereby broader political forces. He placed his personal stamp on the system and consolidated the importance of his own position in it.

The March 1990 **Ukrainian** election saw the entry into the Verkhovna Rada of some members of the most important of the new informal groups that emerged onto the political stage in the late 1980s, the pro-independence social movement, Peoples Movement of Ukraine (Rukh),[163] although the parliament still remained dominated by representatives of the old communist party. Of the 450 seats in the chamber, 248 were held by members of the apparat and security services compared with 117 of the so-called Democratic bloc.[164] But more important than the presence of these deputies was the fact that Rukh's emergence and growth had prompted the development within the Communist Party of Ukraine (CPU) of a section which was sympathetic to the claims of Ukrainian sovereignty if not independence. When party leader Vladimir Ivashko moved to Moscow in July 1990, he was replaced as Chair of the Rada by party ideology secretary Leonid Kravchuk who showed himself to be very sensitive to this. But although the Rada adopted a declaration of state sovereignty on 16 July 1990, the more cautious approach of much of the CPU seems to have been more in tune with popular sentiment than Rukh's independence rhetoric. When Gorbachev's referendum on the future of the USSR was held in March 1991, Ukrainians voted strongly for remaining within a revived union,[165] while the Ukrainian leadership was a full participant in the discussions surrounding a proposed new union treaty. However following the August coup in Moscow, Kravchuk left the CPU and declared Ukraine's independence on 24 August. Kravchuk rejected all efforts to revive any sort of union over the subsequent months. On 1 December there was a simultaneous popular referendum on independence and a presidential election. In the referendum, 90.3% of voters supported independence, and in the election Kravchuk won overwhelmingly against five opponents with 61.6% of the vote. Kravchuk now combined with Yeltsin and Shushkevich from Belarus to end the USSR.

Kravchuk was able to present himself (and the communists) as an acceptable leader to significant segments of the Ukrainian population. He took on a moderate nationalist mantle, playing up his part in the acquisition of Ukrainian independence, demonstrating tough anti-Russian credentials on a series of issues, including the future of the Black Sea Fleet, Crimea and Ukraine's nuclear weapons, and initially being unenthusiastic about the Commonwealth of Independent States. His economic moderation and refusal to follow Russia down the path of shock therapy appealed to many of those ex-communists who, like himself, now found themselves in positions of authority in the new state. Kravchuk was thus able to draw support from the two extremes, the nationalist democrats and the communists. This alliance of reformed ex-communists and nationalist democrats stemming from Rukh[166] dominated the political scene and Kravchuk was able to use them to make himself the leading political figure in Ukraine. As part of this Kravchuk established his primacy over the government through acquisition of the power to reorganise the government, including appointing its personnel, by decree, a power he used on a number of occasions in 1992–93 to remove government ministers. He also shifted decision-making power out of the parliament and into a presidentially-appointed State Council and established presidentially-appointed regional governors throughout the country. It was difficult for alternatives to emerge and gain significant support. But the challenge was to come from within this milieu.

Towards the end of 1992 the economic difficulties led to the replacement of existing prime minister Vitold Fokin by Leonid Kuchma. Kuchma was widely seen as a member of the Soviet economic nomenklatura (he had managed the largest rocket factory in the USSR in the Soviet period) but had a reputation for competence. He appointed gradualists to his government and, bolstered by the granting of emergency powers for six months to combat the economic difficulties,[167] proceeded to carry out measures of moderate economic reform. As the six month period began to draw to a close, the tensions evident at the summit of Ukrainian politics came into the open. Although some work had been done on the question of constitutional change,[168] there had been no agreement on the respective powers of president, government and parliament, and Kuchma's request for an extension of his extraordinary powers seemed to raise this issue. Within Rukh a section had emerged led by Vyacheslav Chornovil which was opposed to what it saw as the maintenance of power by the former nomenklatura, personified by Kravchuk and Kuchma. Accordingly Chornovil had been pressing for new elections, a call now taken up by Kravchuk. In May 1993, with economic crisis building, Kuchma's request for extended powers was rejected by the Rada, so he offered to resign. Kravchuk now suggested that the prime minister's powers should be passed to the president. The Rada rejected both this proposal and Kuchma's resignation. As public dissatisfaction with the continuing economic difficulties mounted, Kuchma again tried unsuccessfully to resign. Searching for a way out of the impasse the Rada now suggested a referendum on public confidence in the parliament and presidency, but Kravchuk rejected this idea. Instead he issued a decree naming himself head of government and Kuchma as head of a special commission on economic reform. Kuchma again tried to resign, and Kravchuk was forced to withdraw the decree. The referendum proposal lapsed. Finally in September Kuchma was allowed to resign, Kravchuk took over effective leadership of the government on an interim basis, and the Rada voted for new parliamentary elections in March 1994 and presidential elections three months later.

This complex elite manoeuvring did little to build public confidence in politicians. Nor did it assist the development of effective political organisations. Party development remained retarded. In the initial stages of independence Rukh had decided not to transform itself from a social movement into a political party, yet its presence inhibited the growth of such a party among nationalist democrats. Two successor parties had emerged from the communist party, the Socialist Party of Ukraine (SPU) and a new CPU. A range of other parties had also emerged, but their performance in the 1994 election showed how weak they were. In the parliamentary election, 450 deputies were to be elected,[169] all on a majoritarian SMC basis, although Rukh and some other groups had wanted a PR component in the electoral system. After the first round of the election, which despite some manipulation and harassment was generally judged to be fair,[170] 338 deputies were returned, the vast majority were independents; according to one study, only 26.3% of those elected were nominated by parties or party groups; the CPU nominated most candidates (59) and only three other parties nominated more than 12.[171] When the Rada met, most deputies organised themselves into factions,[172] but these clearly had little connection with society as a whole. The Rada elected SPU leader (and former leader of the communist deputies in the pre-1991 soviet) Oleksandr Moroz Chairman of the Rada, and Kravchuk's preferred candidate (and premier 1987–90) Vitaly Masol as prime minister. The continued dominance of former Soviet officials seemed assured.

There were three major candidates in the presidential election. Kravchuk ran on a platform of independent statehood and moderate economics, Moroz wanted closer links with Russia, a parliamentary system and gradual economic reform with strong state involvement, and Kuchma favoured closer links with Russia, a presidential system and more radical economic reform.[173] Moroz and Kuchma gained most support from the centre, east and south, while Kravchuk gained support from the west where the proportion of Russians in the population was much less. Moroz was eliminated in the first round, and much of his support went to Kuchma, who then defeated Kravchuk in the second round. But Kuchma's election propelled the presidency into dispute with the Rada, a conflict which was central to the structuring of Ukrainian politics in the middle of the decade.

Kuchma wanted a new constitution to establish a presidential system, while most in the Rada favoured a parliamentary system of government; some even wanted to do away with the presidency entirely.[174] Kuchma's tactic was similar to that initially used by Kravchuk, direct populist appeal to the people over the heads of competing politicians, thereby seeking to rest his authority upon an image of popular support. In August 1994 Kuchma expanded his powers by taking over supervision of central and local government, thereby ensuring that the Masol government's agenda was not set in a way to which he was opposed. He also asserted his control over appointments to state organs. Four months later he presented a draft law to the Rada which would have given him the power to dissolve it, but he was unable to gain the required level of support. A constitutional commission had been established by the Rada to produce a new constitutional draft, but there was a lack of agreement within both the commission and the Rada over this draft. When deadlock developed, Kuchma threatened a referendum on a bicameral parliament, something the Rada factions believed would have undercut their power. As a result they accepted a draft which strengthened the president but left the Rada unicameral.[175] The new constitution was thus a result of elite bargaining in which people stemming from the old regime dominated. The weakness of the party system, which was in part responsible for the lack of popular input into high politics, was shown again in the parliamentary elections of March 1998. Despite the change in the electoral system to have half the deputies elected by PR with a 4% threshold, some eight party groups crossed the threshold, producing a fragmented chamber; the largest party fraction (the successor CPU) had only 122 of the 450 seats.[176] In October 1999 a presidential election was held which in the run off saw the incumbent Kuchma defeat the communist (a supporter of closer links with Russia) Petro Symonenko 57.4% to 37.7%. While the voting was considered to be fair, international observers said that the campaign was dirty, the media strongly pro-Kuchma, and many state officials worked actively for the incumbent. The election was therefore not fair. The re-elected Kuchma sought to use his renewed authority to reduce the powers and importance of the parliament, an act which divided the parliament and rendered it virtually hamstrung as an institution. In April 2000 he introduced a referendum which reduced the number of seats in the Rada, transformed it into a bicameral parliament in which the second chamber was to be filled by regional officials appointed by the president, abolished the legal immunity of deputies, and expanded presidential powers to disband the

Rada. All questions were overwhelmingly supported, thereby consolidating presidential dominance.

So in Ukraine the post-communist scene was dominated by an alliance of former communists and nationalists, with the former exercising most influence over the course of developments. No strong opposition forces emerged, and those who remained most influential had strong roots in the old regime. Within this context, successive presidents have sought to expand their power, using in part a populist appeal over the heads of the parliamentarians. By the late 1990s, presidential primacy had been established, but it remained much more weakly based than in Russia. Thus while Ukraine qualifies as a plebiscitary democracy, it is a much less robust one than that which emerged in Russia.

In the **Kyrgyz Republic** the republican election in February 1990 resulted in nearly all seats in the Supreme Soviet being filled by communists associated with the ruling party. There were no social movements that could have any real impact. In the presidential election in October, victory went to former physicist and head of the Academy of Sciences Askar Akaev. Akaev's victory followed the failure of the republican elite to engineer the election of party leader Masaliev to this post a year earlier, resulting in Akaev's election by the parliament in October 1990. Twelve months later he won in a popular election.[177] The Kyrgyz leadership did not press for independence from the Soviet Union, preferring to maintain membership of the revised union Gorbachev was trying to bring about. However when Soviet power collapsed, the Kyrgyz elite turned to the construction of a new state. A key early issue was a new constitution. Both Akaev and the Supreme Soviet (through a constitutional commission) had been working on separate versions of a new document, the main difference between them being the powers of the presidency, government and parliament. Agreement was finally reached, with the parliament adopting a new constitution on 5 May 1993.[178] Among other things, this transferred the responsibilities of head of government from the president to the prime minister. During this early period, the Kyrgyz political form was an oligarchy with its precise nature, open or closed, as yet undetermined because of the balance between president and parliament.

Opposition parties did emerge during the early stages of Kyrgyz independence, but they were neither strong nor united. They were not able to bring much pressure to bear for new elections, for economic reform or for political liberalisation, such as the removal of restrictions on the press. The question of elections was particularly important because, following the adoption of the constitution, it was argued that neither president nor parliament had a legitimate mandate. Towards the end of 1993 Akaev took a step designed to bolster his position both against such arguments and *vis-à-vis* the government. Also important here was the collapse of the cooperative relationship between parliament and president, and the rise of much criticism in the wake of increasing economic difficulty. He announced that a referendum on confidence in his presidency would be held, and although this was opposed by the parliament, it went ahead in January 1994. On a turnout of 95.9%, he received a 96.3% vote of approval.[179] In mid-1994 Akaev moved to restrict the freedom of the media in an attempt to limit the growing attacks being made on him.

In autumn 1994 a political crisis erupted. Criticism of the parliament as a body which did nothing and represented the past had been growing and was brought to a head when 143 (of 350) deputies urged on by Akaev[180] announced they would boycott the coming session to protest its opposition to reform. This rendered the parliament inquorate. The government also resigned, but Akaev issued a decree authorising it to continue until new elections were held. He also announced the bringing forward of those elections and that prior to them a referendum would be held on a number of constitutional amendments, including the means of constitutional amendment (by popular referendum rather than vote in the parliament) and replacing the existing Soviet-era parliament with a new one. The referendum approved the changes overwhelmingly (80% on an 86% turn out). In December Akaev convened a constitutional convention including parliamentarians, regional representatives and representatives from various political and functional organisations[181] at which he proposed a new constitution which would have shifted power away from the parliament and to the presidency. These proposals were to be put before public discussion prior to the election of the new parliament in February. Akaev had thus used the parliamentary crisis to enhance his own powers. When the election was held in February 1995, the overwhelming majority of seats was won by governing officials, intellectuals and clan leaders; political parties were not important actors although eight had small representation in the new parliament. There were complaints about the fairness of the election, both in terms of the speed with which it was brought on (and therefore the little time the opposition had to prepare) and the actual procedures used, including intimidation, bribery and the exercise of influence by regional officials. However the importance of this was downplayed by international observers.[182] The parliament soon became bogged down in arguments about the respective powers of the two houses, increasing Akaev's frustration. Akaev now sought to avoid facing the voters himself; he proposed that a referendum should be held on whether his tenure as president should be extended until 2001. This proposal was opposed by opposition groups, and in September the parliament rejected it. Akaev immediately pressed for a new presidential election. This was held in December 1995, and Akaev with 71.5% of the vote easily defeated his major rival, communist era party leader Masaliev. Although most thought the election free and fair, the opposition pointed to the barring of three potential candidates from participating. Akaev now sought to extend his powers further. In July 1995 the Constitutional Court determined that Akaev's first term as president should not be counted because of the new constitution introduced in 1993, thereby making him eligible to run for the presidency in 2000 despite the constitutional limitation of two terms. In February 1996 he sponsored a referendum which supported enhanced powers for the president, including his right to appoint all senior officials except the prime minister, whose appointment would still have to be confirmed by the parliament. Accompanied by increased pressure on the media,[183] and the arrest of some opposition figures, the referendum was passed 94.5% on a turn out of 96.5%. Akaev pushed through a further referendum over parliamentary opposition which increased the number of deputies in the upper house and reduced those in the lower house. Parliamentary elections were scheduled for February 2000, and in the lead up in late 1999, four parties were banned.[184] When the election was held, the communist party won 27.7% of the vote and a quarter of the seats to be the largest party in the legislature, although Akaev supporters won a majority of seats. The election was accompanied by a range of irregularities, including the pre-marking of ballot papers and the removal of candidates from ballots. In October 2000, a presidential election was held. Despite the constitutional provision limiting the president to a maximum of two terms, Akaev presented himself as a candidate. The Constitutional Court ruled that his first term began in 1995 rather than 1991, because on the earlier occasion he had run unopposed. With the rules thereby clearly bent in his favour, Akaev went on to win 74.5% of the vote in a field of six, reduced by the stringent application of a Kyrgyz language test to would-be candidates. The election was adjudged not to have been fair, and NGO observers were barred from observing the count.

The weakness of organised opposition forces enabled successor elements from the old regime to maintain a strong position in the parliament and effectively put a brake on many of the initiatives of the more reformist president. He in turn has been forced to rely on the powers of the presidency and his direct mobilisation of popular support to carry out the policies he has supported. Plebiscitarian democracy has been the result.

Slovenia was able to avoid direct involvement in the wars of the Yugoslav succession because it had no Serbian minority within its borders. While there was border tension with Serbia in late 1989 and there were concerns that the conflict in Croatia and Bosnia-Herzegovina might overflow the borders into Slovenia, this did not happen. The process of construction of a Slovenian political system was therefore able to proceed without the disruption evident in its neighbours to the south.

Slovenia had developed a vibrant civil society during the latter part of the 1980s, a development in which the republican communist party had played an important part. For some time the possibility of Slovenian independence had been on the agenda of civil society forces in the republic.[185] In December 1989 an umbrella organisation of opposition parties had been formed, the Democratic Opposition of Slovenia (Demos), while in early 1990 the ruling League of Communists of Yugoslavia broke away from its Yugoslav parent and, in February, became the Party of Democratic Revival (PDR) led by the reformist Milan Kucan. That same month Round Table discussions were held between the ruling PDR and Demos in preparation for elections scheduled in April. Such discussions took place against a background of heightened public activism and interest, since the earlier confrontation with Serbia and the disintegration of federal authority had mobilised much of the population into the political sphere; politics was not considered just an elite preserve.[186] Consequently when the elections were held in April 1990, there were both established autonomous parties and a reformist communist party in the field. The election produced a mixed result: although the PDR won the highest proportion of votes (17.3%) and seats (17.5%) of any single party, it was defeated by the Demos coalition which won 55.3% of votes and 58.6% of the seats in the parliament[187] and formed a broad centrist coalition government. The presidency was won by PDR leader Kucan with 44.3% of the vote, compared with his nearest competitor 26.3%.

Although elsewhere the election of a parliament and government from one side of the political spectrum and the president from another has produced conflict, this was not the case in Slovenia. One of the reasons for this is that the differences between these sides were narrower to begin with than was the case elsewhere in the region, largely because of the longer-term liberalisation of Slovenian society and the shared perception of the challenge from Belgrade; both president and government shared a commitment to Slovenian independence and a recognition that this still had to be achieved. As conflicts with Belgrade over budgetary, military and general inter-republican matters escalated, the drive for independence gathered pace with general support from virtually all political elites. On 2 July the government issued a declaration of sovereignty, and the effect of this was reinforced by a popular referendum on 23 December 1990 when 95.7% on a turnout of 92.5% voted in favour of independence.[188] On 25 June 1991 the government declared Slovenian independence, provoking intervention by federal, Yugoslav, troops. Following negotiations with Belgrade, independence was formally achieved on 8 October 1991. This was followed by the introduction of a new constitution in December 1991, which provided for a popularly-elected president with a five-year term, and a government accountable to the parliament. In the lower house, the National Assembly, 88 of the 90 seats were to be filled by PR from eight multi-member constituencies with a 3% threshold; the remaining two seats were to be for the Italian and Hungarian ethnic minorities. In the upper house, the National Council, 22 members were to be elected by SMC and 18 by electoral colleges representing functional groups.

Following the adoption of the constitution, Demos began to disintegrate. Slovenia experienced a number of moderate rightist coalitions like Demos in the lead up to the December 1992 elections. Following those elections and those of November 1996 and October 2000, moderate right wing coalition governments exercised power,[189] while Kucan was re-elected president in December 1992 and November 1997. Despite some splintering of the parties, the party system has remained broadly stable.

Thus in Slovenia a reformist regime elite negotiated with civil society forces prior to elections which brought some of those civil society forces to power, but which also entrenched a segment of the old regime elite, in the person of the president, in power. So in contrast to Ukraine and Kyrgyzstan, the old regime (albeit reformist) retained a hold on power through the presidency rather than the parliament and the president did not pursue a confrontationist course with the parliament.

From the outset, **Macedonia** faced major problems of its own identity, with its two neighbours Greece and Bulgaria questioning its right to exist as an indepenent state, its name and its state symbols. Elections in November 1990 saw the oppositionist Internal Macedonian Revolutionary Organisation (IMRO) as the most successful party with 38 seats in a chamber of 120, with the reform communists coming second with 31 seats. The parliament elected former communist official

Kiro Gligorov as president in December. Given the electoral split, majority government was impossible, so a government of non-party experts was established. In January the parliament declared the republic's sovereignty and right to secede and, following a referendum in September in which 95% supported independence, the parliament proclaimed Macedonian independence in November 1991. A new constitution was introduced in November. Using his leadership of the communist successor party the Social Democratic Union of Macedonia (SDUM), usually in alliance with other parties, Gligorov was usually able to get his way in the parliament and to dominate the political scene. In October 1994 he was popularly elected president, while his SDUM became the largest party in the parliament with 58 of the 120 seats. The opposition claimed the outcome was fraudulent, a claim not supported by international observers although they did note a series of irregularities in the process.[190] The SDUM alliance dominated in the parliament, with 95 of the 120 seats, while the major opposition party IMRO was not represented. The dominating figure in Macedonian politics remained Gligorov, who was popularly seen as a force for stability, except among sections of the Albanian population. He retained his dominance, despite injury in an assassination attempt in October 1995, until he stepped down at the end of 1999. In these latter stages he was more restricted by the return to power in the 1998 parliamentary elections of IMRO in coalition mainly with the Albanian Party for Democratic Prosperity, with whom he frequently clashed. In 1999 Gligorov stepped down and in the ensuing presidential election in October-November, IMRO candidate Boris Trajkovski beat the Social Democrat Tito Petkovski 53%:46%. Due to claims of large scale fraud, the voting had to be repeated in mainly Albanian areas, but even the repeat voting, in which the result was almost identical to the first time, there was significant ballot box stuffing, multiple voting and unrealistic claimed turnouts.

Thus principally through Gligorov, the communist successor forces were able to come to power, displacing the initial post-communist mixed government through the ballot box. Rule has remained by an open oligarchy.

In these five countries, then, products of the old regime have played a significant part in shaping the political outcomes. Political forces independent of the old regime have been able to play a continuing role in the Kyrgyz Republic in the form of the president and in Slovenia through the parties, but in Russia, Ukraine and Macedonia the presidents have had old regime pedigrees and the successor communists have remained prominent in the parliaments.

Pattern Six

In this pattern, the second echelon elite of the old regime seizes power and seeks to consolidate its control. In Romania, the only non-federal state experiencing this pattern, such control could not be maintained, with civil society forces ultimately ousting this old regime elite. In the other cases of this pattern, the Former Republic of Yugoslavia (Serbia and Montenegro), Azerbaijan, Belarus, Kazakhstan, Tajikistan, Turkmenistan and Uzbekistan, the old regime elite was better able to stabilise its hold on state power, even if in Azerbaijan there was a period in which control was wielded by the popular front. This old regime elite used its control over state power to depress the development of civil society forces.

In **Romania** the Ceausescu regime fell in December 1990 as a result of popular protest and the splitting of the regime as a section based principally on the military threw its support behind the opposition. But the fall of Ceausescu did not lead to the opening of political power to civil society forces. Instead that second echelon of the regime which had split from Ceausescu organised itself into the National Salvation Front (NSF) led by Ion Iliescu and took over the state administration, effectively preventing the disintegration of political control. Basing itself upon the old party and taking over many of that organisation's personnel[191] and much of its structure, the NSF refused to engage in negotiations with other groups; it simply declared that it was in charge until elections for the presidency and the parliament in May 1990. Although the body created to exercise national leadership, the Provisional Council for National Unity, did coopt some figures ostensibly from the opposition, it was stacked by the NSF and did not reflect a pluralism of political interests. This body adopted an electoral law under which the president and lower house were to be directly elected, the latter by PR. The presidential election saw a sweeping victory for Iliescu, who won 85.1% of the vote, and in the parliamentary election for the NSF which won 66.3%; the next highest party's total was 7.2%. Not only was this election called too soon for opposition to organise, but it was administered by a participant (the NSF) and was characterised by violence, intimidation and fraud on a major scale.[192] The election of the NSF did not bring to power a government that was either committed to economic reform or able to deal with the country's serious economic problems. As a result, popular protest was a common feature, although the regime used violence and coercion in an endeavour to keep it under control. This early period in government also saw tensions within the NSF, especially between Iliescu and the prime minister Petre Roman, who was the head of an opposing faction. This led to Roman's forced resignation in late 1991. The Front formally split in March 1992, when Iliescu left to form the breakaway Democratic National Salvation Front (DNSF).

Despite the entry of some non-NSF people including members of some small parties into the government at the end of 1991, the NSF remained solidly in control. It was able to introduce into the parliament a draft constitution establishing a presidential system and get this adopted by popular referendum in December.[193] But little else was achieved. However the opposition made little progress in the struggle to present a viable alternative. A number of parties had emerged,[194] and in November 1991 they had come together in an umbrella organisation called the Democratic Convention (DC).[195] Although this had enjoyed some success in the local elections of 1992, it remained plagued by disunity. New elections for both presidency and parliament were called for September 1992, with the electoral law introducing a threshold of 3% rising by 1% for each party in an electoral bloc to a maximum of eight. Iliescu was again the clear winner in the presidential election, with 61.4% of the vote to his main rival Emil Constantinescu, who belonged to one of the main parties in the Democratic Convention (the Christian Democratic National Peasants' Party), who received 38.6%. In the parliamentary election,

Iliescu's DNSF won the largest share of the vote, 27.7%, followed by the DC with 20% and the NSF (which had become the Democratic Party-NSF) 10.2%. Almost a fifth of the votes went to nationalist parties. There was some independent support for opposition claims about fraud and irregularities in the election.[196] The election thus confirmed the dominance of Iliescu and his party, and although he lacked a majority in the chamber, he was able to rely upon the support of the Party of Romanian National Unity and the Greater Romanian Party. The situation was therefore similar to that in Slovakia: a strong man was in power supported by a large umbrella organisation in alliance with extremist parties to form a traditionalist-nationalist coalition.[197]

The government formed following the elections was headed by the non-party Nicolae Vicariou, and was able to survive the whole electoral cycle. It was able to survive the tensions that wracked the coalition arrangement[198] in part because the partners shared views on economic issues (an economic policy involving continued state involvement) and a broadly nationalist perspective. The continuing divisions within the opposition were also important here.[199] While there were some changes in the composition of the government, it was able to see out its term until new elections in November 1996. In the presidential election Iliescu was defeated by his 1992 opponent Constantinescu, while in the parliamentary election the DNSF (since 1993 called the Social Democratic Party of Romania) was defeated by the DC 30.2% of the vote to 21.5%. The successor regime had thus been overthrown at the ballot box by forces stemming more immediately from society at large. However this result was overturned at the November-December 2000 elections. Constantinescu did not take part in the election, leaving Iliescu to defeat the candidate of the zhenophobic Greater Romania Party, Corneliu Tudor 66.8% to 33.2%. In the parliamentary election, a coalition of leftist parties supporting Iliescu called the Democratic Social Pole of Romania (comprising the Democratic Social Party, Iliescu's Social Democratic Party and the Humanist Party of Romania) won 36.6% of the vote and 44.8% of the seats. In second place was the Greater Romania Party with 19.5% of the votes and 24.3% of the seats. A minority government was formed by the Democratic Social Pole of Romania, which sought the support of a number of the smaller parties in the parliament. Support for Romanian nationalist parties had increased, and with it Iliescu's position was consolidated.

So in Romania, the collapse of the old regime led to the seizure of power by some from the second echelon of that regime who were able to legitimise their act by gaining electoral validation. Even though it was more bureaucratic bloc than a political party, the NSF sought the sheen provided by democratic success. But ultimately the need for electoral validation brought them down, with the opposition able to form a government and fill the presidency following the third post-communist election. In this sense, the course of the regime's development was shaped overwhelmingly by old regime elites, although the strength of opposition did enable them to play some part in these negotiations and, ultimately, to displace the old regime elite and the open oligarchy it constituted and move Romania to democracy.

The **Former Republic of Yugoslavia** consists of the republics of Serbia and Montenegro, with the former being more important in setting the political tenor of the federation. With the initial Yugoslav federation dying in 1990, elections were held in **Serbia** in the December before opposition forces had time to organise.[200] Given the control of the media by old regime personnel and the favourable conditions for a nationalist appeal created by the break up of the country and the presence of so many Serbs outside Serbian borders, it is not surprising that the existing republican government of Slobodan Milosevic with its strong nationalist message was returned to power. The Socialist Party of Serbia (SPS) which was the Serbian successor party to the former ruling Yugoslav Communist League, won 194 of the 250 seats, while its leader Milosevic won 63% of the vote in the presidential poll. Opposition to Milosevic was not negligible, as shown by the street demonstrations in Belgrade in March 1991. Milosevic skilfully used nationalism to consolidate his position,[201] especially with the break up of the old Yugoslav federation and the outbreak of the wars of the Yugoslav succession. But also important was the way in which he set the political agenda in such a way that opposition parties found it difficult to escape from his nationalist themes.

However Milosevic's dominance, which was based on the projection of personal charisma, manipulation of the media and electoral structures,[202] playing on Serbian nationalism in the context of the war in Bosnia, and strong arm tactics, was not enough to guarantee his party a majority in the first 'post-communist' December 1992 parliamentary elections. The SPS won only 28.8% of the votes but 40.4% of the seats, while in the concurrent presidential election, Milosevic won 55.9%. An attempt to gain a majority in the parliament through elections a year later failed, with the SPS winning 123 seats in a chamber of 250 (36.7% of the votes).[203] Opposition forces were thus clearly able to garner support and gain representation in the chamber, but the plebiscitarian style of Milosevic and the powers vested in the presidency, added to his control of the media and coercive arms of the state[204] meant that they had no real power. However at the time of the September 1997 election, won by the SPS with 40% of the seats, an opposition alliance of three parties (the Serbian Renewal Movement, the Democratic Party, and the Serbian Civic Alliance) won power in a number of simultaneous local elections, including in Belgrade. The authorities tried fraudulently to deny them this victory. The response was massive local and international protests from November 1996– February 1997, which forced Milosevic to back down and accept the verdict. However the opposition then split, with part of it allying itself with Milosevic, and those in positions of authority proving themselves no less incorruptible in office than the SPS had been.[205] Furthermore in the September 1997 parliamentary election, the divided opposition was again defeated as the SPS won 44% of the seats with 34.3% of the votes. In July 1997 Milosevic, who was prevented by the constitution from standing again for the presidency of Serbia, was elected president of the FRY; but he remained the main political force in Serbia. Despite opposition, even the military defeat in Kosovo in 1999 and the subsequent opposition mobilisation against him, did not shake his plebiscitarian leadership.

However in 2000 Milosevic miscalculated. He introduced constitutional amendments providing for the direct election of the Yugoslav president instead of election by parliament and for him to be eligible for two terms in office. He then brought on a presidential election in the belief that he could manipulate and control its outcome, just as he had been able to do before. But this time, instead of splintering and fighting among themselves, the bulk of the opposition combined behind a single candidate, Vojislav Kostunica of the Democratic Party of Serbia. Only Vuk Draskovic's Serbian Renewal Movement did not join this coalition, but nor did it campaign against the united front. Following the first round of voting and the clear groundswell of support for Kostunica, the Milosevic-controlled electoral commission declared that no candidate had received a majority and a run off election would have to be held. This prompted the mobilisation of popular forces onto the streets: students, NGOs, political parties, trade unions and ordinary citizens rallied in support of Kostunica. In the face of such widespread opposition and the wavering of the army and police, the regime buckled. Milosevic conceded defeat and Kostunica was sworn in as president with 51.7% of the vote to Milosevic's 38.2%. Parliamentary elections were called in December 2000 in Serbia, with opposition forces routing the ruling party and throwing out the communist successor regime which had dominated in Belgrade. Milosevic's Socialist Party received only 13.8% of the vote compared with 64.1% for the 18–party opposition alliance, the Democratic Opposition, allied to Kostunica. The real task was now to hold this coalition together.

In **Montenegro**, a more reformist figure, Momir Bulatovic, had taken over the leadership of the communist party in 1989, and he led this to electoral victory in the parliamentary elections of December 1990; the communist successor Democratic Socialist Party (DPMS) won 83 of the 125 seats. Bulatovic worked closely with Milosevic in establishing the FRY in 1992 and in consolidating his control in Montenegro. His DPMS won further parliamentary elections in 1992 and 1996 when the opposition was fragmented, while Bulatovic was re-elected president in 1992/93.[206] But the control of the successor party was broken with the split of the party in 1997 and the presidential election of October 1997 when Bulatovic's former close colleague in the DPMS Milo Djukanovic beat him and, in the May 1998 parliamentary election, Djukanovic's coalition won 42 of the parliament's 78 seats.[207] Bulatovic moved on to become prime minister of the federal republic, thereby working again closely with Milosevic, while Montenegro under Djukanovic has become increasingly critical of Milosevic and the federal authorities, and began to loosen its ties with its federal partner. The Djukanovic leadership has also favoured some liberalisation of society and the political system, and may thereby have begun to move away from the initial closed oligarchy in a democratic direction.

So in the FRY, communist successor forces played the major part in shaping political outcomes. In both republics they were able to stabilise their rule, enabling the Serbian authorities (because of the massive imbalance in size and strength of the two republics) to dominate the political scene. However this dominance slipped with the splitting of the successor forces in Montenegro and the expulsion of the Milosevic regime in Serbia and of Milosevic himself at the federal level.

In **Azerbaijan** the Soviet regime had been able to keep a tight rein on the development of independent political forces,[208] with the result that when republican elections were held in September 1990, the communist party won an overwhelming majority of seats in the 360 seat chamber[209] while the opposition Azeri Popular Front (APF) won only 25. The old regime remained in control, with party leader Ayaz Mutalibov[210] elected unopposed as state president in May 1990 and then again in September 1991. This administration participated in Gorbachev's attempt to develop a new union structure for the USSR, opposed the break up of the union, and reluctantly embarked on independence after the Moscow coup. But independence did not remove the greatest challenge that had been confronting Azerbaijan since 1988, that of Nagorno-Karabakh. Fighting over this erupted again in January 1992, and the tense and conflictual relationship with Armenia continued to shape Azeri politics late into the decade.

Mutalibov responded to this latest bout of fighting by imposing direct presidential rule on the region and proposing a new peace settlement. The terms of this proposal, and the massacre of some Azeri citizens by Armenian forces caused outrage in the capital Baku; demonstrators took to the streets demanding his resignation. With his proposal rejected by the parliament, Mutalibov resigned in early March 1992, being replaced by an interim president (Mamedov) who was to rule until new elections in June. At this time, the APF leader Abulfez Elchibey pressed for power to be passed to a new National Council, in which the APF would have half the seats, but he was ignored. However in May the Azeris suffered new reverses on the battlefield and conflict broke out in Nakhichevan, the Azeri enclave on Armenia's southern border. The Supreme Soviet blamed these reverses on Mamedov, and Mutalibov's supporters in that body reinstated him in the presidency. Mutalibov immediately declared a state of emergency and cancelled the coming presidential elections, which were widely expected to bring Elchibey to power. But the same day, popular demonstrations by APF supporters, with the support of elements in the military, drove Mutalibov from office. A new coalition government led by the APF was formed. The closed oligarchy initially established appeared to have been overthrown.

When the presidential election was held on 6 July 1992, Elchibey easily beat four opponents; in a turnout of 76%, he gained a vote of 59.4%. Although there was no widescale fraud, the APF had a distinct advantage because of its control over the governmental apparatus, substantial media assistance, and support from the outside, especially Turkey.[211] But Elchibey's rule soon led to disappointment among opposition forces which, despite the creation of a number of new parties, remained poorly organised and lacking in unity. In December 1992 a demonstration by opposition forces was dispersed by the security forces, and in January 1993 a leading opposition figure (Nemat Panakhov) was arrested. There was also tension between Elchibey and his prime minister Penag Guseinov over a proposed reduction in prime ministerial powers. In April 1993, in response to an Armenian offensive, Elchibey introduced a state of emergency. But Elchibey's rule came to an abrupt end in June when a rebellion led by Colonel Surat Guseinov forced Elchibey to flee Baku. The prime minister and the Chair of the Supreme Soviet both resigned, with the latter being replaced by former Soviet Politburo member and leader of Azerbaijan, Heidar Aliev. The parliament also voted to impeach Elchibey and pass his powers to Aliev, and to appoint Colonel Guseinov as prime minister and commander-in-chief of the armed forces.

Aliev set about consolidating his position and restoring closed oligarchical rule. He moved supporters into leading posts in the security and interior structures, and publicly cracked down on the APF. Against claims of an attempt to assassinate Aliev, leading APF figures were arrested, APF rallies were broken up, and the police sought to close down Front headquarters in Baku. In an attempt to provide Aliev with some legitimacy, in August 1993 a referendum was held asking people about their confidence in the Elchibey presidency. A reported 97.5% of a 92% turnout expressed no confidence in him. The APF had boycotted the poll and claimed that its results were rigged. New presidential elections were called for 3 October, but against a background of continuing arrests of APF activists, the Front and the Moslem Democratic Party (Musavat) declared they would boycott the poll. In the event, no major party nominated a candidate (although two others stood), and Aliev claimed the support of 98.8% on a 97% turnout. Helsinki Watch adjudged the election to be undemocratic.

The authorities continued to seek to cripple the opposition. There were continued attacks on opposition supporters and leaders, and in May 1994 the only independent television station in the country was ordered to cease broadcasting. Attempted coups in October 1994 and March 1995 were put down, but only encouraged the repression of the opposition. Following the announcement of simultaneous parliamentary elections and a constitutional referendum for November 1995, there were mounting protests over the authorities' refusal to register some 15 parties, including the APF, for the election. There were further protests when the parliament announced the election regulations, which provided for a unicameral parliament of 125 deputies with 80% elected by SMC and 20% by PR; the opposition had wanted a larger chamber with half the seats elected by PR. During October increased restrictions were placed on parties seeking to contest the election: some party leaders were arrested, and four parties were banned from participating (although the Supreme Court did reverse an earlier ban on the participation of the communist party). In the same month five journalists were imprisoned for defaming Aliev. Eight parties participated in the election, but Aliev's New Azerbaijan Party won a crushing victory with 78% of the votes; only three parties exceeded the 8% threshold. Opposition parties rejected the election as unfair and undemocratic, and characterised by many irregularities, a view endorsed by OSCE observers.[212] The new constitution establishing a republic with a strong presidency was reportedly endorsed by 91.9% of registered voters.

In succeeding years, Aliev's grip on power did not weaken. Against claims of planned coups and assassination attempts, the pressure was kept up on opposition forces, and although there were attempts by those forces to create a greater sense of unity of purpose, they were not able to challenge the authorities. Aliev did not seek to eliminate opposition, but to weaken and control it. At times this took the form of minor concessions by Aliev to opposition viewpoints, as in the changes to electoral regulations to lower the minimum level of voter participation to 25% and to allow voters to express a preference for more than one candidate. Similarly in the lead up to the presidential elections in October 1998, negotiations were held with the opposition to try to head off a proposed boycott, opposition rallies were allowed to take place (although some were the scene of violent clashes between demonstrators and police), and press censorship was officially (although not in practice) lifted. But these sorts of concessions did not obscure the fact that Aliev remained in charge. When the election was held, most major parties boycotted the poll. Of the six candidates, only three exceeded 1% of the vote, with Aliev gaining 76.1%. The opposition claimed the vote was rigged and characterised by fraud, but it remained unable to unite effectively and thereby to influence the course of political life.[213] This problem recurred at the time of the parliamentary election in November 2000. Although final results seem not to have been issued, the ruling New Azerbaijan Party claimed more than 70% of the vote. International observers adjudged the election to be 'seriously flawed' and to have failed 'to meet even minimum international standards'.[214] Claiming massive fraud, opposition forces pledged to boycott parliament and popular rallies were mounted in the streets, but the regime remained unmoved.

So in Azerbaijan the course of developments has been shaped overwhelmingly by old regime forces, with the opposition being too weak to be able to combat the aggressive use of the advantages of incumbency and the wielding of state power. Except for some twelve months of APF rule in 1992–93, a closed oligarchy of old regime forces has been able to stabilise its control in Azerbaijan.

The communist regime in **Belarus** kept a tight rein on political developments in the republic,[215] with the result that when elections were held in March 1990, the Popular Front of Belarus (PFB) did not do well;[216] it won only 25 of the 360 seats in the parliament. Despite achieving this result, principally through manipulation of the process, the anti-reform communists could not be sure of controlling the parliament because although most deputies were party members, communist unity had fractured on the eve of the election.[217] Consistent with this was the election of PFB member Stanislau Shushkevich as the parliament's first deputy chair. But the communists were lagging behind the popular mood. Despite the declaration of state sovereignty issued in July 1990, the Belarus leadership showed little inclination to proceed down the path of reform. They continued to participate in discussions about a revived union, and they did not oppose the Moscow coup and its aim of keeping the union together. However this discredited the old regime, and opened the way for Shushkevich to become Chairman of the Supreme Soviet, and therefore effective head of the republic. But he was restricted in what he could do. The government headed by Vyacheslau Kebich (a party official and then prime minister during the Soviet period who had resigned from the party after the coup) remained dominated by members of the former Soviet nomenklatura, and received solid support from the conservative majority in the Supreme Soviet.[218] Shushkevich was virtually helpless when confronted by this bloc. In August 1992 the Constitutional Commission produced a draft constitution which included a presidency despite Shushkevich's open opposition to this,[219] the Supreme Soviet simply ignored a legally-valid petition mounted by the PFB calling for new elections, the Kebich government used its support in the chamber to take over some of the powers formally accorded to the parliament and to press for closer relations with Russia,[220] and in April 1993 the Supreme Soviet voted to sign the CIS collective security agreement against Shushkevich's wishes.[221] Shushkevich refused to sign this agreement (although he eventually signed it in January 1994), and called for a referendum on Belarus' neutrality. Instead the Supreme Soviet launched a vote of no confidence in its chairman, which failed only because the PFB deputies had withdrawn and left the chamber inquorate.

In January 1994 the closed oligarchy that had ruled Belarus since independence began to crumble as a result of pressure from within. A vote of no confidence was called in that month against Shushkevich and Kebich. The precipitating factor was allegations of corruption made against them by the chairman of the Supreme Soviet's commission on corruption, Aleksandr Lukashenka. Kebich survived the vote, but Shushkevich was defeated 209:36[222] and was replaced by Kebich's ally Myetshislav Hryb. In March the Supreme Soviet adopted the latest constitutional draft placed before it, containing a strong presidency,[223] and in April Kebich signed a treaty of monetary union with Russia. The adoption of the new constitution made a presidential election necessary, and this was held in June 1994. The leading candidates were Shushkevich, Kebich and Lukashenka, and in the second round Lukashenka soundly defeated Kebich 85.0%:15.1%. International observers declared the election to be free and fair. With this strong mandate, Lukashenka set about expanding his powers. He was able to persuade the Supreme Soviet to pass a law on local administration which effectively brought it under his direct control, and although part of this was later ruled invalid by the Constitutional Court, it did not undo the effect of the law: to create a vertical chain of command from the local administrations to the presidency.[224] In December restrictions were imposed on the press, including the removal of one major newspaper's editor and the closure of eight other newspapers. In April 1995 violence was used to break up a PFB demonstration, and Lukashenka continually sought to use the security organs to consolidate power.

However conflict was also brewing between president and parliament. In January 1995 the Supreme Soviet adopted rules for impeachment of the president. But the tension between a president with an expansive view of his powers and a parliament anxious to protect its role and interests took shape around the parliamentary elections due in May 1995. There were two areas of contention. First, the electoral system. By the end of 1994 there were some 26 parties and movements in existence,[225] and their leaders favoured a mixed PR-SMC system in order to encourage the development of party organisations. Lukashenka believed that parties were insubstantial and therefore election by party list through PR was unnecessary. Second, Lukashenka wanted to combine the election with a referendum on four issues: a presidential right to suspend the parliament if it violated the constitution, relations with Russia, the re-introduction of Russian as a state language, and the re-introduction of Soviet-era state symbols. The only one of these the parliament accepted was that on relations with Russia. Lukashenka now threatened to suspend the Supreme Soviet and the elections, and had some PFB deputies who had gone on a hunger strike forcibly removed from the parliamentary building. The Supreme Soviet backed down, although it did declare that the question on the president's right to suspend the parliament would not be legally binding.

74 Negotiating regime change

The credibility of the parliament as an institution was undermined by the referendum and election results. All the referendum questions were passed overwhelmingly, the lowest vote being 75% for the re-introduction of Soviet-era state symbols. In the election to the parliament, only 18 of the 260 seats were filled in the first round,[226] with another 102 in the second. This left the parliament without a quorum. It took until December, seven months later, for successive rounds of voting to elect enough deputies to make the chamber quorate. This process was hindered by Lukashenka's attempts to keep the institution helpless by encouraging people not to vote. Following the voting, which international observers said was neither free nor fair,[227] the largest parties were the Communist Party and the Agrarian Party,[228] but the weakness of the party system is reflected in the fact that the deputies of both of these parties together did not equal half the number of deputies in the chamber.

Lukashenka used the vacuum created by the election to expand his position. He refused to recognise the parliament as a legitimate body. In July 1995 he unilaterally passed the budget by presidential decree, he broke a metro workers strike by force and arrested 15 trade union leaders, he removed parliamentary immunity by decree and arrested an opposition deputy for helping to organise the strike, he appointed two members of his administration as deputy prime ministers, and he instructed state employees to ignore Constitutional Court rulings against the validity of his decrees. In April 1996 he signed an agreement establishing a Community of Sovereign Republics with Russia, an act which provoked violent demonstrations which were vigorously put down, thereby provoking further demonstrations. Two months later Lukashenka faced criticism from the head of the Supreme Soviet, Sharetsky, over his failure to deal with the growing economic crisis,[229] and a threat from Sharetsky that if the president did not act, the parliament, which following run off elections in late 1995 had a quorum, would. In response Lukashenka announced that he would call a referendum to extend his term in office, create a new two-tier parliament with many presidential appointees, and increase presidential control over judicial appointments. This action generated much opposition among the parliamentary opposition and international opinion, but Lukashenka bulldozed over the top of it. His referendum proposals were formally adopted in a poll characterised by widespread fraud and manipulation,[230] thereby consolidating his personal control. He disbanded the parliament in 1996 and continued to rule by strong arm methods, using force to suppress opposition demonstrations and remove opposition.[231] When Lukashenka's term of office ran out in July 1999, he ignored this constitutional provision and continued to rule in defiance of protests. These included an opposition-staged presidential election which attracted 58% of the voters but which Lukashenka ignored.[232] During this whole period he continued to press for unification with Russia, culminating in the signature in December 1999 of a treaty designed to bring about a confederal union. In September 2000, parliamentary elections were held. They were neither free nor fair. Of the 565 candidates standing for seats, only 54 did not support Lukashenka. The opposition parties boycotted the poll, but security forces ensured there were no mass manifestations of opposition to disrupt proceedings.

So in Belarus the weakness of the opposition was reflected in the dominance in the parliament of old regime forces. But even these were not able to restrain the ambitions of the president, who himself came from this milieu, and who used his control of the state and willingness to use force to get what he wanted. In this way, the split between old regime forces led to personal authoritarianism as closed oligarchy gave way to sultanism.

The republican election in March 1990 in **Kazakhstan** did not disturb the control exercised by the old regime (the communist party won 95% of the 360 seats), and when Nursultan Nazarbaev was elected president unopposed at the beginning of December 1991, he came to the post as one of the leading politicians in the USSR. Indeed, he had been a major figure in trying to retain the USSR in the revived form Gorbachev hoped to see emerge from the new union treaty negotiations. However when the leaders of Russia, Ukraine and Belarus effectively ended the USSR in December 1991, the Kazakh leadership reluctantly embarked on independence. Nazarbaev's standing as a prominent Soviet politician (and one who was perceived to be pro-Russian in orientation) was a source of considerable discontent on the part of opposition forces in the republic, and was the origin of the public demonstration which delayed the opening of the Supreme Soviet in June 1992. But the opposition was very weak, despite the merger of three small opposition parties (the Azat, National Democratic, and Republican parties) in October 1992.

Nazarbaev set about consolidating his position. In October 1992 a presidential party, the People's Unity Union (PUU), was formed and Nazarbaev became its head.[233] Nazarbaev saw the task of this organisation to be the uniting of all Kazakhs around a common goal and thereby the overcoming of divisions and petty politicking.[234] At the beginning of 1993 a new constitution was adopted. The draft had been drawn up by a constitutional commission headed by Nazarbaev and adopted by the parliament for public discussion in June 1992.[235] The new constitution gave the president the power to appoint the prime minister, deputy prime minister, and foreign, defence and interior ministers, the chairman of the National Security Council, all ambassadors and the administrative heads of the country's 19 regions (which supervised elections). It made provision neither for the impeachment of the president nor presidential closure of the parliament. In December 1993 the Supreme Soviet approved the abolition of elected local and regional soviets in the wake of the self-proroguing of many of these bodies. They were seen as representative of the old order, and were to be replaced by administrators appointed by the president. The Supreme Soviet was then prorogued and elections scheduled for March 1994. In the interim, Nazarbaev was to rule by decree.

There was widespread support for these elections, because with a new constitution it was clear that the parliament needed a new mandate. But Nazarbaev also wanted a more tractable parliament. The election was a sweeping victory for Nazarbaev supporters.[236] As well as the 42 seats filled from names entered onto a special presidential list (and therefore within the personal gift of Nazarbaev), of the 135 seats filled by SMC, the PUU won the most seats of any party; its 33 seats was triple that of the second group, the Confederation of Trade Unions. There were 59 independents. Independent monitors noted serious inadequacies in the conduct of the poll, including gerrymandering, disqualification of independent candidates, high levels of proxy voting, fraud, harassment of critics and a biased media.[237] When the new parliament met, Nazarbaev pressed for the granting of additional powers to the president. But despite its mode of election, the parliament began to oppose Nazarbaev. In April-May an opposition bloc of some 32 deputies (Respublika[238]) was formed, and became the spearhead of opposition within the parliament to the largely president-appointed government. By late 1994 the parliament saw itself as the main limit on presidential power, passing a vote of no confidence in the prime minister and government, blocking reform measures, and openly discussing the need to restrict presidential power.[239]

A political crisis developed in 1995. On 6 March the Constitutional Court, on Nazarbaev's encouragement,[240] declared that there had been procedural infringements in the conduct of the election, and that its results were therefore invalid. Initially Nazarbaev made a purely formal objection to this on the grounds that it would destabilise Kazakhstan, while the Speaker of the parliament ordered the suspension of this judgement. On 11 March the parliament approved a constitutional amendment allowing it to overrule Court decisions and suspending the Court until June. The same day Nazarbaev dissolved the parliament and the government resigned, with the president declaring he would rule by decree until a new government was formed. He also signed decrees forbidding demonstrations and rallies, but members of the parliament ignored these to demonstrate against the dissolution of that body. Nazarbaev again called for a stronger presidency in order to be able to deal with the declining law and order situation, and announced a referendum on extending his presidential term beyond the scheduled December 1996 election until December 2000. On a reported turnout of 91.3%, 95.4% agreed to the extension of Nazarbaev's term.[241] In May Nazarbaev established a council of experts under his leadership to draft a new constitution. The draft, which was made public in early July, was denounced by the Constitutional Court, leaders of minority groups and the trade unions. It also concentrated power further in the president's hands; he could appoint all ministers (the prime minister with the parliament's approval), dissolve the parliament in times of 'severe disagreements' and issue decrees having the force of law, while impeachment was made very difficult and his 'honour and dignity' were declared sacrosanct.[242] Among other things, it proposed changing the country's name to the Kazakh Republic (an ethnically-exclusivist formulation that was later dropped), recognising Kazakh as the only official language, preventing dual citizenship, banning trade unions in state institutions, and restricting the foreign funding of trade unions. In a referendum on the draft in August, 89.1% of voters (on a turn out of 90.6%) were said to have approved of it. The same month Nazarbaev announced that the Constitutional Court would be abolished and replaced by a Constitutional Council whose decisions would be subject to presidential veto. Elections for the parliament were scheduled for December 1995. Nazarbaev had clearly used the 1995 crisis to expand and consolidate his power and position.

When the election was held, the majority of deputies returned to the lower house of the Majlis[243] were either notionally independents or members of the PUU;

other parties were barely represented.[244] Observers noted numerous violations of electoral procedures, including multiple voting, no witnesses to the counting of votes, the banning of some candidates and the listing on the ballots of only candidates' (not parties') names. There was also pressure against parties, including refusal of registration, harassment of opposition figures and pressure on the non-state media.[245] The composition of the parliament limited its ability to oppose the president effectively, although in late 1998 when deputies did threaten the president with impeachment, he reversed his opposition to constitutional amendments moved by the parliament which included holding early parliamentary and presidential elections in 1999.[246] The presidential election was held in January 1999, with Nazarbaev being returned for a seven year term with 82% electoral support in a field of four. The election was widely criticised both by the opposition and by international observers: three candidates including Nazarbaev's only realistic rival were barred from participating, pressure was brought on the media, there was fraud in the gathering of signatures for nomination, and claims about fraud in the counting of votes.[247] Similarly when the parliamentary elections were held in October 1999, in which opposition parties performed poorly,[248] OSCE observers acknowledged that the actual vote was relatively free, but the intimidation and obstruction of opposition candidates and parties and violations in counting the votes seriously undermined democratic principles. Furthermore the main opposition party, the Republican People's Party boycotted the poll because its leader and the main opposition figure, former prime minister Kazhegeletin, had been banned from participating. The election was neither free nor fair.[249]

So in Kazakhstan the weakness of the opposition enabled old regime forces, and especially the president, to dominate the political process. Indeed, it was Nazarbaev's personal ability to dominate political life which was the main shaping figure in the course of Kazakh development and the emergence of a sultanist regime.

In **Tajikistan** orthodox communist control was not shaken by the republican election of February 1990, although control did have to be restored when it slipped in the wake of the 1991 coup in Moscow. The party leader K.M. Makhkamov who had supported the coup was forced from office, but those who had removed him were in turn displaced by a coup in September which brought former party secretary (he had been removed from office by Gorbachev in 1985) Rakhmon Nabiev to power. This elite around Nabiev continued to work for the maintenance of the USSR, only giving up on that goal when the country was effectively dissolved in December 1991. Consequently the country entered the independent era with a president (Nabiev) and parliament rooted in the old structure. However they were not without opposition. In the presidential election in November 1991, which was characterised by fraud and manipulation,[250] Nabiev received 58% of the vote against six opponents, while political parties had begun to emerge earlier in the year.[251] Popular demonstrations between March and May 1992, including the capturing of part of the capital Dushanbe by armed groups opposed to the government, led to negotiations which produced a coalition government (the opposition had eight of 24 ministries) and a new transitional parliament, the Majlis, which was to include representatives of opposition parties. But the establishment of such a coalition arrangement did not bring stability. Fighting broke out in various parts of the country, mounted by groups opposed to the new government, and opposition demonstrations continued to demand Nabiev's resignation. The civil conflict forced Nabiev from office in early September; he was captured by a dissident group and forced to resign. However the Nabiev-supporter who was made acting-president, Akbarsho Iskandarov, survived only until November. Under pressure from pro-Nabiev forces and unable to solve the growing crisis, Iskandarov resigned. The presidency was now abolished, and the Supreme Soviet chairman became the head of state. This was former communist leader and Nabiev-supporter, Imomali Rakhmonov. Iskandarov took up arms against the new government. The country outside the capital was effectively divided into antagonistic clan areas run by local warlords, and central control collapsed.[252]

With fighting widespread throughout the country, Rakhmonov attempted to consolidate his position. During 1993–94 opposition parties were banned and their leaders imprisoned, the broadcast media were placed under the direct control of the president, the coercive arms of the state were strengthened, many of Rakhmonov's supporters were moved into official positions, all events of a 'mass character' were banned, and a state of emergency was introduced. In April 1994 the People's Party of Tajikistan (PPT), a communist successor party including many local officials and industrial managers, was established. In the same month Rakhmonov introduced a draft constitution which re-introduced the presidency. This was adopted by the Supreme Soviet for placement before the people in a referendum to coincide with the presidential election.[253]

The election had originally been scheduled for 25 September, but in late August this was postponed, reportedly under Russian pressure, to give opposition forces more time to organise. In the lead up to the election, the state of emergency expired, a ceasefire was signed with the opposition (although this did not end all of the fighting), and an attempt was made to persuade opposition forces to participate in the poll. However when the election was held on 6 November 1994, most opposition forces boycotted it. Rakhmonov reportedly won 58.3% to his opponent, former prime minister Abdullojonov's, 35%. The result was accompanied by widespread claims of falsification, intimidation and fraud, claims supported by international observers.[254] It also showed the starkly regionalised nature of Tajikistan: Rakhmonov's support came from the south, Abdullojonov's from the north. In the constitutional referendum, it was claimed that 90% of voters approved of the draft. With parliamentary elections due in February 1995, Abdullojonov established a new political party, the Party of Popular Unity and Justice. However as the election approached, Abdullojonov was barred from participating, and he withdrew his party as well. This was part of a widespread opposition boycott which resulted in 40% of the seats being uncontested. Most candidates were former officials of the state administration, and although their party affiliations were not clear, many were communists. In any event, most were in positions where they were beholden to the president. The election was widely faulted for fraud, intimidation, censorship of the opposition and refusal to register opposition parties.

The election did not bring peace. Fighting between government and opposition supporters continued. Following the collapse of discussions designed to bring an end to the conflict, in negotiations from December 1996 until May 1997, Rakhmonov reached agreement with the leader of the banned Islamic Renaissance Party, Said Abdullo Nuri, about the establishment of a National Reconciliation Commission including opposition representation to discuss constitutional amendments, legalisation of opposition media and parties, an amnesty, and participation by members of the United Tajik Opposition (UTO, the opposition umbrella organisation) in a new government. Despite armed rebellions in part of the country opposed to this agreement, in the twelve months following it negotiations between the government and the UTO continued. By November 1998 there was agreement on 11 of the 14 ministerial posts the opposition was to fill, but it took a further six months before final agreement was reached. This, and the relegalisation of four opposition bodies (the Islamic Renaissance Party, Democratic Party, Rastokhez, and Lali Badakhshan) in August 1999 paved the way for a referendum on constitutional reform. The referendum was held in September, and involved the replacement of the unicameral by a bicameral parliament, extension of the presidential term from five to seven years, and revocation of the ban on religious parties. A presidential poll was held in November 1999, but a number of potential challengers (including the leading opposition figure) were ruled ineligible to contest the ballot, leaving Rakhmonov as the only candidate. He won 96.9% of the vote. International observers were critical of the election as clearly breaching the principles of democracy. The February 2000 elections for the lower house were also considered to be seriously flawed.[255] Only three parties gained representation, and the only opposition party, the Islamic Renaissance Party, gained only 7.5% of the vote. Rakhmonov's control of the official structures of the state had clearly been strengthened, and after the election he removed opposition UTO members from the government.

The control of the main institutions of state by representatives of the old regime and the outbreak of conflict based principally on regional/clan considerations, meant that the opposition was accorded no legitimate role in the working out of the contours of the new state. This came about only with the settlement at the end of the civil war, but even then it is not clear that closed oligarchic control has been modified.

In **Turkmenistan** control by the Soviet regime remained tight, with the republican elections in January 1990 not shaking that control; communist functionaries dominated the parliament and party leader Sapuramad Niyazov was elected president unopposed. The Turkmen leadership supported the attempt to keep the Soviet Union together, only agreeing to follow the independence path when there was no alternative. The control exercised by the old regime elite was maintained once independence was achieved. None of the power structures of the Soviet system in the republic were abolished; in December 1991, the communist party turned itself into the Democratic Party of Turkmenistan.[256] Manifestations of opposition were suppressed, the press strictly controlled, and elections were generally not competitive; the total number of candidates usually exceeded the number of seats by one, and the emergence of parties prevented. When Niyazov stood for the presidency in June 1992 following the introduction of a new constitution in May which made the president both head of state and head of government,[257] he was the only candidate and reportedly received 99.5% of the vote. His personality cult blossomed. In January 1994 in a referendum on extending his term until 2002, a reported 99.9% of voters favoured this. Although elections have been held regularly for the parliament, they have provided no opening for opposition activity; in the December 1994 election there were 50 candidates for 50 seats and the counting of votes was crudely manipulated,[258] while in 1999 there were 104 candidates for 50 seats but almost all came from the DPT. In any case, parliament was a rubber stamp. There has been room for no one except the president and his supporters in the political system,[259] and it is the president who has been in undisputed control in this sultanist regime.

The control exercised by the Soviet authorities in **Uzbekistan** remained tight right through the perestroika period, so that few civil society forces were able to emerge and develop any strength. The parliament elected in the January 1990 election was dominated by conservative party officials, while the party first secretary Islam Karimov, was elected president by the Supreme Soviet in March 1990 and by the populace in December 1991, receiving 86% of the vote.[260] In the election he had been opposed by only one person, whose campaign had been seriously hindered by the authorities, while the candidates of two other parties (Birlik and the Islamic Renaissance Party) were prevented from participating. The Uzbek leadership had favoured the maintenance of the USSR, accepting the reality of independence only when the USSR was dissolved by the heads of the three Slavic republics. When independence was achieved, little changed as the authorities maintained their harassment and repression of the opposition, especially its two main manifestations, the parties/social movements Erk and Birlik. In November 1991 the communist party had become the People's Democratic Party of Uzbekistan, and continued as the effective ruling structure, while in the early months of 1992 Karimov consolidated his personal power through both institutional means and the suppression of opposition.[261] In January 1992 the post of vice-president was abolished and a new post of prime minister established, to which a loyal ally of Karimov was appointed. The post of presidentially-appointed governor was created throughout the country. In July 1992 the Supreme Soviet approved the details of a new draft constitution[262] that was strongly presidential. Uzbekistan was referred to as a secular, democratic, presidential republic in which the president could not be removed from office except as a result of illness, but could dissolve parliament. The draft guaranteed freedom of thought, conscience and religious conviction, of political parties and public associations, and respect for human rights, all of which flew in the face of the systematic harassment of opposition forces that had been occurring throughout 1992. The constitution was adopted on 8 December 1992. Soon after, political parties, including Birlik, were banned.[263] In May 1993 the posts of president and prime minister were combined, thereby giving the president direct control over the government.

Pressure was maintained against opposition forces.[264] Individual dissidents were arrested (some were even seized while attending a human rights conference in Bishkek in the Kyrgyz Republic), or beaten up in the streets, opposition parties and independent media outlets were refused registration, non-government print media were banned, independent organisations were raided and subjected to threats, all against a continuing emphasis upon the need for unity and support for the government. When elections were called to the new parliament, the Oly Majlis, between December 1994 and January 1995, only two parties were allowed to participate: the People's Democratic Party (PDP) which was the communist successor party led by Karimov, and Fatherland Progress which was allied with the PDP. Although all but five seats were contested, no one opposed to government policy was able to stand.[265] Of the 250 seats, the PDP won 69 and Fatherland Progress 14. The other 167 seats went to the nominees of local authorities, of whom some 120 were PDP members. The other 47 members formed themselves into an opposition bloc, the Adolet (Justice) Social Democratic Party, but they were clearly overwhelmed by Karimov supporters. The parliament remained little more than a rubber stamp. In March 1995 a reported 99.6% (on a turnout of 99.3%) in a referendum vote approved extending Karimov's term until 2000. Parliamentary elections were held in December 1999, and although all seats were formally contested, none of the five parties opposed the government. International observers thought the elections were not free, fair, equal or transparent; two independent parties were banned and no independent parties could participate, there was interference in candidate selection by authorities, and local electoral commissions were neither unbiased nor independent. In the presidential election of January 2000, Karimov determined both the rules of the election and the identity of his 'opponent'. Karimov received 91.9% of the vote on a turn out of about 95%.

Formally opposition has remained possible in Uzbekistan, but in practice it is suppressed. Although nominally independent groups have appeared, in practice they have been closely allied with Karimov.[266] The opposition also suffers because the different groups have been unable to come together to present a united front. As a result, the rule of old regime forces has continued and Karimov has exercised sultanist control.

It is clear that there is a relationship between the involvement of opposition, non-old regime, civil society forces and the political outcome in these states. This is illustrated in Table 2.1 which shows the pattern of development in association with the type of regime each country has had throughout much of the 1990s.

While the fit is not exact, the tendency is clear: the greater the involvement of non-old regime civil society forces in the negotiations at the initial stage, the greater the prospects for democracy. *Per contra*, the more the decisions about regime form are made by forces emanating from within the old regime to the exclusion of civil society forces, the greater the likelihood of an authoritarian outcome. The type of authoritarian outcome is shaped by the dynamics of those forces ruling in the new states. The question is why civil society forces have been better able to play a determining role in some countries than in others. This will be discussed in the following chapter.

Table 2.1 Patterns of development and regime types

Regime type	Democracy	Façade democracy			Non-democracy		
Pattern of development		Ethnic democracy	Open oligarchy	Plebiscitary democracy	Closed oligarchy	Plebiscitary democracy	Sultanism
Pattern 1	Poland						
	Hungary						
Pattern 2	Bulgaria		Albania				
Pattern 3	Czech Republic		Slovakia				
Pattern 4							
(i)		Latvia					
		Estonia					
		Moldova					
(ii)	Lithuania						
(iii)				Georgia			
(iv)				Croatia	Armenia		
Pattern 5	Slovenia		Macedonia	Russia		Kyrgyz Republic	
				Ukraine			
Pattern 6			Romania		Tajikistan	FRY	Belarus
					Azerb.		Kazakhstan
							Turkmenistan
							Uzbekistan

3 Civil society and the onset of negotiations

The previous chapter has shown how the political trajectory of the post-communist states has been shaped by the circumstances of the initial process of regime change. Crucial here has been the role played by civil society forces in bringing about the change of regime. To understand why such forces were able to play a significant part in some countries but not in others, attention should be turned to the history of the development of civil society in this region.

Civil society has become one of the most important concepts in the social sciences over the past decade or so. But it has also been accompanied by significant ambiguity about what it means. Most agree that the core of civil society is the existence of organisations and groups autonomous from the state which act to defend the interests of their members, including against state intervention. But few seek to extend the concept further than this sort of counter-position to the state. Yet if we are to understand why civil society forces are powerful in some places and not in others and at some times and not at others, the conception of civil society must be richer than this.

There are three levels of the structuring of human activity in society. The first level comprises those networks of interrelationships which structure people's pursuit of their immediate, usually personal, concerns; they grow out of the immediate conditions and problems of people's lives. These networks are essentially primary and face-to-face; they are concerned with those matters which are of a private nature, and they rest on personal, often kinship and friendship, bases. They do not relate to the public sphere nor do they interact in any direct way with the power of the state. These are the essential building blocks of a society. Without these personal linkages, society could not exist because the basic units of that society, the people, rely upon these for the structuring of their own personal lives. These are the bedrock of social existence, and occur in all societies. If they did not exist, society would not exist. Examples of such groups would include friendship associations, hobby groups, and discussion groups/study circles. These will be called primary groups.

The second level comprises those organisations which are generated to enable individuals to pursue their interests and concerns in the public sphere. These rest upon and may be extensions of the first type of networks,[1] but their essence is quite different. These may not involve face-to-face relationships, they project people's concerns beyond the private sphere into the public sphere, and this form of association is often manifested through formal organisational structures. This associative behaviour thus has as its arena of operation the society more generally, and its major focus of concern tends to be much more generalised than in the first type. Furthermore the interactions of organisations of this sort tend to be much more competitive and more likely to be zero sum than those of the first type. This is because the matters with which they are concerned usually have a more generalised significance for the society as a whole or for segments of it. These groups are not essentially political in nature, in the sense of seeking to play a continuing role in the political sphere and to put pressure upon government, but at times they may play a political role in seeking to advance and defend the interests of their members. In this sense, they can mediate between state and individual, protecting the latter against the former and engaging in dialogue with the state. Examples would include trade unions, professional associations, and employer groups. These will be called secondary groups.

The third level comprises those organisations and associations which are designed specifically to seek to exercise political influence. Such organisations seek to advance and defend the interests of particular groups through activity in the political sphere. While at times they may seek to play a role in other than political matters, their primary focus and raison d'etre is to be active within the political field. The principal form such organisation takes is the political party. These will be called tertiary groups.

For civil society to exist, all three levels of the structuring of human activity must be present. The first level, the primary groups, is fundamental for society itself to exist. The second level, secondary groups, involves what most people see as the essence of civil society: organisation in the public sphere independent of the state to defend corporate interests. But it makes no sense to talk about civil society and the effective defence and promotion of interests unless that defence and promotion can take a political form. Unless people are free to organise politically to defend their interests and to develop tertiary groups, the defence of those interests is both insecure and incomplete. This means that civil society cannot exist without the right of organisation and action within the political sphere. Unless the state acknowledges the legitimacy of political organisation and activity, unless there is the right to organise and pursue one's interests politically, civil society cannot exist. This means that the absence of civil society is not the same as the absence of all forms of social organisation. Just because political organisation is forbidden, it does not mean that the other forms of organisation will not exist. Clearly primary groups will always be present, but secondary groups can also survive in the absence of a legitimate sphere of political activity. Indeed, political organisations can also exist in the absence of state acceptance of their legitimacy, but they will usually take an illegal or underground form. But when secondary and tertiary groups exist in the absence of recognition of the legitimacy of political organisation, they do not constitute a civil society. They are civil society forces, organisations that would constitute part of a civil society were the state to acknowledge the legitimacy of independent political activity and therefore of civil society, but in themselves they do not equal civil society. This means that civil society forces may exist in a country without the existence of a civil society. Such forces usually have primacy in a temporal sense, their existence being necessary before a civil society can emerge.

There is a logical relationship between the three levels of structuring of activity. Expansion of horizons from the personal to the public social to the public political is a logical progression. The link between primary and secondary groups is both facilitative and generative. It is facilitative in the sense that the sorts of patterns of associational behaviour intrinsic to primary groups feed into the activity of secondary groups, providing a structure which is expanded and strengthened on the larger scale. It is generative in the sense that the sorts of concerns which are the focus of primary groups can lead on to more general, community-wide interests, and thereby generate the causes around which secondary groups can form. Similarly this can generate the activity of the tertiary groups. Promotion of interests logically extends from the private sphere into the social and political. In institutional terms, this means that the development of social and political organisations is a logical, and therefore highly likely, product of social life. The issue is the attitude taken to this by the state. Where the state welcomes and recognises the legitimacy of political activity, this sort of development is likely to lead to the emergence of civil society. Where the state stands in the way of such a development, civil society forces are likely to emerge, but state intervention will prevent their extension into political activity (and may even constrain their activity in the public non-political sphere) and will thereby prevent the emergence of civil society. It is this relationship between the logic of the development of civil society forces and the attitude of the state that is crucial in structuring the course of historical development.

But if the development of civil society forces and the structuring of their relationship with the state have been important in shaping society's development, two aspects must be borne in mind. First, while the development of civil society forces is usually the progenitor of civil society, not all such forces may actually support the development of a civil society. To the extent that a civil society embodies the recognition of rights and obligations and implies both tolerance and adherence to the rules, some civil society forces emerge which are not supportive of or conducive to the development of such a society. The freedom of organisation which underpins the growth of all civil society forces facilitates the development of groups which refuse to accept the accords with which a developed civil society is associated. Such groups are usually extremist, sometimes nationalist, organisations which seek to make use of the space created by civil society forces more generally to build up their positions and strength. Thus although they may appear as regular civil society forces, their aim is often a society devoid of the principles underpinning civil society. This is a paradox of civil society force development. Second, the presence of civil society forces is not the same as their strength. The latter stems from such things as levels of popular support, degree of organisation, possession of resources, and levels of commitment of its members. In relative terms most forces, at least initially, are unable to challenge the strength of the state. They rely upon the state to leave them scope to develop and thereby increase their strength.

But this is relational. The weaker the state, the weaker civil society forces can be and still exercise influence upon it. As is evident from the post-communist cases, ultimately it is this relationship rather than any measure of the civil society forces' internal strength which is crucial in the capacity of civil society forces to play an influential role in regime change.

Some factors have historically been crucial to the functioning of a civil society. The first, essential, condition is a state in both senses of the word, a territorially-defined entity and an administrative structure which enjoys sovereignty and exercises authority within the bounds of that territorially-defined entity. Territorial boundaries have been important in the sense that people within them usually accept that they represent the limits of their community, that their interests are defined in part through membership of that community, and that satisfaction of those interests can be achieved by working through the structures, mechanisms and processes of that community. Perhaps more importantly, if sufficient numbers of people do not share this perception of community membership but instead see their future bound up with some other community, usually defined in terms of different territorial boundaries, their activities can undermine the development of civil society. Where people do not accept inclusion within the boundaries of a particular community, their actions will not usually strengthen civil society but may instead fuel the disintegration of the state. The clearest instance of this is minority ethnic groups who reject the power of the territorial state within which they dwell in favour of giving their allegiance to another state. Such groups may organise to press their interests, but rather than this being evidence of a strengthening of civil society, it may assist the break down of the society within which they dwell, and thereby the domestic civil society also. This does not mean that civil society is impossible where there is ethnic difference. Ethnic difference can contribute to the proliferation of interests that underpins civil society. But where a group seeks to pursue its interests in the context of another society, its activities are more likely to disrupt than to assist the growth of civil society in its society of location.

But more important is the notion of the state in the other sense of the word, a sovereign administrative structure. The administrative state is essential because of the regulatory functions it performs. A civil society means not only groups independent of the state acting to promote and defend the interests of their members. It also means that those groups must act in a civil way. Negotiation, compromise, recognition of the rights of others, eschewing violence, obedience to laws, rules and norms and generally acting with restraint, are all characteristic of civil society. Without this sort of pattern of civil conduct, competition between interests would become conflict of interests and would threaten social stability. While such a pattern of behaviour cannot be imposed from above, because it is a culture and therefore can become embedded only through practice and iteration, it does depend upon the presence of an effective state. The state must provide, at minimum, a sense of certainty and predictability through the provision of law and order. The state is the body which, ultimately, is the sanction against unacceptable behaviour. It ensures that those organisations which go about pursuing their interests in accord with the existing rules of the game are not going to be harmed by others who refuse to play by those accepted rules. Without the state, the strongest would be supreme and the very notion of a civil society in which all may seek to realise their ends would be undercut. Only if an effective state can provide the underpinning of certainty (in all spheres from weights and measures to personal safety) can the culture of a civil society develop. Where such certainty is missing, the development of civil society is distorted.

However certainty alone is insufficient. An authoritarian, highly penetrative state can provide certainty, but by not leaving room for civil society to develop, it can undermine that process. The state must acknowledge a sphere within which independent organisations have a right to organise to press their interests, including through political activity. If the state does not recognise the right of free organisation and political activity, civil society cannot exist. In this sense the state needs to take a permissive view of civil society activity. If it either denies the appropriateness of such activity or interferes in the playing out of such activity, it will be difficult for civil society to develop. Furthermore because of the dominant place in the political sphere occupied by the state, it must act as a crucial partner to civil society if the latter is to develop fully. If the promotion and defence of interests politically is an essential criterion for the existence of civil society, this must involve interaction with the state. Pursuit of those interests politically cannot avoid coming into contact with the state, and therefore makes the state's attitude to such activity central. The state is thus a crucial factor in the development of civil society. It is the single most important factor; if it seeks to prevent civil society from developing, the domestic sovereignty it possesses usually endows it with the means to prevent that development. Thus while it cannot of itself create a civil society, it can destroy one, or the prospects for the emergence of one.

Another crucial factor in the development of civil society has been urbanisation. The development of cities, and in particular a capital city which has also been a commercial/industrial centre, has provided an important stimulus for the development of civil society. One element in this has been the way in which cities bring together large numbers of people sharing common interests. Geographical propinquity creates the conditions under which those who share interests can organise to pursue them. If people mostly live in villages or rural hamlets widely scattered throughout the countryside, their capacity to come together in groups and organisations to pursue those interests is very limited. Peasants may be mobilised, but their rural location and the culture of peasant life gives them something of an outsider status; while they may form the electoral basis of a party, they are usually unable to play a positive part in the generation of civil society. In towns and cities the capacity for organisation is greatly expanded, especially if the means of urban transport are well developed. Cities provide the infrastructure, chiefly in the form of transport and communication, but also that indefinable raw energy that comes from urban life, which can be crucial to the development of the sorts of networks of interactions and interrelations at the centre of civil society.

Another important historical factor in the growth of modern civil society has been the development of industrial capitalism. Based on private ownership of the means of production, this has generated a whole set of interests stemming from the resulting structure of production. An urban working class which sold its labour and a bourgeois middle class which employed that labour on the basis of profits generated from investment and the use of that labour both emerged as a result of industrial capitalism. Their different life situations, prospects and perspectives were important sources of the generation of interests, which in turn spawned organisations of many different types. Many of those organisations naturally had to function in the public sphere because to the extent that they were concerned with matters that involved relations between employer, employee and state in some combination, those matters were of necessity to be found in the public domain. Even those matters which did not stem directly from the employee-employer-state triad were often propelled into the public domain as part of the way in which political life was transformed by the process of industrialisation. The greater openness of politics compared with the pre-industrial period meant that the groups that emerged were forced to interact and function in ways that created patterns of activity not formerly seen. In this sense, industrial capitalism both helped to form new interests and to shape the way they interacted. Furthermore the capitalist nature of this industrialisation has been crucial in one area: the ideology accompanying industrial capitalism which focused upon the efforts of the independent entrepreneur reinforced the sense of the need for the pursuit of interests independent of the state. It thereby confirmed the division essential to the notion of civil society, that between legitimate spheres of non-state and of state activity.

This emphasis upon life situations (rather than the ownership/non-ownership dichotomy) as the basis of associative behaviour means that even in economic systems where private ownership was not the legal basis, the relationship between different components of those systems could be the basis for organised activity. In this sense, industrial development itself may make a contribution to the development of civil society independent from the capitalist form much of that industrialisation historically has taken. The implication of this is that the communist system itself, and the program of economic development that such systems implemented everywhere they came into existence, in effect unleashed those pressures which historically have been so important for the emergence of civil society forces. Despite the internationalism of the ideology, throughout much of the communist world the system emphasised the creation of new or re-formed national communities, and in multi-ethnic states, sought to submerge ethnic difference within (supra-) national identity. But more importantly, communism everywhere hastened the linked processes of urbanisation and industrialisation. By emphasising the need for rapid economic development, communist regimes fostered both industrialisation on a large scale and a process of major and rapid urban expansion. This in turn created pressures for the development of civil society forces. In this sense, the communist development pattern fuelled the sorts of social developments which the communist regime was intent on suppressing. This contradiction was to become clear in the experiences of some of the Eastern European states in the 1980s.

At base, then, association together in organisations to pursue common interests is a natural response to the challenge posed by the desire to realise those interests. Such associative behaviour on a large scale may be encouraged by urban development and by industrialism, especially its capitalist variant, but it is fundamentally shaped by the state. An effective state that is open to such a development can channel such associative behaviour into acceptable forms and assist in the embedding of a culture of civility so essential to civil society. Indeed, it is this notion of civility, a recognition of the appropriate ways to behave, an acknowledgement of rules of proper conduct which emphasise the importance of acting according to established rules and norms, which finds it most difficult to emerge. Even after the long suppression of independent organisation, the fact that people find it useful to their ends to associate in organisations explains why such organised activity becomes a feature of public life. The emergence of civil society forces should therefore not be a surprise. However the form in which they emerge and their strength will be profoundly affected by the legacy of such civil society forces stemming from earlier and the vigour with which the state has sought (and been able) to suppress them. The importance of pre-communist civil society forces stems from the fact that once such forces are established and are functioning, the patterns of both activities and expectations that are thereby set up will be likely to continue unless they are specifically interrupted. But it is these self-sustaining and self-replicating patterns which communist regimes sought to eradicate in their quest for the new society. However the deeper and more embedded those patterns were, the greater, more extensive and possibly violent the state's intervention had to be to destroy them. The difficulty the state faced in destroying such patterns should not be under-estimated. The complete destruction of these patterns is much more difficult than their suppression. Although the institutions through which groups function and interests seek their satisfaction may be destroyed and collective action by group members may be banned, their history and memory of them is likely to be embedded in the collective consciousness of the culture generally and the particular community more especially. It may be transmitted through generations along with more general cultural values, and given the difficulty in eradicating cultural legacies, may remain embedded in the society despite regime attempts to extirpate it. If patterns of civil society activity are simply suppressed, and this is the usual result of the imposition of authoritarian power, once state power is weakened, those patterns may re-emerge.[2] If we are to understand why civil society forces were able to play an important role early in the process of regime change in some post-communist countries and not in others, it is to this legacy of civil society forces that we must look.[3] This comprises both the growth of civil society forces in the pre-communist period and the capacity of civil society forces to develop during the communist period. Central to the latter is the attitude of the communist state.

Roots of civil society

In the East European and former Soviet regions, there was not a strong precommunist tradition of political democracy. In the Russian Empire, the hesitant steps in a democratic direction following the 1905 revolution were choked off by the conservative reaction spearheaded by Stolypin and then by the outbreak of war. Throughout most of Eastern Europe, by the end of the 1920s a pseudo-democratic façade hid the reality of authoritarian rule, with only Czechoslovakia able to maintain a democratic system until it was displaced by the Nazi takeover in the lead up to the war.[4] But the absence of a democratic political system is not the same thing as the absence of civil society, so the absence of a democratic tradition in the region is conclusive evidence neither for nor against the development of civil society forces. In historical terms, the growth of civil society forces reflecting the capacity of the infrastructure of primary groups to generate broader patterns of associative behaviour and the range of secondary groups intrinsic to civil society, has often been associated with the growth of a bourgeois middle class. This group, united around their economic interests, possessing the resources and means to come together to defend those interests, and usually congregated in the large towns (and especially the capital), sought to pursue its interests by carving out a space independent of the state, and thereby creating a shell within which a more broadly-based and diverse range of social organisation could blossom. But such a bourgeois middle class was not well-developed in the East European region or former Russian Empire.

This region was essentially one of economic backwardness and late development (with corresponding lower levels of urbanisation[5]), with the state playing a significant role in economic development and independent social forces comparatively weak.[6] The indigenous bourgeoisie generally was weak, reflecting the domination of commerce and business in some countries by foreigners,[7] the propensity of those large landowners who left the land to seek to enter government service rather than commerce (although in Russia they generally eschewed both government service and commerce), and an anti-entrepreneurial ethos throughout much of the region.[8] The middle class tended to be aligned with the state, principally through employment in the large government bureaucracies or heavy reliance on state subsidies and support, and therefore lacked the sort of autonomy from the state evident in the classic model. Industrial development was patchy, with the main impetus coming from the state and foreign investment. The predominant role of the state was reflected in the fact that in all of the countries of Eastern Europe except for Czechoslovakia and Hungary, the dominant group was the state bureaucracy and the growing intelligentsia which staffed it. This constituted what one observer has called the 'bureaucratic 'political class',[9] a group which was able to use its dominance of office to serve its own interests. It was the search for office among the intelligentsia (the expansion of which could not be accommodated by an expanding industrial economy) which spawned the large number of patronage-oriented (as opposed to policy-oriented) parties[10] and the large, corrupt and inefficient state bureaucracies.[11] Generally rule was authoritarian, culminating in many countries in the rise of fascism in the inter-war period.[12] But within this general pattern, there were significant country differences.

Similarly, in the communist period, each country had imposed upon it a pattern of rule in which the institutional features were broadly similar. Dominated by a communist party whose tentacles penetrated all walks of life, legitimated by a formal ideology, with opposition suppressed and pursuing a program of industrial development justified by a millenarian end, the individual countries' systems had broadly standard features. However here too there were significant differences, most importantly in the scope allowed for independent social organisation and in the room provided within each regime for the emergence of reformist political forces. Even in the context of general bloc-wide lessening of the state's pressure on society in the 1970s and 1980s, there were clear country differences. These different aspects of the experiences of the various countries, the presence of civil society forces and the nature of the regime, will be discussed briefly and schematically in terms of the patterns of development identified in Chapter Two.

The process of regime change in the countries in **Patterns One** and **Three**, Poland, Hungary and Czechoslovakia, saw civil society forces present right at the outset and more powerful than the regime which controlled the respective countries. In all three countries, there was a legacy of civil society force development.

In Poland, the traditional gentry had fallen on hard times during the nineteenth century, and this had encouraged them in increasing numbers to leave the land[13] and enter state service, the professions, the army or the intelligentsia. While retaining a land-based dominance in the countryside, they became a particularly important force as the intelligentsia, coming to symbolise Polish nationhood during a period when Poland was part of the Russian Empire and taking over the running of the state once independence was achieved in 1918. With commerce dominated by a small, bourgeois middle class principally of German and Jewish origin,[14] the main basis for Polish middle class development remained the state and the expansion of its responsibilities. But although the state thereby constituted the main basis of Polish middle class development, and therefore the latter lacked autonomy from the state, sections of the intelligentsia remained important as an arena for the discussion of issues relating to the shape of Polish society. This was in part responsible for the proliferation of Polish political parties between the wars; by 1926 there were 26 Polish and 33 ethnic parties, of which 31 had achieved parliamentary representation.[15] This contributed to the parliamentary instabiliy and deadlock, which in turn contributed to the Pilsudski coup in 1926. Some parties continued to operate after the coup, despite the regime's best efforts to introduce a technocratic, avowedly non-political administration after Pilsudski's death in 1935. The Church was an important element in the public sphere. There was also an industrial working class, which by 1930 constituted almost a quarter of gainfully employed males, but this class and its organisations (especially trade unions) remained weak.

The functioning of civil society forces in communist Poland was more dramatic than anywhere else because of the succession of crises that arose in relations between the state and these forces. In the wake of the unrest in 1956, which led to the replacement of the hard-line Ochab leadership by the Gomulka-led national communists,[16] the regime sought to reach accommodation with the society, and although this did not involve official sanctioning of autonomous organisation, a range of these emerged and were reluctantly tolerated. This also involved recognising a private sector of the economy, agriculture. Discussion clubs among intellectuals were significant here,[17] again forming the nucleus of what in Czechoslovakia had come to be called a parallel polis,[18] the generation and circulation by intellectuals of a morality based on values autonomous from and critical of the official values of the regime. Attempts were also made to establish links with other sectors of society, most importantly in the emergence of the Workers' Defence Committee (KOR), which was formed to defend the strikers against the state in the wake of the June 1976 strikes. KOR's stance stimulated the emergence of a large range of other autonomous groups in Polish society,[19] but more important in the longer term were the pressures for independent organisation on the part of industrial workers. Riots and strikes occurred in response to price rises in 1970 (which resulted in the replacement of Gomulka by Gierek) and 1976, but the organisation of such activity reached its peak with the creation of Solidarity in 1980.[20] Solidarity's strength lay in the fact that although it was solidly based in the working class, it was able to reach out to other sections of Polish society and to mobilise them to place pressure on the regime, and it could act as an umbrella under which a range of oppositional groups could shelter.[21] Despite its outlawing with the imposition of martial law in 1981, Solidarity remained a major social actor, a significant moral force, and an important negotiating partner when the crisis of power reached its peak in 1988–89. Also important as a manifestation of civil society forces in Poland has been the Catholic Church.[22] Historically the Church was symbolically associated with the idea of the Polish nation and thereby had a popular legitimacy that transcended religious belief. With strong commitment on the part of believers, the Church was a continuing, if not always highly vocal, critic of the regime's record on human rights and a defender of its own (and by implication that of others) institutional autonomy. This became particularly important following the banning of Solidarity.

Like their counterparts to the north, large parts of the nobility in Hungary had left the land to go to the cities and enter government service, the professions and the intelligentsia. But despite many leaving the land, the absence of land reform meant that they still dominated the countryside through their large estates. The traditional rulers of Hungary, they were able to maintain that control through their dominance of the bureaucratic apparatus. Furthermore they were able to reassert this control following the disasters of the war and Bela Kun's soviet republic. They continued throughout to see themselves as the bearers of national culture and identity. Once off the land, they entered the mainstream of one of the imperial capitals, and, perhaps reflecting the high literacy levels, one with a tradition of vigorous intellectual life. There was a small bourgeois middle class, chiefly Jewish in origin but becoming increasingly Magyarised in the inter-war period, but the main basis of middle class development remained the state. In the inter-war period there was a range of political parties which competed in the parliamentary elections of the 1920s and 1930s, but the most important was the government party. There was also a trade union organisation based on the expansion of the working class on the back of military industry during the war, although it was not particularly strong. The tradition of discussion and debate in the capital constituted the focus around which a public sphere could turn.

A parallel polis functioned in communist Hungary following the relaxation of the early 1960s, with intellectuals very influential in shaping the debate surrounding the nature of communist regimes in the region both within the communist states themselves and, through their continuing links with a substantial émigré intellectual population, in the West as well.²³ The importance of the Hungarian intellectuals in sustaining a general sense of morality autonomous from the regime should not be underestimated.²⁴ But also important in Hungary was the large range of civil organisations which emerged and developed in response to the more liberal atmosphere fostered by the regime in its attempt to build bridges to the population following the crushing of the 1956 revolution. That regime acknowledged the legitimacy, even value, of the open manifestation of group interests in society, and accepted with equanimity the view that those interests could come into conflict. In practical terms it legalised a private sphere in the economy, and encouraged such a sphere more broadly in the social domain, with the result that a wide diversity of groups was able to play a public part in Hungarian life.²⁵ Although there were clearly some limits on what groups could do and many of those groups were small and fragmented, they did constitute a much more vibrant arena of civil life than anywhere else in the communist world.

In Czechoslovakia there was a clear split between the industrialised Czech lands of Bohemia and Moravia and the more traditional agricultural lands of Slovakia. Gentry dominance of the Czech lands had been long smashed, with the result that when the country gained its independence in 1918, it was dominated by a native bourgeoisie and intelligentsia. A long history of industrial development had produced a strong commercial bourgeoisie which was closely allied to other commercial, intellectual, professional and bureaucratic elements of the middle class, and, in a development rare in the region, which also played a part in local administration.²⁶ There was also a strong working class movement with a substantial trade union structure. The Czech lands had what one observer has called 'a well articulated and modern' class structure.²⁷ This provided the basis for a developed system of programmatic parties, although the large numbers of such parties made coalitions both essential and complex to arrange.²⁸ Regardless of this, politics remained stable and remarkably civil in its conduct throughout the inter-war period, with Czechoslovakia being the only country in the region to maintain a democratic system throughout this period.

This basis of civil society activity was vigorously suppressed when the communists came to power in 1948. The Czechoslovak regime was one of the most hard-line in the bloc, maintaining unrelenting pressure on any manifestation of autonomous activity despite periods of relaxation experienced elsewhere. However over time, increasing dissatisfaction with this course both inside and outside the ruling party led to some liberalisation in the mid-1960s, and ultimately to the removal of veteran leader Antonin Novotny in December 1967. Under the new leader Alexander Dubcek, the capacity of Czechoslovak society to generate civil society forces was clearly evident in the Prague Spring,²⁹ when the further relaxation of regime control (and the explicit encouragement of leading regime figures) led to a massive explosion of autonomous group activity. These groups radicalised the political agenda, threatening to displace the party from its ruling position, and introducing a much more pluralist political environment than anywhere else in the communist world. Ultimately this provoked armed intervention by Warsaw Pact forces. The speed with which these groups emerged and the diversity of them suggests that, despite the best efforts of the authorities especially in the 1950s, civil society forces had been suppressed rather than destroyed; many secondary groups continued to exist despite regime pressure. This is the case too for the period of 'normalisation'[30] that followed the suppression of the Prague Spring. The emergence of groups like Charter 77 and the associated Committee for the Defence of the Unjustly Prosecuted (VONS) in the late 1970s and their survival into the 1980s reflects the continuing importance of the civil society impulse.[31] These were significant bodies too for the way in which they helped to provide an infrastructure for a parallel polis. Although these organisations were the home of intellectuals and never developed mass roots,[32] they did continue to constitute an expression of civil society, and, particularly in the form of the parallel polis (weak though it was), constituted the sort of ersatz moral limitation on the state that civil society elsewhere was expected to provide.

The pre-communist basis for the growth of civil society forces was stronger in these three countries than anywhere else. In the Czech lands the main basis for this was the growing economic position of the bourgeoisie, in Poland and Hungary it was chiefly the moral authority of the intelligentsia. In all three countries, this development was largely restricted to the major urban centres. The capacity for civil society force development evident in these countries was not destroyed by communist rule despite significant attempts to do so. Indeed, civil society forces developed in all three countries under communist rule. The greater development of civil society forces over a long period of time in Poland and Hungary was a function of the way in which both regimes sought to reach a *modus vivendi* with their respective societies following the events of 1956. After an initial crackdown following its installation by Soviet troops in 1956, the Kadar regime in Hungary sought to win support among the populace by relaxing control in a range of areas, thereby creating space for the emergence of some autonomous social groups and creating a sense of dialogue between populace and regime. In Poland, the Gomulka regime also sought to stabilise its relationship with the populace through liberalising measures, including the decollectivisation of agriculture and the lightening of excessive political controls. These attitudes of the ruling parties facilitated the development within their ranks of the acceptance of the need for some flexibility in policy, and thereby legitimated the possibility of heterodox opinion, albeit still within prescribed (if shifting) bounds. The basis therefore existed for the acceptance of reformist elements within leadership ranks in these two countries. This linkage between the development of civil society forces and regime attitude was even more marked in Czechoslovakia. The hardline repressive Novotny regime began to change in the mid-1960s, but it was not until the emergence of the Dubcek leadership in 1968 that the regime positively welcomed independent social activism. But this development was shortlived, and when the following Husak regime implemented the policy of 'normalisation', the toleration of independent activity ceased. This policy also served to drive reformism and any adherents it may have had out of party ranks, thereby leaving it substantially dominated by conservative elements. But the suppression of civil society forces did not mean their destruction, as 1989 was to show.

Civil society and the onset of negotiations 95

So the countries which followed patterns one and three had a pre-communist tradition of some civil society force development, a history of the operation of some such forces under communism, and a regime which had tolerated this, in the cases of Poland and Hungary for over thirty years and of Czechoslovakia for a much shorter time. The Polish and Hungarian regimes were also the most liberal in the region, although this does not mean that they countenanced open opposition. This history facilitated an activist role by civil society forces from the beginnings of the process of regime change.

The countries following **Pattern Two**, Bulgaria and Albania, experienced a process of regime change whereby civil society forces emerged at the beginning, were not sufficiently powerful to be able to displace the regime, but were too powerful to be either ignored or suppressed. Both countries had a history of much weaker development of civil society forces than those states in Patterns One and Three. By the outbreak of the First World War, neither country had much in the way of modern industry, and although some did develop during the inter-war period, this was largely in state or foreign hands owing to the weakness of the native bourgeoisie. In 1930 in Bulgaria 75% and in Albania 80% of the populace was dependent on agriculture for their livelihood.[33] The peasantry remained the largest class in Bulgaria, locked in the countryside on small and inefficient family farms, although they did constitute the basis of the cooperative movement and of the political movement launched by Stamboliskii early in the twentieth century. Urban development was stunted and the working class and trade unions weak, especially following the increased state pressure after 1923; the trade unions were abolished in 1934. The education system was widely accessible and facilitated social mobility,[34] so that the political, bureaucratic and military elites were overwhelmingly indigenous. Literacy levels in Bulgaria were the highest in the Balkans: 79.6% for males and 57.2% for females in 1934.[35] However the middle class consisted principally of military men, shopkeepers, artisans and rich peasants, was geographically dispersed and weak as a class. It was not a sound basis for the growth of civil society forces. Although there were many parties in Bulgaria, they tended to be personality-based and designed to act as power-bases for the leaders who were often already in official positions. In Albania the basis for civil society forces was even weaker. As the least developed country in Europe, Albania had no real industry and was divided along what were essentially clan lines. In the north, the Ghegs remained clan-based, were ruled over by tribal chiefdoms, and worked in a pastoral economy. In the south, Tosk society was agriculturally-based with a strong class of large landowners and a large number of tenant farmers. There was little urban development, with only 15% of the population living in localities of more than 5,000 people, while only 20% of those over seven years of age were literate.[36] Some industrial development occurred in the inter-war period, but this was mainly financed from Italy. There was no bourgeois middle class,[37] and no basis upon which any notion of civil society forces could rest.

Under the communist regimes in both countries, there was not the sort of development of civil society forces evident in Hungary, Poland or Czechoslovakia. Certainly the policies of economic development fostered by both regimes created conditions which were favourable to the generation of such forces: industrialisation, urbanisation, education, improved communications all helped to create a favourable infrastructure for the emergence of civil society forces. However, despite discussion groups among some intellectuals and occasional isolated acts of dissident activity, there was little evidence of the emergence of civil society forces. This was because of the attitude of the respective regimes. Neither regime was willing to accept that any form of independent social organisation or activity was legitimate. The Albanian regime was particularly harsh, using widespread police control actively to both destroy and discourage independent activity. Although there was some lightening of this control following the death of Enver Hoxha in 1985 and his replacement by Ramiz Alia, there was still little room for independent social activity. In Bulgaria too control remained tight throughout much of the communist period, although it was not as penetrating as in Albania, and here too there was some lightening of this in the second half of the 1980s. As the Zhivkov regime, which had begun in 1954 and was the most slavishly obedient to the USSR of all of the states of Eastern Europe, became increasingly tired the longer it remained in power, elements within the leadership did begin to think about the need for liberalisation. This was not translated into acceptance of the right of civil society forces to function openly; indeed, it was accompanied by increased pressure on the Turkish part of the population. However it did create the groundwork for greater flexibility on the part of the leadership, and in the final year before the fall of communism some civil society force organisations did begin to appear.

So civil society forces were weak in Bulgaria and Albania. In neither country was there a developed pre-communist tradition of this sort of activity, and it was not allowed to emerge during the communist period. Both regimes had maintained tight control throughout most of this period, but the longevity of the respective communist leaders (Hoxha and Zhivkov) facilitated the build up within each regime of some pressures for change, or at least the capacity to recognise the need for change when there was no alternative. Such pressures were stronger in Bulgaria than Albania. Civil society forces were therefore late in emerging and were not as powerful as in Poland, Hungary and Czechoslovakia, and therefore less able to influence regime action at the outset.

In the countries experiencing **Pattern Four**, the smaller western republics of the FSU (Latvia, Lithuania, Estonia, Moldova, Georgia and Armenia) and Croatia, the identity of the initial negotiating partners was determined by membership of the official political institutions of the state (legislature and executive), and this had been decided by elections in 1990. In all republics, nationalist forces had gained the upper hand and, to varying degrees, were able to sideline old regime forces. In all of these states except for Moldova, which prior to 1940 was mostly part of Romania, there was a basis for the development of civil society forces. This basis was stronger in the Baltic region than in Transcaucasus. The three Baltic countries had been part of the Russian Empire until they gained their independence in 1918, which lasted until their incorporation into the USSR in 1940. All three countries had seen increasing levels of urbanisation during the second half of the nineteenth century, fuelled in part by the industrial expansion occurring in the

Empire as a whole. Estonia and Latvia in particular benefited here, with the Latvian ports becoming important centres of trade with Europe, although this also meant increased Russian immigration;[38] Lithuania was largely deprived of industry because of its location as a vulnerable border area with East Prussia. But these parts of the Empire differed from regions elsewhere because of the strong legacy of foreign influence. In all three, the landed nobility was foreign, Baltic German in Estonia and Latvia, Polish in Lithuania, rather than indigenous in its ethnic identity and cultural milieu. Baltic Germans were also prominent in the emergent nineteenth century middle class in Estonia and Latvia and Poles and Jews in Lithuania, with the result that the indigenous population found itself locked out of both political and economic power in its own country. This fuelled popular resentment, which seems to have been directed more sharply against the more obvious Germans and Poles than the Russians, whose role in the administrative structure did not bring them into as direct and immediate a relationship with the local population as did that of the established German nobility and middle class.[39] This resentment helped to fuel a surge of nationalist sentiment in all three countries in the last half of the nineteenth century.

The heightened national consciousness was in part a function of the growth of a native intelligentsia, but also important was the spreading of literacy and of publishing in the indigenous language. This expanded significantly, aided by increasing education levels.[40] In addition, by the turn of the century, indigenous middle classes had begun to displace the Germans from their commercial dominance in Estonia and to encroach upon this in Latvia.[41] The conditions were therefore favourable for the development of civil society forces in these countries when they gained independence in 1918. The independent era saw greatly increased opportunities for indigenes to move into positions of power and authority in both political and economic spheres. This was associated with open political activity and the consequent organisation of a large number of political parties[42] and interest associations. Literacy levels were high in the mid-1930s in Estonia and Latvia, respectively 96% and 90%, but less so in Lithuania (70%).[43] The network of organisations that emerged was not destroyed by the imposition of dictatorships in 1927 in Lithuania,[44] 1933 in Estonia and 1934 in Latvia. In all three cases, although vigorous action may have been taken against the communists, generally the opposition was kept in check rather than destroyed. Public organisation continued to be permitted provided it did not take an activist stand against the regime.

When these countries were incorporated into the USSR, they were subjected to a particularly vigorous and brutal process of Stalinisation, with significant sections of the population transported to the camps or killed and all independent organisation crushed. The pressure destroyed those bases of autonomous activity which had survived the inter-war dictatorships and consolidated communist party rule throughout these states. Party rule refused to countenance autonomous activity and was particularly severe on any manifestations of independent nationalism. However the pressures on nationalist sentiment did not destroy its roots; it only served to force it underground. In the major cities, intellectuals continued to talk about nationalist themes, albeit in subdued and secretive terms. Their activity was sustained with the assistance of emigre communities abroad which were particularly assiduous in trying to keep alive the dream of independence. As a result, the nationalist strand of thinking was never destroyed, but was even given added impetus in Latvia and Estonia by the large scale Russian immigration. This sentiment, carried principally in intelligentsia circles and manifested in various aspects of cultural activity, did not have a very wide public resonance, although the development policies pursued in these republics, including industrialisation, urbanisation, increased education and social mobility, created a milieu in which, when the opportunity arose, it would thrive.

In all three republics, the local regime tended to closely follow the Moscow line. Unlike in some of the other republics where local authorities were prone to follow their own lines to some degree, the small size of these republics, their proximity to both Moscow and the second city of the USSR Leningrad, and their contiguity both geographically and culturally to Europe, ensured that the centre maintained a close watch over the activities of its local authorities. Reformist wings did not emerge in the parties until the perestroika period, but then, they were at the forefront of seeking a change in the Soviet political structures; the Lithuanian and Estonian parties were the first to split formally with the CPSU.[45] These regimes, or at least elements within them, were clearly affected by the way in which nationalist sentiment ballooned in the republics from 1988, a development which rested upon the foundation provided by the pre-Soviet and Soviet structures.

The two Transcaucasian republics, Georgia and Armenia, both had long histories and rich cultures, with a strong sense of identity shaped in part by their visions of themselves as Christian outposts in a predominantly Islamic region. This sense of identity remained soundly based, at least among the intelligentsia, even while the countries were swallowed up by the Russian Empire and, in the case of Armenia, the Ottoman Empire. In Georgia, this was reinforced by the way in which throughout much of the nineteenth century, the urban areas were dominated by Armenians. Commerce was primarily in the hands of an Armenian urban middle class which was becoming increasingly powerful and wealthy towards the middle of the century and was a source of continuing Georgian resentment; Armenians remained dominant in the economy of the capital Tiflis at the end of the century.[46] The Georgian middle class was very weak. Nevertheless during the second half of the nineteenth century Georgian national consciousness developed significantly, partly owing to the promotion of cultural pursuits by the local Russian administrators, and partly to the efforts of the native intelligentsia; intellectual life flourished.[47] This was accompanied by the emergence of a range of political parties and movements, including a powerful social democratic wing which was able to gain power following the 1917 revolution and institute a democratic republic. Its rule was brief, with Georgia being incorporated into the USSR in 1922.

In Armenia, commerce provided the basis for a vigorous and energetic bourgeoisie to develop. However again it was national issues which were most important for the development of a sense of autonomous activity. Under Russian rule, and with many of their compatriots under Ottoman rule and therefore outside the political unit, the Armenian intelligentsia during the nineteenth century were instrumental in a flowering of national consciousness. Aided by the network of schools established by the Armenian Church and sustained by increased publication in the indigenous language, national sentiment soon took a political form.[48] Organised political parties emerged in the last decades of tsarist rule, and when that rule collapsed in 1917, they seized power and established the Armenian Republic. However like its Georgian neighbour, this was shortlived and the country was incorporated into the USSR in December 1920.

Under Soviet rule the bases of autonomous activity, especially of a nationalist type,[49] in both countries were suppressed, although generally this was less vigorous in Armenia which was, in the words of one observer, 'Moscow's showpiece to the world',[50] and where a higher level of tolerance of civic organisation was in evidence. In neither country were they destroyed, and when the pressure was relaxed as part of the personnel policy adopted by the Brezhnev administration, nationalist stirrings were once again evident. The atmosphere favouring the development of some form of autonomous public activity was strengthened in Georgia during the leadership of Eduard Shevardnadze, 1972–85. The most obvious instance of this was the popular demonstration against the removal of the Georgian language from the republican constitution in 1978. Among intellectuals in particular in both republics, a form of dissident nationalism emerged. This was matched by the development of new bases of autonomous activity in the second economy. While such activity did not contribute to the development of a new sense of autonomous civil society forces, it did give a popular legitimacy to activity independent of the state. But clearly in both republics, the principal theme of non-state action was nationalist. For the Armenians this was reinforced both by the memory of the 1915 genocide and by the fate of their compatriots in Nagorno-Karabakh, that part of Azerbaijan inhabited predominantly by Armenians.[51]

In both republics the strength of this underlying nationalist sentiment was reflected in the way the local regimes sought to reach accommodation with it. Republican leaders often sought guardedly to ally themselves with this sentiment, with accusations of nationalism sometimes accompanying their removal from office.[52] Political leaders were also often involved in the sorts of corruption that were linked with activity in the second economy.[53] This means the linkages that political elites had into the society more generally did create a basis upon which such elites could see an alternative path of development to that provided by the Soviet system, while the strength of nationalist sentiment in the society could both throw up nationalist activists when the opportunity arose with perestroika and provide a welcoming milieu for such elites.

Moldova lacked the pre-Soviet past of these other countries, being an artificial creation of the Soviet rulers after the end of the second world war. However because its population was predominantly ethnically Romanian and spoke Romanian, the basis existed for the development of a nationalist movement. A mainly rural and agrarian area, there was no tradition of civil society pre-dating 1945, and although Soviet development policies did help to create the socio-economic milieu within which civil society forces might have emerged, they were prevented from doing so by the strength of regime control. When Gorbachev opened the way for the emergence of autonomous organisation, there was little established basis upon which such organisation could stand except nationalism inspired initially by the Romanian connection.

In pre-communist times, Croatia had an emergent Croatian middle class concentrated in Zagreb[54] and a state administration that was dominated by former members of the gentry. Situated on the border between the Austro-Hungarian and Ottoman empires, the Croats did have a sense of their own identity which was only sharpened by the continuing rivalry with the Serbs when they were joined in the Kingdom of Serbs, Croats and Slovenes (from 1929 Yugoslavia) and, after the second world war, the Federal People's Republic then Socialist Federal Republic of Yugoslavia. Pre-war trade unions were controlled by the Peasant Party and had a distinctly nationalist hue. A range of political parties existed in Croatia, having emerged when the country was part of the Austro-Hungarian Empire. In 1921 the literacy level was 67.7%.[55] The basis for civil society forces was strengthened by the attitude of the Yugoslav communist regime. As in Hungary, the Yugoslav authorities accepted the legitimacy of organised, autonomous interests. Indeed, the official ideology of self-managed socialism was predicated upon a degree of pluralism and the organisation of interests. The result was a more liberal, relaxed, attitude to the freedom of discussion (albeit still within bounds) and expression of heterodox views, with a press that for much of the time was significantly freer than anywhere else in the communist bloc.[56] Nationalist sentiment did strengthen in Croatia, with the so-called Croatian Spring of 1971 being an important manifestation of it. Its suppression was a setback to the development of civil society forces in Croatia, but with a favourable environment in the capital and with the support of the republican administration, civil society forces continued to develop.

So none of the countries in Pattern Four had the level of civil society forces that was present in Poland or Hungary, but in the Baltic republics and Croatia in particular, the basis existed for such development and it was utilised. That basis was much weaker in Armenia and Georgia, and virtually non-existent in Moldova. But in all countries, the backbone of potential autonomous activity was nationalist consciousness. Even where autonomous social activity did not assume major dimensions, the creation of a sense of national awakening or sentiment was crucial. And importantly, in all cases elements within the regime associated themselves with this development, especially during the closing years of communist rule.

In the countries experiencing **Pattern Five**, Russia, Ukraine, Kyrgyz Republic, Slovenia and Macedonia, when the federal centre falls, oppositionist forces share power with old regime forces. The history of civil society force development was very different in these countries. The traditional rulers were still in power in Russia at the time of the cataclysm which led to the communist seizure of power. However those traditional rulers were being forced during the latter part of the nineteenth century increasingly to share power with an emergent commercial and industrial bourgeoisie. In the decades before the first world war, a developing bourgeoisie and a growing professional sector of society was coming to constitute an increasingly important middle class, concentrated in the major cities and aware of their interests and willing to act to defend them.[57] As industrial development accelerated, the power of this group grew. There was also within Russia a tradition of intelligentsia discussion and debate, which helped to form a public sphere within which issues of national import could be discussed. This was sustained by a press which, while acting under some restrictions, could still discuss many issues in a free and hard hitting fashion.

During the communist period, after the suppression of NEP at the end of the 1920s, there was little evidence of activity on the part of civil society forces. This was chiefly because of the way in which the revolution imposed on Soviet society by its rulers (agricultural collectivisation, industrialisation and the terror) was far more extensive, penetrative and violent than anywhere else, with the result that the bases of civil society development were far more deeply affected. By the time the excesses of regime control were being wound back, the 1950s and 1960s, throughout the USSR civil society was something beyond the collective memory of the people.[58] While the first-order organisations existed,[59] they were rarely translated into the second order.[60] A partial exception to this was the dissident movement which lasted from the mid-1960s until the end of the 1970s, but this hardly constitutes solid evidence of civil society: it was illegal activity which involved a comparatively few individuals and, unlike the notion of the parallel polis, did not include a vibrant and continuing process of debate and discussion. Even when the regime had become tired and complacent under Brezhnev, it had the strength to suppress this development. However this changed completely with the liberalisation introduced by Gorbachev. The changes in policy he brought enabled the mushrooming of large numbers of informal groups, proto-parties and movements onto the Soviet, and since many of these were based in Moscow, the Russian scene.[61] This was accompanied by the growth of a sphere of public discussion and debate which, as time passed, became increasingly less restricted. Civil society forces (with significant support from within the regime) thus began to carve out for themselves a real sphere of civil society. However by the time of the August 1991 coup, these forces were still very weak.

The Soviet regime did have a significant tradition of reformism within its ranks.[62] The changes wrought by Khrushchev constituted an important element of this, although its clearest manifestation was Gorbachev's perestroika. The latter was in part a result of the frustration that had developed under Brezhnev, and the recognition by many that change was needed. But it is important to recognise that commitment to the view that change is essential, to the reformist principle, went far deeper than just the leader. It was upon this support that the changes embodied by perestroika depended. However as the perestroika period demonstrated, this commitment to change was not always shared by party leaders at the republican level. But over the course of Soviet history many such leaders, although not supporting measures of liberalisation, were sympathetic to nationalist sentiment. For non-Russian republican leaders, appeal to local nationalism was sometimes seen as a viable way of establishing or consolidating a personal power base. In this sense, then, alongside the strand of reformism within Soviet history there was also a strand of support for local nationalism which potentially provided room for the growth of the sorts of nationalist movements that had come to the fore in the Pattern Four regimes.

Ukraine had been a part of the Russian Empire for some three centuries with almost no history of independent statehood, and although it had developed some industry during the nineteenth century, mostly based around the coal deposits of the Donbass and the oil industry in Galicia's Carpathian foothills, it remained primarily agricultural. The emergent Ukrainian bourgeoisie remained very small and in competition with the Jews. Kiev was a major city of the empire with its own public, economic and intellectual life, but it was clearly far less important than either the imperial capital St Petersburg or the second city, Moscow. The most important element of a potential independent civil society was Ukrainian national sentiment, which was given a focus by the revival of national culture and traditions during the second half of the nineteenth century. However this remained stunted with little pressure for Ukrainian separation from Russia; a vibrant civil society had not emerged by the time of the revolution.

In Soviet times, official policy worked very effectively to blunt the development of civil society forces or of anything approaching a civil society in Ukraine. The destruction of the bases of traditional Ukrainian society was complete, with the republic taking the brunt of collectivisation, experiencing forced pace industrialisation and being subjected to campaigns to eradicate so-called 'bourgeois nationalism'. This was quite successful in preventing the emergence of autonomous group activity, although it did not prevent the emergence and growth of Ukrainian national consciousness.[63] This became particularly important in the late 1960s–1970s when it even infected the republican government, with one of the principal reasons for the removal of party leader Shelest his association with and succouring of nationalist sentiment.[64] It was thus nationalism which was best placed to fill the space opened up by the Gorbachev reforms.

The future Kyrgyz Republic was a region with no history of being an independent state and no clear boundaries distinguishing it from those people who lived in most of the neighbouring Soviet republics. Like the other republics of Central Asia, the Kyrgyz state was a creation of the Soviet authorities. In pre-Soviet times, the land was inhabited primarily by pastoralists with very little urban development. The culture was mainly oral and there was no industrial development. Certainly adherence to Islam gave a focus to collective life, but there was little to stimulate civil society development. The Soviet development program did remedy some of these deficiencies. It stimulated urban development, introduced some manufacturing, increased education and literacy levels, and improved the means of communication. But this did not lead to the emergence of strong civil society forces even during perestroika, principally because the regime did all it could to stifle such a development. The Kyrgyz regime maintained tight control over society and hindered the emergence of autonomous social activity.[65] Like the other republics of the region,[66] Kyrgyzstan was particularly marked by the operation of informal clans, cliques and closed associations, but these were far from the building blocks of civil society. They were the mechanisms through which those in positions of authority exploited the Soviet structure for their own ends. In this sense, they were part of the regime rather than independent of it. Thus both civil society and nationalist forces were weak in Kyrgyzstan at the time of the end of the USSR.

In Slovenia during the nineteenth century, urban and industrial development (and therefore the working class and trade unions) had been stronger than elsewhere in the future Yugoslavia. An indigenous Slovene bourgeois middle class had displaced the dominance of ethnic Germans and provided significant support for the idea of Slovenian independence in the period leading up to the first world war. Once in a single country with the Serbs and Croats, this continued to provide a sense of Slovene identity in contrast with the other two major nationality groups. With a public culture that encouraged discussion of issues, a vibrant civil society was taking root in Slovenia before the outbreak of the second world war and subsequent establishment of communist Yugoslavia; in 1921 the literacy level was 91.2%, by far the highest in Yugoslavia.[67] Slovenia benefited from the attitude taken by the Yugoslav communist authorities to freedom of discussion and organisation discussed above with regard to Croatia. Its advantage compared with Croatia was that its regime was not scoured of reformist thinking by any equivalent of the Croatian Spring, with the result that the regime was liberal even by Yugoslav standards throughout the 1980s. By the late 1980s, one author declared that Slovenia had 'developed a strong opposition movement and a true civil society made up of alternative movements, nationally-minded intellectuals, and a powerful youth movement.'[68]

In Macedonia, which had been part of the Ottoman Empire until just before the first world war, there was little basis for civil society development prior to the communist period; the illiteracy level in 1921 was 83.8%.[69] Under communism it experienced the same sort of liberal attitude as the other republics, with the result that there was a basis for autonomous group activity within broadly defined bounds, but this was weaker than in most other parts of the country. Nationalist feeling was significant, partly because of the historical relationship with Greece and Bulgaria.

So of the countries in Pattern Five, Slovenia had the soundest basis for civil society force development, with a history of this both prior to and during the communist period while the Kyrgyz Republic had the weakest with no history of significant civil society development either before or after the communist takeover. Russia's nascent civil society was snuffed out by the communist regime, while that of Ukraine was able to maintain a thin thread in nationalist form. Macedonia, although lacking a pre-communist tradition of this, did develop weak civil society forces under Yugoslav communism.

In the countries experiencing **Pattern Six**, Azerbaijan, Belarus, Kazakhstan, Tajikistan, Turkmenistan, Uzbekistan, Romania and the Federal Republic of Yugoslavia, power remained in the hands of the old regime at the second, mostly republican level after the collapse of the federal centre, with weak civil society forces effectively sidelined. The history of civil society force development was much weaker in most of these countries. None of the former Soviet republics had a pre-Soviet history characterised by the development of powerful civil society forces. Although the Azerbaijani capital Baku was the scene of major industrial development during the latter part of the nineteenth century in the form of oil extraction, this was dominated by foreign and Russian firms which had little interest

104 Civil society and the onset of negotiations

in the development of the sort of environment that would stimulate civil society development. Nevertheless, on the basis of an educated elite which had been emerging during the nineteenth century, after the fall of tsarism a multi-party republic was established, although its government was severely restricted by British occupation forces from November 1918 to August 1919. The republican experiment collapsed with Soviet incorporation in 1920. The area that was to be Belarus remained a backwater of the Russian Empire, with little sense of an independent national identity and none of national independence,[70] while the states of Central Asia too were artifices of the Soviet authorities. During the Soviet period, although all experienced the effects of the Soviet development program, regime control was sufficiently tight to prevent the emergence of civil society forces.[71] Even during Gorbachev's perestroika, autonomous group activity seems to have been much less in these republics than elsewhere.[72] Nationalist movements did emerge, encouraged in Azerbaijan by the dispute with Armenia over Nagorno-Karabakh, and in Belarus by the effects of Chernobyl,[73] but they were kept largely in control by the respective regimes. The regimes in the Central Asian republics were particularly affected by the sorts of informal groups, clans and cliques noted above with regard to the Kyrgyz Republic.

In Romania the pre-communist basis for civil society development was weak. There was little industrial development, with only 11% of males gainfully employed in manufacturing in 1930.[74] The traditional landed class mostly either left the land during the nineteenth century to enter state service, the professions or the army, or (at least until the land reform of the 1920s) operated their holdings on an absentee basis. A weak commercial middle class had developed, chiefly Jewish but with an increasingly Romanian component late in the century. This Jewish prominence in commerce and in the professions prompted Rothschild to write '(t)he 'alien' middle class was economically essential but politically resented and socially unassimilated...'.[75] The main industry, oil, was substantially foreign owned. A Romanian intelligentsia had emerged, but they preferred state service, politics and the professions to commerce, and were a vehicle for the expression of resentment against the Jews. The literacy level was only 57.1% in 1930, and significantly lower in some areas.[76] The state remained the main bastion of the middle class, being its main source of employment and an important instrument of economic development. There was clearly little middle class autonomy and therefore limited scope for the development of a wide range of civil society forces. There was a large number of political parties during the inter-war period, but in the words of one observer, they were 'led by members of the intelligentsia and most of them were congeries based on personalities and class'.[77] Power and influence remained focused in an 'intelligentsia-bureaucratic 'middle class'[78] that rested upon the state, and the state was generally controlled by a series of short term authoritarian regimes.

When the communist regime came to power, and especially after the replacement of Gheorgiu-Dej by Ceausescu in 1965, a policy of the vigorous suppression of any manifestation of civil society development was followed. While the economic policy of forced pace industrialisation was accompanied by higher levels of urbanisation and education which should have had a positive impact on the prospects for civil society development, any shift in this direction was blunted by the regime. Its oppressive policies and highly intrusive presence, reflected in the activity of the security service within Romanian society, ensured that there was no opportunity for autonomous social organisation. Furthermore as personal control became consolidated increasingly in the hands of Ceausescu and his family,[79] the elimination of those who questioned or opposed him created an environment which stifled any manifestation of reformism or dissidence both within the regime and society more broadly. Such control became increasingly oppressive and intrusive in the last years of his rule.

Of the two parts comprising the FRY, Serbia and Montenegro, the former was clearly the much more important. In Serbia, as in Bulgaria, land reform in the nineteenth century had eliminated the class of large landowners, leaving the countryside dominated by a class of independent smallholding peasants.[80] There was limited urban development, with the middle class that emerged consisting principally of military officers, small town shopkeepers, artisans and rich peasants. State employees were the dominant group. This was not, therefore, a middle class which was concentrated in a large city and which could generate the sorts of networks and patterns of interaction which would stimulate civil society; the literacy level in 1921 was only 34.6%.[81] Serbia did, however, have a strong historical tradition of its own identity, and when it became part of the joint kingdom after 1918, its ruling elite saw this as little more than an extension and expansion of the old Serbia.[82] This provided a basis for a significant number of political parties during the inter-war period. Like the rest of the country, Serbia benefited from the more liberal policies of the communist regime, with the result that a range of autonomous bodies and organisations did emerge to structure public life. The presence of the federal capital, Belgrade, in Serbia and the increased range of activities that flowed from this probably increased the richness and diversity of such organisations. The nature of the communist regime, as in the other republics, with its wider perspective on what was acceptable behaviour and greater tolerance for heterodox opinion meant that it was able to accommodate different points of view and therefore some reformist sentiment. However because of Serb dominance of much of the federal structure, at least in aspiration, the nationalist theme which was so important in Croatia and Slovenia for the break up of Yugoslavia, in Serbia had an integrative rather than a disintegrative thrust. Serb nationalism, as manifested in the ranks of the republic's leadership, involved the maintenance of the Yugoslav federation and, if this could not be achieved, the unification of all Serbs within Serbian borders. This was a higher priority than civil society concerns, and this was to have tragic consequences.

So the countries of Pattern Six did not have a pre-communist history that was favourable to the development of civil society forces, and only in Serbia (and Montenegro/FRY) was the one communist regime which could accommodate such a development. As a result, nowhere were civil society forces able to have a major impact at the time of regime crisis. In the FRY any impact they may have been expected to have as a result of their development during communist times was shortcircuited by the way in which old regime forces took over the nationalist mantle to consolidate themselves in power.

Patterns of development

Comparison of the growth of civil society forces in the pre-communist and the communist periods with the patterns of change identified in the previous chapter shows some clear consistencies.

1 *Pattern One* (Poland and Hungary) where civil society forces were able to displace the regime early in the process of negotiation and ultimately resolve the final form of the system without old regime participation. In both countries there was a history of substantial civil society force development prior to communism and, particularly in its final decades, strong civil society growth under communism. The regime in Poland tolerated this development, while in Hungary for much of the time it facilitated it. Along with Slovenia, only these countries had this combination.
2 *Pattern Two* (Bulgaria and Albania) where civil society forces were not powerful enough to be able to displace the old regime, and old regime forces were therefore able to maintain their position for a time and play a major part in the negotiations before being forced to share power with civil society forces. In both countries there was weak development of civil society forces in both the pre-communist and communist periods, although they did begin to emerge in the final stages of communist rule. During the communist period the firm control of the regime was an important factor in this course of developments.
3 *Pattern Three* (Czechoslovakia) where the regime disintegrated at the outset, leaving the negotiations up to civil society forces. Strong pre-communist civil society development was followed by the rigid suppression of it during much of the communist period, but a flowering when regime control weakened.
4 *Pattern Four* (Latvia, Lithuania, Estonia, Moldova, Georgia, Armenia and Croatia) where an opposition nationalist group was in power in the republican capital when federal authority collapsed. This was able to sideline old regime forces, at least for a time. In the three Baltic states there was strong and in the other four weaker pre-communist civil society development. During the communist era there was weak development in all the states except Croatia where the growth of civil society forces was facilitated. However what was important here was the nationalist form this development took towards the end of the respective regimes' lives.
5 *Pattern Five* (Slovenia, Russia, Ukraine, Kyrgyz Republic and Macedonia) where, when the centre collapsed, power lay in the republican capital with an elite comprising both oppositionist and old regime forces, with the latter usually split between reformist and conservative forces. In Slovenia the pattern of civil society development was the same as for those countries in Pattern One, strong pre-communist and communist development. Russia experienced strong pre-communist development in some of the major cities but very little under the communists, while in the other three countries it was a case of weak development in both periods, although in Ukraine the growth of nationalist forces was significant. In Russia and the Kyrgyz Republic, the post-communist

elite had little civil society representation, instead being overwhelmingly a reflection of splits within the state structure.
6 *Pattern Six* (Romania, FRY, Azerbaijan, Belarus, Kazakhstan, Tajikistan, Turkmenistan and Uzbekistan) where the second echelon of the old regime seized power and consolidated its control, sidelining weak civil society forces. In all countries except for FRY, the pattern was one of weak development during both pre-communist and communist periods. In the FRY, weak pre-communist development preceded stronger development under communism.

In a practical sense, if we are trying to explain why the different patterns occurred and why they led to the identified outcomes, what is important is the relative strength of civil society forces and old regime forces at the opening of negotiations. The notion of strength in this context refers to the ability to achieve one's ends, including the commitment on the part of elites to the achievement of those ends. In Patterns One and Three, civil society forces were clearly stronger than the regime and democracy resulted, while in Pattern Six the reverse situation applied, with authoritarian rule the outcome. In Pattern Two, although the civil society forces were not well formed at the time of regime crisis, the weakness of the regime (and most particularly the loss of the will to rule on the part of its leaders) ultimately rendered that regime much weaker than the oppositionist forces. In Pattern Four, nationalist forces took over the state before the collapse of the old regime. Where civil society forces based on civic considerations were able to enter the political scene, democracy resulted (Lithuania). Where nationalist forces continued to dominate and define the agenda, the result was façade democracy of either the ethnic (Estonia, Latvia and Moldova) or plebiscitarian (Georgia and Croatia) kind. Where such civil society forces were unable to enter the political arena in a major way, non-democracy resulted (Armenia). In Pattern Five the nature of the coalition between old regime and oppositionist forces depended on the strength of civil society forces and divisions within the state. In Slovenia civil society forces played an important structuring role, leading to a democratic outcome. In Russia, Ukraine and Macedonia they were much less important, leading to a façade democracy, while in authoritarian Kyrgyzstan they played no role. In Russia and Kyrgyzstan, the crucial thing given the weakness of civil society forces was the split within the state apparatus.

The general message from this is clear: the greater the role played by civil society forces at the time of regime crisis, the greater the likelihood of a democratic outcome; the less the role played by such forces, the greater the likelihood of a non-democratic outcome. In those countries where civil society groups were strong at the time the regime entered what proved to be the final crisis, the old regime elite could not hang on to power but were compelled to hand it over, or at least to share it. Where civil society groups were weak, the old regime was able to maintain its hold, sometimes undergoing some change itself, but often substantially remaining in its old form. What is striking about this pattern is the correspondence between the pre-communist history of civil society development and the role played in the initial shaping of the new system by civil society forces. In those countries where the history of pre-communist civil society development was strongest, civil society forces were most prominent in shaping the new post-communist regime (Poland, Hungary, Czechoslovakia, Slovenia, Latvia, Lithuania and Estonia). Where the pre-communist period witnessed little civil society development, civil society forces played no effective role in the shift from communism (especially the Pattern six countries).[83] This correspondence is not accidental. The development of a civil society constitutes the creation of a dense network of associations, organisations and patterns of action and expectation which encase the public activity of the citizenry. Civil society forms a kind of shield which can deflect or weaken attempts by the state to penetrate too deeply into the society and order its life. In this sense, the vigorous development of civil society could represent a significant barrier to a state elite which sought to penetrate society, to re-order its structures and to closely control the life of its citizens. This was precisely the aim of the communist regime.

When the communist regime came to power in each of these states, it sought to smash the existing structures, destroy much of the existing elite, and establish a system in which there was no room for independent initiative or activity. While substantial progress was made in some aspects of this enterprise, particularly in some states, it could not be fully realised in all the communist states. Two factors stood in its way. First, the generative impulse embedded in the primary group structure discussed at the outset of this chapter meant that while society itself continued to exist, its citizens were always going to seek to create secondary and even tertiary groups to realise their interests. The logical imperative embedded in the search to defend and realise personal interests provided a continual stimulus to autonomous group formation. It is intrinsic to the notion of society itself that such levels of organisation should structure public activity, and given the diversity of individuals' interests and demands, such a development could not be monopolised by the state. The only way the state could prevent this was through the exertion of massive and continuing terror, of the type manifested in Pol Pot's Kampuchea. None of the European communist regimes mounted this sort of campaign; the waves of terror mounted in the Soviet Union in the 1930s and Eastern Europe in the late 1940s, extensive though they were, did not reach the scale or intensity needed to break down the social networks which kept the society together and provided the incubus for autonomous group development. This means that while in the countries of Eastern Europe where there was a strong tradition of civil society development, the state could destroy the main public institutions of the society (like political parties, free trade unions and an independent media), it could not destroy the basic patterns of social action and expectation upon which they rested. While the communist regimes and the development programs they introduced brought about substantial change in the society, including the generation of new patterns of interaction and new social networks, these rested on the basis of pre-communist structures and patterns of inter-personal relations. Furthermore, where the pre-communist tradition was one of strong civil society growth, there was also the memory of this to reinforce the maintenance of these pre-communist perceptions and patterns of activity. The pre-communist past could not be obliterated from the collective memory of the society (especially when it was within the lifespan of a single generation), and where that past culminated with the growth of civil society, it remained a potent force in the search for the realisation of autonomy from political control. This would have been reinforced by the model of the West to which regime opponents looked.

Second, the ambiguous effects of communist rule. This ambiguity consists in the way in which the regime sought political control through the elimination of personal and group autonomy while the economic development program it promoted set in train forces generating such autonomous groups. Thus while the regime set about trying to destroy the existing network of civil society forces, its economic policies created pressures for such forces to re-emerge. Where there was a pre-communist legacy of civil society development, this would have reinforced and perhaps shaped the growth of civil society forces generated by the communist development model. Those forces would thereby have been made stronger than they would have been in the absence of such a legacy. In most of the countries of Eastern Europe, they took on a predominantly civic form; in the Baltic republics they had a nationalist tinge. In a practical sense, then, the strength of civil society forces placed clear restrictions upon the capacity of the state to penetrate and control civil society. This was most evident in Poland and Hungary after 1956 when the respective regimes sought a *modus vivendi* with their societies based upon recognition of a sphere of autonomous activity outside tight state control. A similar situation applied in Slovenia. In Czechoslovakia tight control was maintained until 1968 when, with its loosening, civil society forces threatened to burst the regime apart leading to a reimposition of control. In the Baltic republics emergent civil society forces placed fewer constraints on the state than in these other countries because the source of central control was Moscow rather than the republican capital. There was less sensitivity to the demands of the society and less perceived need to reach accommodation at least partly on its terms. This was one reason why, when opposition forces became openly active, they took a nationalist form. A pre-communist legacy thus strengthened the effects of communist development policies to create a more powerful network of civil society forces which could emerge as central actors during the period of old regime crisis and help to structure the transition from communist rule.

The strength of civil society forces under communism stemming from the pre-communist tradition and the effects of the communist development program may also have been instrumental in the emergence within the regime of a reformist wing more inclined to seek accommodation than confrontation with those forces. Recognition of the strength of such forces encouraged some within the regime to see the advantages of cooperation rather than confrontation, especially since the effect of their own development policies was to strengthen such autonomous networks. The existence of such sentiments within the regime would be important not only in structuring the eventual shift from communist rule, but also in promoting the development of such groups under communism.

The pre-communist legacy of civil society development was therefore clearly important in determining the role civil society forces would play in the transition from communism. A pre-communist tradition of strong development enabled such forces to sustain themselves (albeit at a lower level and in a less public institutional form) despite pressure from the state and play a leading role in the shift from communism. Where such a tradition was lacking, including where it had been subjected to state pressure for a much longer time as in most of the USSR, civil society forces were less influential. What is clear is that the more involved civil society forces were in the transition, the more likely a democratic outcome was. This democratising effect of civil society forces does not assume a deep commitment on their part to the ideology or principles of democracy. Such commitment could exist and often does so, but it is not crucial to the explanation. What is important is that civil society forces seek to project, promote and protect the interests of their constituents and, given the variety of these, a pluralistic system is the only way they can be accommodated. In the absence of particular civil society forces being able to guarantee that they will always be able to achieve their ends, their interests will lie in establishing a system which is open, competitive, and gives them the chance to succeed when they need to act. In this sense, it is the logic of civil society itself which is democratic, not the values of its participants.

This also means that the outcome of the initial sets of negotiations is not set in stone. These can change, and indeed in those cases where civil society forces were not sufficiently powerful to nudge the system in a democratic direction at the outset, it is in their interests to seek to do so once that system has been set up and is running. Similarly, in those cases where a democratic set of arrangements was agreed from the outset, there is the perceived need to consolidate them. The struggle to establish and consolidate civil society continues after the fall of the communist regime. It is to this which we must turn.

4 Creating civil society?

Previous chapters have shown how the political trajectories of the post-communist states have been shaped by the course of negotiations between old regime actors and civil society forces at the time of regime change. The overwhelming majority of post-communist states have remained on the basic trajectory established at the time of the crisis of communism. At the end of 2000, of the 26 states, only four had clearly shifted between regime types: Belarus had moved from a closed oligarchy to sultanism, Azerbaijan had shifted from closed to open oligarchy and back to closed oligarchy, and Georgia had moved from a plebiscitary democracy to a closed oligarchy and back to a plebiscitary democracy. These changes had all been between sub-types of façade democracy. A more substantial shift, from the open oligarchy type of façade democracy to full democracy, occurred in Romania. By 2000 Croatia may also have been in the process of shifting from a plebiscitary democracy towards a full democracy, while Slovakia may have been making the same journey from open oligarchy. The Romanian experience is most striking: of the nine states which experienced a pattern 6 type of regime change, it is the only one (with the possible exception of Montenegro whose trajectory remains unclear) that did not remain a non-democracy. The issue that these cases raise is why have some regime trajectories changed and others have not? The reverse question is also important: why have the overwhelming number of initial trajectories been confirmed by later development? Explanation of the adoption of the initial trajectories emphasised the importance of civil society forces. The development of civil society also has a part to play in explaining the consolidation or shifting of these trajectories.

The elements of a civil society have been outlined above, but given the attempt to be made now to establish the progress civil society has made in both consolidating and strengthening itself in the post-communist countries, it may be useful to list those elements once again. There are three central struts to the notion of civil society:

1 Groups autonomous from the state which act to project and defend the interests of their members/constituents.
2 Recognition by both the state and the groups that the other has a legitimate role in society and that both have a sphere within which they should be able to act independent of the other.

3   Among the groups that are able to function are those with specifically political ends.

It is upon these struts that the substance of civil society rests. Their existence assumes the presence of a vibrant public sphere within which issues of general importance are discussed. It assumes a public that is aware of political issues and willing to act through their institutions to play a part in the working out of those issues. It assumes a process of public debate, structured in part by the expression of interests through the efforts of those autonomous groups which constitute the heart of civil society. Because of the centrality of public debate and its quality, the strength of civil society cannot be measured simply by looking at the number of groups which are present or the state regulations governing their activity. Nevertheless these are crucial factors in determining the prospects for the development of civil society.

A public sphere?

Formally all of the post-communist states except Tajikistan and Turkmenistan allow for a legal sphere of activity independent of the state. Provision is made for this either through recognition of the right of free association in the constitution or through laws or regulations seeking to regulate group activity. In Turkmenistan there is no provision for freedom of organised activity, while in Tajikistan this is limited to groups supporting the government. Similarly with the exception of these two countries plus Uzbekistan, formal provision has existed for free trade unions. However these formal provisions were frequently modified in practice, with pressure from the state sharply restricting the capacity of such organisations to function freely. The clearest case of this has been Uzbekistan, where technically all forms of group activity were permitted but in practice none was allowed; the promotion of the 'government-organised, non-government organisations', which were effectively instruments of the Uzbek regime, was important here. Elsewhere too various forms of pressure have been evident: disruption of meetings, harassment of activists, refusal of registration, and limitations on the types of permissible activity have all been used to disrupt the emergence and functioning of groups in many of these countries, including some classed as democracies.

Crucial in the capacity of civil society groups and a sphere of public discussion and debate to develop is a free press. In all post-communist countries except Turkmenistan and Uzbekistan, where all the media are state-owned and controlled, the media are in mixed ownership: while the state maintains full or partial ownership over some media outlets, many are in non-state, private, hands. In most countries the media are predominantly privately-owned, although the state-controlled media often has the widest reach and, technically, the best coverage of the country as a whole.[1] This is because the state media usually rest on the former communist state media networks, and these were designed explicitly to provide access to all parts of society. But even though particular media outlets have not been in state hands, this has not meant that they have been public advocates or independent voices;

much of the media in these countries has been in the hands of powerful, usually commercial and business, interests, and has represented those interests through their activities.

But probably more important than the issue of ownership is that of control, and especially the presence or otherwise of state pressure on media outlets. Freedom House has conducted regular surveys of the extent of media freedom.[2] Using the categories 'not free', 'partly free' and 'free', Freedom House has situated the countries for each year. Based upon the Freedom House judgements, we can establish rough trends over the period as a whole as shown in Table 4.1.

It is clear that over this period, the trend in different countries has been mixed. Only in the Czech Republic, Poland[3] and Slovenia did the media remain untrammeled by government over the whole period, while in Azerbaijan, Tajikistan, Turkmenistan and Uzbekistan the media remained under state control. In Bulgaria, Kyrgyz Republic, Macedonia, Moldova, Romania,[4] Russia and Ukraine the media was subject to significant pressure during the period. Although Freedom House does not give full data, the same judgement applies to the FRY throughout the period. In the other countries there was movement, in a positive direction towards greater freedom in Croatia and Estonia, and in a negative direction towards greater pressure and control in Armenia, Belarus and Kazakhstan. In Albania, Georgia, Hungary, Latvia and Slovakia (although this has not been picked up in the Freedom House statistics) there was a movement in both directions. Only in Albania, Hungary, Kyrgyz Republic, Latvia and Lithuania was there an independent regulatory body.[5] Those countries with a media consistently classed as 'free' and those where there was movement in a positive direction experienced developments in the media field consistent with a strengthening of civil society. But the essential aspect of this remained group activity.

If, in principle, the existence of autonomous groups is a key indicator of civil society, in practice their identification is not always straightforward. Problems of definition can be substantial, especially in terms of establishing the autonomy of groups from the state. Many groups receive subsidies of one form or another from state (often local) bodies,[6] and it is not clear that there is a boundary of such support which in principle renders a group dependent or autonomous. Furthermore there are in many societies bodies which are semi-governmental in nature but which should not be seen as instruments of the state. Possessing autonomy of action, they can contribute significantly to the richness of civil society.[7] There can also be a very real difference between groups which are active and those which are inactive. In most of the post-communist states, groups must register, but it is not clear how many of those groups which do register are active or how many active groups do not register. Similarly the different levels at which groups operate may be significant; groups with a local focus and perspective may be very important in building up and maintaining a sense of local community but have no role at all to play on the national stage. The size of the different groups is also important; should a small group organised around a common hobby be equated with a nationally-organised environmental group with thousands of members? These problems of definition and identification make any figures about the number of

Table 4.1 Freedom of the media

	Not free	Partly free	Free
Albania	1990, 1992–3, 1995–8	1991–2, 1994, 1999	
Armenia	1996	1992–5, 1997–9	
Azerbaijan	1992–9		
Belarus	1994–9	1992–3	
Bulgaria		1990–9	
Croatia	1992–3	1994–9	
Czech Republic			1990–9
Estonia		1992	1993–9
Georgia	1994–6	1992–3, 1997–9	
Hungary		1993, 1995	1990–2, 1994, 1996–9
Kazakhstan	1994–9	1992–3	
Kyrgyz Republic		1992–9	
Latvia		1992–3	1991, 1994–9
Lithuania			1993–9
Macedonia		1992–9	
Moldova		1992–9	
Poland			1990–9
Romania	1990	1991–9	
Russia		1991–9	
Slovakia		1993–9	1990–2
Slovenia			1991–9
Tajikistan	1992–9		
Turkmenistan	1992–9		
Ukraine		1992–9	
Uzbekistan	1992–9		

autonomous groups in any one country problematic. And yet the number of groups is crucial for establishing the density of civil society.[8] The greater the number and range of groups, the higher the density of the particular civil society. Consequently, bearing in mind the qualifications above, it would be useful to try to establish the size of the non-governmental organised sector in the post-communist states.

One comparative study[9] encompassing all of the post-communist states except Yugoslavia (Serbia and Montenegro) and Bosnia-Herzegovina, included in its survey the number of non-government organisations which had come into existence since 1988. This seems generally to have been interpreted to mean how many were functioning at the end of 1996.[10] The figures in Table 4.2 for the total numbers of NGOs and for the national populations come from this source; the number of NGOs per million of the population is calculated on the basis of those figures.

Given the uncertainty surrounding figures of the type in the table, care must be taken in using them; they can only be approximations, lacking real precision.[11] However, one thing is apparent: in none of the countries which has been classed as democratic is the level of NGO per million of population lower than 300, and in most it is substantially above that.[12] Certainly in some of the façade democracies

Table 4.2 Non-government organisations

Country	No. of NGOs	Population (in millions)	NGOs per million of population
Albania	>300	3.4	88
Armenia	>1000	3.7	270
Azerbaijan	600	7.3	82
Belarus	900	10.3	87
Bulgaria	2900	8.4	345
Croatia	4000	4.5	888
Czech Republic	27500	10.3	2669
Estonia	4000–8000	1.5	2666–5333
Georgia	60	5.4	11
Hungary	40000	10.2	3921
Kazakhstan	700	16.8	42
Kyrgyz Republic	50	4.4	11
Latvia	1200–1500	3.4	352–441
Lithuania	3000–4000	3.7	811–1081
Macedonia	150	2.1	71
Moldova	'several hundred'	4.3	c70
Poland	25000	38.6	648
Romania	12000	22.7	529
Russia	>50000	147.5	339
Slovakia	9709	5.4	1797
Slovenia	'few'	2.1	?
Tajikistan	300	5.7	53
Turkmenistan	'none'	4.5	–
Ukraine	4000	52.0	77
Uzbekistan	'none'	22.7	–

it is also above that level,[13] but this merely reflects the fact that a dense network of groups alone is insufficient to create consolidated democracy; what is important here is the degree of public activitism of the groups. In regional terms, the numbers of groups is very low in all the states of Central Asia,[14] the Caucasus except for Armenia,[15] the southern part of the Balkans, and the south west borderlands of the FSU (Ukraine, Belarus and Moldova).

If the figures in the table are an accurate reflection of the number of groups active in these societies, they do not reflect vigorous civil societies comprising dense networks of autonomous organisations. Even in the country where the average number of groups is greatest, Hungary, the ratio of groups to people (and therefore potential members) is very low 1:255. This situation is considerably worse in most other countries, and is consistent with high levels of apathy and disaffection within the population at large.[16] This low density group network is accompanied throughout the region by a low level of activism on the part of these groups. Many are little more than names without any organisational substance, while many of those which do have some real presence, rarely meet or function effectively. In those countries where group activity has been permitted, activism has generally been restricted to a few of the better organised groups. The sector of autonomous group activity as a whole has generally been demobilised compared with the role it played in many of the individual cases of the collapse of communism.

The causes of this demobilisation of groups have been various,[17] including:

1. Many of the groups which emerged initially were not based on the material interests of their members but on post-material values like environmentalism. When the economy deteriorated and people's interest in such issues was displaced by more immediate economic concerns, such groups had little in the way of solidly-based commitment upon which to rely.
2. Emergent political elites have sought to focus political life on the party system and the new institutions of the state, often legitimised by the rhetoric of liberal democracy. Such a focus, by emphasising the importance of the party system and formal notions of representation, effectively delegitimised much of the sort of activity in which autonomous groups could engage. Their role was squeezed out and their very legitimacy placed in question.
3. Many activists who had been prominent in the development of these organisations sought to further their political careers (or to press the interests they believed in) by joining the parties and the mainstream of political life. Many groups thereby became largely denuded of political talent.
4. Many of the groups were small and localised in their scope and interests, and therefore had little capacity to develop linkages broadly across the society or the spectrum or to expand their membership beyond their immediate bounds.
5. There was often a highly conflictual culture enveloping such groups. Debate within individual bodies over the appropriate roles and structures could lead to fragmentation, while these discussions plus the public pursuit of their interests did lead to rivalry and competition between groups.
6. Most groups had small memberships, a result of the growth of popular withdrawal from politics (see pp. 116–23), a perception that the groups did not represent their interests, and a shortage of people with the skills or resources to sustain continuing activity.
7. Funding shortages, especially in a context of economic difficulty.

These factors have been evident throughout the entire region. At the source of many of the problems of civil society forces, including the decline of group activity, was the development of popular alienation from politics reflected in broad popular demobilisation.[18]

Public activism generally has declined in the post-communist countries following the fall of communism. This demobilisation of the populace may be seen in a number of ways. One of the most easily seen is through declining levels of participation in elections. Table 4.3 shows participation levels for many of the different elections. In some countries participation has been skewed by regime control. Where two rounds of election are held, the figure is for the first round (in which turn out was in most cases higher), where the electoral system is mixed the figure is for the party list, and where the election is for the presidency, the figure is marked by *.[19]

Table 4.3 Levels of participation in post-communist national elections

	1990	1991	1992	1993	1994	1995	1996	1997	1998	1999	2000
Albania		98.9	90.4				89	73	55.7		
Armenia						54.9	60.3*				
Azerbaijan			79.4*	97.6*		79.8					68.7*
Belarus					70.0*	64.7					
Bulgaria	90.8	84.1	75.4*		75.2		63.3*	58.1			
Croatia	84.5		75.6			68.8		57.6*			
Czech Republic	96.7		85.1				75.7				
Estonia			67.8 / 68.0*			68.9				55.8	
Georgia	63.1		74.8			64.0					82.1*
Hungary					68.9				57		
Kazakhstan					73.5	79.3				61.5 / 86.3*	
Kyrgyz Republic						62.0					73* / 64.4
Latvia	84.8			89.9		72.6			72.7		
Lithuania			75.2	78.1*			52.9	71.5*			58.2
Macedonia					77.3		c67*				
Moldova					79.3		67.1				
Montenegro	75							47.9	75		
Poland	60.6*	43.2		52.1		64.7*	76.1				61.9*
Romania	86.2		76.3 / 76.2*				76.0* / 69.7*				56.5 / 56.5*
Russia	71.5			54.8		64.4	69.7*			62.0	64.2*
Serbia			69.7 / 69.7*	63.7				57.5 / 67.4*			57.7
Slovakia	96.8		84.2		75.2		73.2		84		
Slovenia	83.5		85.8 / 85.7*					68.6*			69.9
Tajikistan	83.0*		99.5			84					
Turkmenistan					99.8						
Ukraine					74.7				70.8	69.8*	
Uzbekistan					93.6						

Note: The figures for the Czech Republic and Slovakia for 1990 and 1992 refer to the lower house of each republic, not to that of Czechoslovakia as a whole.

In most countries where voting has remained a voluntary activity, the level of participation has declined. Although with the exception of Poland,[20] and possibly Lithuania (at least in parliamentary elections) and Estonia, this has not reached levels significantly lower than some of the more established democracies in the West, it does represent a measure of popular demobilisation as increasing numbers of people chose not to exercise their democratic right to vote. Furthermore this demobilisation has been very rapid, given that less than a decade had passed since the collapse of communism and the flowering of popular activism associated with that. This sort of turning away from political involvement could have stemmed from a number of factors: dissatisfaction with politics and the political process, resignation and the belief that their involvement changed nothing, exhaustion from the rigours of economic change,[21] or perhaps dissatisfaction with the course events were taking. Whatever the reason, this withdrawal from politics does have implications for the effort to construct a vigorous civil society.

The withdrawal from politics that seems to be reflected in the figures for voting, a measure which relates to active involvement in politics, has occurred against a background of a low, and in many countries declining, level of affective attachment to the political system. Although we do not have reliable opinion poll data for all of the post-communist countries, such data does exist for different periods for most of the countries of central Europe and some of the western republics of the former Soviet Union. Respondents were asked to rate the former communist system of government, and the present system of government now and how they believed it would be in five years time. Their responses were as in Tables 4.4–4.9.[22]

These figures show a number of things. One of the most striking is the contrast in evaluations of the present system between the countries of central Europe and the FSU. In all countries of the former region, positive evaluations are greater than negative, but the reverse is the case in the former Soviet republics. Furthermore the evaluations of the future, and therefore the degree of optimism pervading the society, are much more negative in the FSU than in central Europe. Comparison of the trends of change in both positive and negative evaluations over the period of the figures shows that with the exception of Russia, Poland and the Czech Republic, there has been less than 10% movement;[23] in Belarus, Bulgaria, Croatia, Hungary, Romania and Slovenia this constituted a drop in overall approval of the regime, while in the Czech Republic, Poland, Russia, Slovakia and Ukraine there was increased approval. But in most cases the shift in opinion has been so small as to mean little. More generally, approval ratings in many countries are not high: in Belarus, Croatia, Hungary, Russia and Ukraine[24] about 50% or less of the population has approved of the current system of government, while in Bulgaria, Romania, Slovakia and for most of the time Slovenia that approval rating has been less than two-thirds of the populace. Comparison of the evaluation of the present and future systems of government shows that the latter has higher positive and lower negative scores than the former, suggesting that the approval for the present regime may rest more on the hope of what it may become than of what it is. The communist system is also much more popular than the present system in the states of the FSU

Table 4.4 Communist system of government, positive rating

Year	Bel	Bul	Cro	CR	Hu	Pol	Rom	Rus	Slk	Slv	Ukr
1992		30		23	51	34	26	50	44	41	
1993	60	42	13	29	68	42	35	62	48	41	55
1994	64	51	28	23	58	38	33	51	50	32	55
1995	77	58	34	24	56	25	28	67	52	36	75

Notes:
Bel = Belarus   Bul = Bulgaria   Cro = Croatia
CR = Czech Republic   Hu = Hungary   Pol = Poland
Rom = Romania   Rus = Russia   Slk = Slovakia
Slv = Slovenia   Ukr = Ukraine

Table 4.5 Communist system of government, negative rating

Year	Bel	Bul	Cro	CR	Hu	Pol	Rom	Rus	Slk	Slv	Ukr
1992		54		60	31	53	55	37	60		
1993	28	46	70	62	25	47	56	26	39	53	32
1994	28	38	57	68	30	54	62	36	39	49	34
1995	18	37	53	61	34	68	57	18	36	43	22

Table 4.6 Present system of government, positive rating

Year	Bel	Bul	Cro	CR	Hu	Pol	Rom	Rus	Slk	Slv	Ukr
1992	35	61		64	46	44	65	14	64	68	25
1993	35	55	42	71	43	56	68	36	58	77	25
1994	29	59	51	78	51	69	60	35	52	55	24
1995	35	66	45	76	50	76	60	26	61	66	33

Table 4.7 Present system of government, negative rating

Year	Bel	Bul	Cro	CR	Hu	Pol	Rom	Ru	Slk	Slv	Ukr
1992	48	19		23	22	33	18	74	23	20	54
1993	48	31	37	18	51	32	22	49	27	23	54
1994	58	27	31	13	35	20	31	48	36	30	62
1995	55	28	41	13	28	15	21	54	27	19	60

and in Hungary.[25] This is hardly a ringing endorsement of the political system, nor one which would encourage widespread participation.

This picture is confirmed when we look at the extent of popular trust in the institutions (Tables 4.10a–l).[26]

The low levels of trust in these major components of the political system are marked. The levels of lack of trust or scepticism are greater than those of trust in all years for which there are figures in all countries for the parliament[27] and political

Table 4.8 Future system of government, positive rating

Year	Bel	Bul	Cro	CR	Hu	Pol	Rom	Rus	Slk	Slv	Ukr
1992		71		82	62	57	81	50	82		
1993	46	72	73	88	72	69	82	52	80	87	49
1994	56	70	73	88	76	84	77	49	79	72	53
1995	66	83	69	86	68	90	73	40	78	75	52

Table 4.9 Future system of government, negative rating

Year	Bel	Bul	Cro	CR	Hu	Pol	Rom	Rus	Slk	Slv	Ukr
1992		6		7	6	13	6	37	7		
1993	22	13	11	7	19	18	9	24	12	13	25
1994	24	10	12	6	14	8	13	17	12	12	21
1995	22	8	21	5	19	5	10	31	13	9	39

Note: 1992 figures for Czech Republic and Slovakia are those for Czechoslovakia.

parties, the avenues into the system which usually are seen as most open to the populace. Only in Slovenia do more of the populace trust civil servants than not, and only in the Czech Republic and Slovenia (for one year) have those lacking trust in the government been smaller than those trusting it. The presidency and to a lesser extent the media seem to enjoy most trust generally, but the overall picture is one of little popular trust in the institutions of the system. However low levels of trust in formal institutions are not unique to the post-communist world. Trust in many public institutions has been on the decline in many Western societies for some decades, and by some measures for some institutions is below that in the post-communist states.[28] But in most cases where comparisons are directly made, the post-communist states cluster in the lower part of the register of trust in institutions. Furthermore the disillusionment with the institutions has set in very quickly after the euphoria of the fall of communism, betokening a dramatic disappointment of expectations.

This lack of trust in institutions operating in the public domain is consistent with expressed low levels of interest in politics. In 1993 only 31% of Russians expressed any interest in politics,[29] in 1995 29%[30] and 35% in 1996.[31] Although levels of interest may be somewhat higher in central Europe[32] and the Baltic republics,[33] they seem to constitute a significant decline compared with the enthusiastic involvement many showed at the time of the collapse of communism. Perhaps this reflects the conviction, reported by many (in Russia 83%, Ukraine 83%, Czech Republic 72%, Slovakia 78%, Hungary 84%) in late 1993 that politics was so complicated that they often could not understand what was happening.[34] Or perhaps it reflects the view that ordinary people can have little effect upon the government of the day; a significant number of people (70% in the Czech Republic, 85% in Slovakia, 73% in Hungary, 70% in Poland and 63% in Romania in 1994) believed the post-communist system was no better than its predecessor in enabling ordinary people to influence what the government did.[35] This sort of context not

Table 4.10 Trust in institutions

Year	Belarus	Bulgaria	Croatia	Czech Republic	Hungary	Poland	Romania	Russia	Slovakia	Slovenia	Ukraine
a) Trust in government											
1993	23	13		57	22	26	27		32	36	12
1994	17	13	36	57	21	25	27	10	32	34	13
1995	15	36	36	43	18	21	26		30	43	15
b) Little or no trust in government											
1993	51	69		24	57	47	52		43	42	77
1994	61	70	39	24	57	47	52	76	43	43	77
1995	65	50	40	31	57	47	55		49	33	62
c) Trust in president											
1993	21	40		67	64	20	48	33	62	46	16
1994	23	40	33	68	65	20	48	18	62	44	16
1995	38	38	51	36	37	29	48	12	26	58	31
d) Little or no trust in president											
1993	52	37		19	19	60	41	66	22	34	73
1994	51	38	47	18	19	59	41	71	22	36	72
1995	47	45	33	33	33	45	32	75	44	24	44
e) Trust in parliament											
1993	24			28	22	23	22	20			14
1994	16	7	44	29	22	23	22	12	21	26	14
1995	13	26	30	23	22	24	25	13	25	27	11
f) Little or no trust in parliament											
1993	49			44	57	48	56	80			73
1994	62	81	29	44	57	47	56	72	53	42	73
1995	69	58	46	51	54	44	53	68	52	47	67

(continued)

Table 4.10 (continued)

Year	Belarus	Bulgaria	Croatia	Czech Republic	Hungary	Poland	Romania	Russia	Slovakia	Slovenia	Ukraine
g) Trust in civil servants											
1993	22	16	45	27	33	23	28		27	38	17
1994	20	16		28	33	23	28	11	27	37	17
1995	4	14	26	25	29	25	26	8	20	40	22
h) Little or no trust in civil servants											
1993	47	66	29	42	40	47	50		44	31	64
1994	57	66		41	39	46	50	73	44	32	63
1995	85	66	47	44	38	44	50	74	49	35	46
i) Trust in media											
1993	35	32	63	44	31	35	22		35	31	35
1994	32	31		45	32	34	22	36	35	32	33
1995	31	12	18	57	46	43	46	23	37	54	27
j) Little or no trust in media											
1993	38	45	18	29	42	36	57		38	39	43
1994	43	46		29	42	36	57	64	37	40	44
1995	45	74	62	17	28	24	30	60	30	18	39
k) Trust in political parties											
1993	15	11		25	12	8	19		16	11	7
1994	13	11		24	11	7	19	7	16	11	8
1995	8	19	19	21	10	9	22	6	14	13	7
l) Little or no trust in political parties											
1993	64	74		38	66	71	64		59	66	76
1994	67	73		38	65	71	63	93	58	66	76
1995	78	62	55	44	69	71	53	83	58	62	73

only did not reflect a vibrant public domain of politics, but neither did it encourage the development of such a domain.

In seeking to evaluate the development of civil society in these countries, these opinion poll data suggest that the value basis upon which such a society could rest is not very robust. But this situation does differ between countries and although it is difficult to pull the results of these diverse public opinion polls together into a conglomerate picture of the profile of each country, some conclusions can be reached. The generalisations that follow are based on what appears to be the predominant trend over the years rather than any one particular year. It needs also to be recognised that in some cases the countries are marginal in the categories.

In all the countries for which results have been reproduced, the level of trust in the parliament and in civil servants has been below 50%, and for political parties it has been below 25%; trust in the media has also been below 50% for all countries except for one year in the Czech Republic. Only in the Czech Republic (and Estonia – see below) has the figure for trust in the government exceeded 50%,[36] and then only for one of the two years for which figures are given. In all of these cases, the levels of little or no trust in these institutions have been higher than the levels of trust. The results are more differentiated concerning trust in the president, but it is striking that in those countries where the president has been particularly activist and powerful (Belarus, Poland, Romania, Russia, Slovakia and Ukraine), levels of trust have been below 50%. These results are relevant to the issue of the development of civil society because they reflect the low levels of trust in two major channels for popular involvement in political affairs, political parties and the media, and the arms of the state with which ordinary citizens are seen to have most contact, the government, parliament and civil servants. The picture is not as universally negative when it comes to evaluations of the present system. A positive rating (50% or more) of the present system occurred in a majority of the countries for which data has been presented: Bulgaria, Czech Republic, Estonia (see p. 166), Poland, Romania, Slovakia and Slovenia; Hungary's rating was right on the margin.

Comparison of these data with that for the NGOs shows that the countries with a positive rating for the present system of government all have an average of 300 or more NGOs per million of population, including the four countries with the highest such figures. They have also had a media upon which state regulation has been most limited. It seems that a generally low evaluation of the worth of the leading political institutions has not led to a tendency to generate and become involved in the activities of unofficial groups. Instead the response seems to have been apathy.

A private economy?

In historical terms, one of the central pillars of civil society has been private economic activity.[37] The development of such activity has been central to the growth of such a society in a number of ways. It has promoted the development of interests which have been intent on pursuing their concerns in the political arena and therefore have in turn generated organisations to realise this aim. Such interests have, through their economic activity, been able to accumulate the resources necessary to pursue their concerns politically, and have thereby stimulated the growth of a sector independent of state control. Possession of economic resources independent of the state has also provided these interests with the capacity to exercise a limiting or moderating effect upon the state. Furthermore, through their economic activities, private economic interests foster the development of economic markets which, in order to function effectively, strengthen the development of other sorts of markets, particularly in information and ideas. In this way, the development of a private economic sector out of a formerly state-dominated sector may be a step towards the strengthening of civil society elements in the country.

With the generally-professed intention of transforming the communist system into a democratic, capitalist economy,[38] all countries have adopted policies of privatisation of state assets. Attempts to privatise small concerns, such as shops, restaurants and small workshops, preceded the privatisation of medium and large enterprises in nearly every case. The years of the beginning of the privatisation programs are indicated in Table 4.11,[39] although it is not as straight forward as the dates alone suggest. In some cases (e.g. Armenia and Azerbaijan) laws on privatisation were introduced significantly earlier than the actual process of privatisation was begun. In some countries (e.g. Tajikistan) privatisation was started, then stopped, then begun again. And the pace and vigour with which the respective programs have been pursued has differed significantly between countries. Furthermore in many cases of privatisation the state has retained a significant shareholding;

Table 4.11 Dates of commencement of privatisation programs

Date	Small scale enterprises	Medium and large scale enterprises
1990	Poland	Hungary, Poland (90/91)
1991	Albania, Armenia, Belarus, Czech Rep., Estonia, Hungary, Kazakhstan, Kyrgyz Rep., Latvia, Lithuania, Slovakia, Tajikistan	Kazakhstan, Lithuania, Tajikistan
1992	Romania, Russia, Ukraine, Uzbekistan	Croatia, Czech Rep., Estonia, Kyrgyz Rep., Romania, Russia, Slovakia, Slovenia (92/93), Ukraine
1993	Bulgaria, Georgia, Moldova, Turkmenistan (93/94)	Belarus (93/94), Bulgaria, Macedonia (93/94)
1994		Georgia (94/95), Latvia, Moldova, Uzbekistan
1995		Albania, Armenia
1996	Azerbaijan	
1997		Azerbaijan, Turkmenistan

Creating civil society? 125

although usually below 50%, it nevertheless means that privatisation levels may in effect be significantly lower than the figures cited below suggest.[40]

While all countries have introduced programs of privatisation, the extent to which they have been implemented differs considerably across the countries. One way of looking at the pace and dimensions of privatisation in the different countries is to compare the share of GDP provided by private sector output as in Table 4.12.[41]

Another way of looking at this is in terms of the proportion of enterprises privatised between the beginning of the program and 1998 as in Tables 4.13 and 4.14.[42]

Although many of the categories are not precise, it is clear from these tables that while significant progress has been made in privatising small enterprises, the record for large enterprises is much more mixed, with six countries having barely started and none having privatised more than three-quarters of their medium and large enterprises.[43] The extent of privatisation of small enterprises across the region is generally high and has been done relatively quickly, and these may be expected to constitute an important underpinning of autonomous group formation and activity. However it is not clear in practice the extent to which such enterprises, which include a heavy representation of small retail outlets, did take the lead in

Table 4.12 Private sector output of GDP, in %

	Mid-1995	Mid-1996	Mid-1997	Mid-1998	Mid-1999	Mid-2000
Albania	60	75	75	75	75	75
Armenia	45	50	55	60	60	60
Azerbaijan	25	25	40	45	45	45
Belarus	15	15	20	20	20	20
Bulgaria	45	45	50	50	60	70
Croatia	45	50	55	55	60	60
Czech Republic	70	75	75	75	80	80
Estonia	65	70	70	70	75	75
Georgia	30	50	55	60	60	60
Hungary	60	70	75	80	80	80
Kazakhstan	25	40	55	55	55	60
Kyrgyz Republic	40	50	60	60	60	60
Latvia	60	60	60	60	65	65
Lithuania	55	65	70	70	70	70
Macedonia	40	50	50	55	55	55
Moldova	30	40	45	45	45	50
Poland	60	60	65	65	65	70
Romania	40	60	60	60	60	60
Russia	55	60	70	70	70	70
Slovakia	60	70	75	75	75	75
Slovenia	45	45	50	55	55	55
Tajikistan	15	20	20	30	30	40
Turkmenistan	15	20	25	25	25	25
Ukraine	35	40	50	55	55	60
Uzbekistan	30	40	45	45	45	45

Table 4.13 Privatisation of large enterprises

< 25%	25%–50%	51%–75%	> 75%
Albania, Azerbaijan, Belarus, Tajikistan, Turkmenistan, Ukraine	Armenia, Bulgaria, Croatia, Georgia, Kazakhstan, Kyrgyz Republic, Latvia, Lithuania, Macedonia, Moldova, Poland, Romania, Russia, Slovenia, Uzbekistan	Czech Republic, Estonia, Hungary, Slovakia	

Table 4.14 Privatisation of small enterprises

Little progress	Substantial share privatised	Nearly comprehensive	Complete privatisation
	Belarus, Tajikistan, Turkmenistan	Armenia, Azerbaijan, Bulgaria, Moldova, Tajikistan, Ukraine, Uzbekistan	Albania, Croatia, Czech Republic, Estonia, Georgia, Hungary, Kazakhstan, Kyrgyz Republic, Latvia, Lithuania, Macedonia, Poland, Romania, Russia, Slovakia, Slovenia

fostering civil society development or quickly generating a public sphere of activity within which this could occur. The principal reason for this is that such entities, especially when they are small family businesses, have had only limited capital and time to devote to activities outside their immediate work concerns. This is especially the case given the difficult economic circumstances with which most have had to cope during the years of economic change. Therefore it may be that it is to the larger enterprises that we should look as an indicator of civil society development.

An important consideration in the question of large-scale privatisation is whose hands the enterprise falls into. This is not easy to generalise about, both because of the opacity and complexity of many of the ownership arrangements (including continuing shareholding by the state) and because of country and regional differences.[44] A number of different methods of privatising enterprises have been used. Their details do not concern us here, but what is important is who is advantaged by the primary method of privatisation used.[45] Using data provided by the EBRD, Table 4.15 shows those countries whose primary method of privatisation benefited those already in the enterprises to be privatised (the chief form of this was the management/employee buy-out, but it also includes schemes which gave significant

Table 4.15 Beneficiaries of primary mode of privatisation of large enterprises

Insiders	Outsiders	Treated equally
Azerbaijan, Belarus, Croatia, Georgia, Kyrgyz Republic, Macedonia, Moldova, Poland, Romania, Russia, Slovakia, Slovenia, Tajikistan, Turkmenistan, Ukraine, Uzbekistan	Albania, Bulgaria, Estonia, Hungary	Armenia, Czech Republic, Kazakhstan, Latvia, Lithuania

other concessions to insiders), those which benefited people not in the enterprises, and those methods which gave advantages to neither group.

In most countries, the primary mode of privatisation has favoured insiders. This has been at the root of much of the discussion of 'nomenklatura capitalism' and 'nomenklatura privatisation',[46] and clearly such characterisations have been relevant for at least part of the privatisation process in many countries.[47] People in positions of responsibility under the communist regime have often been able to turn such positions and the administrative power that went with them into economic ownership. This is important in the current context because people who were well connected under the old regime have not lost all of those connections with the passing of communism. The substantial continuity that has existed in many of the bureaucratic structures of the state has ensured that many of these connections have remained largely intact. They presumably have on occasions facilitated the establishment of new contacts as well. To the extent that the new owners of privatised enterprises are reliant upon such contacts, they have less need for the development of autonomous groups to project their interests. They are able to deal direct with politicians and officials to achieve their ends, and therefore have less need for autonomous group activity than those lacking such contacts.[48]

Is there, then, any link between the density of civil society measured by the number of NGOs per million head of population and the extent and mode of privatisation? There do appear to be some approximate correlations. Low levels of the privatisation of large enterprises appears to be associated with low numbers of NGOs; all countries with less than 25% privatisation of large enterprises had fewer than 100 NGOs per million head of population, while no country with fewer than 100 NGOs per head had privatised more than half of their large enterprises. The four countries with the highest levels of privatisation also had the highest number of NGOs (Czech Republic, Estonia, Hungary and Slovenia). Furthermore three of those (Czech Republic, Estonia and Hungary) had modes of privatisation which did not favour insiders. Low levels of privatisation were also generally associated with methods favouring insiders. The date privatisation began is less important than the vigour with which it was prosecuted.[49] But the general principle is clear: where privatisation has been most developed, NGOs are most numerous and vice versa. This is consistent with the view that privatisation stimulates NGO development, but there is clearly no single direct relationship which applies in all countries.

A further comment on the relationship between the development of civil society and the beneficiaries of privatisation is in order. Important in this is the type of political regime. Of the 16 countries in which the primary mode of privatisation has favoured insiders, only Poland and Slovenia have been democracies throughout, while Croatia, Romania and Slovakia moved in that direction in the second half of the 1990s. The association of insider privatisation with non-democratic regimes is consistent. Former insider owners are well placed to utilise their contacts with remaining old regime officials to advance their interests, and thereby have less incentive to foster the development of public and open politics. The question is, what distinguishes the five countries noted above from their 11 undemocratic neighbours. One important distinction is the much greater number of NGOs present in each country (there are no figures for Slovenia, but qualitative analysis suggests it is comparable with the other democracies) compared with the undemocratic states. The press is also generally freer. What this suggests is that where there is a dense network of civil society which structures and constrains much political life, the possible political effects of insider privatisation may be ameliorated. Insider privatised firms may be forced to act like other civil society organisations by the developing civil society network and the culture of open and competitive policy-making which it fosters. The political culture embedded in a developing civil society, added to the greater sense of a rule of law which goes with this, may thus be more important in shaping the patterns of action of enterprises than the mode of privatisation.

On the basis of an uncertain commitment to the positive value of the system or a positive attitude to its main institutions, there has not been the powerful growth of autonomous group activity in many of the post-communist countries. However there does appear to be a positive correlation between high levels of privatisation and the growth of autonomous group activity. The correlation is not quite as strong, although still significant, when the mode of privatization not favouring insiders is factored in. It is important also to see this in the light of the development of political parties.

Political representation

The standard picture of the communist legacy is of the flattened society, one in which class distinctions were, if not eliminated, at least significantly narrowed, and where the economic basis of private activity was absent. With a regime intent on deep penetration of the society, it was a situation that was not conducive to the development of civil society forces: the material basis was weak and regime opposition strong. But as Chapter three demonstrated, this model of communist society did not approximate reality in a number of communist countries. Especially in the states of East Central Europe (Poland, Hungary and to a less extent Czechoslovakia), civil society forces were able to develop. Even in these countries the basis of civil society forces was somewhat problematic; civil society forces here lacked both the range and depth that similar forces had in societies where there was greater acceptance of civil society by the regime. This means that even in those countries where civil society forces were most developed under communist rule, there was still significant work to do in constructing a vibrant and powerful civil society in the post-communist period. But the construction of such a society was vital for, depending on the cases, the consolidation of democracy or the generation of pressures in favour of democratic development.

A crucial indicator, as well as an important factor in its own right in the construction of civil society, is the development of a party system. Political parties are the quintessential organisations for the projection of private interests in the political sphere, and therefore for the transition from secondary to tertiary group activity which is the hallmark of a developed civil society. Although some communist countries formally permitted a number of political parties to exist (Bulgaria, Czechoslovakia and Poland[50]), these had no independence and did not engage in autonomous political activity. They could, however, be seen as representing distinct interests in the society, with the United Peasants' Party in Poland being the clearest instance of this. But in most countries there was no similar structure of multi-partism, even in a purely formal sense. Rather the assumption that the communist party could adequately represent what diverse interests there were in the society created an environment that did not provide scope for the existence of a variety of political parties. Consequently when the opportunity arose for the creation of independent parties, these had to be built almost completely from scratch. This situation was strengthened by the widespread popular suspicion about political parties. Although much of the respective populations acknowledged that political parties were intrinsic parts of the democratic process as it had been established in the West, their only experience of parties was of those to which they had been exposed under communism, chiefly the communist party itself. With the rejection of that system went a rejection of those parties.

An important factor in the development of political parties is the conditions which produced their emergence. Parties emerged in the former communist world chiefly as the vehicles elites, or potential elites, sought to use to press their claims in the political arena. Those figures from outside the regime who sought in each of the countries to bring about the transformation or replacement of the communist system organised themselves into parties the better to pursue this aim. When the opportunity for involvement in competitive elections came along, the need to organise political parties in order both to mobilise electoral support and to organise action in the parliamentary chamber, could further stimulate party development. In this sense, parties generally were created from the top down, to further interests as perceived and defined by the elites rather than the mass of the population. Parties were conceived as the vehicles for elite activity and the mobilisation of mass support for that activity rather than as mechanisms for the involvement of the masses in political life. This was consistent with one of the consequences of the above-noted greater flatness of communist society. Given that the communist system had not provided great scope for the emergence of private interests or of organisations to protect those interests that did emerge, such interests were generally not well developed or crystallised by the time regime change entered the political agenda.[51] With private interests still in the throes of crystallising, and thereby of establishing secondary groups, they were generally not well placed to contribute to the development of tertiary groups like political parties. Political elites, looking on this landscape of the weak structuring of interests, were therefore encouraged in their development of parties not to seek to rely too heavily upon particular sectors of the population but to spread their appeal broadly across a range of interests.[52] The result in many places was the development of movement parties and a high level of fluidity with, in the view of some, politics not securely anchored in the social and economic structure.[53] These were parties that lacked strong roots in the population and therefore a stable membership, leadership was based on personal authority rather than official position, and programs were vague, emotive, and often syncretic; for example, the HDF appealed to an amalgam of traditional Hungarian values, Christian democracy, statism and nationalism. These parties rested on the vigorous espousal of broad values rather than a range of specific policies, and usually eschewed the label 'party' because of the negative connotation it had from the communist period. They preferred to present themselves as movements, with corresponding less discipline than a normal party and less apparent concern for the institutional aspects of party building.[54] This sort of party lacked a strong branch structure and was focused principally upon national level, usually parliamentary, leaders; parties were principally parliamentary bodies with little structure in the society at large.[55] Their links with the populace as a whole and with their members were often realised more through the mass media than a developed party machinery.[56]

While the movement party was a natural response to the conditions emanating from communist rule, this was always likely to be a transitional form. When the organisation of private and partial interest became legitimate, the movement party was less satisfactory as a vehicle for the realisation and representation of those interests. The movement parties projected broad values based on 'over-ideologised' party programs and, in the view of one observer, engaged in 'culture wars' with other similar parties,[57] but this made them unable to meet the needs of more narrowly-based interests within the society. Increasingly the development of private interests demands scope for the articulation and aggregation of those interests in the political sphere, and this stimulates pressure for the shifting of partisan conflict from broad issues of values to narrower ones of interests. The scope for this will differ from country to country depending upon circumstances,[58] and there is debate over how this is best understood (see p. 131–2),[59] but wherever an effective party system has been allowed to develop, such pressures have been experienced. These pressures for the development of interest-based parties and for the structuring of a party system along interest-based lines were a significant aspect of the stabilisation of the party system.

As will be shown, not all countries have witnessed the stabilisation of such a system.[60] However if the society is to have an effective means of interests participating in and affecting the outcome of political decision-making that is democratic in its nature, the development of a stable and effective party system is essential. If the party system has become stabilised, with the same parties regularly drawing substantial popular support, we can assume that those parties are meeting a need in the community more broadly. Two qualifications are necessary. First, the performance of parties can be influenced by electoral laws, and if these should change between elections, the comparison of performance can be obscured. Second, it is clear that elections provide a major stimulus for the consolidation and shaping of parties.[61] Consequently given that different countries have experienced different numbers of elections and that in some countries elections have been structured in such a way as to hinder the involvement of some parties, our reliance upon election results to gauge party system development must acknowledge that the electoral impetus for partisan development will differ from case to case.

In looking at the role played by party development in the strengthening of democracy, two aspects are therefore relevant.

1 The extent to which the party system which has emerged constitutes a stable structure within which political elites interact. If the political system is to be regularised and conflict kept within structured bounds, there must be institutions which do this. In a democratic system, the main form of such institutions is the political party. If parties are acting as effective vehicles of political engagement for elites, we would expect to see them survive over an extended period of time. We would also expect to see real challenges in elections, if not changes in party government. Stable patterns of competition between parties facilitate popular control and reflect satisfaction on the part of elites with the political structure as a means of realising their aims.

2 The extent to which parties act as effective vehicles for the representation of the interests of defined constituencies. If parties do represent such interests, they are playing a crucial role by providing a channel into the political process for the views of those who are not directly involved in political life. The view that, given the flattened nature of society resulting from the communist experience, voters would be swayed by charismatic and clientelistic appeals rather than by ideological or policy positions based on structured interests,[62] has not in the longer term proved to be correct. Although there have clearly been some politicians whose appeal has been based in part upon charismatic or clientelistic factors (Zhirinovsky in Russia, Milosevic in Serbia, Meciar in Slovakia), studies have shown in a number of countries of the region that there is some correspondence between voters' attitudes and their party preferences.[63] Although the basis of this may be different for different groups of voters (e.g. economic interest, ethnic identity), survey data supports the linkage of attitudes with party preferences. The weakness of the charismatic appeal is given *prima facie* support by the general failure of demagogic politicians in those countries where elections have been freely conducted. Furthermore the argument about clientelism may be less removed from that relating to interests than its proponents think; if the essence of clientelism is swapping support for benefits, the direct provision of goods and services,[64] such benefits may be related to the structural locations, and thereby interests, of the putative supporters. In this sense, there may not be much effective difference in the relationship between party and supporters in a clientelistic and an interest-based relationship.

It is, therefore, these two aspects of the party system, their role as vehicles for elite interaction and mass representation, which are central to an evaluation of the development and stabilisation of the party system. Essentially it is the stabilisation of the system which is crucial. If that system has regularised patterns of party interaction, reflected in the dominance of the competitive electoral process across elections by the same parties and the stability of parties' electoral support, we assume that the elites are content to operate within the bounds of this system and that much of the population believe their interests are being met through these bodies. It is on this issue of the stabilisation of the system that the discussion will focus. However a number of preliminary points must be made.

First, in charting the course of party development, we can distinguish between a number of types of political parties:

a) Successor parties – parties that emerge out of the former ruling communist party; such a party may be the former party with only a name change, the party substantially reworked (usually) in a social democratic direction, or a fragment of that party.
b) Movement parties – the initial, value-based, leadership centred parties which emerged about the time of regime change discussed above.
c) New parties – parties that emerge rather later in the process of regime change; they may be successor parties to the movement parties, emerging when the latter split, or they may be completely new; they may be interest-based parties or they may retain the broader value orientation of movement parties.
d) Historical parties – parties which had existed prior to communist rule and re-emerge in the post-communist period.

These categories blur at the edges and it is not always clear precisely which category best fits particular parties, but the essential difference between the categories is clear and it does capture important differences in party type evident in the region.

Second, the party systems being analysed here are all new systems. They emerged at the earliest at the time of the fall of the communist regime and therefore at the time of writing are barely a decade old. We should therefore expect there to be considerable fluidity in their contours. They did not emerge fully formed from the chrysalis of the communist transition, but have developed and changed over time. This means that there has been substantial fluidity, even instability, in the respective party systems. Levels of party support have fluctuated, often wildly; for example, in Albania the SPA's vote went from 56.2% in 1991 to 25.7% in 1992 to 20.4% in 1996 to 52.8% in 1997 while its opponent the DPA gained 38.7%, 62.1%, 55.5% and 25.7% in the same years.[65] Of all of the parties which have gained at least 1% of the vote in elections from 1990–99 in those countries where elections have been meaningful competitions,[66] fewer than 6% were able to maintain their voting share within a margin of 10% from one election to the next.[67] Many parties were transitory on the political scene; for example in Romania, of the 11 parties getting more than 0.5% of the vote in the first election in 1990, only one, the Hungarian Democratic Union (HDU), participated in the 1996 election in substantially the same form. Of the more than 450 parties gaining more than 1% of the vote in the elections in the region,[68] 133 were new, emerging after the first post-communist election, while a further 104 either disappeared as independent entities or changed their name and identity. In the 17 countries conducting meaningful competitive elections, only some 58 parties maintained their independent existence from the initial post-communist election to the last one. It is clear that the party systems of the region were characterised by high levels of fluidity, with the result that all comments about stability and consolidation that follow must be seen as highly relative.

Third, in a number of the post-communist countries, effective party systems have not emerged. This has been the case in Azerbaijan, Belarus, Kazakhstan, the Kyrgyz Republic, Tajikistan, Turkmenistan and Uzbekistan. In all of these countries except the Kyrgyz Republic, the emergence and development of parties has been stunted as a result of regime pressure and opposition, with the result that the parties that have been able to maintain an existence enjoy neither free access to the political system nor the capacity freely to attract popular support. In the Kyrgyz Republic the failure of a functioning party system to develop is less the result of regime pressure than of other circumstances in the country. These cases where party systems did not develop will not be discussed in this chapter. In the discussion of the party systems, the cases will be discussed in terms of the patterns of transition identified in Chapter Two.

In **Pattern One** countries, the shape of the initial party system was set by the circumstances of the transition, and in particular by the fact that in both Poland and Hungary, civil society forces were organised before the regime fell and they played a central part in the construction of the post-communist system. The basis for party-building therefore existed from the outset, and it was legitimised by the part its components played in the destruction of the communist regime. In both cases, initial parties emerged from among the groups involved in the respective round table negotiations. The basic data on the party system is shown in Table 4.16.[69]

In both countries the movement party prominent in the negotiations with the old regime led a coalition government in the initial stages of the post-communist period. In Poland Solidarity headed a coalition which included representatives of the old regime, but with their departure in mid-1990, Solidarity began to fragment. This process was fuelled by a number of factors: the transformation of the former ruling communist party into Social Democracy of the Polish Republic (SDPR) seemed to remove the communist threat which had been so essential for the unity of Solidarity,[83] the conflict between the Solidarity Mazowiecki-led government, Solidarity's parliamentary deputies, and Walesa at the head of the trade union wing, and the impact of radical economic shock therapy, all contributed to the break up of the movement party. Between 1990 and 1993 a dozen parties emerged from Solidarity, and went through a process of continuing fission and unification;[84] parties independent of Solidarity also emerged. At the outset, the only parties with any sort of mass base were the regime successor parties, which following the disaster of the 1989 election had been forced to fundamentally reconfigure

Table 4.16 Party system data for Poland and Hungary

Country, movement, party, elections	% votes, largest party	% votes, two largest parties	No. of parties over threshold	No. of parties in legislature	Largest parties (in terms of votes)	Government
Poland Solidarity						
1st election 10/91 (PR, no threshold)[70]	12.3	24.3	9	28	FU, DLA, H, CA, PPP,CIP, LDC, PA, S[72]	Coalitions led by Solidarity successors
2nd election 9/93 (PR, 5% threshold)[71]	20.4	35.9	7	7	DLA, PPP, FU, UL, H, CIP, NPRB[73]	Communist successor DLA-PPP coalition
3rd election 9/97 (as for 9/93)	33.8	60.9	5	6	AWS, DLA, FU, PPP, MRP[74]	Coalition of new (Solidarity successor) parties AWS and FU
Hungary Democratic Forum						
1st election 3/90 (mixed system, 4% threshold)[75]	24.7	46.1	6	7	DF, AFD, IS, HSP, AYD, CDPP[78]	Movement party-led coalition with new parties – DF and ISP and CDPP
2nd election 5/94 (as for 3/90, 5% threshold)[76]	33.0	52.7	6	8	HSP, AFD, DF, IS, CDPP, AYD[79]	Successor communist party HSP led coalition with AFD[81]
3rd election 5/98 (as for 5/94)[77]	32.9	62.4	5	6	HSP, AYD IS, AFD, HJL, DF[80]	New party-led coalition – AYD and IS and DF[82]

themselves, the SDPR and the Peasants' Party; most parties were little more than organisational titles attached to prominent politicians. In the first election, where there was no threshold and no experience of partisan competition, a very large number of party groups shared the vote.[85] The resulting fragmentation contributed to the instability of elite politics at this time. With the introduction of an electoral threshold at the next election, this fragmentation was dramatically reduced, but at the expense of the distortion of voters' preferences; the DLA and PPP with almost 36% of the votes won almost 66% of the seats, while 29.5% of the votes was wasted on parties that failed to cross the threshold. There was much less distortion in the following election, with only about 12% of the vote wasted, while the seats won by the leading parties more closely approximated the share of the vote they received.[86] With that vote being shared between communist and movement party successors, there seems to have been a consolidation of support around these positions. Indeed, throughout the post-communist period, the leading party groups in each election have been successor parties of either Solidarity or the communists, and over the three elections, support for both groups has increased. This has also been part of a general consolidation of the party system over the three elections; the share of votes for the two largest political parties/coalitions increased, while the number of parties exceeding the threshold and gaining representation in the parliament decreased, and the votes cast for parties which failed to gain parliamentary representation decreased (34.4% in 1993 to 12.8% in 1997). This consolidation is most clearly reflected in the way that, for the 1997 election, the anti-communist side was reorganised with the formation of Electoral Action Solidarity, a coalition of many Solidarity successor and other centre-right parties and groups[87] which was able to defeat the communist successors at the polls. However following this success, the coalition split (as did the Freedom Union). Despite the splintering, the main axis of party competition has been Solidarity successor-communist successor, with a communist successor administration[88] attaining government between two Solidarity successor administrations. This consolidation of the structure of the party system (albeit with some fragmentation of parties and coalitions within it) along the lines broadly reflected in the round table negotiations suggests that it is acting effectively as a means of structuring elite competition.

Turning to mass representation, the initial fragmentation of the party system shows that there had been little connection between the crystallisation of broad interests in society and the capacity of the parties to aggregate those interests into definable electoral coalitions. This is confirmed by the fact that in 1992 only 3% of respondents in one survey believed that there were political parties 'which are acting on behalf of people like you'.[89] The reconfiguring of the party system over the course of these three elections, and in particular the disappearance of some 17 parties and the emergence of some eight new ones,[90] suggests that many of the parties have remained unconnected to a substantial social base. However the continuing prominence of the two types of successor groupings, Solidarity and communist, suggests that they may be meeting the demands of particular constituencies. Given the rhetorical positions both sides took on economic reform during the early period, this would be consistent with the view that this party system has come to represent popular constituencies that define themselves chiefly (although not exclusively) in terms of issues of economic distribution.[91] Alternatively, this sort of division would be consistent with the view that ideological self-placement (perhaps reflected in the attitude to the communist past) and the values one adopts are important in determining partisan support, at least for considerable sections of the population.[92] But if such identification does occur, it does not seem to be particularly strong. The electoral turnout figures for the three parliamentary elections[93] do not show an electorate energised to go and support the parties which represent their interests or an electorate which feels sufficiently attached to a party to place a high priority on supporting it at the polls.[94] Poland has the lowest turnout level for any of the countries for which we have runs of figures. So while the party system may be an effective means of structuring the activity of political elites, it is less clear that it as yet acts as a vehicle for the carriage of popular interests.

In Hungary too the party system arose out of the forces represented in the round table negotiations. The Hungarian Democratic Forum, which led the first post-communist government, suffered from a series of splits and a process of declining electoral support: from 24.7% in 1990 to 11.7% in 1994 and 3.1% in 1998. This decline coincided with two developments: the rebounding of the communist successor party newly reformed after the collapse of 1989, and the growth in strength of a diversity of non-communist forces. The communist successor party, the HSP, was able in both the 1994 and 1998 elections to attract about a third of the vote and thereby to stabilise itself as a major player in Hungarian politics. In both elections it was the largest single party, and formed the government in 1994. On the non-communist side, the most striking development was the rise of the AYD which went from 9% of the vote in 1990 to 28.2% in 1998, thereby effectively replacing the AFD which went from 21.4% to 7.9%. Although both were liberal centrist parties, the AFD was rent by disputes over both policy and personality and also lost favour owing to its participation in the government from 1994, while the AYD was able, beginning in 1993, to transform itself from a social movement into a political party.[95] Although all parties in the Hungarian system, as elsewhere, experienced internal arguments and splits, the party system has generally been very stable. Hungary was the only country in which the parliament ran its full term twice, there were no changes of government between elections, and the six largest parties in the first election were also the six largest in the second; and in the third election four of those parties were the four largest.[96] In the first two elections, except for the two winners (HDF and HSP), the results for the other parties were almost the same. Over the three elections there has also been a decline in voter support for parties which did not exceed the threshold (12.8% in 1990, 11.4% in 1994 and 6.6% in 1998) and for independents.[97] During the same time only two parties disappeared and two new ones emerged. The parties which have dominated the Hungarian political scene were the first parties established, suggesting the advantages to be gained by adopting positions on the political spectrum at an early stage in the open crystallisation of interests in Hungarian society. These parties did change, however, with policy and tactical disagreements causing them to change their positions on issues at various times.[98] But the general stability of the system and the containment of politics within its bounds suggests that it has been an effective vehicle for elite interaction.

This stability would also be consistent with the parties accurately reflecting the views of particular constituencies. The development of the Hungarian system looks like the archetype for the region: the decline of the movement party, the resurrection of the communist successors, and the development of stable centre-right parties. However it is not clear that this represents the embedding of the particular parties in their own defined popular constituencies. After its initial rejection in 1990, the communist successor HSP won about a third of the vote in the two subsequent elections. Furthermore it seems to enjoy a high level of continuity of voting support. A survey of voters showed that the percentage of a party's voters who voted for that party in 1990 and also voted for it in 1994 was as follows: HSP 95.1%, IS 61.3%, CDPP 56.0%, AYD 55.6%, AFD 41.3% and HDF 37.6%.[99] The communist successor party seems to have had a much higher level of party loyalty among its supporters than any of its competitors. None of the other parties has been able to achieve the sort of consistency the HSP has achieved in terms of the proportion of votes it received in the last two elections. The fluctuations suggest that even if Hungarians make their decisions about who to vote for on the basis of the similarity of party programs to their own attitudes,[100] most are not locked into positions of partisan support. Electoral turnout levels are consistent with this view that the parties are not seen as effective representatives of the interests of particular constituencies: 1990 65%, 1994 69%, 1998 57%. As in Poland, while the party system may perform well as a mechanism for elite activity, it is not clear that all the parties effectively serve to represent the interests of defined constituencies among the populace.

The party systems in the **Pattern Two** countries were also profoundly affected by the circumstances of the fall of communism, and particularly the absence of strong organised civil society forces prior to the collapse of the regime. The result was that in both countries the ruling communist party was able initially to maintain itself in power and, subsequently, continue to play a major role in the political system, see Table 4.17.

In both countries the successor communist party and the movement party were able to stabilise their positions in the political spectrum and maintain a place as major political actors. In Bulgaria the oppositionist UDF was an umbrella organisation comprising a large number of parties and groupings,[118] but despite the heterogeneity of its membership and bouts of disunity and splits, especially in 1991 and 1994, and despite difficulty reaching agreement on policy issues, it has been able to maintain itself as a viable competitor to the BSP. This capacity to maintain itself largely intact may reflect the challenge posed by the continued strength of the BSP,[119] which was able to avoid excessive internecine squabbling following its fall. As the figures show, these two party groups have together dominated Bulgarian politics, in no election gaining less than two thirds of the votes and alternating in power at each election, although the support for each has oscillated significantly (see p. 140). The inability of these two parties to work

Table 4.17 Party system data for Bulgaria and Albania

Country, movement, party, elections	% votes, largest party	% votes, two largest parties	No. of parties over threshold	No. of parties in legislature	Largest parties (in terms of votes)	Government
Bulgaria Union of Democratic Forces						
1st election 6/90 (mixed system, 4% threshold)[101]	47.2	83.4	4	5	BSP, UDF, BANU, MRF[102]	Successor communist party BSP[106]
2nd election 10/91 (PR, 4% threshold)	34.4	67.5	3	3	UDF, BSP, MRF[103]	Movement party UDF[107]
3rd election 12/94 (as for 10/91)	43.5	67.7	5	5	BSP, UDF, BANU, MRF, BBB[104]	Successor communist party BSP[108]
4th election 4/97 (as for 12/94)	52.3	74.4	5	5	UDF, BSP, UNS, EC, BBB[105]	Movement party UDF
Albania Democratic Party						
1st election 3–4/91 (SMC)	56.2	94.9	2	4	SPA, DPA[112]	Successor communist party SPA[116]
2nd election 3/92 (mixed system, 4% threshold)[109]	62.1	87.8	3	5	DPA, SPA, SD[113]	Movement party DPA
3rd election 5–6/96 (mixed system, 4% threshold)[110]	55.5	75.9	5	5	DPA, SPA, RPA, NF, UPHR[114]	Movement party DPA
4th election 6–7/97 (mixed system, 3% threshold)[111]	52.8	78.5	2	8	SPA, DPA[115]	Successor communist party SPA[117]

easily together[120] gave greater scope for influence to the MRF, especially when neither had a majority in the parliament following the 1991 election. However the ethnic (Turkish) basis of the MRF effectively served to limit its capacity to become a major player in Bulgarian politics (see p. 163); it was not seen as a viable coalition partner by either of the other major parties. The party system has therefore been quite stable in terms of the dominance of these two major party groups. The initial communist:post-communist division has thereby become frozen, while the pluralisation of politics which many expected has been blunted. The decline in support for parties which failed to gain representation in the parliament (24.9% in 1991, 15.6% in 1994 and 7.6% in 1997)[121] and the decline in the number of parties winning at least 1% of the votes (10 in 1991 and 1994, 5 in 1997) is consistent with this. The 1997 election was significant in this regard, witnessing the transformation of the other two most important parties during the first three elections (MRF joined with a number of other groups to form UNS, while BANU had split with one part joining the BSP and the other the Popular Union which was in coalition with UDF) and the emergence of two new ones gaining parliamentary representation. This suggests that the system has settled into a pattern which the dominant political elites find congenial. The fact that not all with political aspirations agree is suggested by the fact that between 1990 and 1997 some ten new parties (which were big enough to gain at least 1% of the vote in a national election) were created; in the same time twelve disappeared.

However the relative stability of the vote shared by the two leading parties over this period (with the exception of 1991) masks the oscillation in their individual vote from election to election, especially between 1994 and 1997, see Table 4.18.

This pattern suggests that these major parties are not soundly based in stable interest structures in society more broadly, and while it may be that people vote on the basis of party programs, it would appear that, if so, their own views have been changing quite substantially. One party, the MRF, does have a clearly defined constituency, the Turkish section of the population, and it may be that the BBB is developing such a constituency (the Bulgarian Business Bloc had a very stable vote between the last two elections – 4.7% and 4.9%). However there appears to be little prima facie evidence that the populace sees the parties as effective vehicles for the realisation of their interests.[123] The decline in voter turnout (1990 90%, 1991 80%, 1994 74% and 1997 63%) is consistent with this view.

In Albania too the successor communist party and movement party have dominated the political process, with only one other party grouping exceeding the threshold in three elections. However Albanian politics has been blighted by authoritarian action by the DPA and its leader Sali Berisha while in office, by substantial electoral fraud in the 1996 election, and by popular unrest, so that the party system has had to develop in conditions that did not favour the emergence of regularised rules of the political game. Nevertheless the continuing primacy of these two parties and the weakness of others suggests that for the dominant political elites, insofar as they chose to work through party structures, these are satisfactory vehicles for political activity. Turning to popular representation, the dramatic oscillation in the levels of electoral support enjoyed by both major parties is not

140 *Creating civil society?*

Table 4.18 Shares of votes for BSP and UDF

	1990	1991	1994	1997
BSP	47.2%	33.1%	43.5%	22.1%
UDF	36.2%	34.4%	24.2%	52.3%[122]

Table 4.19 Shares of votes for SPA and DPA

	1991	1992	1996	1997
SPA	56.2%	25.7%	20.4%	52.8%
DPA	38.7%	62.1%	55.5%	25.7%

consistent with the view that they have come to represent large clearly defined constituencies who are attached to them, see Table 4.19.

The increased number of parties gaining representation in the parliament at the 1997 election also suggests some dissatisfaction with the two leading parties. Nevertheless the high figures on voting turn out prior to 1997, when participation may have been affected by reaction against the fraud at the last election and subsequent conflict, if genuine, suggests that the populace does see merit in its continued involvement in the electoral process, and therefore in offering partisan support. Although only five new parties have emerged between 1991 and 1997, there is no evidence that they have been able to carve out a clear constituency any better than the two major parties. But despite the stable pattern of competition reflected in the apparent crystallisation of the party system around the communist successor and movement successor parties, the wild swings in support for these parties may mean that the populace votes mainly for these parties less because of an affective tie with them than because they are the two main parties in existence.

In the **Pattern Three** countries, the collapse of communist rule and sidelining of the former ruling party left the new party system to be shaped largely by the process of fragmentation of the initial movement parties, see Table 4.20.

In both republics of Czechoslovakia, a movement party filled the gap created by the disintegration of communist rule, but each of these parties disintegrated before the next election in 1992. The second elections in both republics were won by new parties emerging from the movement parties, in the Czech republic by the right-centrist CDP of Vaclav Klaus and in Slovakia by the populist nationalist MDS led by Vladimir Meciar. The parties also won the subsequent election, but in the one after that (the fourth) in Slovakia, the MDS was displaced by a coalition of new parties and in the Czech Republic the CDP was defeated by the SDs. The party systems in both republics have shown considerable stability. After the first election the largest party has been the same one in each republic except for the 1998 Czech election, and on each occasion it has gained over a quarter of the vote, but because it has not gained a majority, coalition governments have had to be formed. In the Czech Republic, a moderate leftist party, the Social Democrats, has

Table 4.20 Party system data for the Czech Republic and Slovakia

Country, movement, party, elections	% votes, largest party	% votes, two largest parties	No. of parties over threshold	No. of parties in legislature	Largest parties (in terms of votes)	Government
Czech Republic Civic Forum						
1st election 6/90 (PR, 5% threshold)	49.5	62.7	4	4	CF, CPBM, MSM, CDU[126]	Movement party CF[130]
2nd election 6/92 (PR, 5% threshold[124])	29.7	43.7	8	8	CDP, CPBM, SD, LSU, CDU, AR, CDA, MSM[127]	New party (CDP – CF successor) led coalition with CDU
3rd election 5–6/96 (PR, 5% threshold[125])	29.6	56.0	6	6	CDP, SD, CPBM, CDU, AR, CDA[128]	New party (CDP – CF successor) led coalition
4th election 6/98 (as for 1996)	32.3	60.0	5	5	SD, CDP, FU, CDU-PP, CPBM[129]	Historical party (SD) minority government
Slovakia Public Against Violence						
1st election 6/90 (PR, 3% threshold)	29.3	48.5	5	7	PAV, CDM, SNP, PDL, HC, DP, GPS[132]	Movement party (PAV) led coalition

(continued)

Table 4.20 (continued)

Country, movement, party, elections	% votes, largest party	% votes, two largest parties	No. of parties over threshold	No. of parties in legislature	Largest parties (in terms of votes)	Government
2nd election 6/92 (PR, 5% threshold[131])	37.3	52.0	5	5	MDS, PDL, CDM, SNP, HC[133]	New party (MDS – PAV successor); then MDS-SNP coalition; then opposition coalition.[136]
3rd election 9/94 (as for 6/92)	35.0	44.7	7	7	MDS, CC, HC, CDM, DUS, AWS, SNP[134]	New party MDS-led coalition with SNP and AWS
4th election 9/98 (5% threshold for parties)	27.0	53.3	6	6	MDS, SDC, PDL, HC, SNP, PCU[135]	New party coalition: SDC, PDL, HC, PCU[137]

Note: Prior to the dissolution of Czechoslovakia at the end of 1992, the figures are for the lower houses of the individual republican (Czech and Slovak) parliaments.

emerged as the major alternative to the centre-right CDP. The historical SDs were able to displace the successor communist party, the only country in the region where this has occurred, perhaps reflecting the strength of the pre-communist democratic tradition, the weakness of reformism within the former ruling party as a result of the post-1968 'normalisation', and the effect of the lustration laws implemented in the Czech Republic. The strong association between the CDP and economic policies of marketisation may also have assisted the growth of this SD identity. This may indicate a stabilisation of the party system around a moderate left–right axis.[138] The relative stability of the communist party's vote (1990 13.2%, 1992 14.0%, 1996 10.3%) suggests that it has had a stable constituency among the voters. The decline in support for parties failing to gain a seat in the parliament (18.8% in 1990, 19.2% in 1992, 10.6% in 1996, and 9.4% in 1998) also suggests some stabilisation of the system as a whole. This process was aided by the split with Slovakia by making the country more homogenous in ethnic and socio-economic terms. This would be consistent with the argument that Czech electors had come to see their parties in terms of their own interests, although one survey did suggest that 86% of respondents believed that their representatives quickly lost touch with them;[139] in 1994 only 12% of people were members of political parties.[140] Despite a decline in voter turn out, the figures are consistent with continuing popular acceptance of the electoral system as a viable means of realising voters' interests and of parties as means for doing this. That some of the parties were seen to fill a need is also suggested by the fact that four[141] of them (the CPBM, CDU,[142] SD and the Free Democrats) participated in all elections, and although some 11 new parties were formed, nine disappeared during this time.

In Slovakia, a broad bloc of parties from both left and right emerged to challenge (and ultimately defeat) the populist MDS, although this party did remain the largest after each election. With its focus upon nationalism and building on the momentum it created through the split with the Czech Republic, the MDS remained largely a movement party, and although the individual components of the other bloc appealed to definite constituencies, their unification in the alliance obscured their capacity to act as interest-based organisations. An important contrast between the Czech and Slovak party systems is the strength and importance in the latter not only of nationalist influences (the SNP gained parliamentary representation at all elections and was part of a governing coalition on a number of occasions), but of religion; the Christian Democrats have been stronger in Slovakia than in any other post-communist country. The party system in Slovakia thus remains more weakly linked to social interests, with the polarisation currently being essentially one of nationalist versus a-nationalist. The decline in support for parties which did not gain parliamentary representation (7.8% in 1990, 23.6% in 1992, 12% in 1994, and 5.8% in 1998)[143] is consistent with some stabilisation of the party system.[144] So too is the relative stability of the vote for some parties across the elections, see Table 4.21.

This sort of stability (although the judgement with regard to the MDS may have to await the next election) is consistent with a situation in which Slovak voters see their interests being represented through major political parties. The high levels

144 *Creating civil society?*

Table 4.21 Share of votes in Slovakia

	1990	1992	1994	1998
Party of Democratic Left	13.3%	14.7%	9.7%[145]	14.7%
Hungarian Coalition	8.6%	7.4%	10.2%	9.1%
MDS		37.3%	35.0%	27.0%

of voter turn out (1990 95%, 1992 84%, 1994 76%, 1998 84%) are also consistent with this, although in 1999 only 8% said they belonged to a party.[146]

So both the successor countries in Pattern Three have developed stable party systems, reflecting general satisfaction with the parties on the part of elites and masses.

The party systems in the countries of **Pattern Four** were shaped by the fact that at the time of the collapse of the communist regime, government was in the hands principally of a nationalist movement. The capacity of these movements to adjust to the transition to real power with the collapse of a federal centre clearly shaped the forms adopted by the respective party systems. In three of the countries (Latvia, Armenia and Croatia) the movement party or a movement party successor was able to win power in the first post-communist election. In Moldova and Lithuania a communist successor party won the first election. In Estonia it was won by a new party, while in Georgia the election produced a fragmented parliament. Only in Croatia was a party able to establish continuing electoral dominance, and this was the movement party which had gained power in the last communist era election. In all other states where there was more than one election, each election brought a change of government and, except for Lithuania where the movement party successor won the second election, this resulted in power being gained by a new party or coalition of new parties.

In the Baltic States, elections have been held regularly, but the party systems have not developed stable competitive structures. In Latvia, the Popular Front, which had held power at the time of the Soviet collapse, began to fragment soon after independence was gained. The accompanying process of party development accelerated with the announcement of the election for June 1993. The election was won by the successor movement party, Latvia's Way Alliance, with almost a third of the vote, but the party system remained fragmented; a further seven parties crossed the threshold to gain representation. The level of fragmentation is even more marked in light of the fact that some 34% of voters were disenfranchised because of the rules relating to citizenship (see p. 165–6), most of whom were Russians. The continuing fragmentation of party competition is reflected in the relatively low votes received by the largest party in the second and third elections and by the closeness of those vote tallies with those of a number of other parties: in the 1995 election the proportions of votes received by each of the top four parties ranged from 12.0% to 15.2%, while in the 1998 election the votes of the top five parties ranged from 12.95% to 20.79%. Only LWA has been able to maintain a position near the top of the vote-gathering list, and even support for

Table 4.22 Party system data for Latvia, Lithuania, Estonia, Moldova, Georgia, Armenia and Croatia

Country, movement, party, elections	% votes, largest party	% votes, two largest parties	No. of parties over threshold	No. of parties in legislature	Largest parties (in terms of votes)	Government
Latvia Popular Front						
1st election 6/93 (PR, 4% threshold)	32.9	46.5	8	8	LWA, LNC, NHP, LFU, ERM, FFF, LCD, ADP[147]	New party LWA (PF successor) and historical party LFU coalition.[150]
2nd election 9–10/95 (PR, 5% threshold)	15.2	30.2	9	9	DP, LWA, NML, FFF, LUP, UL, LNC, NHP, LSP[148]	Broad new party coalition: DP, LWA, FFF, LUP, LNC, LFU, LCD, Greens[151]
3rd election 10/98 (as for 9–10/95)	20.8	39.3	6	6	PP, LWA, NHP, FFF, SDA, NP[149]	Broad new party coalition: LWA, FFF, NP, SDU
Lithuania Sajudis						
1st election 10/92 (mixed, 4% threshold)[152]	44.0	65.2	4	9	LDLP, HU, CDP, SDP[154]	Successor communist party
LDLP[157]						
2nd election 10/96 (mixed, 5% threshold)[153]	31.3	41.4	5	14	HU, CDP, LDLP, CM, SDP[155]	New party coalition: HU (Sajudis successor) and CDP[158]

(continued)

Table 4.22 (continued)

Country, movement, party, elections	% votes, largest party	% votes, two largest parties	No. of parties over threshold	No. of parties in legislature	Largest parties (in terms of votes)	Government
3rd election 10/00 (as for 10/96)	31.1	50.7	4	16	SDC, NU-SL, LU, HU-LCT[156]	New party coalition: LU, NU-SL, CU and CDU[159]
Estonia Popular Front 1st election 9/92 (PR, 5% threshold)[160]	22.0	35.6	7	9	FU, CPRU, ECP, M, ENIP, FP, BE[161]	New party coalition: FU, M and ENIP[164]
2nd election 3/95 (as in 9/92)	32.2	48.4	7	7	CPRU, ERP, ECP, FU, M, OHE, RWP[162]	New party coalition: CPRU and ECP[165], and later CPRU and ERP
3rd election 3/99 (as in 3/95)	23.6	39.6	7	7	ECP, FU, ERP, M, CPRU, CPP, UPP[163]	Broad new party coalition: FU, ERP, M
Moldova Popular Front 1st election 2/94 (PR, 4% threshold)	43.2	65.2	4	4	DAPM, SP, P-IB, CDPFA[166]	Communist successor DAPM[169]

(continued)

Table 4.22 (continued)

Country, movement, party, elections	% votes, largest party	% votes, two largest parties	No. of parties over threshold	No. of parties in legislature	Largest parties (in terms of votes)	Government
2nd election 3/98 (as for 1994)	30.1	49.3	4	4	CPM, DCM, BDPM, PDF[167]	Movement party-led coalition DCM, BDPM, PFD[170]
3rd election 2/01 (PR, 6% threshold)	49.9	63.3	3	3	CPM, BEAB, PPCD[168]	CP successor-led government
Georgia Round Table						
1st election 10/92 (mixed, no threshold)	20.4	31.1	—	23	PB, 11OC, NDPG, UB, DP, GP[173]	Appointed by president; not responsible to parlt.
2nd election 11–12/95 (mixed, 5% threshold)[171]	23.7	31.7	3	10	CUG, NDPG, AGUR[174]	CUG-led, not responsible to parlt.
3rd election 10–11/99 (mixed, 7% threshold)[172]	52.0	78.5	2	?	CUG, AGUR[175]	CUG-led, not responsible to parlt.

(continued)

Table 4.22 (continued)

Country, movement, party, elections	% votes, largest party	% votes, two largest parties	No. of parties over threshold	No. of parties in legislature	Largest parties (in terms of votes)	Government
Armenia Armenian Pan-National Movement						
1st election 7/95 (mixed, 5% threshold)[176]	42.7	59.6	5	7	RB, SWP, CP, NDU, UNSD[177]	Movement party successor RB[179]
2nd election 5/99 (as for 7/95)	41.7	53.8	6	10	M, CP, RU, ARF, CL, NDU[178]	Movement successor: M[180]
Croatia Croatian Democratic Community						
1st election 4–5/90 (SMC)	42	77	–	5	CDC, LCC[181]	Movement party – CDC[185]
2nd election 8/92 (mixed, 3% threshold)	43.2	60.7	7	8	CDC, CSLP, CPR, CPP, SDP, CFP, Bloc, SPP[182]	Movement party – CDC[186]
3rd election 10/95 (as for 8/92, 5% threshold)	45.2	63.5	5	5	CDC, OEA, CSLP, SDP, CPR[183]	Movement party – CDC[187]
4th election 1/00 (as for 8/92)	47.0	77.5	3	6	SDP-CSLP, CDC, cps[184]	New party coalition SDP-CSLP + 4 centrist parties

this party has fluctuated (32.9%, 14.7% and 18.5% in 1993, 1995 and 1998, respectively). Support for the other parties has also fluctuated considerably. Attempts were made to bring about some consolidation of the party system in 1994–95 through the construction of broad left and right parliamentary blocs, but these alliances fractured in the lead up to the 1995 election.[188] An electoral bloc was formed in 1996, and in the 1998 election a reduced number of parties crossed the threshold, but, as the figures above show, the votes remained fairly evenly shared among the top five parties. There has been little stability of party competition except for the position of the LWA.

Few parties in Latvia have been designed to appeal to particular constituencies, the Latvian Farmers' Union being the only one with an obvious sectoral appeal, although this only contested the first election in its own right; it was part of the United List in 1995. The disenfranchisement of the Russian population eliminated one potential basis of sectoral party support. The most successful party, the LWA, appeared reluctant to change from a movement party to a more tightly focused programmatic party. The parties do not appear to have developed strong roots in the populace, with none able to sustain stable levels of support across the three elections, while eleven new parties have appeared during this period. Uniquely, support for parties which did not cross the electoral threshold has not fallen in Latvia: 10.9%, 12.2% and 12.1%. Turnout levels fell but have remained the highest in the Baltic region. Thus although there does not appear to be a strong link between parties and particular constituencies, popular support for the electoral process has not palled in the way it has elsewhere. Nor have elites sought to go beyond the party system, thereby implicitly affirming that they see value in its maintenance, even given the instability of many individual parties.

Lithuania seemed unique among post-Soviet states because at the time of independence it seemed to have the germ of a stable party system with strong bodies on both the left and right. On the left was the communist party successor LDLP, which had split from the CPSU in 1989 and supported the push by the movement party Sajudis for independence. On the right was the ruling Sajudis. However strains began to appear in Sajudis once independence was achieved, and these increased after the LDLP's electoral success in 1992. The result, in part, of this was the fragmentation of the party system in Lithuania, as shown by the large increase in the number of parties gaining representation in the parliament in the second (1996) election and by the drop in support for the two largest parties. While some parties showed some stability in their vote (CDP 12.6% and 10.4% and SDP 6.0% and 6.9%), the vote of the two largest parties fluctuated quite considerably: LDLP 44.0% and 10.0% and HU 21.2% and 31.3%. Indeed, the collapse of the LDLP vote in 1996 upset what many saw to be the consolidation of this classic left–right divide that had seemed implicit at the time of independence.[189] The apparent stability reflected in the fact that all four of the largest parties in 1992 were among the largest five in 1996 was belied by the restructuring of the party system evident in 2000: none of the four leading parties in 2000 was in the same form it had been in 1996, even though this was in part a function of rebadging and new coalition arrangements. What this election also showed was a continuing tendency for significant variation in levels of support of individual parties (eg. the HU vote dropped from 31.3% to 8.6% while the SDC received 31.1% in 2000 compared with the LDLP's 10% in 1996), and the associated fluidity of left–right support. Thus while the left–right division has become established, the levels of support for both sides remain fluid.

The fluctuation in voting support for the apparent major parties and the increased number of parties gaining representation in the second election compared with the first suggests that there is no strong tie between parties and particular large constituencies. The appearance of nine new parties and the disappearance of only one supports this view. There was a decline in voting for parties which did not reach the electoral threshold (from 14.2% to 5.6%),[190] but much of this seems to have shifted to smaller parties rather than consolidating the votes of the larger party groups. This may reflect dissatisfaction with the larger parties, something which is also consistent with the decline in turn out level. A lack of attachment between citizens and much of the party system seems apparent. Two elections are insufficient to enable a robust judgement about the stability of the party system, but the magnitude of the changes in electoral support between these elections and the changing party identities in 2000 suggests a significant degree of fluidity within a more broadly stable left–right division.

Estonia too has seen considerable fragmentation, in part because of strains within the Popular Front. Like Latvia, at no election has the combined vote for the two largest parties constituted a majority of the electorate. However in each election in Estonia, one party has emerged clearly as the front runner, with two parties falling some way behind but with similar votes: 1992 FU 22.0%, CPRU 13.6% and ECP 12.2%; 1995 CPRU 32.2%, ERP 16.2% and ECP 14.2%; 1999 ECP 23.4%, FU 16.1% and ERP 16.0%. In the lead up to the 1995 elections there seemed to be some consolidation in the centre of the political spectrum,[191] but the effect of this was offset to some extent by the emergence of the Our Home is Estonia electoral alliance based on the Russian part of the population. There was further restructuring of some parties in 1996[192] but there were still seven parties which exceeded the threshold in 1999. To the extent that four parties have been prominent in all elections (FU, CPRU, ECP and ERP), there has been significant stability in the system.

Over the three elections there was significant variation in support for the individual parties. With the bulk of the votes going to the centrist parties and with few policy differences between them,[193] distinct popular constituencies do not appear to have come into existence. This is consistent with the polls which show that Estonian voters place little reliance on the parties in deciding who to vote for, preferring to make their decisions on the basis of the identity of the candidates.[194] The proportion of votes going to parties not achieving the threshold fell (14.6%, 12.7% and 8.4%) but so too did the turn out level. There does not appear to be a close attachment between particular parties and popular constituencies in Estonia, but there has been some stability in the identity of the leading parties.

In Moldova, the party system has shown little evidence of stability over the two post-communist elections that have been held. Party structures have been weak with little organisation.[195] Party support had become more fragmented, with seven parties sharing 84.1% of the vote in 1998 compared with four sharing 91.9% in 1994 and support levels for the leading parties dropping until the 2001 election when the leading party gained almost half the vote, although the remainder of the vote was splintered among other parties. None of the four leading parties in 1994 gained representation in their own right in 1998; only CDPFA gained representation as part of DCM, while the leading party in 1994, DAPM, saw its vote drop from 43.2% to 3.7%. However the leading vote getter in 1998 was also the leading party in 2001, but this was the only party from two years earlier which gained representation in the new parliament. The party system shows little stability and shallow roots in the broad populace.

The party system in Georgia has remained highly fragmented, with most parties lacking grassroots organisations and a defined social interest base.[196] In 1995, 54 parties and blocs participated in the election, with only three exceeding the threshold. In 1999 for the first time Shevardnadze's CUG won a majority of the vote, but this seems to have been based overwhelmingly upon popular support for him personally. The growth of an effective party system has clearly been hampered by the civil conflict and the consequent unstable situation, with the result that the party system itself is unstable and not rooted firmly in society more broadly. The personality-based nature of the CUG is consistent with this. The party system remains overwhelmingly an arena of elite activity, with no stable patterns of competition or of interest articulation.

In Armenia, four of the six leading parties which gained parliamentary representation in 1999 had either not been represented in 1995 or had been transformed into new entities, including the largest party. Although the vote for the leading party had been reasonably stable, overall there was some fragmentation of the party system; support for the two leading parties decreased, while the number of parties exceeding the threshold and gaining representation both increased. Armenian parties are very small, based overwhelmingly on powerful individuals and their networks, and cast their public appeals on a broad national basis rather than to different social constituencies.[197] The system has not become stabilised into a regular pattern of party competition.

In Croatia, the leading party was able to maintain its position of dominance and its share of the vote over the first three post-communist elections, losing power to a coalition in January 2000. Similarly, the top five parties in 1992 were also the top five in 1995, and the votes of most (CSLP dropped by a third) did not vary greatly from one election to the next, although in 1995 the CPP was present only through its involvement in the OEA. In 2000 the top four party groups remained the same, although the components of the alliance of minor parties did undergo some change. The party system in Croatia seems to have attained some stability, although the results in 2000 suggests that the CDC's electoral support was heavily reliant upon Tudjman and may now dissipate. Given the prominence of some of the same parties over successive elections, at least some of the parties in Croatia may have come to represent relatively stable constituencies.[198] Few new parties emerged. However electoral turn out did drop.

In the countries of **Pattern Five**, with the exception of the Kyrgyz Republic which has lacked effective parties, the development of the party systems has been shaped in part by the way in which at the time of the fall of communism, power was shared between elements of the old regime and movement parties. Despite the similarity of the starting point, different patterns have emerged.

There has been no real consolidation of the party system in Russia, even though the CPRF has been able to maintain its position among the most popular parties over all three elections. The LDPR, a new party (although it was set up with money from the former ruling communist party), was the biggest party in the first election, the second biggest in the second election, but if the electoral figures are accurate, only scraped in to the Duma in the third election in the form of the Zhirinovsky Bloc. The emergence of a system of regularised party competition has been hindered by the circumstances precipitating the 1993 election (the president's unconstitutional closure of the parliament) and by the concentration of power in the presidency, which has undercut some of the rationale for the development of parliamentary parties. Also important has been the creation of parties from within the executive, OHR in 1995 and Unity in 1999. Both were focused on individuals (respectively Chernomyrdin and Shoigu/Putin), as was the third largest party in 1999, OVR (Luzhkov and Primakov). There has been significant fragmentation of the party system, as reflected in both the increase in numbers of parties competing in elections and gaining parliamentary representation, and in the fact that in the first two elections the two largest parties gained only just over a third of the national vote, and in the third election they fell short of gaining a majority.[223] There has also been a big turnover in parties; of the 43 competing in 1995, 35 did not contest the election in 1993.[224] Nor have party memberships been stable: between 1993 and 1995 103 of the 450 Duma deputies changed parties, while between December 1995 and the organisation of the Duma in early 1996, 100 changed their party affiliation.[225] The large number of parties standing in elections has also meant significant vote wastage; in 1993 the proportion of votes for parties which failed to attain the 5% threshold was 8.0%, but in 1995 this was 49.5%. While there has been some consolidation at the parliamentary level through the reduction in the number of parties exceeding the threshold and gaining representation, there is still significant fragmentation in terms of parties gaining support but failing to win party list seats.[226] Although some parties in Moscow have moved toward a programmatic basis (and these include the LDPR and CPRF – see p. 155), a stable national party system has not emerged.[227]

There has been little stabilisation of any relationship between party and particular constituency,[228] despite evidence of some correlation between parties' policies and supporters' attitudes.[229] Certainly in all elections the policy positions of some of the parties have been reasonably distinct; Russia's Choice/Democratic Russia's Choice, Yabloko, the LDPR and perhaps the CPRF (although the message of the CPRF was actually tailored to different audiences), and all offered strong programmatic (as opposed to charismatic; although again there is a qualification with regard to the LDPR) choice.[230] But the weakness of the link between program and party in the voters' minds is suggested by the performance of Unity in 1999.

Table 4.23 Party system data for Russia, Ukraine, Slovenia and Macedonia

Country, movement, party, elections	% votes, largest party	% votes, two largest parties	No. of parties over threshold	No. of parties in legislature	Largest parties (in terms of votes)	Government
Russia						
Democratic Russia 1st election 12/93 (mixed, 5% threshold)[199]	22.9	38.4	8	12	LDPR, RC, CPRF, WR, AP, Yab, PRES, DPR[200]	Non-party, headed by new party RC chief
2nd election 12/95 (as for 12/93)	22.3	33.5	4	23	CPRF, LDPR, OHR, Yab[201]	Non-party headed by OHR chief
3rd election 12/99 (as for 12/95)	24.3	47.6	6	13	CPRF, U, OVR, URF, Yab, Zhir[202]	Non-party.
Ukraine						
Rukh 1st election 1994[203] (SMC, no threshold)	12.7	*		15	CPU, R, PPU, SPU[205]	Appointed by president[207]
2nd election 3/98 (mixed, 4% threshold)[204]	24.7	34.1	8	8	CPU, R, SPPB, G, PDP, H, PSP, SDP[206]	Appointed by president
Slovenia						
Demos 1st election 4/90 (mixed)[208]	17.3	31.8		9	PDR, LD, CDP, SPP, DPS, GS, SDP, SPS[210]	Movement party Demos[214]

(continued)

Table 4.23 (continued)

Country, movement, party, elections	% votes, largest party	% votes, two largest parties	No. of parties over threshold	No. of parties in legislature	Largest parties (in terms of votes)	Government
2nd election 12/92 (PR, 3% threshold)[209]	23.5	38.0	8	8	LD, CDP, ULSD, SNP, SPP, DPS, GS, SDP[211]	New[215] party coalition led by LD with CDP and ULSD
3rd election 11/96 (as for 12/92)	27.0	46.4	7	7	LD, SPP, SDP, CDP, ULSD, DPP, SNP[212]	New party coalition led by LD with SPP and DPP
4th election 10/00 (as for 11/96)	36.3	49.1	8	8	LD, SDP, ULSD, SPP, NSCPP, DPP, SNP, PSY[213]	New party coalition led by LD with ULSD, SPP and DPP
Macedonia IMRO[216]						
1st election 11–12/90 (SMC)	22.0	42.4	–	6	IMRO, LCM-PDR, PDP, ARF[218]	Government of 'experts'; then PDP-led coalition
2nd election 10–11/94 (SMC)	48.3	72.4	–	9	SDUM, LP, PDP, SPM[219]	Communist successor SDUM led coalition with LP and SPM[221]
3rd election 10–11/98 (mixed, no threshold)[217]	28.1	53.2	–	6	IMRO, SDUM, PDP, DA, LDP[220]	IMRO-PDP coalition[222]

Note: * Only about 25% of candidates had a party affiliation.

Formed a couple of weeks before the election, lacking clear policy positions and closely associated in the popular mind with the prime minister Putin, this gained nearly a quarter of the votes. But the weakness of the connection between parties and voters is reflected in the proportions of voters voting for a party in 1995 who also supported that party in 1993: CPRF 37%, LDPR 59%, Yabloko 33%, Agrarians 29%, RDC 55% and Women of Russia 31%.[231] This shows that, for most parties in 1995, a majority of its supporters had not supported it in the earlier election.[232] Stable attachments have therefore not been made, and support for parties has fluctuated significantly; for many small parties, the bulk of the votes they received were for the party leader him/herself in the territorial constituency in which they stood.[233] Unusually for the region, the electoral turn out increased between 1993 and 1995 (54.8%, although there is doubt about this figure and 64.4%), reflecting the unusual circumstances of the 1993 election, before dropping back slightly in 1999. No stable pattern of party competition has emerged, despite the consistent strong showing of the CPRF.

In Ukraine, the largest party in both elections was the communist party successor CPU, although in the first parliament 202 of the 450 deputies were non-party; in the opinion of one observer, this was probably because voters were unaware of the different parties' programs.[234] Parliamentary politics was therefore very fluid and based upon a series of blocs organised for the most part after the balloting had been completed. Following the second election, there had clearly been a strengthening of party positions generally with only 41 deputies unaffiliated and fewer parties in the parliament, but this had been associated with a proliferation of parties rather than a consolidation; 22 parties, receiving 34.3% of the vote, failed to reach the 4% threshold. Apart from the ethnic/regional factor which has seen considerable stability throughout the independence period (see p. 166–7), there appears to have developed no clear linkage between parties and constituencies; indeed, in 1994, party labels were not used to assist voters.[235] Levels of party identification among voters have been low,[236] with one observer arguing that voters have tended to support deputies on a clientelistic (support in return for individual benefits) rather than a programmatic basis.[237] The party system has remained weak and highly fluid with no stable patterns of competition.

There does appear to have been some consolidation in Slovenia. One party, Liberal Democracy, was the second largest party in the first election, coming in behind the reformist communists, and the largest in all subsequent elections (gaining a similar level of support in the first two and increasing it substantially in the third). Furthermore three of the top five parties in the first election remained in the top five in all subsequent elections, including the reformed communists (PDR/ULSD). The dissolution of the initial electoral bloc Demos in December 1991 did not, therefore, lead to the sort of fragmentation that accompanied the dissolution of such umbrella organisations elsewhere; the former members of the bloc were able to make their own way as independent parties, suggesting that they had a basis of popular support in their own capacity. There has also been a high level of continuity of parties: of the thirteen which gained votes in 1990, eight competed in the 1996 elections. There has been some fluctuation in the votes wasted on parties that did not achieve the electoral threshold – 7.8%, 12.8% and 9.5%. Although there has been a drop in voter turn out over the four elections, this has remained high.[238] This consolidation is consistent with a growth of stability of association of parties with constituencies.

In Macedonia, no clear patterns are visible. However the continuing importance of the communist successor LCM-PDR/SDUM is evident, as is the comeback of IMRO in 1998 after it did not run in 1994. There was a reduction in support for the leading parties in 1998. However here too there was considerable fluidity in the identity of the parties; only two of the five largest parties in 1998 were present in that capacity in 1994. The only party able to sustain an impact across both elections was the PDP, which was primarily Albanian. There is little sign of stability in the Macedonian party system.

In the **Pattern Six** countries power initially was seized by the second echelon of the old regime. This fundamentally shaped the course of party system development and was partly responsible for the absence of an effective party system in Azerbaijan, Belarus, Kazakhstan, Tajikistan, Turkmenistan and Uzbekistan.

In Romania, a communist successor group won the first election and a fragment which split off from that won the second. But in the third election, an opposition movement party formed in February 1992 and comprising 18 organisations, was victorious before the former communists returned in 2000. Of those party groups winning over 5% of the vote, only the very small ethnically-based HDU's vote remained relatively stable over the four elections (7.2%, 7.5%, 6.6% and 6.8%). The vote of the communist successors declined significantly, while that of the main opposition group increased by some 50% between 1992 and 1996, but this was reversed in 2000. There has been no crystallisation of parties around defined interests.[267] Even the nationalist vote (except for the Hungarians and the HDU) has fluctuated wildly: the GRP's vote increased from 3.9% in 1992 and 4.5% in 1996 to 19.5% in 2000. The identity of the leading parties has changed at each election. Furthermore although the number of parties gaining representation has fallen, the number receiving at least 1% of the vote has remained relatively stable – nine, 11 and 11 in the last three elections. Electoral turn out has declined but remains high. The system has not become stabilised, although the communists seem to have consolidated their position as the leading political force.

In both republics of the FRY, communist successor parties dominated most of the post-1989 period, winning all elections in Montenegro and all but the last in Serbia. In Serbia, Milosevic's Socialist Party dominated, with its ultra-nationalist ally the Radical Party and the opposition movement party SRM lagging behind until 2000 when the opposition was able to unite and drive it from office. The main parties are nationalist-oriented and leader-centred, including the broad alliance that came to power in 2000. Similarly in Montenegro where the main parties are also leader-centred, the Socialists have dominated with other parties unable to gain a solid position. However the ruling party did split prior to the 1998 election and a fragment came to power. In both states, the president is more important than the parliament, and many parties have come into existence only at election time. In Serbia the pattern of competition was relatively stable and undemocratic until

Table 4.24 Party system data for Romania, Serbia and Montenegro

Country, movement, party, elections	% votes, largest party	% votes, two largest parties	No. of parties over threshold	No. of parties in legislature	Largest parties (in terms of votes)	Government
Romania						
1st election 5/90 (PR, no threshold)[239]	66.3	73.5	–	18	NSF, HDU, NLP[243]	Communist successor NSF[247]
2nd election 9/92 (PR, 3% threshold)[240]	27.7	47.7	8	8	DNSF, DC, DP, RNUP, HDU, GRP, SLP, ADP[244]	Effective communist successor DNSF[248]
3rd election 11/96 (as for 9/92)	30.2	51.5	6	6[241]	DC, SDPR, SDU, HDU, GRP, RNUP[245]	Movement party DC in coalition with SDU[249]
4th election 11/00 (as for 11/96)	36.6	56.1	5	5[242]	DSP, GRP, DP, NLP, HDU[246]	Successor party coalition DSP[250]
FRY						
Serbia						
Serbian Renewal Movement[251]						
1st election 12/92 (mixed)[252]	28.8	51.4	–	9	SPS, SRP, Depos[253]	Communist successor SPS[260]

(continued)

Table 4.24 (continued)

Country, movement, party, elections	% votes, largest party	% votes, two largest parties	No. of parties over threshold	No. of parties in legislature	Largest parties (in terms of votes)	Government
2nd election 12/93 (PR)	36.7	53.3	7	7	SPS, DMS, SRP, DP[254]	Communist successor SPS in coalition with ND[261]
3rd election 9/97 (PR)	34.3	62.4	7	7	SPS, SRP, SRM[255]	Communist successor SPS[262]
4th election 12/00 (as for 9/97)	64.1	77.8	4	4	DOS, SPS, SRP, PSU[256]	New party coalition DOS[263]
Montenegro 1st election 12/92 (PR, 5% threshold)	42.6	55.3	5	5	DPMS, PPM, LAM, SRP[257]	Communist successor DPMS[264]
2nd election 11/96 (PR)	51.2	76.8	5	5	DPMS, NUC, LAM[258]	Communist Successor DPMS[265]
3rd election 5/98 (PR, 3% threshold)	49.5	85.6	5	5	FBL, SPP, LAM, DAA, DUA[259]	Communist successor FBL[266]

the ousting of the Milosevic regime at the end of 2000. There has been less sign of stability in Montenegro.

Analysis of the emergent party systems in the post-communist states in terms of their success in achieving a degree of stabilisation yields the following results:

- Some evidence of stabilisation: Poland, Hungary, Bulgaria, Albania, Czech Republic, Slovakia, Lithuania, Estonia, Croatia, Slovenia, Serbia.
- Little evidence of stabilisation: Latvia, Moldova, Georgia, Armenia, Russia, Ukraine, Macedonia, Romania, Montenegro

The division of the different states in this way makes the distinction between the two categories sharper than it actually is. For example, the results of the last two elections in Georgia and Ukraine does show some stability of the position of the leading parties, but the parties themselves are so weak as organisations (they have little relevance in the chamber and the number of non-party candidates, especially in Ukraine, remains high) that it would be misleading to say that the system had stabilised. Similarly in Macedonia, the absence of IMRO from the second election obscures what otherwise would have been significant continuity. And in Lithuania what appeared to be developing as a stable situation was cast into doubt by the most recent election. On the other side, in many of those countries which are shown as having made progress toward stabilisation, the two leading parties regularly gain much less than half the total vote: only in Albania, Bulgaria, Croatia and Serbia have the two leading parties won a majority of the votes at each election. Furthermore where there has been fragmentation of parties, minor shifts in electoral support can produce a different constellation of leading parties and thereby a different impression of the system's stability. But even given these reservations, the above categorisation is sufficiently robust for our purposes.

The stabilisation of the party system seems to be linked to the institutional form adopted for the new political system. All countries in which the party system has achieved a measure of stabilisation are either parliamentary or semi-presidential in form (the institutional structure is discussed further in Chapter Five) while five of the nine with little evidence of stabilisation have been presidential; only Latvia and Macedonia are parliamentary. This suggests that where the parliament is a major arena of meaningful political activity, there is a greater tendency for parties to become consolidated in order to strengthen their capacity for action, and the system to thereby become stabilised.

There may also be a link with the fate of the former ruling communist parties. These parties suffered one of three fates following the collapse of the old regime: substantial reformation in a social democratic direction, refusal to change and marginalisation, or rejection of major change and consolidation as a significant actor in the new political system. Which of these paths was followed was shaped to a considerable degree by the outcome of the initial post-communist election. Where the party did very badly, it tended either to be reformed or marginalised; where it did well or was not challenged because the election was not truly competitive, it tended to eschew internal change and was able to remain as a major

160 *Creating civil society?*

actor.[268] Of the thirteen countries in which the former ruling communist party has been either reformed (Estonia, Hungary, Lithuania, Macedonia, Poland, Slovakia and Slovenia)[269] or marginalised (Armenia, Croatia, Czech Republic, Georgia, Kyrgyz Republic and Latvia), nine had stabilised party systems. Of the twelve where the communist party was not reformed, only four had stabilised party systems, and only one of those, Bulgaria, is a democracy. But it is not clear that there is a causal relationship between these two factors, stabilisation of party system and fate of communist party. Rather, both seem to be a result of the pattern of regime change and the capacity of old regime forces to maintain their position in the face of opposition.

The stabilisation of the party system is part of the issue of the more general development of civil society. This will be taken up after discussing one factor which can impede civil society development, ethnic difference.

The ethnic issue

The creation of a civil society can be profoundly influenced by ethnic questions. Paradoxically, the conditions of civil society development can facilitate the emergence of forces which are, at base, antithetical to the growth of civil society and democracy. Such forces are intolerant, divisive, and usually seek to replace a culture of compromise and agreement with one emphasising unity on the basis of a particular set of (usually exclusivist) principles. Nationalism is often identified as such a force, but a distinction needs to be made here between two types of nationalism, civic and ethnic.[270] Nationalism is a means of defining membership of a particular community. Civic nationalism usually defines that membership in terms of attachment (usually through residence) to the state; ethnic nationalism defines it in terms of ethnic identity, of belonging to a group defined in ethnic terms. The former is inclusionary, compatible with individual rights, and sympathetic to democratic arrangements. The latter is exclusionary, subordinates individual rights to collective rights, and is not conducive to democracy. Ethnic conflict and tension usually accompany ethnic nationalism.

There are two main aspects of the ethnic issue which are relevant. First, the outbreak of ethnic conflict. Many observers believed that, with the collapse of communism and especially given the crucial role played in this by ethnic factors,[271] the former communist world would be wracked by ethnic conflict. It was assumed that, with the collapse of the communist value system, people would be searching for another source of identity and would find this in ethnicity. Given the patchwork of ethnic identities that existed across the former communist world,[272] the perception of a history that was marked with ethnic antagonism and the problematic nature of many of the borders, it was assumed that the rise of such identity-based politics would lead to conflict on a wide scale. And such conflict has occurred. Bitter civil wars have been fought in Yugoslavia (Kosovo), Tajikistan, Russia, Moldova, Georgia and Albania, while conflict has occurred between Serbia and Croatia, Serbia and Bosnia-Herzegovina, and Armenia and Azerbaijan. In socio-political terms, the onset of war is usually accompanied by pressures for increased discipline in society, a development which not only suppresses dissident activity and criticism of the government, but also limits the development of the sort of public politics essential for civil society. In this way, conflict can inhibit the development of civil society forces and stunt the growth of civil society. This has clearly been evident in Tajikistan, Serbia, Moldova, Georgia, Armenia, Azerbaijan and Albania, where incumbent elites have sought to use military conflict to hinder the growth of opposition forces. In Bosnia-Herzegovina, the conflict so completely shaped the course of development as to render analysis of the role of other factors in the course of that development meaningless. It has been much less marked in Russia, where the conflict was limited in its territorial coverage and a long way from the major urban centres, and Croatia where the war occurred right at the start of the period and was relatively brief in duration. In those countries identified as having been significantly affected by war, the development of NGOs has been limited, press freedom restricted, and viable democratic party systems have yet to emerge. These characteristics are not attributable to war alone, being shared by some states which did not experience such conflict, but the fact that all of those countries experiencing war could be thus characterised suggests a link.

Such ethnic-based conflict, or at least conflict between groups which could be distinguished on ethnic grounds (Albania and Tajikistan are partial exceptions here, with the wars waged less on ethnic than on political and clan bases), is the most extreme manifestation of ethnic differences. But in many parts of the region where there was no such military conflict, ethnic differences within countries have created tensions and problems.[273] This is the second aspect of the ethnic issue relevant to civil society creation. The essential relevance of this for the creation of civil society lies in two factors: the extent to which ethnic difference generates different definitions of what the relevant societal unit is, and therefore the degree to which different parts of the community see themselves as belonging together in a single state, and the way in which ethnic difference and tensions are handled. Central to this question is the ethnic composition of the state.

It is clear that in a range of these countries, the ethnic dominance of the titular nationality could in no way have been construed to be under threat from minority nationalities: Albania, Armenia, Azerbaijan, Belarus, Bulgaria, Croatia, Czech Republic, Hungary, Lithuania, Poland, Romania, Russia, Slovakia and Slovenia. In the other countries, the ethnic balance was more delicately poised. In three countries, a still substantial titular nationality was confronted by a number of much smaller national groups: Georgia, Turkmenistan and Uzbekistan. In a number of other countries, the titular nationality was confronted by a minority (although in Kazakhstan it was a majority; although by 1998 official figures claimed Kazakhs were in a majority) population with one (in Moldova two) major ethnic group dominant in it, and, given the size of the titular nationality, sometimes perceived by it as a potential challenger: Estonia, Kazakhstan, Kyrgyz Republic, Latvia, Macedonia, Moldova, Tajikistan and Ukraine.

While these ethnic patterns may constitute the raw material of ethnic conflict, they do not of themselves produce such conflict. Roeder exaggerates when he says that 'the larger the ethnic minority relative to the core (majority or titular)

162 *Creating civil society?*

Table 4.25 Ethnic composition in % in 1989[274]

	Titular nationality	Second nationality		Third nationality	
Albania	96	3	Greek		
Armenia	93	3	Azeri		
Azerbaijan	82	7	Russian	5	Armenian
Belarus	79	12	Russian	4	Polish
Bulgaria	86	9	Turkish	4	Roma
Croatia	77	12	Serb	1	Bosnian
Czech Republic	94	3	Slovak	2	Roma
Estonia	62	30	Russian	3	Ukrainian
Georgia	70	8	Armenian	6	Russian
Hungary	96				
Kazakhstan	43	35	Russian	6	Ukrainian
Kyrgyz Republic	54	28	Russian	15	Uzbek
Latvia	52	34	Russian		
Lithuania	80	9	Russian	8	Polish
Macedonia	65	22	Albanian	5	Turkish
Moldova	64	14	Ukrainian	13	Russian
Poland	98				
Romania	88	9	Hungarian		
Russia	82	4	Tatar	3	Ukrainian
Slovakia	82	11	Hungarian	5	Roma
Slovenia	91	3	Croat	2	Serb
Tajikistan	62	23	Uzbek		
Turkmenistan	73	10	Russian	9	Uzbek
Ukraine	73	22	Russian		
Uzbekistan	71	8	Russian		
FRY	62	17	Albanian	5	Montenegran
Serbia	63	14	Albanian	6	Montenegran
Montenegro	62	15	Moslem	9	Serb

nation, the more likely it was that conflict would erupt.'[275] Of the twelve countries where minorities constituted more than 25% of the population in 1989, only in the FRY, Georgia and Moldova has ethnic-based military conflict broken out. While, as indicated the other nine countries may have experienced ethnic tensions and differences, these have been kept within the bounds of civic politics. What is important for the likelihood of ethnic conflict is the relationship between ethnic groups, the degree to which these different groups perceive themselves in ethnically-exclusivist terms, the institutional mechanisms established to structure access to the political system on the part of minority ethnic groups, and the political stances taken up by political elites.[276] This means that even in countries where the titular ethnic group's dominance is not under threat, ethnic issues may become politically relevant.

The countries in which ethnic issues have played little role include most of those where the titular nationality in 1989 constituted at least 80% of the population. In some of these countries, individual issues relating to ethnic matters have arisen from time to time, but have not dominated the agenda. For example, in the Czech Republic the definition of citizenship in a way that many thought discriminated against the Roma and actions undertaken by local authorities which discriminated against the same group, in Hungary the emergence of nationalist parties the Hungarian Life and Way Party and the Smallholders Party, and in Poland the appeal to nationalist sympathies in the 1990 and 1995 presidential elections, all reflect a politics in which nationalist/ethnic issues became salient, although in none of these cases has this become the dominant mode of discourse and none has a significant minority ethnic party.[277] In Albania, despite a law forbidding ethnically-based parties, the Greek population has gained representation through Omonia, later the Unity Party of Human Rights. But the position of the Greeks has not been a major political problem. More important has been regional and tribal differences among the Albanians, which helped to structure the low intensity conflict of 1997. In Slovenia the 1989–91 tension with Serbia and the subsequent conflicts near its borders helped to consolidate a sense of community and identity. Provision was made for the special representation of Italian and Hungarian minorities in the parliament, but not for Serbs and Croats. Lithuania's Russian and Polish populations are neither geographically concentrated nor represented by their own major parties (neither the Russian Union nor Electoral Action for Lithuania's Poles has gained majority support from their respective target populations), but the inclusive nature of Lithuanian citizenship provisions ensured that these groups, despite complaints about the treatment of their cultures and languages, were conceived of as part of the polity.

In Bulgaria ethnic issues became prominent in the years before the collapse of communism when the Zhivkov regime waged a campaign to force the Turkish section of the population to integrate into the larger Bulgarian part. This was unsuccessful, but did create significant resentment among Turks while highlighting for Bulgarians the salience of this issue. When a range of constitutional amendments and new laws on elections and political parties were introduced for the June 1990 elections, ethnic or religious parties were banned, a ruling which severely restricted the primarily Turkish-based Movement for Rights and Freedoms which was allowed to participate only after a ruling by the Constitutional Court. During the lead up to the October 1991 election, local attempts were made to ban the MRF on the basis that it was an ethnic party, but these were overturned by the Supreme Court, and the MRF was the only party to increase its vote. The MRF enjoyed the balance of power in the parliament, until the UDF government fell and was replaced by a government of technocrats. As further parties developed, the MRF lost its pivotal role, but it was nevertheless able to act as a symbol and a representative of the Turkish minority, which seems to have accepted that it had a part to play within the Bulgarian polity.

In Russia, nationalism has not been a major force, even though its appeal did underpin the electoral performance of the Liberal Democratic Party in 1993. It has been an object of appeal for many groups in the political spectrum, but has not shaped the political landscape. Some issues have been prominent which have touched a nationalist nerve, most importantly the fate of Russians in the 'near abroad', but even this has not aroused political passions. The most important way in which ethnic concerns have been politically important has been the relationship between the centre and the ethnically-based subdivisions of Russia. Much of this has been resolved at the constitutional level (including the Federal Treaty of 1992), with the obvious exception of Chechnya, which has resulted in wars on two occasions, 1994–96 and 1999–2000. But even here, the effect has not flowed over into the political system as a whole. In this sense, national issues have not been a prominent feature of political life. In part this has been a function of the way in which the Russian state adopted a civic rather than an ethnic definition of citizenship, and, by inheriting the Soviet administrative structure, provided an identifiable state form for many of its major ethnic groups.

In four states the position of ethnic minorities has been a major factor in political life. In Moldova early pressure stemming from within the Moldovan Popular Front to unite with Romania was blunted by the adoption of a new constitution in March 1993 under the leadership of former communist party first secretary Lucinschi. This was confirmed by popular referendum in March 1994. More troublesome than the question of relations with Romania, and in part stimulated by that issue, was that of the position of ethnic minorities within Moldova, especially the Russians of Transdnestr and the Gagauz.[278] Both of these groups had begun to mobilise in 1990, in response to the raising by the MPF of the possibility of unification with Romania. In January 1990 the residents of the Transdnestr capital Tiraspol declared independence, a stance taken by the whole region in the September. In October and November elections were held in both Transdnestr and the Gagauz region, and anti-Moldovan deputies were elected. In March 1991, in contrast to Moldova as a whole, both regions participated in Gorbachev's referendum on the future of the union, and both supported it. Both regions also boycotted the presidential election which brought Snegur to power in December 1991. Conflicts had broken out in these regions during the year, as para-military groups supported by the old 14th Soviet army acted to protect Russian interests in Transdnestr. In summer 1992 the Moldovan authorities sent troops into Transdnestr, but they were soon defeated by the rebels supported by the former Soviet forces. A ceasefire ensued and, following the rejection of the possibility of unification with Romania, a new constitution was introduced (July 1994) which guaranteed minority rights and autonomous status for Transdnestr. However this did not satisfy local inhabitants, who pressed for independence; in December 1995 a referendum declaring independence was approved by 82% of the region's population. The authorities in Chisinau declared this to be unconstitutional and, following negotiations, Transdnestr was accorded republican status within Moldova. So the Transdnestr issue was clearly a major one in Moldovan politics, with the population of that region for a considerable time rejecting membership of the Moldovan polity. The state of uncertainty which prevailed between these two regions clearly affected the course of Moldovan politics and hindered the growth of a republic-wide sense of political community.

The question of identity and membership of the new state's political community was also an issue in Estonia. As in Moldova, the ethnic Russian portion of the population was geographically concentrated, in Estonia in the north-east. This group consisted mainly of recent immigrants, who had entered Estonia only during the Soviet period since the end of the war and had not sought to integrate on a large scale with the local population; five years after independence, some 60% of Russians still lacked a working knowledge of the Estonian language and saw measures to strengthen that language[279] as a threat.[280] The citizenship law introduced in 1992 was highly restrictive, stipulating a residency period (initially effectively three years, in 1995 extended to five years), linguistic competence and an oath of allegiance. Furthermore only citizens could vote in national elections, and since the residency requirements were to date from 1990, the Russian population was effectively disenfranchised; in the 1992 election, all 101 seats in the parliament were held by ethnic Estonians. In May 1993 non-citizens were barred from standing in local elections (although they could vote). They were also unable to form social movements with political objectives. This meant that almost a third of the population was restricted in its ability to participate in national political life. The response among the Russian community was a strengthening of sentiment in favour of increased autonomy; in a referendum in the Russian dominated towns of Narva and Sillamae in late 1993, on a low turnout 98% voted for autonomy.[281] Over time, numbers of Russians have been able to gain citizenship, and Russian parties have been able to participate at the national level, most importantly Our Home is Estonia/ United People's Party. However Russian parties remain weak; in the 1995 national election, only about one-third of the 18% of Russian speakers in the electorate voted for Our Home is Estonia,[282] and this coalition gained only six seats and was highly factionalised;[283] a Russian party (United People's Party) also won only six seats in 1999. In the face of reluctance on the part of the Estonian political establishment to change the citizenship provisions, Russian political organisations have been able to bring about little improvement in the political status of the Russians.[284] The continued lower sense of attachment to the Estonian polity is reflected in the lower levels of trust in and positive evaluations of Estonia's political institutions among Russian speakers than Estonian speakers. In 1996 the views of these two constituencies differed (see Table 4.26).[285]

The strong sense of community among the population in north-east Estonia and the continued recognition of its distinctiveness from the Estonian population, has continued to pose a major barrier to the development of a sense of common political community throughout the republic.

In Latvia, where the titular nationality was in an even weaker demographic position than the Estonians, the Popular Front of Latvia called for the 'decolonization' of the country through the departure of Russians, and enacted a similar citizenship law to Estonia which limited this to pre-1940 inhabitants and their descendants. Naturalisation was also restricted by the passage of a new law in July 1994 which imposed an effective quota on the number of non-Latvians who could become citizens in any one year; there was also a ten-year residency requirement. This policy of ethnic exclusion has meant that Russian political organisation in the republic has been quite weak. Non-citizens have been unable to participate even in local elections. It also has meant that Latvian nationalism has been an acceptable mode of discourse for many of the other parties, although this has not taken on an extreme form. Part of the reason for this may be that Russians are much more spread throughout the country (and the Latvian people) than they are in Estonia,

Table 4.26 Political orientations in Estonia

		Estonian speakers	Russian speakers
Present system of government			
	Positive	69	49
	Negative	21	41
Government	Trust	62	39
	Little/no trust	38	60
President	Trust	78	49
	Little/no trust	22	50
Parliament	Trust	54	35
	Little/no trust	45	65
Civil servants	Trust	40	16
	Little/no trust	59	84
Media	Trust	57	63
	Little/no trust	43	37
Parties	Trust	16	13
	Little/no trust	84	87

Table 4.27 Political orientations in Latvia

		Latvian speakers	Russian speakers
Present system of government			
	Positive	37	30
	Negative	45	55
Government	Trust	47	36
	Little/no trust	53	64
President	Trust	67	56
	Little/no trust	33	44
Parliament	Trust	32	32
	Little/no trust	67	68
Civil servants	Trust	36	28
	Little/no trust	63	71
Media	Trust	69	60
	Little/no trust	31	40
Parties	Trust	14	15
	Little/no trust	85	85

and they are more socially integrated and more speak the language,[286] and therefore they are less identified as a coherent and potentially irredentist group. Nevertheless native Russian speakers remain less wedded to Latvian institutions than Latvian speakers, as the following figures for 1996 show:

While the level of Russian attachment to Latvian institutions is higher than that of their counterparts in Estonia and closer to the levels of Latvian speakers, the gap between the two remains significant and shows that a sense of a single Latvian political community does not exist.

Creating civil society? 167

In Ukraine, the ethnic balance differs considerably from that in Estonia and Latvia, but the Russian minority remains substantial. However unlike the two Baltic states, many of the ethnic Russians had been resident in part of Ukraine for centuries, so there was not the same sense of recent arrival which did so much to fuel the charges of 'colonization' which were so common in parts of the Baltic region; indeed, many Russians even claimed they were indigenous to the region in which they lived.[287] There are regional concentrations of the different ethnic groups: the west and centre are primarily Ukrainian-speaking, while the east is Russian-speaking and highly urbanised and in the south there are Russian-speaking cities and an inactive Ukrainian peasantry.[288] What is important about this regional basis is that it reflects not just an ethnic division but a linguistic one also; in the more Russian inhabited east and south, local Ukrainians speak Russian, with the result that language is more accurate as the marker of division than ethnic origin.[289] But unlike in the Baltics, there have been no legal restrictions on the participation of Russians in the political system. In October 1991 citizenship and voting rights were given to all residents,[290] no restrictions were placed on political activity by non-ethnic Ukrainians, and liberal laws were established on party formation and association more generally. As a result of this more inclusive approach, Russians, and Russophone Ukrainians who have been an important segment of the population,[291] have not felt the sort of exclusion which elsewhere has fuelled resentment and alienation. Nevertheless, these ethnic divisions have been manifested in electoral results. In the 1994 presidential election, 75% of Ukrainian-speakers supported Kravchuk and 75% of Russian-speakers supported Kuchma.[292] In the parliamentary election, leftist parties, including the CPU, were strongest in the heavily industrialised, primarily Russian east, while 'national democratic' forces were strongest in the west; the centre was split between the two. This regional division has not been consolidated into a firm boundary between the different communities, but it does mean Ukraine has a series of local party systems rather than a national system.[293] Despite differences with Russia over such issues as Crimea, the Black Sea Fleet, nuclear weapons and fuel supplies, the Ukrainian political elite does not appear to have been worried about the possibility of split loyalties on the part of ethnic Russians in Ukraine. Similarly, hard line Ukrainian nationalists have been unable to capture the agenda in Kyiv. Despite what many saw as high potential for ethnic-based trouble in an independent Ukraine, such issues have not been a major factor in the course of political life.

In the other states, an important feature of national life has been the way in which titular national elites have sought to play upon and emphasise nationalism to consolidate their own political base, but often at the expense of minority nationalities. In two countries, Armenia and Azerbaijan, this nationalist populism has stemmed from the conflict and tension between these states and been directed against opposition forces more generally rather than just minority ethnic groups. In Azerbaijan, the Nagorno-Karabakh conflict and the associated economic difficulties and refugee crisis was instrumental in the fall of Mutalibov and Elchibey's acquisition of power, and was used as an excuse by the latter to crack down on the media and opposition forces. Setbacks in the fighting later precipitated Elchibey's

168 Creating civil society?

fall. In Armenia too the conflict and associated difficulties helped to shape the political agenda, increasing the tension between Ter-Petrossian and the Armenian Revolutionary Federation, and the subsequent suspension of the latter. The Nagorno-Karabakh issue also led to the break up of the ruling Republican Bloc in 1998. Nationalism centred on the Nagorno-Karabakh issue was thus an important factor in the structuring of national politics and the suppression of the opposition. Elsewhere in the Caucasus region, ethnic issues have been instrumental in generating civil war. In Georgia there have been major problems with secessionist forces in Abkhazia and South Ossetia. Fighting broke out in both regions in 1992, in response to the drive (beginning in 1992) by local elites to secede from Georgia, exacerbated by the nationalising policies that the Georgian Gamsakhurdia regime sought to impose. The military struggle went badly for the Georgians, especially in Abkhazia from which their forces (and many ethnic countrymen) were expelled, and with the introduction of peacekeepers the fighting ceased, but did not bring these regions back under the control of the Tbilisi government. As a result the political process in Georgia had to develop with the cloud of ethnic hostilities hanging over it.

In the FRY war based on ethnic difference was also significant. The drive by the Milosevic regime first to unite all Serbs in Slovenia, Croatia and Bosnia-Herzegovina under Belgrade's rule and then to cleanse Kosovo of ethnic Albanians meant that Serbian forces were in the field for much of the 1990s. The effect on Slovenia was negligible, but the conflict with Croatia[294] and the subsequent Croat intervention in the Bosnian conflict provided a significant fillip to the nationalism espoused by Tudjman. Indeed, it was this nationalism which became the chief symbol and mode of political discourse for the Tudjman regime. In Serbia, the relentless emphasis upon Serbian nationalism was used by the regime to promote Serbs at the expense of other ethnic groups, and to consolidate the regime's control by suppressing opposition movements. Such suppression could not be successful at all times, as shown by the campaign against Milosevic's refusal to recognise the results of local elections in 1996 and after the end of the NATO bombing in the Kosovo conflict. But the consolidation of central control was facilitated by both the threat and reality of Balkan conflict. In Macedonia, long-held concern about and on the part of the Albanian minority was heightened by the Kosovo conflict, but Albanians were able to participate in the political system through their own parties, the Party for Democratic Prosperity and the National Democratic Party; the former became a partner in government in 1998. However the Constitution has continued to emphasise Slav supremacy, public service jobs have remained largely closed to Albanians, and Albanian has not been recognised as an official language in the parliament, the courts or the public service. There has been a significant sentiment favouring autonomy among the Albanians,[295] and this provided the basis for armed clashes on the border with Kosovo in early 2001.

Similar to Croatia, nationalism was used as an instrument for the building of popular support by Meciar in Slovakia. His MDS had guided Slovakia into independence on the basis of a program of nationalism, centralism and economic dirigism.[296] Following the MDS' return to government in October 1994 in alliance with the Slovak National Party and the Association of Slovak Workers, the government tried both to centralise power even more in its hands and to reward its supporters. This was accompanied by a vigorous campaign directed against the Hungarian and Roma minorities; with its two coalition partners on the extreme right and left, Slovak nationalism was the unifying element in the government's agenda. Nationalist parties in Slovakia were able to play an influential role in the government before Meciar's fall in 1998, with the protection of notions of Slovak national interests and honour against non-Slovaks a key theme in political life. Following Meciar's fall, pressure on the rights of minorities eased considerably.

In Romania, where the problem of Hungarians in Transylvania was long-standing and had been a factor triggering the toppling of the Ceausescu regime, nationality politics was evident in the formation of a party to represent Hungarian interests (the HDU) and a range of nationalist Romanian parties. The activity of the latter in particular helped to maintain ethnic tension at a discernible level, especially after they became partners in government in late 1994–early 1995; the Party of Romanian National Unity wanted to ban the HDU on the grounds that it was an ethnic party. The nationalist populism fostered by such parties continued to alienate the Hungarian minority and fuel broader fears about possible irredentist pressures (and a favourable local response) from within Hungary itself. The success of the Greater Romania Party in 2000 can only exacerbate this situation and ensures that the ethnic factor remains a continuing element in Romanian political life.

In the Central Asian states, all of which have substantial national minorities, state power has been wielded in such a way as to prevent the emergence of any major expressions of minority nationalities' sentiment. All governments have emphasised the historical and cultural traditions of the nations they claim are the antecedents of the current states (including Islam, with the exception of Kazakhstan[297]), and have implemented a range of measures to give priority to the titular nationality and its culture.[298] Although all denizens of these countries were given citizenship and voting rights at the point of independence, the capacity of national groups to participate effectively has been undercut by restrictions on their organisations and their ability to function in the public sphere.[299] Instead that sphere has been dominated by a nationalist populism focused on the titular nationality and in particular its leader whose political position has been consolidated upon such national mythology.[300]

A contrast to this national populism designed to consolidate an independent state has appeared in Belarus. Initially there was a major attempt to establish a national mythology which established the independent origins and history of the Belarusian people.[301] However following Lukashenka's election as president in 1994, he pressed for the reunification of the country with Russia, and a series of steps were made toward this end. Despite a level of popular opposition to this, the Belarusian leadership continued to champion it, in effect denying the existence of a native Belarusian nationalism.

The ethnic issue has thus had an impact upon the capacity of the post-communist countries to generate a genuine sense of national civic identity which could provide the under-pinning of a civil society. The exclusivist nature of nationalist populism has constituted a major barrier to the emergence of a sense of a political community which embraced all groups within the country. Instead it projected a sense of community which was ethnically exclusivist and therefore hostile to the participation of certain sections of the population in political life and it emphasised the way in which one part of society was linked intimately with the state (which is the obverse of the conditions for civil society) and the other part was excluded. In three of those countries where the position of substantial minority groups has been an issue, the result has been an ethnically-divided polity; in Estonia and Latvia the minority nationality has refused to accede to the essentially discriminatory demands of the majority in order to gain full access to the polity, while in Moldova the minority rejected the very idea of such inclusion. In Ukraine, the Russian minority has gained inclusion within the polity, and acts simply as one of the cleavages structuring political life. In a final group of countries, ethnic identity has not been a major barrier to the development of a sense of over-arching political identity embracing all citizens of the state. It is in this final group that the prospects for civil society development have been least hindered by ethnic factors.

What does all of this mean for the creation of a civil society? The existence of civil society is to be found in the patterns of action which characterise the public and political life of a community and those patterns cannot accurately be captured by looking alone at the institutional structures which facilitate such activity. Nevertheless, although the existence of these institutional structures does not guarantee the growth of a civil society, it is unlikely that civil society could exist without them. These institutions are: an inclusive conception of the political community which enables all sections of the population to participate equally; a substantially free press to provide a vehicle for public debate and discussion; a range of autonomous organisations to facilitate participation in public life; and a stable party system to provide systematic representation of interests and the accountability of political elites to the populace. Based on the analysis above, a number of the post-communist states seem to have a favourable institutional infrastructure for civil society development:

- Press freedom: Czech Republic, Estonia, Hungary, Latvia, Lithuania, Poland, Slovakia, Slovenia
- NGOs: Bulgaria, Croatia, Czech Republic, Estonia, Hungary, Latvia, Lithuania, Poland, Romania, Russia, Slovakia, Slovenia
- Party system: Albania, Bulgaria, Croatia, Czech Republic, Estonia, Hungary, Lithuania, Poland, Serbia, Slovakia, Slovenia
- Pol. Community: Albania, Bulgaria, Czech Republic, Hungary, Lithuania, Poland, Russia, Slovenia

Five countries score highly on all of these aspects of the development of what may be called a civil society infrastructure: the Czech Republic, Hungary, Lithuania, Poland and Slovenia. All of these countries also have high levels of privatisation (although this is less the case for large enterprises in Lithuania, Poland and Slovenia) and in three of the five (Czech Republic, Hungary and Lithuania) the method of privatisation did not favour insiders. These are five of the six countries which have been classed as democracies. The sixth is Bulgaria and the area of civil society development in which it appears deficient is press freedom. The Freedom House evaluation of press freedom in Bulgaria has it as 'partly free'. This seems to be based less on a judgement about editorial independence than upon state control of major printing and distribution outlets.[302] Because ownership diversity and editorial independence are the key factors in the projection of a wide diversity of views, and therefore of a vigorous public opinion, and because these exist in Bulgaria, the state's putative role in printing and distribution may not be a major barrier to the growth of a vibrant civil society in that country. So all of those countries which are democracies have been characterised by the growth of civil society infrastructure; they all had substantially free media, a dense network of NGOs, a generally high level of privatisation, a reasonably stable party system, and a developed sense of inclusive political community.

The façade democracies rank in very different ways on these criteria. Estonia ranks highly on three of these civil society infrastructure aspects, but is lacking in the sense of political community, because of the place of the Russian minority. This is consistent with its designation as an ethnic democracy. The other two ethnic democracies, Latvia and Moldova, are also deficient in this respect, but the strength of the remaining civil society infrastructure is much greater in Latvia than in Moldova. The former ranks higher in terms of press freedom and has a denser network of NGOs, but in neither has the party system become stabilised. Slovakia was also lacking in a sense of political community because of the stance taken by the Meciar government, although this changed with that government's ouster, but, like Estonia, the other struts of a civil society infrastructure have been in place. Albania only has two aspects of this infrastructure well-developed, a stabilised party system and a sense of political community, although the regional division in the country may qualify the sense of being a single community. The network of NGOs in the country remains weak while the press has oscillated between being partly and not free. In Romania, only a dense network of NGOs is present, although the media has consistently been classed as partly free and, despite attempts to muzzle some media outlets at some times, has been able to promote public debate. Although the Romanian party system has not become stabilised, it has enabled vigorous competition for power and been the vehicle through which change of government has been brought about. The dense network of NGOs plus vigorous party conflict and a partly free media, allied to elite commitment to play by the rules of the game, seem to have been sufficient to push the country to democracy. Croatia and Russia are lacking in two of these struts. The media in both countries is classed as partly free but, despite official pressures at times, has been a major source of public exposure and debate. In Croatia the sense of political community has been lacking, chiefly because of the populist nationalism espoused by Tudjman, and it is not clear, especially in the light of the 2000 election results, that ethnic concerns are structurally significant in the community. The party system in Russia remains unstabilised, and its future may depend upon the contours the political system adopts under a Putin presidency. In the façade democracies levels of privatisation have generally been lower and the favouring of insiders more apparent than in the democracies.

Three of the façade democracies (Georgia, Macedonia, Ukraine) lack all four elements of civil society infrastructure, but in all three the media has been classed as mostly partly free. Of those countries classed as non-democracies, only Serbia appears on this list as possessing any component of civil society infrastructure, and this is because a 'competitive' party system dominated by the ruling party has become stabilised. In all of the other non-democratic countries, civil society development has been retarded, although in Armenia and the Kyrgyz Republic the media has consistently been classed as partly free and Armenia does have a significant network of NGOs. But the Armenian party system lacks stability and populist nationalism has been an important weapon of regime-building. In the other countries the media has been non-free, there has not been a competitive party system, NGO development has been weak, privatisation least developed, and (perhaps with the exception of Belarus) populist nationalism has been used to consolidate power.

While the fit is not exact, the broad pattern is clear. Where civil society is most developed, the state has assumed a democratic form; where civil society is weakest, non-democratic political forms have been evident. The façade democracies fall between both in terms of civil society development and political form. As argued in Chapters 2 and 3, initial political forms were shaped by the circumstances of regime change. Where civil society forces were strongest at the time of regime crisis, democracy was the likely outcome. Where state elites could ignore civil society forces, non-democratic regimes emerged. The subsequent development of civil society forces, which was itself affected by state action (see Chapter five), served in most cases to consolidate the patterns set in train at the time of regime change. The strengthening of civil society in the democracies reinforced those democracies, including placing limits on the autonomy of elite action; a free press, an active sphere of public debate, the right of independent organisation, and the strength of opposition parties all posed a constraint upon ruling elites. The weakness of civil society in the non-democracies enabled the elites to play out their politics in the ways they saw fit and with little popular involvement. In the façade democracies the partial development of civil society forces could exert some pressure on elites, but this generally was insufficient to overturn existing patterns of politics. In the six countries identified at the beginning of the chapter as having shifted between regime types (Belarus, Azerbaijan, Georgia, Romania and perhaps Croatia and Slovakia), the state of civil society development has been important in shaping those changes. In Belarus the shift in an authoritarian direction was made possible by the capacity of those in control of the state to roll over weak opposition from within society. In Azerbaijan the apparent shift from closed to open oligarchy and back to closed oligarchy also reflects the relationship between state and civil society forces: when state control was weakened by the consequences of military setbacks, civil society forces could force a change, but this was overturned when the old political elite was able to restabilise itself. In Georgia, plebiscitary democracy gave way to closed oligarchy as a result principally of the failings of the former, and then shifted back to plebiscitary democracy under the impact of a forceful political personality with civil society forces playing little part. Romania, which seemed to be on track towards closed oligarchy, became a democracy as a result of the use of the electoral weapon by opponents in society. A similar force has been at work in the unfinished[303] shift of Croatia from plebiscitary democracy and Slovakia from open oligarchy towards full democracy. All three countries had a dense network of NGOs and a media which was either free or partly free.

So civil society development has been important in shaping regime forms principally through strengthening the regime types established at the time of the fall of communism. But as all of these cases suggest and those of Azerbaijan, Belarus and Romania highlight in different ways, the role of civil society forces must be seen in relation to the role of the state. This will be discussed in the following chapter.

5   Paths to democracy?

The role of civil society has clearly been central to the trajectories of the post-communist states. But the recent history of these countries has also been moulded by decisions taken by political leaders with regard to economic reform and political institutional arrangements.

Economic reform

One of the most common themes in the study of the growth and consolidation of democracy has been the relationship with economic development. A number of aspects of this are significant for the question of the political trajectories followed by the post-communist states. What is particularly important here is the combination in the former communist world of political change with economic transformation. All former communist states publicly adhered to a policy of fundamental transformation of the economic system, moving away from the centrally-directed command structure of the classic communist model in the direction of a more market-based economic system, at least initially. The speed and extent of economic change potentially had two immediate consequences for the course of political development:

a) The full implementation of marketising reforms, it was assumed, would create a new layer of winners who would constitute a solid support base for the democratic reformers. These would include, but not be restricted to, those gaining property as a result of the policies of privatisation and who thereby would constitute the sort of private interests which often are seen as providing the base for democratic politics (see Chapter 4).
b) It could cause such disruption and hardship as to render the government highly unpopular. Under such circumstances one might expect democratically-elected governments to avoid economic reform or, having introduced it, to be ejected from office at the subsequent election and its successor to pull back on economic change. This would be a recipe for one-term reforming government and the subsequent erosion of reform.[1]

These questions are important for the shaping of the trajectories of the post-communist states. What is the experience of those states?

Paths to democracy? 175

The former communist countries (excluding FRY) can be listed in rank order in terms of the progress made in economic reform by 1995.[2] This is referred to as the scope of economic reform and refers to the extent to which change has been brought about in the different sectors of the economy. The following rank ordering has those where change has been greatest at the top and least at the bottom:

1 Czech Republic, Hungary
2 Estonia, Poland, Slovakia
3 Slovenia
4 Lithuania, Kyrgyz Republic
5 Latvia, Croatia
6 Russia, Moldova
7 Macedonia, Romania, Bulgaria
8 Albania, Uzbekistan
9 Ukraine
10 Armenia, Belarus, Kazakhstan
11 Georgia
12 Azerbaijan, Tajikistan
13 Turkmenistan.

Also important is the speed of recovery from the periods of economic dislocation which accompanied economic change. In terms of the recovery of the economy following the imposition of economic reform, two measures have been used. First, the year when the economy stopped contracting, and second, the year when inflation fell to double figures (see Tables 5.1 and 5.2). Both are very rough measures, not only because of the dubious nature of some of the economic statistics, but also because improvements were not without hiccups: the economy in Albania experienced negative growth in 1997, Bulgaria 1996–97, Croatia 1999, Czech Republic 1997–99, Estonia 1999, Kazakhstan 1998, Latvia 1995, Lithuania 1999, Moldova 1998–2000, Romania 1997–99, and Russia 1998, and Bulgarian inflation again achieved three figure levels after dropping to two in 1993. Nevertheless, these measures do give some sense of the way in which different economies picked up following the serious downturns they experienced at the time of the introduction of economic reform.

Although there is not an exact correspondence between the scope of economic reform, the speed of economic recovery, and the type of political regime, there is clearly a relationship. All of the non-democracies with the exception of the Kyrgyz Republic have been lagging in the scope of economic reform and most have been slow to recover. All of the democracies with the exception of Bulgaria have been in the vanguard of economic reform, along with Estonia, Slovakia (whose reforms began before the break up of Czechoslovakia) and the Kyrgyz Republic, and many of these countries experienced rapid recoveries, especially the Czech Republic and Poland.[5] There is no dominant pattern for the façade democracies. What does this mean?

While the association of the democracies with deeper and faster economic reform and the non-democracies with a slower pace is consistent with arguments about a

Table 5.1 First year of economic growth (when change in the GDP ceased to be in the negative)[3]

1992	1993	1994	1995	1996	1997	1998
Poland	Albania	Armenia	Estonia	Azerbaijan	Moldova	Turkmenistan
	Czech Rep.	Bulgaria	Georgia	Belarus	Russia	
	Romania	Croatia	Lithuania	Macedonia	Tajikistan	
	Slovenia	Hungary		Kazakhstan		
		Latvia		Kyrgyz		
		Slovakia		Uzbekistan		

Note: Ukraine achieved positive growth in 2000.

Table 5.2 Price rises of consumer goods: year they dropped to double figures[4]

1991	1992	1993	1994	1995	1996	1997
Czech Rep.		Albania	Croatia	Macedonia	Armenia	Tajikistan
Hungary		Bulgaria	Latvia	Kyrgyz	Azerbaijan	Turkmenistan
Poland		Estonia	Lithuania	Moldova	Belarus	
Slovakia		Slovenia		Romania	Georgia	
					Kazakhstan	
					Russia	
					Ukraine	
					Uzbekistan	

link between democracy and the market, this link is not the one usually identified in the literature. Rather than a market system generating democratic politics, the post-communist case is one where the political regime has introduced marketising reforms, and those reforms have been carried furthest and fastest in the more democratic states.[6] It is therefore the preferences of the political decision-makers for economic reform and the commitment to carry such reform through which are crucial, although the fact that such reform has gone furthest in the democratic polities is consistent with the argument that the shift in a market direction helps to stabilise democratic politics. But this also means that another of those accepted arguments is subject to question.

Many have argued that radical economic reform, which would of necessity impose considerable hardship on large numbers of people, would not be introduced by a democratic government but instead required authoritarian rule, the so-called 'firm hand'.[7] Others have suggested that, should a democratic government introduce such measures, it would lose office and those reforms would be wound back.[8] The evidence from the post-communist states is inconclusive in this regard. As Joel Hellman has shown,[9] those countries in which economic reform has been most far-reaching have had more frequent executive (prime minister or president) and government turnovers than those where reform has been more retarded. This means that, in practice, those politicians who have enjoyed a shorter tenure of office have introduced more far-reaching reforms than those whose tenure has been longer.

This has not been true in all cases, as the experience of the Klaus government in the Czech Republic demonstrates, but this tendency does suggest that fear of retribution through the ballot box (a fear which has been well founded) has not generally been a significant retardant to economic reform. Moreover even in those cases when a reformist government has been replaced by one less enthusiastic about such reform, there has been no wide scale winding back of reform. Certainly large scale privatisation was slowed in Lithuania and Poland following the election of the communist successor party and voucher privatisation was delayed in Slovakia after the break up of Czechoslovakia,[10] but nowhere was reform put into reverse following the ousting of the original reformers.

So the course of economic development in these countries, both in terms of the scope of economic reform and the speed of recovery from it has not had an independent effect upon the shaping of the political regime. Decisions about economic reform were made either during the last stages of the communist regime's crisis (e.g. in Russia) or after the regime had fallen and initial political arrangements had been set in place. In this sense, the economic arrangements were a function of the political imperatives rather than vice versa. It may be the case that the course of economic reform has strengthened certain forces favouring democratic politics. The creation of a private sector generates interests which may see their future better served by a set of open political arrangements than some sort of exclusionary, closed politics, but the effect of this would need to be tempered by recognition of the way in which economic difficulty can also stimulate extremist, anti-democratic politics. In any case, there is little evidence that in the non-democracies economic reform has stimulated the development of pro-democracy forces. The primacy of political imperatives seems clear.

The quest for marketising economic reforms in all of the post-communist countries is the result of a number of important considerations. One is the evident failure of the command economic system as it had been established in these states. It is clear that economic decline throughout the region was an important factor in bringing on regime change. This was a decline which was widely interpreted as being one which could not be arrested through mere tinkering. The time for that had passed, and there was wide assent to the view that what was required was something more than minor adjustments to the structure. In looking for viable alternatives, would-be reformers needed to look no further than the economies of the West. While many of these had been experiencing difficulties in the 1970s and 1980s, their performance was still seen as being superior to that of the communist world, with the result that the paradigm of a market economy came to dominate the thinking of political elites in all the newly post-communist countries. Certainly sections of those elites in each country had considerable reservations about organising the economy along market lines, especially in terms of the inequality and economic hardship that that would involve, but some of this feeling was related more to the means of introducing the market than of the market itself. Despite the reservations, few in leading positions in these countries offered realistic alternatives to a market-based economy. Furthermore for some of those political elites which acquired power with the regime change, a market system appeared as an effective means of destroying the power of the old structures and limiting the scope for independent activity on the part of unelected bureaucrats. In this sense, marketisation was seen as a political tool for the consolidation of the new order and the destruction of the old. This commitment to a market economy did not mean that elites wanted to see their countries become replicas of 'the West', although they did want what they saw as a 'normal' political system and way of life, characterised by democracy and high living standards.[11] Indeed, elites in much of the FSU in particular were adamantly opposed to a perceived 'Westernising' outcome. But a more efficient economy was the aim of all, and this was seen overwhelmingly in market terms.

However for some countries, the market was not the only consideration. For many of the countries of ECE, a market economy was only part of the process of returning to what they saw as the European mainstream. Particularly for Poland, Hungary, the Czech Republic, Slovenia and perhaps to a less extent Slovakia, Bulgaria, Croatia and Romania, the communist period was seen as an interregnum, dividing them off from the broad sweep of European history of which they saw themselves intrinsically part. For them, the collapse of communism was synonymous with a 'return to Europe' (also reflected in the replacement of the term Eastern Europe by East-Central Europe), and rather than being seen in terms of a copying of the West, this was perceived as a reassertion of traditional principles. A democratic political system therefore constituted not just a rejection of communism but an expression of their membership of the common European heritage. 'Democracy' was not just the international hegemonic paradigm which constituted the standard against which all measured themselves in the last part of the century, but the definition of European identity to which they aspired. In a practical sense, this was also the necessary qualification for acceptance into the European club. This was clearly expressed in the terms of the preconditions established for signature of the so-called 'European Agreements': establishment of the rule of law, respect for human rights, the introduction of multi-party democracy, the holding of free and fair competitive elections, and the development of market-oriented economies.[12]

For the countries of ECE, this was an important consideration. It was manifested practically in their desire to join the main institutional structures which united the western part of the continent, the EU and NATO. The drive by the ECE countries and the Baltic states to join these bodies achieved some success with the announced expansion of NATO membership in 1998 to include Poland, Hungary and the Czech Republic, the opening of negotiations between the EU and the Czech Republic, Hungary, Poland, Slovenia and Estonia in 1997 for the entry of these countries into the Union,[13] and the announcement in October 1999 that similar negotiations would open in 2000 with Slovakia, Latvia, Lithuania, Romania and Bulgaria. The aspiration to join these bodies was one factor in the commitment to democratic construction and the choice of a democratic system in the first place. But more directly, the need to be seen to be acting in accord with democratic principles in order to gain the approval and support of the EU states was one factor which moderated domestic political behaviour in some of these states. For example, Western criticism of proposed quotas on naturalisation in Latvia in 1993 and the proposed new and more restricted aliens law in Estonia in the same year led to intervention by the respective presidents and the moderation of both proposals.[14] For those countries which have harboured realistic aspirations to join the European institutions, this sort of pressure and criticism may have been significant at times in helping to shape political action. But this would have been a second order effect, and does not appear to have played a major role in shaping the basic contours of the systems as a whole.

Constitutional engineering

A similar conclusion can be reached with regard to the impact of the nature of the political institutional arrangements on the development of democracy. There is a considerable literature on the advantages and disadvantages of the presidential and parliamentary systems for democratic government.[15] Critics of the presidential system argued that it was likely to facilitate undemocratic outcomes because of the rigidity of the political process it created through the combination of fixed terms and the winner-take-all nature of elections, the way in which it reduced the capacity for the representation of societal interests, the division of authority between executive and parliament, and a fragmented party system. It was believed that the resultant stalemate combined with the concentration of power was likely to increase the likelihood of the resort to non-democratic, perhaps forceful, means of resolving disputes.[16] Proponents of presidentialism argued that in contrast to parliamentarism which dispersed power, presidentialism concentrated it and thereby provided the capacity for decisive leadership and decision-making, enabling the system to cope with difficult situations (and feeding into the arguments about a strong hand) and facilitating stability. It is this supposed capacity for decisive action which is contrasted with the presumed problems that can be created by a strong parliamentary system which can create instability, immobilism and the excessive power of particularistic interests. The argument remains essentially unresolved, although most seem to accept the arguments about the advantages of parliamentarism.[17]

The choice of institutional structure made in the post-communist states illustrates a broadly consistent pattern. Generally, most countries of the FSU opted for a presidential system while those of ECE and the Balkans did not. More importantly, there is a link between institutional form and the nature of the regime (see Table 5.3).

All of the democratic regimes are either parliamentary or semi-presidential in form while all of the non-democracies are either presidential or semi-presidential; façade democracies are spread across all three types.[18] Furthermore most of these countries have retained the basic type of institutional structure established at the origin of the regime, although some have introduced changes. Poland, Lithuania and Belarus began with parliamentary systems[19] and then respectively in 1992, 1993 and 1994 shifted in a presidential direction, while Georgia and Tajikistan both began as presidential, abolished this office during civil war, and reinstated it after the respective conflicts ended. Russia began with a parliamentary-presidential

Table 5.3 Institutional forms and types of political systems

	Presidential	Semi-presidential	Parliamentary
Democracy		Poland Lithuania	Bulgaria Czech Republic Hungary, Slovenia
Façade democracy	Georgia, Moldova Ukraine	Croatia Romania, Russia	Albania, Estonia Latvia, Macedonia Slovakia
Non-democracy	Armenia, Azerbaijan, Belarus Kazakhstan, Kyrgyz Republic Tajikistan Turkmenistan Uzbekistan	FRY	

hybrid system, although this was under dispute, and shifted in a presidential direction in 1993. The other countries retained the initial types of structures basically intact.

Given that most countries have maintained the basic system they began with, the decision about what form of institutional structure was made by the political actors during the phase of regime negotiation discussed in Chapter Two is crucial. The factors structuring those negotiations, and in particular the identity of the elites involved, was fundamental here. In all cases where old regime elites were able to maintain their positions and power (Pattern 6), a presidential, or (in the case of Romania) a semi-presidential, regime was set in place. In all of those cases where non-regime elites resting on civil society forces were predominant (Patterns 1 and 3), parliamentary systems were established. In those cases where the old regime elite transformed itself and negotiated with emergent civil society forces (Pattern 2), a parliamentary system emerged. Where nationalist forces were dominant (Pattern 4), or there was a mix between old regime and non-regime elites (Pattern 5), all three types of system were established. For old regime elites who were able to maintain themselves in power, a presidential system may have appeared as the better option for sustaining their positions.[20] Where a diversity of forces played a part in the negotiations, in most cases either a parliamentary or a semi-presidential system was adopted, both of which ensured a division of power and of spoils between a number of political forces, and therefore seemed better suited than a presidential system to ensuring that no one missed out completely. Where a diversity of interests was involved meaningfully in the discussions, the system established was designed to enable continued access into the system by those forces. It is not an accident that it was in these systems that such access has become consolidated through the stabilisation of the party system.

But in seeking to establish whether the political trajectory of the regime was shaped in a major way by the institutional infrastructure, it is to the period after the regimes' establishment that we need to look. What is most important here is those regimes which have moved in a more democratic or an increasingly non-democratic direction. Romania is a case of the former. Given the circumstances of the Romanian regime transition, a non-democratic outcome in the form of a closed oligarchy seemed most likely. However it has been able to move to a democracy, principally because the old regime rulers permitted the development of parties and the holding of elections which they did not control. Crucial here was the position of the parliament in the semi-presidential system, a position which enabled the opposition to project itself as a viable alternative to the existing rulers. Had this been a presidential system, with a lower status for the parliament, such efforts may have been inhibited. In Belarus, the shift to a presidential system, and with it the consolidation of it as a sultanist rather than a closed oligarchic non-democracy, was brought about under pressure from the president who was able to expand the powers which inhered in that office. So in this sense, the nature of the system (or more specifically the existence of a post of president in Belarus and the position of the parliament in Romania) facilitated the shift of these regimes. In the other cases, the institutional infrastructure may have facilitated the consolidation of the regime on its initial trajectory. In the presidential non-democracies, the post of the presidency has clearly been used to consolidate the position of the leader and to suppress divergent political forces. In the semi-presidencies where vigorous party development has occurred, those independent political forces have acted as a check upon any presidential aspirations, often using the parliamentary institutions to achieve this. Even in some of the presidential systems, like Ukraine, the parliament has been used in an attempt to check expansive presidential power. So the institutional infrastructure has been a factor shaping political development, but it does not generally appear to have had an effect independent of the circumstances of initial regime change.

Development trajectories

It is clear that the different political trajectories followed by the post-communist states have been shaped overwhelmingly by the circumstances of the fall of communism. The patterns of development that have unrolled since 1989/91 have been directly related to those circumstances, producing outcomes which, as at the time of writing, constitute very different styles of political regime. It is these patterns of development and their relationship to the modes of regime change which are the focus of the remainder of this chapter. The crucial factor in shaping subsequent development has been the nature and role played by non-regime forces in the process of regime transition, and the implications that had for the structuring of political life. Important too for the longer term development has been the capacity of such forces to continue to play a role in the post-communist period. This capacity is related not just to the level of development such forces achieved, but also the extent to which state power has been used to frustrate or promote that development. Crucial in the shaping of the political trajectory of each country has therefore been the relationship of civil society forces to the state.[21]

In those countries which experienced Pattern One modes of transition, Poland and Hungary, civil society forces were strong at the time of the onset of regime transition, and were seen as appropriate negotiating partners by that section of the regime elite which believed such negotiations were necessary. In Poland, the position and status Solidarity had achieved as a result of its part in the upheavals of 1980–81 and its capacity to survive in the underground in the intervening period, both of which rested on the basis of substantial popular support, projected it as the most logical interlocutor when the regime elite sought to reach some sort of arrangement with the society. In Hungary, the proliferation of civil society forces, including political parties, stemming from the more liberal Hungarian model of communism threw up an opposition Round Table which was the logical interlocutor for the regime. In both countries, the regime elite believed that, through reaching an accommodation with opposition forces, they could secure some guarantees about their future. The resulting Round Table discussions led to elections which, by delegitimising the ruling communist party, effectively removed it from the political game.

The massive defeat sustained by the communists in Poland was the stimulus for the transformation of that party as reformist communists left their hard line colleagues to form a social democratic party. Similarly in Hungary, the communist party split as reformists left to form the socialist party in preparation for the election which brought to power an alliance of opposition parties led by the movement party, the HDF. In both cases, elections thus removed the old regime from power and put control over the restructuring of the system into the hands of former oppositionists. Furthermore those oppositionists were civil society forces, with their ideological legitimation resting upon broad-based appeals to 'the people' conceived in either democratic or mythologised national terms. Both movement parties (Solidarity and the HDF) were sensitive to the need to foster the growth of a strong civil society. They recognised the need to fashion a robust public sphere and introduced measures which facilitated rather than hindered the growth of both a vigorous press and a diverse range of NGOs. Neither set of rulers took any steps to limit the development of political parties. But the party system that emerged in both countries differed in its course of development. In Poland the principal force in its growth was the fragmentation of the movement party Solidarity, a development which both weakened the power of anti-communist forces and contributed to the fragmentation of the political spectrum. In Hungary, while the HDF did not fragment as severely as its Polish counterpart, in the face of a resurgence of communist support and the strength of other centrist political forces (initially AFD then AYD), its electoral position declined. Importantly in both countries, the reform communists were returned to power in coalition in the second post-communist election, although they lost power at the following election. Nevertheless the communist successor party in Hungary was able to consolidate itself as the largest party, capturing almost a third of the vote.

The emergence of the reform communists as ruling parties in 1993 and 1994 did not change the direction in which the systems had been developing. The democratic rules of the game brokered during the initial negotiations at the time of the collapse of both regimes remained intact, with the reformed communists adhering scrupulously to them. In addition, despite concerns to the contrary, there was no major halting of the radical economic reforms that the new elite had introduced upon coming to power, although large-scale privatisation did slow in Poland following the communists' electoral success.[22] The question of economic reform and its social implications was not therefore, despite the initial hardships in Poland as the big bang strategy took effect, a sufficiently divisive issue as to call into question the basic direction of economic policy set in 1989–90. Nor was there any substantial appeal to populist nationalism, in part because of the integration of the reform communists into the political spectrum (and the associated marginalisation of hard line elements) but also because both countries had a high level of ethnic homogeneity.

So the course of development of Pattern One countries was set firmly on track by the marginalisation of extremist elements, the domination of the political process by civil society forces, and the restrained and essentially limited exercise of state power by successive ruling elites. In Pattern Two countries, Bulgaria and Albania, the course of development was somewhat different. In neither country were civil society forces strongly developed at the time of regime crisis, with the result that a reformist leadership of the communist party was able substantially to structure the emergent political process. In Bulgaria, Round Table talks were held between regime and opposition, but the regime was in a much more powerful position than its counterparts in Hungary and Poland had been. As a result, it was able to have a decisive say in the working out of subsequent arrangements, which the opposition forces broadly accepted. The communist party did not substantially transform itself, although it did change its name, and it was able to win the first and third post-communist elections. In Albania, although there were generally weak civil society forces, when popular mobilisation forced the regime to accede to a multi-party system, a new major competitor did emerge in the form of the DPA. But the new rules of the game were designed substantially by the old elite. In the first election the communist successor party was victorious. Unlike in Bulgaria, the Albanian opposition objected to the way in which the communist successors sought to structure political life but, having brought about the fall of the government and being elected to replace them, the chief opposition party sought to impose an increasingly authoritarian system. The result was the effective collapse of the political system, with the wide-ranging complaints of fraud and the consequent boycott of the 1996 election, and then the descent into violence in 1997.

The key difference here was the greater capacity of civil society forces to emerge in Bulgarian society and to place restraints upon political actors than in Albania. Where political life was rooted in a public sphere resting upon substantial civil society development as occurred in Bulgaria following the regime change in 1989, a stable party system was able to develop and a sense of restraint prevailed. In contrast, in Albania the leading parties felt themselves less constrained to seek to reach compromise or to act in a restrained fashion themselves, leading to a politics in which there was considerable brinkmanship and a significant degree of continuing instability. Whereas in Bulgaria the state was used by successive governing elites to reinforce the emergent rules of democratic politics, in Albania it was used for partisan advantage: restrictions on press freedom, the occasional harassment of opposition, and the manipulation of the electoral process. The continuing role played by barely reformed communists in these two countries also had different effects in the symbolic/policy sphere. In Albania the ethnic dominance of the titular nationality and the absence of earlier conflict over ethnic issues meant that there was little scope for the regime to promote populist nationalism, except insofar as it was directed against the Serbs and in favour of the kin in Kosovo. But this was not a major dividing issue in domestic politics. In Bulgaria, where there was a significant Turkish minority which had been at the centre of political controversy in the last years of communist rule and which directed most of its electoral support to an openly-acknowledged Turkish party, there was scope for the mobilisation of such sentiment. The communist successor regime did indulge in this sort of rhetoric from time to time, and the ethnic issue was used to try to consolidate support, but this did not become a defining element in Bulgarian politics.

Economic reform has also been shaped by the continuing prominence of the communists after official regime change. Major economic reform has been slower to get started in both countries than in those where the old elite was removed from the scene at an early stage. Large scale privatisation did not get under way until 1993 in Bulgaria and 1995 in Albania but, perhaps reflecting the greater difficulties confronted by the Albanian former communists, such reform has moved more rapidly in that country than in Bulgaria. But clearly, the course of development in political and economic life has been shaped substantially by the continuing strength of the barely reformed communists, although in Albania the former opposition must shoulder much of the responsibility for the authoritarian characteristics the regime acquired in the mid-1990s. But even so, Albania has remained an open oligarchy with changes of government occurring through the electoral process.

In the two countries of Pattern Three, the Czech Republic and Slovakia, similar starting points were complicated by the effects of the split of Czechoslovakia and the economic implications that had. In Czechoslovakia, the regime passed from the scene with hardly any prior negotiations with opposition forces, which had been late to gain prominence in an organised form. Power devolved in the two republics to movement parties, which dominated the negotiations about new political forms. Following the initial election, these movement parties found themselves in power, alone in the Czech Republic and in coalition in Slovakia. However once in power, both movement parties began to fragment, spawning a range of centrist and rightist parties which came to dominate the political spectrum. It was the leaders of two of these parties, the CDP in the Czech Republic and MDS in Slovakia which negotiated the splitting of the country.

In both countries, centre-right parties have remained dominant electorally, although in Slovakia following independence the MDS did move substantially to the right. The communists were marginalised by the circumstances of the collapse of the old regime, having effectively dealt themselves out of the game at the outset, a position confirmed by the passage of lustration laws in October 1991. However the course of politics in both countries has diverged sharply. In the Czech Republic, which was more developed and had a stronger tradition of civil society activity than Slovakia, the CDP was able to maintain itself in power despite imposing upon the country rapid and wide-ranging economic reform, so that by the end of 1995 the Czech Republic was judged to have gone furthest of all the post-communist countries in terms of economic transformation.[23] Politics has remained civil and stable. In Slovakia, where the break with the Czech Republic had negative economic effects and where economic difficulty has been deeper and more sustained, the initial ruling MDS sought to base itself on populist nationalism. This was designed both to justify the split and to offset potential popular disaffection arising from economic difficulties. Unlike in the Czech Republic where the titular nationality constituted more than 90% of the population, in Slovakia there was a substantial, politically-active Hungarian minority. This was a perfect foil for the populist nationalism of the MDS and its leader Meciar, especially when in coalition with the Slovak National Party.[24] In this way although the former communists were marginalised, a form of nationalist extremism pervaded Slovak politics. Under Meciar too Slovak economic reform was slower than in the Czech Republic, but it did go faster and further than in many of its neighbours. But the key in Slovakia is that although Meciar held power for much of the decade and he did use the state to project his populist nationalist message, he did not use the state either systematically to suppress civil society or to restrain its development. The press remained subject to some pressure throughout this period and although there was some harassment of opposition, a competitive party system was stabilised, and a dense network of civil society organisations developed. Thus state power was not used to permanently transform the open oligarchy in an undemocratic direction, and therefore away from the trajectory the country seemed to be on at the time of the collapse of communism. So in the Czech Republic and Slovakia, crucial to the structuring of post-communist development was the underlying strength of civil society forces, reflected most clearly in the dominance of movement party successor parties, and the refusal of successive governing elites to use state power to cut down the competitive arena of politics.

In the Pattern Four countries (Latvia, Lithuania, Estonia, Moldova, Georgia, Croatia and Armenia), at the time of the collapse of the federal centre, nationalist movements were in power in what were the republican capitals. Elections held over a year before independence had led to the entry into government of these nationalist forces and, especially in the Baltic republics and Georgia, had discredited communist rule. The consequences of this varied in the different countries.

In Estonia and Latvia, the movement parties which emerged from the nationalist movements used the positions they had attained to structure political life in an ethnically discriminatory way. The definitions of citizenship they imposed, added to the laws relating to political participation, resulted in the injection of the ethnic principle into a central place in political life. This was reflected most clearly in the barriers to effective Russian involvement in politics. The restriction of the political sphere in this way, although it was not a complete closure, does mean that political life was more circumscribed than it could have been and shows the state being used to structure political life in a way which both clearly discriminated against one section of the populace and contradicted the broadly liberal principles upon which the main part of the polity rested. The fracturing of the initial movement party in both countries resulted in the fragmentation of both party systems and the political spectrum more broadly. In both countries the communists were discredited at the time of regime crisis, despite the fact that both parties had split in 1990 over the question of independence, with the result that no communist successor party was able to gain a prominent place in the new polity; indeed, in Latvia the communist party was banned. The absence of old regime elites may be reflected in the pace and extent of economic reform, especially in Estonia which was one of those countries which had gone furthest by 1995 in this regard.[25] The political trajectory of both countries was thus clearly shaped by the way in which one wing of the emergent civil society has used the state to construct an ethnic democracy whose principles severely compromise the basis upon which civil society usually rests.

In Lithuania, the Popular Front government was confronted by a strong successor communist party which had been the first in the USSR to split from the CPSU in 1989 and to take up a pro-independence stance. This meant that it was not discredited in the same way as its sister parties by the collapse of communism, and that in the newly-independent Lithuania it was seen by many as a credible alternative government. The effect of the prominence of the nationalists through the Popular Front was to push the communist successor LDLP in a more nationalist direction and away from the rigidities and style of thinking typical of unreformed parties elsewhere. The LDLP became a genuine social democratic party with a nationalist tinge. Its position was strengthened by the fragmentation of the nationalist movement party Sajudis, with the result that it achieved power in October 1992. It was under its auspices that the new constitution embodying the formal rules of the game was introduced (although it was drafted before the election bringing the LDLP to power). Although there has been some fragmentation of the party system, with the significant increase in parliamentary representation in the 1996 election despite the higher threshold, the leading four parties in the first election also appeared in the leading five in the second. These parties were thus able to create some stability in their identity over time. National exclusivism did not become a major factor structuring political life because the relatively small size of the non-Lithuanian population ensured that the ethnic Russians were not perceived as a threat and neither major party group saw much political advantage to be gained in making this an issue. Despite some slowing of the pace of large scale privatisation as a result of the LDLP victory,[26] radical economic reform did not suffer any serious setback as a result of the former communists' win. Thus when the initial political arrangements were made by civil society forces that, while including a prominent nationalist movement also had many more broadly-based organisations, the outcome was a liberal structure in which none of the political elites sought to use the power of the state to configure that structure to their permanent advantage.

In Croatia, the movement party which held power at the time of the break up of the Yugoslav federation continued to use nationalism to consolidate its position in power. Its success is reflected in the continuing dominance of the Croatian political scene the CDC and its leader Tudjman were able to achieve. To do this they resorted to electoral manipulation, pressure on opposition and the use of nationalism as a unifying symbol. Stable alternative parties were able to emerge and function within the sphere permitted by the regime, but until Tudjman's death they were able to make little electoral impact upon the ruling party. The communist successor party was sidelined. Ethnic difference has been a factor in structuring the political scene, but its effect has been complicated by the conflicts in Bosnia and Kosovo. The largest minority in Croatia at the time of independence was Serbian, and therefore the emphasis upon Croatian nationalism and the discriminatory attitude implicit in that was seen as much in foreign policy terms as an issue about domestic political or economic arrangements. Plebiscitarian democracy thus emerged on the basis of initial movement party hegemony, using state power and populist nationalism to consolidate its dominance. That dominance only slipped when the plebiscitarian leader passed from the scene.

In these four countries where nationalist movements inherited power, the political trajectory has differed. In Latvia and Estonia, the splintering of the nationalist movement party resulted in government by weak coalitions within an ethnically exclusionary polity. Within this context, independent civil society forces were able to generate significant parties which could challenge the government. In Lithuania the splintering nationalist movement party was confronted by a series of consolidated parties, including most importantly the reform communists, with the agenda remaining one relatively unaffected by nationalist considerations. In Croatia, the nationalist movement party was able to consolidate its position in power despite the emergence and activities of a number of other significant political parties. What these countries share is the fact that nationalism did not overwhelm a politics based on non-ethnic, civic foundations. Even where politics has been structured in a fundamental way by the ethnic issue, Latvia and Estonia, within the sphere of acceptable political activity, groups have been able to emerge and play a major political role on the basis of non-ethnic considerations. In this sense, nationalism neither banished from the political scene nor significantly diminished the role of civil society forces. The same cannot be said for the other Pattern Four countries.

In Georgia the increasingly authoritarian approach of the nationalist regime and the attempt to use the state to get rid of its enemies was instrumental both in fuelling the secessionist drive of some ethnic minorities and in bringing about the collapse of the structure of civil politics. As a result, a stable political structure could not emerge, as populist nationalism and the reaction to it skewed the agenda. The restoration of some sense of stability following the end of armed conflict was achieved through the emergence of plebiscitarian democracy which remained prone to use populist nationalism to bolster its position. Civil society forces have remained weak. In Moldova, the agenda was overshadowed for some time by the issue of unification with Romania and the problem posed in particular by the Transdnestr, both of which were influential in the splintering of the nationalist movement party which had inherited power, and in the establishment of an ethnic democracy.[27] The ability of the reform communists to gain power through the ballot box reflects the way in which that party had transformed itself following its rejection in 1990, but in the context of a fragmenting party system, it could not sustain itself in government. Within the ethnically majoritarian political sphere, elite politics has been played out competitively, without sustained attempts to use the state to consolidate a particular group in power, but within a context of weak civil society development. In Armenia, the same successor movement party has been able to retain power but the party system has not become stabilised. Nationalist sentiment has been fanned, but this has chiefly been externally directed as a result of the continuing tension with Azerbaijan over Nagorno-Karabakh. This tension, and the economic hardship that has been the spin off of it, has tended to dominate the political agenda and shape the process of political development. The closed oligarchy that has eventuated has used the state to consolidate itself in power by hampering the development and functioning of opposition political forces. Using the nationalist appeal to define the terrain of politics, the rulers have been able to prevent a potential basis of powerful civil society activity (established network of NGOs, partly free media) from realising itself in civil politics.

The difference between these latter three countries and the initial four is that nationalist considerations have overshadowed the development of a politics based on civic foundations. The appeal to nationalist sentiment and the attempt to mobilise it in partisan causes has functioned very differently in Georgia, Moldova and Armenia to the way it has worked in the other four countries. In Lithuania it played no real role after the fall of the USSR. In Estonia and Latvia it defined the political sphere in an ethnically exclusivist way, but within the majoritarian ethnic political arena, competitive politics based on liberal principles has accompanied civil society development. In Croatia it was used to stabilise plebiscitarian democracy, but this was not so harsh as to destroy either civil society or competitive politics. However in Georgia, Moldova and Armenia it has retarded the growth of civil society forces and the emergence of an agenda immune from nationalist concerns. This type of impact of ethnic nationalism in these countries may be explained by two factors. First, in all three countries ethnic issues brought on armed conflict, in Moldova and Georgia with would-be secessionist nationalities and in Armenia with Azerbaijan. Such conflict was not a function of the size of minority populations (after all the titular nationality in Latvia and Estonia was smaller than in all three of these countries) but of the management of the ethnic issue. An unwillingness to compromise, at least initially, by both minority and majority leaders in Moldova and Georgia was crucial to the outbreak of conflict. A similar situation applied in the Armenian-Azeri conflict and in Croatia, although in both cases the main object of nationalist hostility was outside national borders. In the Baltic states such conflict has not occurred, both communities seeking peaceful ways of dealing with the situation. Second (which also helps to structure the first), the tradition of civil society. In the four countries where civic-based parties were better able to establish themselves, there was a stronger tradition of civil society development prior to the communist period which was also able to survive communist rule. The shorter time these countries were under communist control may be relevant here. This clearly helped such parties to establish a basis independent of the nationalist theme.

In the Pattern Five countries (Slovenia, Russia, Ukraine, Macedonia and Kyrgyz Republic), when the federal centre collapsed, the republican ruling elite consisted of an amalgam of oppositionist and old regime elites. Old regime figures who had adopted a more reformist stance during the last years of communist power held the presidency in Slovenia, Russia, Ukraine and Macedonia, and faced a parliament which comprised an amalgam of old regime functionaries, nationalists and 'democrats'. In the Kyrgyz Republic a figure who had not held an official political position in the old regime became president but the parliament was dominated by old regime forces. In all of these countries, communist parties remained prominent but, except for Slovenia, other parties have found it difficult to establish a stable presence or to generate a consolidated party system. In Slovenia this combination of elements in the political elite did not produce any difficulties, principally because the president (Milan Kucan) had moved close to the position of the opposition which dominated in the parliament. This meant that more hard line elements were essentially sidelined as a succession of moderate rightist coalitions held power in conjunction with Kucan who was re-elected in 1992 and 1997. Political elites played politics according to the emergent rules of the political game and, given the absence of sharp division and conflict and the presence of a powerful civil society, civic politics and a democratic polity resulted. In Macedonia, this initial difference between president and parliament disappeared when, at the first post-communist election in 1994, the post-communist successor party fell just short of a majority but was able to form government in coalition. Even before this, the president Gligorov had usually been able to get his way by building coalitions in the parliament based principally upon the communist successor party. An open oligarchy based upon observance of the principles of civic competitive politics combined with some limited use of the state to manipulate that process resting on a weak civil society basis has been the result. In Ukraine, where powerful party blocs did not dominate in the parliament and the initial president followed policies which appealed to the large conservative section of the parliament, there were little grounds for continuing conflict. In this way the different complexions of the two institutions did not have a major early effect on the structuring of political life. However the dominance of the parliament by uncommitted deputies and the nationalist movement Rukh was an important factor inhibiting the development of mass-based parties. The weakness of the party system added to the underdevelopment of civil society and the emergence late in the decade of differences between parliament and president has enabled successive presidents to use the state to exercise a weak form of plebiscitary democracy.

In Russia, conflict soon emerged between the president and parliament. The former's reluctance to build coalitions with sympathetic elements in the parliament meant that when conflict emerged over policy issues and institutional and personal ambitions, it took a clear cut form of a clash between these two institutions of state. Its resolution by force and the imposition of a new set of constitutional arrangements was the most dramatic instance of the sort of conflict which stemmed directly from the balance of leading political forces at the time of the regime's birth. It also reflected the retarded development of civil society and the willingness of part of the political elite to use the state to achieve its political ends. In the Kyrgyz Republic, the dominance of the parliament by representatives of the old regime inhibited party development, and led to clashes with the president. The clashes led to the crisis of autumn 1994 and, in the subsequent election (February 1995), parties were again too weak to have any real impact. It is clear that the predominance of old regime forces in the parliament has acted as a restraint upon party development in the Kyrgyz Republic. But it is also clear that the weakness of civil society has been significant in undercutting strong party development, as has the tendency of the president to use his position and the power of the state to build up a political machine of parliamentary representatives personally loyal to him and to the state.

In the countries experiencing Pattern Six (Romania, FRY, Azerbaijan, Belarus, Kazakhstan, Tajikistan, Turkmenistan and Uzbekistan), when the centre collapsed, power passed to the second echelon of the old regime. In the countries of the FSU and the FRY, power was held by old regime elites who had been able to control the last election before the federal government fell and to ensure that their control was not challenged by newly emergent independent political forces. These elites then used the power of the state to repress in varying degrees the development of alternative political forces, including breaking up the weak, emergent civil society forces. The usual way of doing this was to rig elections, but the forceful suppression of independent political organisation was also evident.[28] In Azerbaijan, Belarus, Kazakhstan and the FRY, some independent political activity was allowed, but the elite was clearly willing to use coercion when it felt its power was threatened. In Romania, power devolved to a second level of the old regime located principally in the security forces and the party, and although in the early years force was used to put down popular opposition, the regime did allow parties to form and to participate in elections. However the regime did not embark on the fraudulent manipulation of the electoral process to a degree sufficient to ensure its domination of office, with the result that in 1996 it was replaced in office by an oppositionist movement party. In part the weakness of civil society forces at the time of the fall of Ceausescu explains the long period of former communist domination before it succumbed to opposition forces, while the subsequent growth of NGOs and the partly free nature of the press did provide a basis for the growth of opposition forces, especially the Democratic Convention which had sought to unite opposition political forces throughout the country.

While the role of the state has therefore been influential in shaping the political trajectories of these regimes, the sort of independent activity on the part of the state's coercive arms (military, police, security services) so evident in cases of regime change elsewhere, has been relatively absent from the former communist world. Valerie Bunce has argued that the military played an independent role only in Yugoslavia, Albania and Romania, and that this was because during communist times the military in none of these countries was integrated into the WTO and therefore restricted in their capacity to use force by Gorbachev's veto.[29] Even if this argument is accurate for the limited period of the transition,[30] it cannot explain events after the initial transition had ended. Part of the answer here is the tradition of military subservience to the civil power that was inculcated into the communist military establishments. These principles have probably continued to apply even after the fall of communism. Certainly they were reinforced by the statements of civilian politicians, who were generally intent both to assert that control and to avoid creating situations which might provoke the military to act. Generally, autonomous military activity has occurred where civilian processes have broken down (Romania and Albania; in the former Yugoslavia such breakdown occurred only after the military had been ordered into action by civilian elites in some of the former republics) and has tended to be short in duration. It has been followed by the reassertion of civilian rule. So the key has been the maintenance of civilian control and the avoidance of the breakdown of civilian processes. This in turn relates to the circumstances of the fall of the communist regime and the strength of civil society forces.

The key determinant of the trajectory adopted by these different countries was the nature of the political elite that gained power at the time of the fall of communism and the decisions made at this time about the future. Where the elite that came to power was closely linked with established civil society forces (reflecting a history of their development in pre-communist and communist times) of a non-ethnic nature, democracy was the outcome. They were able to marginalise the old regime communists (who in most cases responded by transforming themselves in a social democratic direction) and implement policies of political and economic reform which opened the way to a strengthening of civil society. Free media, stable party system and proliferation of independent public organisations within a public context of civic discourse in turn strengthened the democratic impetus imparted by the political elites. In this way, given the initial opening created by the elites, the growth of civil society reinforced the democratic structures set in place by those elites. In contrast, when the elite which came to power was dominated by civil society forces defined in ethnic terms, had a major component from the old regime and was thereby embedded in the existing state structure, or consisted solely of those in that structure, the result was either façade democracy or non-democracy. In these cases, civil society forces (of a civic type) were not strong enough to displace the ethnically-defined forces or the elements of the former elite, and have not subsequently been able to gain sufficient strength to reshape the political structures emanating from 1989–91. In the case of the façade democracies, ruling elites have acted in ways which have undermined the democratic aspirations espoused at the outset, keeping civil society restrained and to a degree destabilised and preventing it from imposing new sets of patterns of action upon the political system. Even economic reform, with its effect of generating independent economic interests, has been carried through in a generally less far reaching fashion than in the democracies, with the result that such interests remain hamstrung and under-developed. In the non-democracies, elements of civil society have been positively repressed as political elites have used the power of the state to try to maintain their autonomy from civil society forces. The more limited scope of economic reform is consistent with this. What is striking in all three broad trajectories is the primacy of political elites in the process, both temporally and causally.

But what is equally clear is that it is the relationship between those elites and civil society forces that is crucial for the sort of role they played.

The central role of political elites is clear in those cases of post-communist regime change. In Belarus, the shift from closed oligarchy to sultanism reflects the drive and power of one man and his supporters and the absence of stable party groups anchored in a robust civil society able to oppose his will. In Azerbaijan, the shift from closed to open oligarchy and back again is the story of a political elite overthrown by popular mobilisation and military action, but the resultant regime was unable to stabilise itself because of the weakness of its supporters among civil society forces. It could therefore be pushed from power by a military revolt which reinstated a closed oligarchical system. These were elite decisions in which civil society forces played little role. Georgia's transit from plebiscitary democracy to closed oligarchy and back again occurred against a background of military conflict, but its chief dynamic was the relationship between successive presidents (Gamsakhurdia and Shevardnadze) and the military. Again, civil society forces had little independent part to play. In Croatia the shift in a democratic direction followed the departure from office of a strong individual leader, a development which enabled civil society forces to emerge and take control of the agenda. A similar course of developments was prompted in Slovakia and in Serbia when the populace, acting through the electoral system, threw out the incumbent personalist government. And finally, in Romania and Bulgaria, which both appeared to have dim prospects for democracy at the outset, the more optimistic outcome has been because of the decision taken by the initial rulers to allow the comparatively free development of civil society forces. In both countries, although much more quickly in Bulgaria than in Romania, those civil society forces were able to take advantage of the opening provided by the ruling elite, build up their strength, and eventually displace the old regime successors from office. A significant shift in a democratic direction has occurred following the seeming consolidation of non-democratic rule (Romania, Slovakia, Croatia and perhaps Serbia) only in those cases where civil society forces were able to develop and where the regime provided them with an opening in the form of a moderately free election which enabled them to mobilise popular support. Throughout the region, therefore, it has been the relationship between ruling elites and those forces based in civil society which has shaped the course of regime trajectory.

Thus it is clear that the constellation of forces present at the time of the fall of the old regime was crucial in structuring subsequent developments. Where independent civil society forces with strong links into the community at large were powerful and prominent, the new regime was built along more open, competitive lines leading to a democratic outcome. Where the passing of the old regime was managed overwhelmingly by old regime elites, the outcome was authoritarian rule. In those cases where the transition from the old regime occurred at the time at which neither old regime nor new elites were clearly ascendant, the result was mixed, with a façade democratic outcome. This does not mean that the patterns set at the outset of the lives of the post-communist regimes were necessarily immutable, as those cases where civil society forces were able to develop and ultimately displace old regime successors show, but the subsequent course of development did in most cases realise the patterns initially established. In those places where an open, democratic, competitive politics was set in place, the consolidation of powerful civil society forces and the tendency for elites to refrain from seeking to use state power for partisan advantage (developments which are linked), enabled those patterns initially established to become embedded in the structure. In those cases where variants of non-democratic regimes (closed oligarchy, plebiscitary democracy and sultanism) emerged from the collapse of the communist structure, their emergence has been facilitated by the propensity of ruling elites to use the power of the state to consolidate their positions in such a way as to render them invulnerable to removal through established political structures and processes. The use of state power in this way undercut and repressed the development of civil society, and its use has generally been more extensive and invasive as one moves from closed oligarchy through plebiscitary democracy to sultanism. In the cases of façade democracy, the structuring of politics and the development of civil society have both been shaped in important ways by the resort to state power, and in some cases exclusivist nationalism, such that political arrangements have been set in train which may meet many of the procedural requirements of democracy but are deficient in others and in some of its substantive aspects. This balance between the mobilisation of state power and the growth of independent civil society activity has been central to the shaping of the political trajectories of the post-communist regimes, but it has been within the context inherited from the communist collapse.

6 Conclusion
Democracy and post-communism

It is clear that the post-communist countries have followed a variety of trajectories in the period since the fall of communism. While some have been able to establish a stable, consolidated democracy, others have produced well-entrenched authoritarian structures while others seem stuck in the morass of façade democracy. One of the things which is striking about these outcomes is the geographical pattern they form. Comparison of the typology of regimes given earlier with a map of the region makes this pattern clear. It can be expressed in a number of general propositions.

1. The further north-west a country is geographically, the more likely the outcome is democratic while the further south-east a country is to be found, the more likely a non-democratic outcome; façade democracies dominate in a band between these two.
2. Democracy is more common in east central Europe (ECE; especially excluding the Balkans) than in the former Soviet Union (FSU), where façade democracy and non-democracy dominate the political forms.
3. Democracy has been more common in the countries with a western Christian tradition, façade democracy with an Orthodox Christian tradition, and non-democracy in countries with a Moslem tradition.
4. Democracies predominate in parliamentary systems and non-democracies in presidential systems.

The correspondence between these general propositions and the location of all countries is not exact; for example, Belarus, Albania and much of the former Yugoslavia seem anomalous. Nevertheless the broad pattern is apparent, and its clearest expression is in the first proposition.

The consistency of this pattern suggests that it is not accidental. But the question is what produced this pattern. Why is it that democracy has been the outcome on the western part of this post-communist territory and non-democracy on the eastern (and southern) part? Many would argue that this reflects the exposure of these regions to different sorts of cultural influences over time, that ECE has always been more closely hooked in to the cultural developments in Western Europe which have been characterised by the rise of democracy than has the territory of the former Soviet Union, which has had its own strong authoritarian tradition. Similarly some would argue that the cultural influences shaping the development of Central Asia have not been conducive to democratic development. This is not an argument about the intrinsic, or necessary, nature of these societies, nor does it posit the view that the West is superior. It is simply a statement of historical fact: democratic political forms developed in the West, and although these were exported from their native heartland, they affected different regions to different degrees. Historically, ECE has been influenced by these cultural and political forces much more than its neighbours to the east and south. But an argument about cultural influences (and the proposition above regarding religion must be included here) is unsatisfactory unless it shows how those influences are manifested and how they shape political development.

This book has argued that crucial in determining the political outcome of the post-communist transition is the identity of those leading political actors who shaped that transition. Where the transition was in the hands of non-regime civil society forces, democracy generally has been the outcome. Where old regime forces remained firmly in control and were able to exclude civil society forces, non-democracy has been the outcome, with the nature of that outcome in turn shaped by the types of political forces which dominated within each regime.[1] Where the transition has been shaped either by nationalist movements with an exclusivist agenda or second-echelon old-regime elites, but under pressure from active civil society forces, façade democracy has been the outcome. The crucial dynamic here has been the strength of civil society forces *vis-à-vis* the regime, and the state of the old regime itself. If the regime split, there was greater scope for the emergence and development of civil society forces than was the case when the unity of the regime elite was maintained intact. But in this dynamic, the principal motor force for democratic development was the civil society forces, and it is in their operation and functioning that the effects of cultural influence noted above may be seen. As the analysis in Chapter 3 has demonstrated, although the communist development model generated pressures for the growth of civil society forces (while at the same time placing substantial political barriers in the path of their growth), those forces were strongest in the countries where there had been a pre-communist history of their development. The growth of such forces in ECE in the pre-communist period, while patchy, did provide a base for the later emergence of civil society forces at the time of regime crisis. While the degree to which these pre-communist developments were internally generated or were a response to contact with emergent democracies in Western Europe may be a matter of debate, what is clear is that those countries with such a history were better placed to achieve democracy upon the fall of communism. Historically the elites in the countries of ECE saw themselves as part of a common European civilisation, and in pre-communist times they acted consciously as part of that culture area. Under such circumstances, cultural influences from the West were bound to enter these countries and have an effect upon their internal milieu. The development of civil society forces is likely to have been encouraged by this.

Regardless of whether the development of pre-communist civil society forces was shaped by Western contacts or not, the presence or absence, and strength, of those forces at the time of communist crisis was crucial to the outcome of that crisis. But it is important to recognise that, although the initial trajectories of these countries were set by the disposition of forces at the time of regime transition, those trajectories have not been set unmoveably in place. Just because one country has thus far emerged as a democracy and another as an authoritarian regime does not mean these countries are condemned to that sort of system forever. A trajectory is a path taken by an object that, in the absence of forces pushing it off course, will lead to that object arriving at a predictable point. Should forces emerge which seek to alter that trajectory, the predicted point of arrival, or in this case course of development, may be changed. In more practical terms this means that a democratic polity today could become either a façade or a non-democracy in the future, just as either of these other two political forms could be transformed into democracy. This capacity to alter the trajectory is reflected in the experiences of a number of the post-communist countries discussed above. The literature on the collapse of democracy[2] has been unable to develop an explanation which would allow prediction, but it has shown that what generally is present is regime performance failure (usually in economic terms) and extremist groups willing to take advantage of this to seize power and institute a new set of political arrangements. Among the established post-communist democracies, there are small, right-wing nationalist groups which offer an agenda consistent with the undermining of democratic political forms. Their electoral support generally has been modest, but should economic difficulty return, it is possible that they could become more significant players in the political game. Under such circumstances, the democracies of the region are as vulnerable as their counterparts in other parts of the world. Indeed, they may be more vulnerable, given the recency of their establishment and the non-democratic political traditions which still reside in the region.

The literature on the collapse of authoritarian regimes and the transition to democracy is much more extensive than that on democratic collapse.[3] The principal factor structuring the transition to democracy more generally (i.e. not only in the post-communist cases) is the strength of civil society forces relative to the regime.[4] Where those forces are powerful, they may be able either to take advantage of a regime crisis resulting from performance failure or leadership succession to press for democratic change, or, where regime elites provide an opening for such forces to operate, may be able to shift the regime in a democratic direction. This was the situation, for example, in Romania, Slovakia, Croatia and Serbia where civil society forces were able to take advantage of free elections to throw the old regime successor elite out of office. Similarly, in many of the façade democracies where civil society forces do function but are relatively weak, their strengthening could stimulate the emergence of the sort of pressure on current elites which could lead to democratic development. This sort of development is also possible in the non-democracies, but because of the weakness of civil society forces and the strength of state repression, it is much less likely. The democratisation of the façade democracies and the non-democracies therefore requires the same sort of dynamic which has led to democracy in the post-communist transitions, the shaping of political forms predominantly by non-regime civil society forces.

A unique process?

One issue that has arisen in the scholarly attempt to understand the regime changes that occurred in this region is their comparability with those transitions to democracy that occurred in Latin America and Southern Europe in the 1970s and 1980s. If these are considered to be comparable, then that growing literature on the transition to democracy, ironically called 'transitology',[5] could be used to examine these later cases. For some, there was no question; they were part of the 'third wave' of democratisation sweeping the globe.[6] But others were more cautious, suggesting that the communist cases differed significantly from those of Latin America and Southern Europe, with the implication that the theoretical tools used to analyse the earlier cases could not be used without change to study the communist transitions. A number of perceived areas of difference were pointed to.[7] A range of differences were perceived to exist in the nature of the starting point of the transition, the nature of the communist regime and the sort of society over which it ruled. The totalist nature of the regime, in the sense that it sought both to penetrate and transform society much more deeply, and to exercise more extensive control over all aspects of life than was the case in the Latin American and Southern European dictatorships, was considered crucial. The clearest instance of this was the way in which the communist political economy effectively melded together the political and economic realms, eliminating the boundary between the two that was characteristic of these earlier cases. The communist regime was thereby seen as a much more formidable foe than the other dictatorships had been because of the brute power which the regime possessed and the way in which its functionaries were lodged in positions of responsibility throughout the entire socio-politico-economic system. In addition, it was argued that society under communist rule had been much more flattened, with sharp class divisions eliminated, the generation of individual interests subdued, and civil society destroyed. Economically, the communist states were seen to be at a much higher level of economic, and especially industrial, development than their putative comparators. It was also proposed that the transition from communism involved a question of identity, as new states sought to establish their identity independent of the overlordship of an imperial power (seen variously as the USSR, the Russians, the Serbs and the Czechs), and a degree of ethnic diversity much greater than in the earlier dictatorships.

As well as these different starting points, there were said to be differences in the mode of transition. These were seen principally as results of the differences in starting point. The role of international factors, in particular Gorbachev's agreement not to interfere in Eastern Europe, was said to be greater, as it presumably had to be because of the greater weakness of domestic opposition forces. This weakness is also reflected in the greater role attributed to mass mobilisation in the streets as a force for change. Furthermore it was argued that the different nature of the pre-transition political system, and in particular the greater strength of the old regime under communism, meant that it was more invasive and threatening to democratic change, and therefore those seeking change had to adopt different strategies with regard to the old regime and its servants. In Latin America and Southern Europe

198 Conclusion

they could seek to co-opt and reassure the old regime functionaries and thereby neutralize them, while in the communist transitions they had to 'break' decisively with them; this was the 'bridge' strategy compared with the 'break' strategy.[8] The communist linkage between the political and economic also had consequences for the transition, in that political democratisation could not be achieved without the destruction of the central command economy and its replacement by an economy run on market lines. Thus in contrast to Latin America and Southern Europe where the economic task was reform of a capitalist economy, in the former communist countries it was the transformation of the whole economic structure.

It is certainly true that many of the differences identified by the critics existed, especially in terms of the nature of the regime and its impact upon society. But the issue is whether this has made a substantial difference to the modes of regime change in these different geographical areas. The first point to recognise is that, while Valerie Bunce may be correct to argue that 'god is in the details'[9] and that these are different between these groups of countries, the details of the transition differed between different countries in the same region. Comparison of Spain with Portugal and Brazil with Argentina, Uruguay and Chile[10] shows the sorts of variations that have been evident in neighbouring states and have been encompassed within the general 'transitology' literature. The issue is not whether transitions are all exactly the same, but whether the differences are so great as to warrant the course of regime change in these regions being considered to be generically different. As the analysis which follows will show, the differences are not sufficiently large to view these as different processes.

One qualification is in order. We need to be clear about which countries we are comparing. On the one hand it is the successful cases of democratisation in Latin America and Southern Europe. These are the focus of the transition to democracy literature. On the other hand, as the preceding analysis has shown, not all of the former communist countries can be classed as democratic. Inclusion of these non-democratic cases, as some of the critics have done, should, one would have thought, have strengthened the critics' case for difference. The argument is that in these non-democratic countries, the classic steps evident in Latin America and Southern Europe (liberalisation, regime split, primacy of opposition forces perhaps in alliance with reformists from the old regime, democratisation) did not take place. But it is not logical to argue that the failure of these countries to follow the established pattern shows that the processes in the post-communist region as a whole were different to successful cases of democratisation elsewhere, because these states did not achieve the same end point (i.e. democracy). Comparison should be like with like, the successful cases. Furthermore, it is important to realise that there is one further crucial difference between the post-communist region and the others. In the ECE/FSU, the process of regime change actually led in three cases to something which did not occur in Latin America or Southern Europe, the collapse and break up of the state. Most of those countries which have not achieved democracy were formerly constituent parts of those states which collapsed, and at least in the Soviet Union and Yugoslavia, at the federal level the transitological pattern seems to have been followed. That it did not occur in the sub-national units that were to become independent states should not obscure this fact. However, in any case, as will be shown below, despite the fact that they did not follow the transitological pattern, the experience of these non-democratic countries is consistent with the view that the basic processes in the different regions are the same.

This study has shown that the most important factor in leading to a democratic outcome has been the pressure applied by civil society forces on political elites. Only where political elites have been closely linked with civil society forces and where those forces were strong enough to overwhelm the old regime at the time of regime crisis was democracy the outcome. The only exception to this was Bulgaria, where the old regime elite agreed to move in a democratic direction, opening space for civil society forces to grow and, within a short space of time, achieve power. This link between elites and civil society forces was also the key determining factor in the cases of democratisation in Latin America and Southern Europe. Although by focusing upon elites, much of the transition literature has not given due attention to the role of such forces,[11] it is clear that those forces played the same essential role as in the communist transitions: they provided the impetus which pushed elite negotiations in a democratic direction. This is where the non-democratic outcome states are relevant. It was in those states that civil society forces were weakest relative to the old regime elite, so that they provide the negative case for the importance of civil society forces to the political outcome. The common role played by civil society forces in democratic transitions in all regions suggests that the very real differences that did exist in terms of the nature of the regime and of the society did not have significant implications for the basic process and its dynamic, although it did have implications for the forms in which this unrolled. Civil society forces were just as important in the communist transitions as in the non-communist. Indeed, in contrast to the view noted above, given the higher levels of economic development of the communist states, it might have been expected that civil society forces would have been even stronger than in the less developed Latin America and Southern Europe areas, although this development was clearly offset by the nature of the communist regime and its greater penetration of society. This reflects the ambiguity of the impact of communism.

While the basic dynamic of the process was the same, there were differences of details between individual cases in all regions. The forms that activity took were shaped by the institutional and political environment within which they were to be acted out. For example, the pacting that took place in Uruguay was very different from that in Spain, which was different from that in Brazil and Peru,[12] which was different again from that in Eastern Europe, where the Round Tables were the institutional form of this. The shape of the new political elites reflected political circumstances, with the left more prominent in Latin America and Southern Europe than, at least initially, in the former communist region. This reflects the political orientation of the respective old regimes. The military was more important as an actor (and a potential threat) in Latin America and Southern Europe than in the former communist region because of the nature of the old regime. In the former regions, the authoritarian government which was overthrown was often a military administration, whereas in the communist regimes the military had been kept under strict control. The role of international factors was clearly important in the case of ECE. This was not as direct in many of the cases in Latin America and Southern Europe (or, for that matter, the USSR), but international factors were important. The so-called domino effect whereby developments in one country stimulate similar developments in another, the influence that was exercised by major external powers like the US and the EU, and the activities of non-state actors were all influential in shaping developments in many of the states of Latin America and Southern Europe.[13] But some variation in detail should be expected between the communist and non-communist cases, just as there were significant differences among the individual cases of both groups.

In the view of some the attitude of the reformers to the old regime was also different between these regions. According to Valerie Bunce, in Latin America and Southern Europe, the reformers sought to build a bridge to the old regime, to include some of its elements in the new politics in order not to so alienate them as to provoke a violent reaction. This attempt at inclusiveness, alongside a clear break with the past by the introduction of democratic institutions with substance, was accompanied by a demobilisation of the populace designed to blunt the radicalisation of change, which would have threatened old regime elements even more.[14] She claims this is in stark contrast to the situation in ECE where the most successful cases of transition saw the exclusion of the former rulers through their defeat in the first election. But this is an exaggeration of the earlier cases and a misreading of the communist ones. While there may have been cooptation at an early stage in Spain and some other countries, this did not always occur (e.g. in Portugal). A bridge was not always built to the old regime and even when it was, it is often not clear that this constituted anything more than a symbolic inclusion beside an effective marginalisation. Indeed, if inclusion means involvement in discussion with emergent political elites, then inclusion has been virtually universal, including in most of the communist cases. In ECE, the most successful cases of transition (Poland, Hungary, the Czech Republic, Slovenia and, in Bunce's view, the Baltic states) all saw some form of pacting, sometimes explicitly in the form of Round Tables, and in the Baltics in the way in which the splinters of the communist party adhered to the nationalist banner. All established competitive electoral systems, and except in Latvia where the communists were banned (and in any case which we have not classed as a democracy) and in the Czech Republic where lustration laws restricted the participation of certain levels of former officials, in which the former communists could participate. In a number of these countries they participated with such success that they won office at the second post-communist election. The demobilisation of the populace occurred throughout the former communist region, thereby blunting a possible source of political radicalisation as in Latin America and Southern Europe. Furthermore the forms in which privatisation were undertaken enabled former communists to gain control of often significant economic assets, often through occupying a privileged position in this process. And in this region there have been few trials of former communist officials. So the perceived difference between 'bridging' and 'breaking' is exaggerated, and it is not clear how 'sharp' the break has been with the communist past; many elements of continuity remain.

It is true that the communist political economy had important implications for successful democratisation that were not present in the other regions. If the old regime's political power was to be broken, the communist economic mechanism had to be replaced by a more decentralised, market system. This is the reason why, in this region, democratisation and radical economic change have gone together, while in the other regions successful political change has been accompanied by less far reaching economic reform.[15] But it is not clear that this is important for our understanding of the process of political transformation. As has been argued above, the course of economic reform was dependent upon the political outcome of transition, not vice versa. Economic reform may help consolidate democracy, but it did not have a role in the initial establishment of a democratic polity.

Ultimately what this means is that the sort of process of regime change that has occurred in the former communist region is generically the same sort of process that occurred earlier in Latin America and Southern Europe. While individual details of the different cases will be different, there is no consistent pattern that would differentiate the earlier cases from the later in any meaningful sense. Furthermore the basic dynamic at work in all cases has been the same: the relationship between civil society forces and political elites. This was the key in the cases of democratisation in Latin America and Southern Europe, despite the failure of much of the writing on these areas to appreciate that fact, and it was the key in the communist transitions as well.

Post-communism

The different outcomes of the post-communist transitions, and the possibility of further changes of regime type in the future, raises the question of the nature of post-communism itself. There have been numerous attempts to give this phenomenon some meaning. The most sophisticated treatment of post-communism has provided a fourteen-point model.[16] This sees post-communism as being a unique blend of: assertion of independence and the rise of nationalism; near absence of a culture of compromise; high expectations of leaders; cynicism towards, and/or mistrust of, political institutions; rejection of teleologism and grand theories; an ideological vacuum; moral confusion; comprehensive revolution; temporality; dynamism; instability; a widespread sense of insecurity; unfortunate timing; and legitimation problems. Although some may argue with these points, about their comprehensiveness and whether all are equally relevant or important, this model does capture some of the flavour of life in the former communist states. But despite its richness and its capturing of aspects of life in the post-communist states, like so many other discussions of post-communism, this model does not broach a key issue: what sort of phenomenon is post-communism?

Post-communism can be seen in three ways:

1 *Post-communism as a system.* This perspective sees post-communism as an integrated set of characteristics which together constitute an interdependent, orderly arrangement within which daily life is conducted. Such a system would

embrace political, economic and social structures, and values and patterns of popular belief. It assumes considerable uniformity across all post-communist countries.
2 *Post-communism as a condition.* According to this perspective, post-communism is a set of qualities or features which are evident in the societies to which the term is applied. This does not assume the sort of integration evident in the view of post-communism as a system, but it does imply that the features are normally found together.
3 *Post-communism as a situation.* In this view, post-communism is simply that period after a country has ceased to be communist, usually defined in terms of the fall of the communist political rulers. This implies nothing about the nature of the society or political system in the country except for its origins. It is also more open-ended than the other two perspectives. It will cease to apply when the specific features of which it is constituted cease to exist, or at least to play the major part in shaping reality. Post-communism as a situation will cease to be useful when the countries to which the term is applied can be better defined in other terms.

These three different perspectives are not necessarily mutually exclusive, although it does not make much sense either to use them interchangeably or indiscriminately, or to fail to see their differences. A failure to discriminate between them in usage will hinder the cause of analysis. This is shown by relating them to the study of political trajectories in this book.

One of the key characteristics of communism as a system was its political aspect. The definition of a communist system always had as a central component rule by a Leninist party.[17] Consequently any analysis of post-communism, which however one sees it (as system, condition or situation) supersedes communism, must have at its core consideration of the political arrangements; moving on from communism must involve transforming its political arrangements. This means that the different political trajectories followed by the post-communist states have direct implications for our understanding of what post-communism means. The spread of the post-communist states from stable democracies to consolidated authoritarian regimes means that the post-communist states exhibit a wide range of different institutional forms in their political arrangements. This sort of diversity means that it does not make much sense to see post-communism as a system. The political systems have become too diverse to be included in a uniform system called post-communism. The same point applies to the political patterns which would be part of the perspective which sees post-communism as a condition. The patterns of political life, including vehicles and types of participation, relationship between rulers and ruled, and elite decision-making institutions, have come to differ such that they cannot be incorporated within the one set of features which would constitute a condition of post-communism. Witness the difference between Hungary and Turkmenistan. Post-communism cannot be equated with democracy.

The most sensible understanding of the notion of post-communism is the minimalist view of it as a situation, as the period following the collapse of communism. What unites the various post-communist countries is therefore nothing about the institutions or patterns of political, economic or social life, but the simple fact that they all emerged from the crisis of communism at the end of the 1980s and they had all had communist regimes prior to that date. They shared a common past (although even this had limits), but not necessarily a common present or a common future. Certainly many of the problems they have had to face have been shared ones, but these are largely a reflection of their common past, the legacy of the communist regime. Recognition of the fact that the individual countries are meeting these problems in their own ways and through this building their own different political systems and societies means that we must acknowledge their growing diversity. Increasingly these countries should be seen less as post-communist, and therefore defined in terms of what they were rather than what they are, and more in terms of their current political forms and trajectories. As time passes, it will become more useful to discuss the countries of ECE in comparison with the countries of Western Europe than with those of Central Asia. This sort of perspective, which will help to integrate the study of these countries even more into the established disciplines than the collapse of communism up until now has done, is recognition of the diversity that is emerging in these regimes. And this, in turn, is a result of the different post-communist trajectories and of the circumstances of the initial shaping of these political systems.

Notes

1 A democratic post-communism?

1. Samuel P. Huntington, *The Third Wave. Democratization in the Late Twentieth Century*, Norman: University of Oklahoma Press, 1991.
2. Bosnia-Herzegovina has been excluded from the analysis because of the way in which the war between 1992 and 1995 shaped the political trajectory of this state.
3. For one useful discussion, among many, of the conditions of democracy, see William R. Reisinger, 'Choices Facing the Builders of a Liberal Democracy', Robert D. Grey (ed), *Democratic Theory and Post-Communist Change*, Upper Saddle River: Prentice Hall, 1997, pp.24–51.
4. Although see below.
5. For one view which conflates procedural factors with guarantees of civil liberties, see David Collier and Steven Levitsky, 'Democracy with Adjectives: Conceptual Innovation in Comparative Research', *World Politics* 49, 3, 1997, p.434.
6. On the general phenomenon of 'democracy with adjectives', see Collier and Levitsky.
7. For example, see Amos Perlmutter, *Modern Authoritarianism. A Comparative Institutional Analysis*, New Haven: Yale University Press, 1981; Juan J. Linz, 'Totalitarian and Authoritarian Regimes', Fred I. Greenstein and Nelson W. Polsby (eds), *Handbook of Political Science. Volume 3. Macropolitical Theory*, Reading/MA: Addison-Wesley Pub. Co., 1975; and Juan J. Linz and Alfred Stepan, *Problems of Democratic Transition and Consolidation. Southern Europe, South America, and Post-Communist Europe*, Baltimore: The Johns Hopkins University Press, 1996. While the categorisation used in this book is unique to it, it is underpinned by a wide and sophisticated literature on comparing regime types. For discussions of comparison see, *inter alia*, Rod Hague, Martin Harrop and Shaun Breslin, *Comparative Government. An Introduction*, Basingstoke: Macmillan, 1992, ch.2, and the classic S.E. Finer, *Comparative Government*, Harmondsworth: Penguin, 1974, first published 1970, Pt 1. Also the very useful Collier and Levitsky.
8. This schema contrasts with the typology given in Philip G. Roeder, 'Varieties of Post-Soviet Authoritarian Regimes', *Post-Soviet Affairs* 10, 1, 1994, pp.61–101.
9. For one discussion of sultanism, see Linz and Stepan, pp.51–4.
10. On the definition of consolidation in terms of two elections, see Huntington, p.267.
11. For details of the methodology, see the methodology section of any of the annual surveys of freedom published by Freedom House. For example, Freedom House, *Freedom in the World 1989–90. Political Rights and Civil Liberties*, New York: Freedom House, 1990, pp.19–21. Also see www.freedomhouse.org
12. Valerie Bunce, 'The Political Economy of Postsocialism', and M. Steven Fish, 'Postcommunist Subversion: Social Science and Democratization in East Europe and Eurasia', *Slavic Review* 58, 4, Winter 1999, pp.756–93 and 794–823.
13. Adrian Karatnycky, Alexander Motyl and Boris Shor, *Nations in Transit 1997. Civil Society, Democracy and Markets in East Central Europe and the Newly Independent States*, New Brunswick: Transaction Publishers, 1997, p.80.

14 Karatnycky et al., p.118. See also Stanislaw Gebethner, 'Free Elections and Political Parties in Transition to Democracy in Central and Southeastern Europe', *International Political Science Review* 18, 4, 1997, pp.381–99; David Olson, 'Dissolution of the State: Political Parties and the 1992 Election in Czechoslovakia', *Communist and Post-Communist Studies* 26, 3, 1993, pp.301–14; Gordon Wightman, 'Czechoslovakia', *Electoral Studies* 9, 4, 1990, pp.319–26.
15 Karatnycky et al., p.179. Also Attila Agh and Sandor Kurtan, 'The 1994 parliamentary elections in Hungary', *Democratisation and Europeanization in Hungary: The First Parliament 1990–1994*, Budapest: Hungarian Center for Democracy Studies, 1995; Gabriella Ilonski and Sandor Kurtan, 'Hungary', *European Journal of Political Research* 28, 3/4, 1995, pp.359–68; Martyn Rady, 'The 1994 Hungarian General Election', *Representation* 32, 119, 1994, pp.69–72.
16 Karatnycky et al., p.247. Also see Richard J. Krickus, 'Democratization in Lithuania', Karen Dawisha and Bruce Parrott (eds), *The consolidation of democracy in East Central Europe*, Cambridge: Cambridge University Press, 1997; Rein Taagepera, 'The Baltic States', *Electoral Studies* 9, 4, 1990, pp.303–11.
17 Karatnycky et al., p.281. Also A.A. Michta, 'Democratic Consolidation in Poland', Dawisha and Parrott; David M. Olson, 'Compartmentalized Competition: The Managed Transitional Election System of Poland', *Journal of Politics* 55, 2, 1993, pp.415–41.
18 Karatnycky et al., pp.355 and 356. Also S. Gaber, 'Elections in Slovenia – April 1990', *Representation* 31, 113, 1992, pp.22–4; Sabrina Petra Ramet, 'Democratization in Slovenia: the second stage', Karen Dawisha and Bruce Parrott, *Politics, Power, and the Struggle for Democracy in South-East Europe* Cambridge: Cambridge University Press, 1997, pp.189–225.
19 Karatnycky et al., passim. For another, more impressionistic, survey, see Mary Kaldor and Ivan Vejvoda (eds), *Democratization in Central and Eastern Europe*, London: Pinter, 1999.
20 Countries are deemed 'free' if they achieve a score of 2.5 or better, 'partly free' 3–5, and 'not free' 5.5 and above.
21 Karatnycky et al., p.27; Fabian Schmidt, 'Election Fraud Sparks Protests', *Transition* 2, 13, 28 June 1996, pp.38–9 and 63.
22 Karatnycky et al., p.97. Also Kenneth E. Basom, 'Prospects for Democracy in Serbia and Croatia', *East European Quarterly* xxix, 4, January 1996, pp.518–20.
23 Karatnycky et al., p.143; J. Ishiyama, 'Electoral Systems Experimentation in the New Eastern Europe: The Single Transferable Vote and the Additional Member System in Estonia and Hungary', *East European Quarterly* 29, 4, 1996, pp.487–507; Toivo U. Raun, 'Democratization and Political Development in Estonia, 1987–96', Dawisha and Parrott, (East Central Europe), pp.334–74; Paul Wilder, 'The Estonian Elections of 1992: Proportionality and Party Organization in a New Democracy', *Representation* 31, 116, 1993, pp.72–6; Taagepara.
24 Karatnycky et al., pp.163–4. See the discussion in S. Neil MacFarlane, 'Democratization, Nationalism and Regional Security in the Southern Caucasus', *Government and Opposition* 32, 3, 1998, pp.405–6.
25 Karatnycky et al., p.232; Philip John Davies and Andrejs Valdis Ozolins, 'The Latvian Parliamentary Election of 1995', *Electoral Studies* 15, 1, 1996, pp.124–8; Andrejs Plakans, 'Democratization and Political Participation in Postcommunist Societies: the Case of Latvia', Dawisha and Parrott (East Central Europe); Taagepera.
26 Karatnycky et al., p.272.
27 Richard Rose, Neil Munro and Tom Mackie, *Elections in Central and Eastern Europe Since 1990*, Glasgow: University of Strathclyde, Studies in Public Policy No.300, 1998, pp.96–7. Also see Dennis Deletant, 'The Romanian Elections of May 1990', *Representation* 29, 108, 1990, pp.23–6; Jonathan Eyal, 'Romania', Stephen Whitefield (ed), *The New Institutional Architecture of Eastern Europe*, London: Macmillan, 1993, pp.121–42; Daniel N. Nelson, 'Romania', *Electoral Studies* 9, 4, 1990, pp.355–66.
28 Karatnycky et al., pp.315–16.
29 Karatnycky et al., p.338; Zora Butorova and Martin Butora, 'Political Parties, Value Orientations and Slovakia's Road to Independence', Gordon Wightman (ed), *Party Formation in East-Central Europe*, Aldershot: Edward Elgar, 1995, pp.107–33.

30 Taras Kuzio, 'The 1994 Parliamentary Elections in Ukraine', *The Journal of Communist Studies and Transition Politics* 11, 4, December 1995, pp.353–6; Karatnycky *et al.*, pp.390–1; Jack E. Matlock Jr, 'The Nowhere Nation', *The New York Review of Books* 24 February 2000, p.41.
31 Karatnycky *et al.*, pp.41–2; MacFarlane, p.405; Nora Dudwick, 'Political transformation in postcommunist Armenia: images and realities', Karen Dawisha and Bruce Parrott (eds), *Conflict, Cleavage, and Change in Central Asia and the Caucasus*, Cambridge: Cambridge University Press, 1997, p.70.
32 Karatnycky *et al.*, pp.54–5; MacFarlane, p.404.
33 Karatnycky *et al.*, p.64.
34 Tim Judah, 'How Milosevic Hangs On', *The New York Review of Books* 16 July 1998, pp.44–5; Basom, pp.518–20.
35 'Parliamentary and Municipal Elections In Montenegro', A Report Prepared by the Staff of the Commission on Security and Cooperation in Europe, August 1998.
36 Karatnycky *et al.*, pp.196–8.
37 Karatnycky *et al.*, pp.216–7.
38 Karatnycky *et al.*, pp.368–70.
39 Bunce (The Political Economy of Postsocialism), p.761.
40 Bunce (The Political Economy of Postsocialism), p.761.
41 Bunce (The Political Economy of Postsocialism), pp.783–4.
42 It is a little ironic that Bunce's explanation focuses upon elites and their values, which is precisely the same focus of that transition literature which she has argued so vigorously has little relevance for the post-communist situation. For example, see the following exchange: Philippe C. Schmitter with Terry Lynn Karl, 'The Conceptual Travels of Transitologists and Consolidologists: How Far to the East Should They Attempt to Go?', *Slavic Review* 53, 1, Spring 1994, pp.173–85; Valerie Bunce, 'Should Transitologists be Grounded?', *Slavic Review* 54, 1, Spring 1995, pp. 111–27; Terry Lynn Karl and Philippe C. Schmitter, 'From an Iron Curtain to a Paper Curtain: Grounding Transitologists or Students of Postcommunism?', *Slavic Review* 54, 4, Winter 1995, pp.965–78; and Valerie Bunce, 'Paper Curtains and Paper Tigers', *Slavic Review* 54, 4, Winter 1995, pp.979–87.
43 And Bunce acknowledges this. Bunce (The Political Economy of Postsocialism), p.778.
44 Bunce (The Political Economy of Postsocialism), p.785.
45 Bunce is aware of the importance of the structuring role that the communist legacy provides. For one example, see Valerie Bunce, *Subversive Institutions. The Design and the Destruction of Socialism and the State*, Cambridge: Cambridge University Press, 1999.
46 Fish (Postcommunist Subversion).
47 Fish (Postcommunist Subversion), p.800.
48 Fish (Postcommunist Subversion), pp.803–05.
49 Fish (Postcommunist Subversion), p.809. For a more extended discussion, see M. Steven Fish, 'The Determinants of Economic Reform in the Post-Communist World', *East European Politics and Societies* 12, 1, Winter 1998, pp.31–78, and M. Steven Fish, 'Democratization's Requisites: The Postcommunist Experience', *Post-Soviet Affairs* 14, 3, July–September 1998, pp.212–47. Also Chapter 4 in this book.
50 A similar point can be made about the analysis of Philip Roeder who sees the configuration of political forces dominating the legislature after the 1990 republican elections in the Soviet Union as the key to the shape of the regime. Roeder (Varieties of Post-Soviet Authoritarian Regimes).

2 Negotiating regime change

1 See the discussion in Stephan Haggard and Robert R. Kaufmann, *The Political Economy of Democratic Transitions*, Princeton: Princeton University Press, 1995.
2 On institutional choice, see Arend Lijphart and Carlos Waisman (eds), *Institutional Design in New Democracies. Eastern Europe and Latin America*, Boulder: Westview Press, 1996.

3 This point is emphasised in Jon Elster, Claus Offe and Ulrich K. Preuss, *Institutional Design in Post-communist Societies. Rebuilding the Ship at Sea*, Cambridge: Cambridge University Press, 1998, pp.11–7.
4 Implicit here is the rule of law and the subordination of political authorities to it. For a discussion of attempts to create institutional structures to achieve this, see John Reitz, 'Progress in Building Institutions for the Rule of Law in Russia and Poland', Robert D. Grey (ed), *Democratic Theory and Post-Communist Change*, Upper Saddle River: Prentice Hall, 1997, pp.144–89. For a discussion of constitution-making in Czechoslovakia, Hungary and Bulgaria, see Elster, Offe and Preuss. For an overview of constitutional provisions, see James P. McGregor, 'Constitutional Factors in Politics in Post-communist Central and Eastern Europe', *Communist and Post-Communist Studies* 29, 2, June 1996, pp.147–66.
5 For one discussion, see Valerie Bunce, 'Presidents and the Transition in Eastern Europe', Kurt von Mettenheim (ed), *Presidential Institutions and Democratic Politics. Comparing Regional and National Contexts*, Baltimore: The Johns Hopkins University Press, 1997, pp.161–76. For a survey and discussion of presidentialism in the region, see the discussion in *East European Constitutional Review* (henceforth EECR) 2 4, and 3, 1, Fall 1993 and Winter 1994, pp.36–9 and 58–98.
6 For example, see Arend Lijphart (ed), *Parliamentary versus Presidential Government*, Oxford: Oxford University Press, 1992; Alfred Stepan and Cindy Skach, 'Constitutional Frameworks and Democratic Consolidation: Parliamentarianism and Presidentialism', *World Politics* 46, 1, October 1993, pp.1–22; M. Shugart and J. Carey, *Presidents and Assemblies: Constitutional Design and Electoral Dynamics*, Cambridge: Cambridge University Press, 1992.
7 For example, Juan J. Linz, 'The Perils of Presidentialism', *The Journal of Democracy* 1, 1, Winter 1990, pp.51–69; Juan J. Linz, 'The Virtues of Parliamentarism', *The Journal of Democracy* 1, 4, Fall 1990, pp.84–91; Adam Przeworski, Michael Alvarez, Jose Antonio Cheibub and Fernando Limongi, 'What Makes Democracies Endure?', *The Journal of Democracy* 7, 1, January 1996, pp.39–55.
8 It is this characteristic which, following Rokkan's explanation, should make it attractive to ruling parties and to challengers; for the former, although it may lose some of its representation it is a guarantee that it will not lose all of it, and for the latter it is a guarantee of gaining at least a share of representation and political power. Arend Lijphart, 'Democratization and Constitutional Choices in Czecho-Slovakia, Hungary and Poland 1989–91', *Journal of Theoretical Politics* 4, 2, 1992, pp.208–9.
9 Not all forms of PR are as strongly favourable to party centres. However the single transferable vote form of PR where voters vote for individual candidates rather than parties was not seriously considered in the region. For a more general discussion which suggests these rules are not as clear cut in their operation in all post-communist countries, see Robert G. Moser, 'Electoral Systems and the Number of Parties in Postcommunist States', *World Politics* 51, 3, 1999, pp.359–84. For a survey of some of these systems in the early post-communist period, see Kimmo Kuusela, 'The founding electoral systems in Eastern Europe, 1989–91', Geoffrey Pridham and Tatu Vanhanen, *Democratization in Eastern Europe. Domestic and international perspectives*, London: Routledge, 1994, pp.128–50; also Elster, Offe and Preuss, ch.4.
10 For some discussion of this in terms of the presidency, see Stephen Holmes, 'A Forum on Presidential Powers', EECR 2, 4, and 3, 1, Fall 1993–Winter 1994, pp.95–8.
11 These have been defined as 'semiformal meetings, of a preconstitutional or quasi-constitutional nature, that took place between leaders of the Communist regimes and spokesmen for dissident and oppositional groups.' Jon Elster, 'Introduction', Jon Elster (ed), *The Roundtable Talks and the Breakdown of Communism*, Chicago: University of Chicago Press, 1996, pp.3–4.
12 See Graeme Gill, *The Dynamics of Democratization. Elites, Civil Society and the Transition Process* Basingstoke: Macmillan, 2000, ch.2.
13 For one argument about elite identity, see Thomas A. Baylis, 'Plus Ca Change? Transformation and Continuity Among East European Elites', *Communist and Post-Communist Studies* 27, 3, 1994, pp.315–28.
14 Although often too the regime splits and a section goes into opposition, sometimes taking up leading posts.

15 The notion of civil society will be discussed more fully in Chapter 3.
16 The initial argument with regard to founding elections will be found in Guillermo O'Donnell and Philippe C. Schmitter, *Transitions from Authoritarian Rule. Tentative Conclusions about Uncertain Democracies*, Baltimore: The Johns Hopkins University Press, 1986, pp.61–4.
17 This has been seen chiefly in terms of economic reform. M. Steven Fish, 'The Determinants of Economic Reform in the Post-Communist World', *East European Politics and Societies* 12, 1, Winter 1998, pp.48–63; M. Steven Fish, 'Postcommunist Subversion: Social Science and Democratization in East Europe and Eurasia', *Slavic Review* 58, 4, Winter 1999, p.809; Valerie Bunce, 'The Political Economy of Postsocialism', *Slavic Review* 58, 4, Winter 1999, p.769.
18 Although these might better be characterised, in Huntington's terms, as 'stunning' elections ie. elections sponsored by the regime in which it did very badly. Samuel P. Huntington, *The Third Wave. Democratization in the Late Twentieth Century*, Norman: University of Oklahoma Press, 1991, p.175.
19 While formally the communist party remained in power up until the election, through constitutional amendment and the practice of politics, the old system had already been replaced by the time the election was held.
20 Those regimes discussed in terms of Pattern 6 pp.65–81.
21 This is the implication of the discussion in Fish (The Determinants of Economic Reform), pp.48–50. This simply reinforces the point about the ambiguity of the notion of founding elections noted in Chapter One.
22 On the Polish Round Table, see Wiktor Osiatynski, 'The Roundtable Talks in Poland', Elster, pp.21–68.
23 Attila Agh, *The Politics of Central Europe*, London: Sage, 1998, p.85. On the significance of Round Table talks in Eastern Europe generally, see Helga A. Welsh, 'Political Transition Processes in Central and Eastern Europe', *Comparative Politics* 26, 4, July 1994, pp.383–8.
24 For an argument which emphasises the false assumptions and misperceptions underpinning both sides in these negotiations, see Joseph M. Colomer and Margot Pascual, 'The Polish Games of Transition', *Communist and Post-Communist Studies* 27, 3, 1994, pp.275–94.
25 On presidential powers, see Maurice D. Simon, 'Institutional Development of Poland's Post-Communist Sejm: A Comparative Analysis', David M. Olson and Philip Norton (eds), *The New Parliaments of Central and Eastern Europe*, London: Frank Cass, 1996, p.63. Also Michael Bernhard, 'Semipresidentialism, Charisma, and Democratic Institutions in Poland', von Mettenheim, pp.177–203.
26 Agh (Politics of Central Europe) p.143.
27 A constitutional amendment three months earlier had made provision for the popular election of the president.
28 Karen Henderson and Neil Robinson, *Post-Communist Politics. An Introduction*, London: Prentice Hall, 1997, p.145. For one discussion of the Walesa–Mazowiecki conflict, see Andrzej Rapaczynski, 'Constitutional Politics in Poland: A Report on the Constitutional Commission of the Polish Parliament', A.E. Dick Howard (ed), *Constitution Making in Eastern Europe*, Washington: Woodrow Wilson Center Press, 1993, pp.93–131.
29 See the discussion in Frances Millard, 'The Shaping of the Polish Party System, 1989–93', *East European Politics and Societies* 8, 3, Fall 1994, pp.467–94.
30 For the establishment of a political council, which was widely seen as an attempt to undercut the government, see Simon (Institutional Development), p.64.
31 Of the 460 seats, 391 were elected in districts without a threshold, and 69 from a national list with a 5% threshold.
32 For details of fragmentation of the political system, see Millard (Shaping), pp.478–80. Eleven groups won only one seat each.
33 For some details, see Krzysztof Jasiewicz, 'Polish Parties on the Eve of the 1993 Elections: Toward Fragmentation or Pluralism', *Communist and Post-Communist Studies* 26, 4, December 1993, pp.387–411. On the effect of the electoral laws, see Voytek Zubek, 'The Fragmentation of Poland's Political Party System' *Communist and Post-Communist Studies* 26, 1 March 1993, pp.47–71. On the failure of Solidarity, see Tomek Grabowski, 'The Party That Never Was: The

Rise and Fall of the Solidarity Citizens' Committees in Poland', *East European Politics and Societies* 10, 2, Spring 1996, pp.214–54.
34 Work on devising a constitution from the competing conceptions of different political forces was the responsibility of a Constitutional Commission of the National Assembly, which began work on 30 October 1992. For its work and the difficulties it faced, see the series of reports in successive issues of EECR beginning 2, 1, Winter 1993.
35 Wojciech Sokolewicz, 'The Relevance of Western Models for Constitution-Building in Poland', Joachim Jens Hesse and Nevil Johnson (eds), *Constitutional Policy and Change in Europe*, Oxford: Oxford University Press, 1995, p.248. For some details, see 'Constitution Watch', EECR 1, 1, Spring 1992, p.2. and 'Poland has a New Constitution as Conflict Between Two Chambers of Parliament Continues', EECR 1, 3, Fall 1992, pp.12–14.
36 See Simon (Institutional Development) pp.66–8 for one discussion of the Little Constitution. Indeed, Walesa sought to amend the Little Constitution to increase his powers in March 1993, less than six months after it was adopted. EECR 2, 2, Spring 1993, p.11.
37 Richard Rose, Neil Munro and Tom Mackie, *Elections in Central and Eastern Europe Since 1990*, Glasgow: Centre for the Study of Public Policy, University of Strathclyde, 1998, pp.91 and 93. This included the conservative, nationalist, free market and Catholic parties. Andrew A. Michta, 'Democratic consolidation in Poland after 1989', Karen Dawisha and Bruce Parrott (eds), *The Consolidation of Democracy in East-Central Europe*, Cambridge: Cambridge University Press, 1997, p.81. For an attempt to explain the successor party's success in terms of the electoral system, the fragmentation of the right-wing post-Solidarity parties, and the desire to moderate the excesses of the reforms, see Frances Millard, 'The Polish Parliamentary Election of September 1993', *Communist and Post-Communist Studies* 27, 3, 1994, pp.295–313. Also see Alison Mahr and John Nagle, 'Resurrection of the Successor Parties and Democratization in East Central Europe', *Communist and Post-Communist Studies* 28, 4, 1995, pp.393–409 and Voytek Zubek, 'The Phoenix Out of the Ashes: The Rise to Power of Poland's Post-Communist SdRP', *Communist and Post-Communist Studies* 28, 3, 1995, pp.275–306.
38 For a discussion of this, see Henderson and Robinson, pp.365–6.
39 Terry Cox and Laszlo Vass, 'Civil Society and Interest Representation in Hungarian Political Development', *The Journal of Communist Studies and Transition Politics* 10, 3, September 1994, pp.153–61.
40 Other groups included the Social Democrats, Ferenc Munnich Society, Hungarian Independence Party, Republican Circle, Endre Bajczy-Zsilinszky Circle, Democratic Union of Scientific Workers, Democratic Teachers' Union, Federation of Young Professionals, Blue Danube Circle, and Democratic Association of Gypsies. Joseph Rothschild, *Return to Diversity. A Political History of East Central Europe Since World War II*, Oxford: Oxford University Press, 1993, p.242.
41 On Hungarian parties, see Bill Lomax, 'The Structure and Organization of Hungary's Political Parties', Paul G. Lewis (ed), *Party Structure and Organization in East Central Europe*, Cheltenham: Edward Elgar, 1996, pp.20–42; Magdolna Balasz and Zsolt Enyedi, 'Hungarian Case Studies: The Alliance of Free Democrats and the Alliance of Young Democrats', Lewis, 1996, pp.43–65; Agh (Politics of Central Europe) pp.104–06.
42 For a discussion by a participant, see Andras Bozoki, 'Hungary's Road to Systematic Change: The Opposition Roundtable', *East European Politics and Societies* 7, 2, Spring 1993, pp.276–308. Also Andras Bozoki, 'Party Formation and Constitutional Change in Hungary', *The Journal of Communist Studies and Transition Politics* 10, 3, September 1994, pp.35–55. On the Round Table also see Andras Sajo, 'The Roundtable Talks in Hungary', Elster, pp.69–98, and Elster, Offe and Preuss, pp.65–7. For a discussion of the negotiations that occurred between different sets of actors in 1988–90, see David Stark and Laszlo Bruszt, *Postsocialist Pathways. Transforming Politics and Property in East Central Europe*, Cambridge: Cambridge University Press, 1998, ch.1.
43 See John T. Ishiyama, 'Electoral Systems Experimentation in the New Eastern Europe: The Single Transferable Vote and the Additional Member System in Estonia and Hungary', *East European Quarterly*, 29, 4, January 1996, pp.499–503. The PR component actually had two

parts: regional lists (152 seats) and a national list (58 seats). Also see Arend Lijphart, 'Democratization and Constitutional Choices in Czecho-Slovakia, Hungary and Poland 1989–91', *Journal of Theoretical Politics* 4, 2, 1992, pp.214–15.
44 The elections were not held earlier in order to give time for further working out of the details of the new system and for viable parties to develop.
45 Attila Agh, 'The Permanent 'Constitutional Crisis' in the Democratic Transition: The Case of Hungary', Hesse and Johnson, pp.302–03.
46 An attempt to reverse this decision through a popular referendum in July 1990 failed when only 13.9% of voters participated. For a discussion of the calculations of the different sides on the issue of the presidency, see Jon Elster, 'Bargaining Over the Presidency', EECR 2, 4 and 3, 1, Fall 1993–Winter 1994, p.96.
47 Henderson and Robinson, p.143. On the nature of the parliamentary representatives, see Akos Rona-Tas, 'The Selected and the Elected: The Making of the New Parliamentary Elite in Hungary', *East European Politics and Societies* 5, 3, Fall 1991, pp.357–93. For an argument that the campaign was charactersed by 'high policy consensus', see John Higley, Jan Pakulski and Wlodzimierz Wesolowski, 'Introduction: Elite Change and Democratic Regimes in Eastern Europe', John Higley, Jan Pakulski and Wlodzimierz Wesolowski (eds), *Postcommunist Elites and Democracy in Eastern Europe*, Basingstoke: Macmillan, 1998, p.8.
48 Bill Lomax, 'Hungary', Stephen Whitefield (ed), *The New Institutional Architecture of Eastern Europe*, London: Macmillan, 1993, pp.87–8; Peter Paloczolay, 'The New Hungarian Constitutional State: Challenges and Perspectives', Howard p.25; Agh (Permanent Constitutional Crisis), p.305.
49 Agh (Permanent Constitutional Crisis), pp.308–11.
50 Lomax (Structure and Organization), p.23.
51 Bill Lomax, 'The 1998 Elections in Hungary: Third Time Lucky for the Young Democrats', *The Journal of Communist Studies and Transition Politics* 15, 2, June 1999, p.119.
52 Anna Seleny, 'Old Political Rationalities and New Democracies. Compromise and Confrontation: Hungary and Poland', *World Politics* 51, 4, July 1999, p.497.
53 Richard Crampton, 'Bulgaria', Whitefield, p.15.
54 For its composition, see John D. Bell, 'Postcommunist Bulgaria', Karen Dawisha and Bruce Parrott (eds), *Politics, power and the struggle for democracy in South-East Europe*, Cambridge: Cambridge University Press, 1997, p.362.
55 On the Bulgarian Round Table, see Rumyana Kolarova and Dimitr Dimitrov, 'The Roundtable Talks in Bulgaria', Elster, 1996, pp.178–212.
56 Although in 1993 a parliamentary commission reported that at least 10% of the votes won by the BSP were of dubious validity. 'Bulgaria', EECR 2, 2, Spring 1993, p.4. Even if this was the case, the BSP still gained significantly more support than its closest rival.
57 For a list of its most important components, see Rose, Munro and Mackie, p.11.
58 For its composition, see Bell, p.372.
59 He was popularly discredited when it became known that he had advocated the use of force against demonstrators in December 1989.
60 On this see Crampton p.20.
61 The MRF had had to survive a challenge to its right to participate given that it explicitly represented the interests of the Turkish section of the population. For a discussion of this, see 'Turkish Party in Bulgaria Allowed to Continue', EECR 1, 2, Summer 1992, pp.11–12.
62 Bell, pp.374–7.
63 He was forced to a second round, where he won 53% of the vote (compared with 44.7% in the first round) against his BSP-supported opponent. Bell, p.380.
64 For a useful study of the UDF, see Michael Waller and Georgi Karasimeonov, 'Party Organization in Post-communist Bulgaria', Lewis, 1996, pp.143–61.
65 Agh (Politics of Central Europe) p.182.
66 On this see Nicholas Pano, 'The process of democratization in Albania', Dawisha and Parrott, (*South-East Europe*), 1997, pp.304–10.

67 A constitutional referendum failed in November 1994. For details of earlier attempts to bring about constitutional change, see 'Albania', EECR 2, 2, Spring 1993, p.2. Also see Pano, pp.326–9.
68 See the discussion in Pano, pp.342–3. Also see Fabian Schmidt, 'Election Fraud Sparks Protest', *Transition* 2, 13, 28 June 1996, pp.38–9 and 63.
69 On the Czechoslovak Round Table, see Milos Calda, 'The Roundtable Talks in Czechoslovakia', Elster, pp.135–77.
70 The threshold for the Slovak National Council was set at 3%.
71 On the proliferation of groups after the collapse of communism, see Sharon Wolchik, 'The Repluralization of Politics in Czechoslovakia', *Communist and Post-Communist Studies* 26, 4, December 1993, pp.412–31.
72 Higley, Pakulski and Wesolowski, p.12.
73 See the discussion in Judy Batt, 'Czechoslovakia', Whitefield, pp.45–6.
74 Henderson and Robinson, p.137.
75 Batt p.39.
76 This had actually been established as an independent party in 1989, joining the CF in 1990.
77 Rose, Munro and Mackie p.33. The Club of Active Non-Partisans had actually been formed in 1968 and joined CF in 1990.
78 For policy differences underlying this, see Batt, p.43. On constitutional discussions, see Elster, Offe and Preuss, pp.71–7.
79 For discussions of this, see Dusan Hendryck, 'Constitutionalism and Constitutional Change in Czechoslovakia', Hesse and Johnson, pp.286–9, and Katarina Mathernova, 'Czecho?Slovakia: Constitutional Disappointments', Howard, pp.57–92. On the role of the federal structure, see Carol Skalnik Leff, 'Democratization and Disintegration in Multinational States: The Breakup of the Communist Federations', *World Politics* 51, 2, 1999, pp.205–35, and Valerie Bunce, *Subversive Institutions. The Design and the Destruction of Socialism and the State*, Cambridge: Cambridge University Press, 1999.
80 For a discussion of the process, see Batt, pp.49–52.
81 For the argument that the future of the state was a major issue in the election in the form of discussion about federalism, see David M. Olson, 'Dissolution of the State: Political Parties and the 1992 Election in Czechoslovakia', *Communist and Post-Communist Studies* 26, 3, September 1993, pp.301–14. Compare with Abby Innes, 'The Breakup of Czechoslovakia: the Impact of Party Development on the Separation of the State', *East European Politics and Societies* 11, 3, Fall 1997, pp.393–435.
82 Henderson and Robinson, p.239.
83 'Czech Republic', EECR 2, 2, Spring 1993, p.5.
84 EECR 2, 4 and 3, 1, Fall 1993–Winter 1994, p.6.
85 'Czech Republic', EECR 2, 1, Winter 1993, p.4. In 1991 Havel had favoured a constitutional amendment giving the president the power to dissolve parliament, but this had been rejected.
86 On the Senate, see 'Czech Republic', EECR 3, 2, Spring 1994, pp.6–8.
87 For a discussion of Czech parties, see Petr Kopecky, 'Parties in the Czech Parliament: From Transformative Towards Arena Type of Parliament', Lewis, pp.66–88; and Ales Kroupa and Tomas Kostelecky, 'Party Organization and Structure at National and Local Level in the Czech Republic Since 1989',' Lewis.
88 For a discussion of the nature of the vote, see Petr Mateju and Blanka Rehakova, 'Turning Left or Class Realignment? Analysis of the Changing Relationship Between Class and Party in the Czech Republic, 1992–96', *East European Politics and Societies* 11, 3, Fall 1997, pp.501–42.
89 For details see EECR 8, 3, Summer 1999, p.10.
90 Darina Malova and Daniva Sivakova, 'The National Council of the Slovak Republic: Between Democratic Transition and National State-Building', Olson and Norton, pp.113–14.
91 For details see Malova and Sivakova, pp.115–16. The MDS worked with the Agrarian Party of Slovakia.
92 On this, see Sharon L. Wolchik, 'Democratization and political participation in Slovakia', Dawisha and Parrott (East-Central Europe), p.211.

93 For a study of the rise of this 'ultra-nationalist, populist, former communist' alliance, see Michael Carpenter, 'Slovakia and the Triumph of Nationalist Populism', *Communist and Post-Communist Studies* 30, 2, June 1997, pp.205–20.
94 For some details, see 'Slovakia', EECR 2, 4 and 3, 1, Fall 1993–Winter 1994 p.19 and 3, 2, Spring 1994, pp.23–4. Also see Spencer Zifcak, 'The Battle Over Presidential Power in Slovakia', EECR, 4, 3, Summer 1995, pp.61–5. Zifcak argues that the combination of extensive but ambiguous powers plus a parliamentary right to remove the president at any time created an unstable constitutional situation.
95 On the Meciar regime, see M. Steven Fish, 'The End of Meciarism', EECR 8, 1–2, Winter–Spring 1999, pp.47–55.
96 In response, the Hungarian Coalition partners united into a single party while the five partners in the SDC combined their candidates into a single front organisation while the individual parties remained dormant.
97 On this see EECR 8, 1–2, Winter–Spring 1999, p.37.
98 This was a front organisation initially comprising the Christian Democratic Movement, Democratic Union, Democratic Party, Social Democratic Party of Slovakia and the Slovak Green Party, formed in response to the raising of the electoral threshold for coalitions from 3% to 5%.
99 Although former communists continued to play a role in the Czech administration while, in the words of one observer, in Slovakia 'onetime communists have taken most of the leading positions in the three post-1992 governments'. Thomas Baylis, 'Elite Change After Communism: Eastern Germany, the Czech Republic and Slovakia', *East European Politics and Societies* 12, 2, Spring 1998, p.279. Also see Lubomir Brokl and Zdenka Mansfeldova, 'Czech and Slovak Political and Parliamentary Elites', Higley, Pakulski and Wesolowski (Postcommunist Elites), pp.139–40.
100 Support for independence among Estonians grew from 64% in September 1989 to 96% in May 1990. Toivo U. Raun, 'Estonia: independence redefined', Ian Bremmer and Ray Taras (eds), *New States New Politics. Building the Post-Soviet Nations*, Cambridge: Cambridge University Press, 1997, p.414.
101 On discussion of the voting system, see Ishiyama (Electoral System), p.490.
102 John T. Ishiyama, 'Founding Elections and the Development of Transitional Parties: The Cases of Estonia and Latvia, 1990–1992', *Communist and Post-Communist Studies* 26, 3, September 1993, p.293.
103 Toivo U. Raun, 'Democratization and Political Development in Estonia, 1987–96', Dawisha and Parrot (eds), (*East-Central Europe*), 1997, p.348.
104 Peet Kask, 'Institutional Development of the Parliament of Estonia', Olson and Norton p.210. Although this had to be applied for within initially two but later four years.
105 The constitutional draft had been written by a special assembly which had begun meeting in September 1991. The assembly had 30 members from the parliament and 30 from the Congress of Estonia, a radical nationalist body. For some details of the constitutional drafting process, see Gerald M. Easter, 'Preference for Presidentialism: Postcommunist Regime Change in Russia and the NIS', *World Politics* 49, 2, January 1997, pp.205–7.
106 Rose, Munro and Mackie, p.49. NB. Henderson and Robinson give different figures. For a discussion of the constitution, see Raun (Dawisha and Parrott, *East-Central Europe*), pp.349–50.
107 Ishiyama ('Founding Elections), p.293.
108 Raun ('Estonia: independence redefined'), p.416.
109 On the election, see David Arter, 'Estonia After the March 1995 Riigikogu Election: Still an Anti-Party System?', *The Journal of Communist Studies and Transition Politics* 11, 3, September 1995, pp.253–4.
110 Meri vetoed 17 of 351 laws passed by the Riigikogu between 1992 and the end of 1994. 'Estonia', EECR 4, 1, Winter 1995, p.12. Also Henderson and Robinson p.321.
111 In the October 1993 local elections, the FU was defeated by good performances by the Coalition Party and by Russian-based parties, which had mobilised for these elections; although debarred

from national elections, non-citizens were able to vote in local elections. 'Estonia', EECR 2, 4 and 3, 1, Fall 1993–Winter 1994, p.9.
112 See Arter.
113 For details, see EECR 8, 1–2, Winter–Spring 1999, p.13.
114 On developments in party and opposition ranks, see Ishiyama ('Founding Elections), pp.284–7. The PFL was founded in 1988. For a discussion, see Nils Muiznieks, 'Latvia: restoring a state, rebuilding a nation', Ian Bremmer and Ray Taras (eds), *New States New Politics. Building the Post-Soviet Nations*, Cambridge: Cambridge University Press, 1997, pp.385–91.
115 Rose, Munro and Mackie, p.66.
116 For one comparison between the positions of the Russian communities in Estonia and Latvia, see Pal Kosto and Boris Tsilevich, 'Patterns of Nation-Building and Political Integration in a Bifurcated Postcommunist State: Ethnic Aspects of Parliamentary Elections in Latvia', *East European Politics and Societies* 11, 2, Spring 1997, pp.366–91.
117 This was amended in July 1992 when a citizenship law established a 16 year period of residency and knowledge of Latvian. Muisnieks, p.401.
118 Amendments included lowering the voting age and introducing a provision for popularly-initiated referenda under strictly circumscribed conditions, namely if the president threatened to dismiss the parliament, if parliament altered the constitution in an undemocratic way, or if 10% of the voters sought to counter a two-month presidential suspension of the publication of a law. 'Latvia', EECR 3, 2, Spring 1994, p.14.
119 General requirements for naturalisation were five years residence after 4 May 1990 and command of the Latvian language, with certain categories of people (e.g. retired Soviet military and KGB) barred permanently from citizenship. Muiznieks, p.392.
120 On the parties, see Andrejs Plakans, 'Democratization and Political Participation in Postcommunist Societies: the Case of Latvia', Dawisha and Parrott (East-Central Europe), pp.270–80.
121 Proposed governments formed by the 'right' and 'left' were both rejected by the parliament before President Ulmanis picked someone from outside both blocs (Andris Skele) to be prime minister and form a government of people from both blocs. See the discussion in Plakans, pp.245 and 282–3.
122 On the composition of the government and the negotiations preceding it, see EECR 8, 1–2, Winter–Spring 1999, pp.19–20.
123 Alfred Erich Senn, 'Lithuania: rights and responsibilities of independence', Bremmer and Taras, p.357.
124 For one discussion, see Stephen Holmes, 'Conflict Between Executive and Parliament Intensifies in Lithuania', EECR 1, 2, Summer 1992, pp.14–15. Landsbergis had lost the support of many Sajudis deputies by this stage. Senn (Bremmer and Taras), p.363.
125 Rose, Munro and Mackie, pp.81 and 83. Homeland Union was founded in April 1993 to be the vehicle for Landsbergis and those sections of Sajudis which supported him. Also see Terry D. Clark, 'The Lithuanian Political Party System: A Case Study of Democratic Consolidation', *East European Politics and Societies* 9, 1, Winter 1995, pp.41–62.
126 Snegur had been a CC Secretary since 1985 and Chairman of the Supreme Soviet since July 1989, but had by early 1990 associated himself with the MPF. William Crowther and Steven D. Roper, 'A Comparative Analysis of Institutional Development in the Romanian and Moldovan Parliaments', Olson and Norton, p.144.
127 Ethnic tensions had been rising for some time and in August 1990 both regions announced the formation of their own republics. William Crowther, 'Moldova: caught between nation and empire', Bremmer and Taras, p.320.
128 Crowther (Moldova), p.323.
129 For a study of the election, see Crowther (Moldova), pp.325–7.
130 For one analysis, see Lincoln Allison, Alexander Kukhianidze, Malkhaz Matsaberidze and Valeri Dolidze, 'Problems of Democratization in the Republic of Georgia', *Democratization* 3, 4, Winter 1996, p.520. Also Stephen F. Jones, 'Georgia: the trauma of statehood', Bremmer and Taras, pp.517–22.

131 Darrell Slider, 'Democratization in Georgia', Karen Dawisha and Bruce Parrott (eds), *Conflict, cleavage, and change in Central Asia and the Caucasus*, Cambridge: Cambridge University Press, 1997, pp.165–7.
132 Local elites in South Ossetia had actually declared the region's sovereignty in August 1990 and organised their own elections in December 1990, boycotting those in Georgia as a whole. When Tbilisi tried to enforce direct rule, fighting broke out which resulted in a brokered deal (with Russian involvement) leaving South Ossetia effectively outside Georgian control. Similar pressure for sovereignty had occurred in the Abkhaz region from 1989. Slider, pp.171–2.
133 Jones, pp.524–5.
134 For one study, see Lincoln Allison, Alexander Kukhianidze and Malkhaz Matsaberidze, 'The Georgian Election of 1992', *Electoral Studies* 12, 2, 1993.
135 Slider, p.177.
136 For the results, see Slider, p.179.
137 On the difficulties of drafting this, see Allison *et al.* (Problems), pp.523–4.
138 This was Shevardnadze's successor as communist party first secretary in 1985, Dzhumber Patiashvili, who received 19.5%.
139 For one study, see Lincoln Allison, Alexander Kukhianidze and Malkhaz Matsaberidze, 'The Georgian Elections of 1995', *Electoral Studies* 15, 2, 1996.
140 Slider, p.189.
141 Attempted coups were reported to have been discovered in August 1995, February 1998 and May 1999.
142 For a brief discussion of the economic situation, see Nora Dudwick, 'Armenia: paradise regained or lost?', Bremmer and Taras, pp.490–1.
143 Nora Dudwick, 'Political transformations in postcommunist Armenia: images and realities', Dawisha and Parrott (Central Asia and the Caucasus), 1997, p.85.
144 Dudwick (Dawisha and Parrott: Central Asia and the Caucasus), p.92. For the charge that the election was manipulated, see S. Neil MacFarlane, 'Democratization, Nationalism and Regional Security in the Southern Caucasus', *Government and Opposition* 32, 3, 1998, p.405.
145 Dudwick (Dawisha and Parrott: Central Asia and the Caucasus), p.93.
146 Dudwick (Dawisha and Parrott: Central Asia and the Caucasus), pp.103–4.
147 See the discussion in Lenard J. Cohen, 'Embattled democracy: postcommunist Croatia in transition', Dawisha and Parrott (South-East Europe), pp.74–80.
148 For a survey of his nationalist world view, see Gordana Uzelak, 'Franjo Tudjman's Nationalist Ideology', *East European Quarterly* xxxi, 4, January 1998, pp.449–72.
149 Cohen, pp.84–9.
150 For the broader Yugoslav dynamic, see the discussion in Leff.
151 'Croatia', EECR 2, 2, Spring 1993, p.5. Also Cohen (Dawisha and Parrott), pp.96–100.
152 Kenneth E. Basom, 'Prospects for Democracy in Serbia and Croatia', *East European Quarterly* xxix, 4, January 1996, pp.518–20.
153 For the views of various opposition leaders, see Stephen S. Markovich, 'Democracy in Croatia: Views from the Opposition', *East European Quarterly* xxxii, 1, March 1998, pp.83–93.
154 For the argument that Tudjman used electoral means to sanction dictatorial action, see Verna Pusic, 'Dictatorships with Democratic Legitimacy: Democracy versus Nation', *East European Politics and Societies* 8, 3, Fall 1994, pp.383–401.
155 The SD-SL coalition (along with two small regional parties) won 71 seats, United List (comprising the Croatian Peasant Party, Istrian Democratic Assembly, Croatian People's Party and the Liberal Party) 24 seats, and the CDC 46 seats.
156 On this process, see John B. Dunlop, *The Rise of Russia and the Fall of the Soviet Empire* Princeton: Princeton University Press, 1993.
157 On this, see Graeme Gill and Roger D. Markwick, *Russia's Stillborn Democracy? From Gorbachev to Yeltsin*, Oxford: Oxford University Press, 2000, ch.4.
158 On this see Michael E. Urban, 'Boris El'tsin, Democratic Russia and the Campaign for the Russian Presidency', *Soviet Studies* 44, 2, 1992, pp.187–207.

159 For an expansion of this argument, see Graeme Gill, 'Elites and the Russian Transition', Graeme Gill (ed), *Elites and Leadership in Russian Politics*, Basingstoke: Macmillan, 1998, pp.134–57.
160 For a good discussion, see Thomas F. Remington, 'Democratization and the New Political Order in Russia', Karen Dawisha and Bruce Parrott (eds), *Democratic changes and authoritarian reactions in Russia, Ukraine, Belarus and Moldova*, Cambridge: Cambridge University Press, 1997, pp.78–87.
161 David Remnick, 'The War for the Kremlin', *The New Yorker* 22 July 1996.
162 For a more substantial discussion, see Gill and Markwick.
163 Rukh was established in September 1989.
164 Sarah Birch, 'Nomenklatura Democratization: Electoral Clientelism in Post-Soviet Ukraine', *Democratization* 4, 4, Winter 1997, pp.43–4. For the organisation of deputies into parliamentary blocs, see Ilya Prizel, 'Ukraine between proto-democracy and 'soft' authoritarianism', Dawisha and Parrott (Russia), p.340.
165 Although they voted even more strongly for a question which asked whether they wanted to be members of a Commonwealth of Sovereign States, entry to which would be based on Ukraine's declaration of sovereignty. Alexander Motyl and Bohdan Krawchenko, 'Ukraine: from empire to statehood', Bremmer and Taras, p.254.
166 This formulation comes from Jose Casanova, 'Ethno-linguistic and religious pluralism and democratic construction in Ukraine', Barnett R. Rubin and Jack Snyder (eds), *Post-Soviet Political Order. Conflict and State Building*, London: Routledge, 1998, p.83.
167 See Stanley Bach, 'From Soviet to Parliament in Ukraine: The Verkhovna Rada During 1992–94', Olson and Norton, p.219.
168 A constitutional commission of the parliament had presented a draft in January 1992, but nothing had come of it. On 30 June 1992 another draft was published. The constitutional commission received more than 46,000 comments and suggestions, leading to the reported modification of 90% of the draft. 'Ukraine', EECR 2, 2, Spring 1993, p.14.
169 The parliament had been made unicameral by parliamentary vote on 7 October 1993. 'Ukraine', EECR 2, 4 and 3, 1, Fall 1993–Winter 1994, p.22. On the election, see Marko Bojcun, 'The Ukrainian Parliamentary Elections in March–April 1994', *Europe-Asia Studies* 47, 2, 1995, pp.229–49; Taras Kuzio, 'The 1994 Parliamentary Elections in Ukraine', *The Journal of Communist Studies and Transition Politics* 11, 4, December 1995, pp.335–61.
170 Kuzio, pp.353–6.
171 Bach, p.225. According to Birch, approximately half the deputies in the final chamber were independents. Birch, p.44.
172 For these see Prizel, p.352.
173 See the characterisations in Henderson and Robinson, pp.317–18.
174 For one discussion, see 'Ukraine', EECR 4, 1, Winter 1995, pp.34–5.
175 Henderson and Robinson, p.319.
176 On the 1998 election, see Melvin J. Hinich, Valeri Khmelko and Peter J. Ordeshook, 'Ukraine's 1998 Parliamentary Elections. A Spatial Analysis', *Post-Soviet Affairs* 15, 2, April–June 1999, pp.149–85; Andrew Wilson and Sarah Birch, 'Voting Stability, Political Gridlock: Ukraine's 1998 Parliamentary Elections', *Europe-Asia Studies* 51, 6, 1999, pp.1039–68; Peter R. Craumer and James I. Clem, 'Ukraine's Emerging Electoral Geography: A Regional Analysis of the 1998 Parliamentary Elections', *Post-Soviet Geography and Economics* 40, 1, 1999, pp.1–26.
177 Eugene Huskey, 'Kyrgyzstan: the fate of political liberalization', Dawisha and Parrott (Central Asia and the Caucasus), p.253.
178 See John Anderson, 'Constitutional Development in Central Asia', *Central Asian Studies* 16, 3, September 1997, p.303.
179 Itar-Tass Daily News, 4 February 1994.
180 Anderson (Constitutional), p.313.
181 For a list see Anderson (Constitutional), pp.313–14.
182 Itar-Tass Daily News 27 February 1995. Huskey, p.261.

216   Notes

183   For a discussion of Akaev's relationship with the media, see Naryn Aiyp, 'Kyrgyzstan: Askar Akayev's Diminishing Democracy', *Transitions* 5, 10, October 1998, p.61.
184   Manes-El, EI (Bei Bechara), Party of Bishkek Residents, and the Labour Popular Party.
185   See the discussion in Adolf Bibic, 'The Emergence of Pluralism in Slovenia', *Communist and Post-Communist Studies* 26, 4, December 1993, pp.369–78; also Sabrina Petra Ramet, 'Democratization in Slovenia and the second stage', Dawisha and Parrott (South-East Europe), pp.190–6. For a comparison of Slovenian nationalism which favoured reformism and independence with that of Serbia which looked for a recentralisation of political control, see Valerie Bunce, *Subversive Institutions. The Design and the Destruction of Socialism and the State*, Cambridge: Cambridge University Press, 1999, pp.92–5.
186   Henderson and Robinson, p.152.
187   For the composition of Demos and the voting figures, see Rose, Munro and Mackie, pp.109, 113 and 115 .
188   Rose, Munro and Mackie, p.107.
189   See Bibic, pp.379–82.
190   Duncan M. Perry, 'The Republic of Macedonia: finding its way', Dawisha and Parrott (South-East Europe), p.235.
191   In the words of one observer, Romania's new leaders were all 'former communist notables.' Jonathan Eyal, 'Romania', Whitefield, p.122.
192   There were other factors in the NSF's victory as well. See Henderson and Robinson, pp.148–9.
193   For details, see Eyal, pp.132–5.
194   For an argument about the growing pluralism in Romania, see Liliana Mihut, 'The Emergence of Political Pluralism in Romania', *Communist and Post-Communist Studies* 27, 4, 1994, pp.411–22.
195   For a discussion, see Steven D. Roper, 'From Opposition to Government Coalition: Unity and Fragmentation within the Democratic Convention of Romania', *East European Quarterly* xxi, 4, January 1998, pp.519–42.
196   See Henry F. Carey, 'Irregularities or Rigging: The 1992 Romanian Parliamentary Elections', *East European Quarterly* xxix, 1, March 1995, pp.43–66. For the argument that most of the media is controlled by the state, see Henry F. Carey, 'From Big Lie to Small Lies: State Mass Media Dominance in Post-Communist Romania', *East European Politics and Societies* 10, 1, Winter 1996, pp.16–45.
197   Agh (Politics of Central Europe), p.184. On Romanian parties, see Steven D. Roper, 'The Romanian Party System and the Catch-All Party Phenomenon', *East European Quarterly* xxviii, 4, January 1995, pp.519–32.
198   For a discussion of some of the issues here, see Henderson and Robinson, p.368.
199   Roper (From Opposition), p.520.
200   On the establishment of political parties, see Nicholas J. Miller, 'A failed transition: the case of Serbia', Dawisha and Parrott (South-East Europe), pp.155–8. A referendum had been held in July asking voters whether they wanted to hold elections before or after the adoption of a new constitution. A reported 97% voted in favour of an earlier constitution. This was adopted by the old parliament in September. It was written by the Milosevic forces and the opposition had no chance to debate it. It involved a powerful presidential position.
201   Bunce (Subversive), pp.93–5.
202   Basom, pp.518–20.
203   The SPS formed a government with the support of former members of the Depos coalition.
204   Miller, pp.172–3. For one discusion of the basis of his power, see Laszlo Sekelj, 'Parties and Elections: The Federal Republic of Yugoslavia – Change Without Transformation', *Europe-Asia Studies* 52, 1, January 2000, pp.59–61.
205   Tim Judah, 'How Milosevic Hangs On', *The New York Review of Books*, 16 July 1998, pp.44–5.
206   The first round was in December 1992, the second January 1993.
207   Dragan Stavljanin, 'Brothers at Arm's Length', *Transitions* 6, 2, February 1999, p.31. Djukanovic's 'For a Better Life' coalition consisted of three parties, the Democratic Party of Socialists (30 seats), People's Party (7 seats) and the Social Democratic Party (5 seats).

Notes 217

208 Although they had been forced to permit the registration of the Azeri Popular Front by striking railway workers in mid-1989. Audrey L. Altstadt, 'Azerbaijan's struggle toward democracy', Dawisha and Parrott (Central Asia and the Caucasus), p.121.
209 The 11 seats from Nagorno-Karabakh were not filled.
210 Since January 1990; he was installed after the Soviet army crashed its way into Baku in the wake of ethnic disturbances.
211 Shireen T. Hunter, 'Azerbaijan: searching for new neighbours', Bremmer and Taras, p.449.
212 See the discussion in Altstadt, pp.130–1.
213 Nathan Hodge and Sharon Weinberger, 'Azerbaijan's Beleaguered Opposition Divides Under Pressure', *Transitions* 6, 2, February 1999, pp.26–7.
214 'Statement of the National Democratic Institute (NDI) International Observer Delegation to Azerbaijan's November 5, 2000 Parliamentary Elections', Baku, November 7, 2000.
215 On the early development of opposition, see Jan Zaprudnik and Michael Urban, 'Belarus: from statehood to empire', Bremmer and Taras, pp.286–9.
216 The Communist Party in Belarus remained hostile to the PFB, which had to be founded formally in Vilnius in Lithuania and party members were forbidden from joining it.
217 Zaprudnik and Urban, pp.289–90.
218 For a discussion, see David R. Marples, 'Belarus: The Illusion of Stability', *Post-Soviet Affairs* 9, 3, July–September 1993, pp.257–8.
219 See the discussion in Alexander Lukashuk , 'The New Draft Constitution of Belarus: A Shaky Step Toward the Rule of Law', EECR 2, 1, Winter 1993, pp.17–20. The third draft presented in May 1993 was even more presidentialist. EECR 2, 2, Spring 1993, pp.2–3.
220 In July 1992 the Kebich government had signed an agreement with Russia establishing a 'common space' in economic, social and political terms, and Russian control over Belarus-based strategic troops and technical and production facilities. Kathleen J. Mihalisko, 'Belarus: retreat to authoritarianism', Dawisha and Parrott (Russia), p.248.
221 Shushkevich favoured closer economic relations, but believed this agreement infringed Belarus' sovereignty.
222 Henderson and Robinson, p.331.
223 The president was to be both head of government and head of state. For his powers, see Zaprudnik and Urban, p.299. On the constitution, see Mihalisko, pp.254–6.
224 Itar-Tass Daily News 18 November 1994. On parties, see Mihalisko, pp.243–6.
225 Itar-Tass Daily News 18 November 1994.
226 To be successful, a candidate had to receive 50% of the vote.
227 Lukashenka even enacted a decree preventing candidates from appearing on television.
228 After four rounds of voting, of the 198 seats filled, 95 were independents, 42 were CPB and 33 Agrarian Party. No other of the 13 parties had more than nine seats. There were 260 seats in all.
229 Under Lukashenko the administration had been re-establishing government control over the economy. Mihalisko, pp.268–9.
230 See the report by Francois Bonnet, 'Belarus leader fights shy of elections', *The Guardian Weekly* April 18, 1999, p.16.
231 On the disappearance of opposition figures, see Alexander Feduta, 'Why Do People in Belarus Keep Vanishing into Thin Air?', *Moscow News* 38, October 6–12, 1999, p.5.
232 For details, see EECR 8, 3, Summer 1999, pp.4–5.
233 On Nazarbaev's attempts to establish a presidential party, see Martha Brill Olcott, 'Kazakhstan: pushing for Eurasia', Bremmer and Taras, pp.557–8.
234 Itar-Tass Daily News 9 February 1993. Ian Bremmer and Cory Welt, 'The trouble with democracy in Kazakhstan', *Central Asian Survey* 15, 2, June 1996, p.185
235 For a short history of its writing, see Anderson (Constitutional), pp.302–3.
236 For the results see Bremmer and Welt, p.189.
237 Bremmer and Welt, p.188. Most candidates were actually on lists proposed by the government. Martha Brill Olcott, 'The growth of political participation in Kazakhstan' (sic), Dawisha and Parrott (Central Asia and the Caucasus), p.220.
238 For its composition, see Olcott (Dawisha and Parrott), p.222.

239 Bremmer and Welt, p.192 and Olcott (Dawisha and Parrott), p.223.
240 Olcott (Dawisha and Parrott), pp.227–8.
241 *Nezavisimaia gazeta* 21 April 1995.
242 For details, see Anderson (Constitutional), pp.312–13.
243 The upper house or Senate was to comprise two representatives from each oblast chosen by the oblast's representative bodies plus seven appointed by the president.
244 For a list of these parties, see Olcott (Dawisha and Parrott), p.232.
245 Timothy Edmunds, 'Power and powerlessness in Kazakhstani society: ethnic problems in perspective', *Central Asian Survey* 17, 3, September 1998, p.468. Also Bremmer and Welt, pp.186–7.
246 The constitutional amendments adopted in November 1998 abolished the limit of two presidential terms and extended the term from five to seven years.
247 Felix Corley, 'Disputed Results', *Transitions* 6, 2, February 1999, pp.8–9.
248 549 candidates competed for 67 SMC seats and 64 candidates representing nine parties competed for the 10 PR seats. The presidential party, Otan won four of the ten PR seats (three other parties won two each) and a majority of SMC seats. Turn out for the first round was 61.5%, for the second 49%.
249 For the report on the first round, see RFE/RL Newsline 3, 199, Part 1, 12 October 1999.
250 Muriel Atkin, 'Thwarted democratization in Tajikistan', Dawisha and Parrott (Central Asia and the Caucasus), p.288.
251 Atkin (Dawisha and Parrott), pp.285–7.
252 On the regional clan basis of this, see Shahram Akbarzadeh, 'The Political Shape of Central Asia', *Central Asian Survey* 16, 4, December 1997, pp.517–42; Also Muriel Atkin, 'Tajikistan: reform, reaction and civil war', Bremmer and Taras, pp.614–16, and Atkin (Dawisha and Parrott), pp.293–5.
253 In effect, the people were being asked whether they wanted a presidency at the same time they were voting for the president. Anderson (Constitutional), pp.303–4.
254 Itar-Tass Daily News 9 November 1994.
255 OSCE, Office for Democratic Institutions and Human Rights, 'The Republic of Tajikistan. Elections to the Parliament 27 February 2000. Final Report', Warsaw, 17 May 2000.
256 John Anderson, 'Authoritarian political development in Central Asia: the case of Turkmenistan', *Central Asian Survey* 14, 4, 1995, p.510.
257 On the constitution and its adoption, see Anderson (Constitutional), p.302. Also Michael Ochs, 'Turkmenistan: the quest for stability and control', Dawisha and Parrott (Central Asia and the Caucasus), pp.318–20.
258 For details, see Murad Esenov, 'Turkmenistan: Saparmurat Niyazov's Invincible Rule', *Transitions* 5, 10, October 1998, p.65.
259 Anderson (Authoritarian), pp.513–15. The situation is summed up by the following title: David Nissman, 'Turkmenistan: just like old times', Bremmer and Taras, pp.634–53.
260 Shahram Akbarzadeh, 'Nation-building in Uzbekistan', *Central Asian Survey* 15, 1, March 1996, p.26.
261 William Fierman 'Political development in Uzbekistan: democratization?', Dawisha and Parrott (Central Asia and the Caucasus), pp.383–5.
262 For some details, see Gregory Gleason, 'Uzbekistan: the politics of national independence', Bremmer and Taras, 1997, p.581.
263 Itar-Tass Daily News 22 January 1993. Felix Corley, 'Uzbekistan: Islam Karimov's Everlasting First Term', *Transitions* 5, 10, October 1998, p.62. Also Fierman (Dawisha and Parrott), pp.388–9.
264 This had actually begun in mid-1992, perhaps stimulated by the unrest against and ultimate fall of Nabiev in Tajikistan.
265 Fierman, p.391.
266 Fierman, p.392. Indeed, the five parties registered at the beginning of 2000 were all formed on Karimov's initiative.

3 Civil society and the onset of negotiations

1. See similar distinctions drawn in Marcia A. Weigle and Jim Butterfield, 'Civil Society in Reforming Communist Regimes. The Logic of Emergence', *Comparative Politics* 25, 1, October 1992, p.1 and Gregorz Ekiert, 'Democratization Processes in East Central Europe: A Theoretical Reconsideration', *British Journal of Political Science* 21, 3, 1991, p.300.
2. For a discussion of this general point in relation to political parties, see Karen L. Remmer, 'Redemocratization and the Impact of Authoritarian Rule in Latin America', *Comparative Politics* 17, 3, April 1985, pp.253–75.
3. For an argument that civil society is important but without recognition that this statement is of little use unless it is explained why civil society forces were able to exercise greater influence in some countries than others, see M. Steven Fish, 'Postcommunist Subversion: Social Science and Democratization in East Europe and Eurasia', *Slavic Review* 58, 4, Winter 1999, pp.800–2.
4. See the discussions in Hugh Seton-Watson, *Eastern Europe Between the Wars, 1918–1941*, London: Cambridge University Press, 1945; Antony Polonsky, *The Little Dictators. The History of Eastern Europe Since 1918*, London: Routledge and Kegan Paul, 1975; Joseph Rothschild, *East Central Europe Between the Two World Wars*, Seattle: University of Washington Press, 1974; Gregory Luebbert, *Liberalism, Fascism or Social Democracy. Social Classes and the Political Origins of Regimes in Interwar Europe*, Oxford: Oxford University Press, 1991.
5. Levels of urbanisation are reflected in the following figures for the population of towns (in 000):

	1800	1850	1900	1940
Belgrade	NA	NA	69	267 (1930)
Bucharest	NA	120	276 (1899)	648
Budapest	54	178	732	1163
Krakow	24	50	91	255
Lodz	0.2	16	315	665
Prague	75	118	202	928
Riga	30	70	256	393
Sofia	NA	19 (1870)	68	401
Warsaw	100	160	638	1266
Zagreb	NA	14	61	186 (1930)
Baku	NA	16 (1860)	112	218 (1910)
Erevan	NA	12	29 (1897)	33 (1910)
Kiev	23	50	247	505 (1910)
St Petersburg	220	485	1267	3191 (1910)
Moscow	250	365	989	1533 (1910)
Tiflis	30	35	161	188 (1910)

B.R. Mitchell, *European Historical Statistics 1750–1970*, New York: Columbia University Press, 1976, pp.76–9.

6. See the classic Perry Anderson, *Lineages of the Absolutist State*, London: New Left Books, 1974, and the stimulating George Schopflin, 'The Political Traditions of Eastern Europe', *Daedalus* 119, Winter 1990. Also see Rothschild (East Central Europe).
7. Keith Crawford, *East Central European Politics Today*, Manchester: Manchester University Press, 1996, p.17.
8. Schopflin, p.65.
9. Rothschild (East Central Europe), p.19.
10. For one survey of these see Seton-Watson (East Central Europe), ch.2.
11. Rothschild (East Central Europe), p.20.

12 On the inter-war period and this trend, see Dirk Berg-Schlosser and Jeremy Mitchell (eds), *Conditions of Democracy in Europe, 1919–1939. Systematic Case Studies*, Basingstoke: Macmillan, 2000.
13 For an argument about the inability of the East European gentry to compete in the international market, leading to large scale urban migration, see Andrew C. Janos, 'The Politics of Backwardness in Continental Europe, 1780–1945', *World Politics* xli, 3, April 1989, pp.331–5.
14 In the inter-war period, almost a third of the population comprised non-Polish minority groups. For figures see Rothschild (East Central Europe), p.36.
15 Rothschild (East Central Europe), p.31.
16 See the excellent discussion in Joseph Rothschild, *Return to Diversity. A Political History of East Central Europe Since World War II*, New York: Oxford University Press, 1993, pp.151–3.
17 For one discussion see Jacques Rupnik, 'Dissent in Poland, 1968–78: the end of Revisionism and the rebirth of Civil Society', Rudolf L.Tokes (ed), *Opposition in Eastern Europe*, London, Macmillan, 1979. In 1968 university students and intellectuals had demonstrated against government censorship and the restrictive cultural policy being pursued.
18 Vaclav Benda, cited in Michael Bernhard, 'Civil Society and Democratic Transition in East Central Europe', *Political Science Quarterly* 108, 2, Summer 1993, p.313.
19 Michael Bernhard, *The Origins of Democratization in Poland: Workers, Intellectuals, and Oppositional Politics, 1976–1980*, New York: Columbia University Press, 1993.
20 On worker organisation, see Neal Ascherson, *The Polish August. What Happened in Poland*, Harmondsworth: Penguin, 1981; Jadwiga Staniszkis, *Poland's Self-Limiting Revolution*, Princeton: Princeton University Press, 1984. For a discussion of this period, see Gregorz Ekiert, *The State Against Society*, Princeton: Princeton University Press, 1996.
21 Almost a third of the population was said to belong to Solidarity at this time. Andrzej Korbonski, 'Poland', Teresa Rakowska-Harmstone (ed.), *Communism in Eastern Europe*, Manchester: Manchester University Press, 1984, p.59.
22 For one discussion, see Suzanne Hruby, 'The Church in Poland and its Political Influence', *Journal of International Affairs* 36, 2, 1982–83, pp.317–28.
23 On the intellectuals see George Schopflin, 'Opposition and Para-Opposition: Critical Currents in Hungary, 1968–1978', Rudolf L. Tokes (ed), *Opposition in Eastern Europe*, London: Macmillan, 1979; Rudolf L. Tokes, 'Hungarian Reform Imperatives', *Problems of Communism* 33, 5, September-October 1984, pp.1–23; Rudolf L. Tokes, *Hungary's Negotiated Revolution. Economic reform, social change and political succession, 1957–1990*, Cambridge: Cambridge University Press, 1996.
24 One author has referred to this in the late 1970s as 'a much more heterodox "democratic opposition"'. Bennett Kovrig, 'Hungary', Rakowska-Harmstone, p.106.
25 For the argument that three prominent, overtly political, organisations which emerged in the 1980s were narrowly-based and neither sought to create nor themselves constituted a civil society, see Bill Lomax, 'The Strange Death of "Civil Society" in Post-Communist Hungary', *The Journal of Communist Studies and Transition Politics* 13, 1, March 1997, pp.44–7. For the argument that an 'incipient civil society' emerged under Kadar, see Andras Bozoki, 'Party Formation and Constitutional Change in Hungary', *The Journal of Communist Studies and Transition Politics* 10, 3, September 1994, pp.35–55; also Terry Cox and Laszlo Vass, 'Civil Society and Interest Representation in Hungarian Political Development', *The Journal of Communist Studies and Transition Politics* 10, 3, September 1994, pp.153–79. Also the discussion in Rudolf L. Tokes, 'Party politics and political participation in postcommunist Hungary', Karen Dawisha and Bruce Parrott (eds), *The consolidation of democracy in East-Central Europe* Cambridge: Cambridge University Press, 1997, pp.112–13.
26 See the discussion in Gale Stokes, 'The Social Origins of East European Politics', Daniel Chirot, (ed), *The Origins of Backwardness in Eastern Europe. Economics and Politics from the Middle Ages Until the Early Twentieth Century*, Berkeley: University of California Press, 1979, pp.217–18.
27 Cited in Joni Lovenduski and Jean Woodall, *Politics and Society in Eastern Europe*, London: Macmillan, 1987, p.36. On the working class, see Luebbert, pp.291–4. It also had significant

ethnic diversity. For some figures, and discussion of their shortcomings, see Rothschild (East Central Europe), pp.88–9.
28 For figures and a discussion, see Rothschild (East Central Europe), pp.94–5.
29 The most important study of this remains H.G. Skilling, *Czechoslovakia's Interrupted Revolution* Princeton: Princeton University Press, 1976.
30 On this, see Milan Simechka, *The Restoration of Order. The Normalization of Czechoslovakia 1969–1976*, London, Verso, 1984.
31 On these see H.G. Skilling, *Charter 77 and Human Rights in Czechoslovakia*, London: Allen and Unwin, 1981; H.G. Skilling, 'Independent Currents in Czechoslovakia', *Problems of Communism* 34, 1, January–February 1985, pp.32–49; H.G. Skilling, *Samizdat and an Independent Society in Central and Eastern Europe*, Columbus: Ohio State University Press, 1989.
32 According to one observer they were 'small and elitist'. Rothschild (Return), p.236.
33 Lovenduski and Woodall, p.32.
34 Rothschild (East Central Europe), p.323. Bulgarian society was the most equal in the region.
35 Rothschild (East Central Europe), p.332.
36 Rothschild (East Central Europe), p.359.
37 According to Staar, 'artisans, government employees, and teachers could be classified as the nucleus of a middle class, although their limited numbers rendered their influence insignificant.' Richard F. Staar, *The Communist Regimes in Eastern Europe*, Stanford, Hoover Institution Press, 1977, p.11.
38 On this, and Riga as a commercial centre, see Juris Dreifelds, *Latvia in Transition*, Cambridge, Cambridge University Press, 1996, p.23. On Russian immigration, see Toomas Varrak, 'Estonia: Crisis and "Pre-Emptive" Authoritarianism', Berg-Schlosser and Mitchell, p.108.
39 Dreifelds, p.22.
40 For a discussion, with some statistics, of the Estonian case, see Toivo U. Raun, *Estonia and the Estonians*, Stanford: Hoover Institution Press, 1987, pp.87–90. For Latvia see Dreifelds p.22 and Alfred Bilmanis, *A History of Latvia*, Westport: Greenwood Press, 1970, ch.13.
41 Raun, p.91 and Emmanuel Nodel, *Estonia: Nation on the Anvil*, New York: Bookman Associates Inc., 1963, p.164. Also Hugh Seton-Watson, *The Russian Empire 1801–1917*, Oxford: Oxford University Press, 1967, pp.414–15 and 497.
42 For one discussion of these in Lithuania see Leonas Sabaliunas, *Lithuania in Crisis. Nationalism to Communism 1939–1940*, Bloomington: Indiana University Press, 1972, pp.5–6. Also see Rothschild (East Central Europe), pp.372–81.
43 Rothschild (East Central Europe), p.369. The figures relate to those over ten years of age.
44 A coup had actually been conducted in December 1926, but the parliament was reconvened to elect the coup leader Antanas Smetona president, and in April 1927 he dissolved the parliament.
45 On this see Graeme Gill, *The Collapse of a Single-Party System. The Disintegration of the Communist Party of the Soviet Union*, Cambridge: Cambridge University Press, 1994, pp.91–4.
46 Ronald Grigor Suny, *The Making of the Georgian Nation*, Bloomington: Indiana University Press, 1988, pp.115 and 118.
47 Suny, pp.93–4 and 125–34. For an interesting older study, see David Marshall Lang, *A Modern History of Georgia* London: Weidenfeld and Nicolson, 1962.
48 Richard G. Hovannisian, *Armenia on the Road to Independence 1918*, Berkeley: University of California Press, 1967, p.16.
49 For the ambiguous effects of Soviet policy on Armenian nationalism, see Nora Dudwick, 'Armenia: paradise regained or lost?' Ian Bremmer and Ray Taras (eds), *New States, New Politics: Building the Post-Soviet Nations*, Cambridge: Cambridge University Press, 1997, pp.477–82.
50 Henry R. Huttenbach, 'Post-Soviet Crisis and Disorder in Transcaucasia. The Search for Regional Stability and Security', Vladimir Tismaneanu (ed), *Political Culture and Civil Society in Russia and the New States of Eurasia*, Armonk: M.E. Sharpe, 1995, p.338.
51 For Armenian dissent in the 1960s, 1970s and 1980s, see Nora Dudwick, 'Political transformations in postcommunist Armenia: images and realities', Karen Dawisha and Bruce Parrott (eds), *Conflict, Cleavage and Change in Central Asia and the Caucasus*, Cambridge: Cambridge University Press, 1997, pp.76–7.

222 Notes

52 Perhaps the most egregious example was Vasilii Mzhavanadze, who was Shevardnadze's predecessor in Georgia and presided over rampant corruption.
53 For a general discussion of this in the Soviet system more generally, see Graeme Gill and Roderic Pitty, *Power in the Party. The Organization of Power and Central-Republican Relations in the CPSU*, Basingstoke: Macmillan, 1997.
54 Hugh Seton-Watson, 'The Political System of Eastern Europe Between the Wars', Stephen Fischer-Galati, *Man, State, and Society in East European History*, New York: Praeger Publications, 1970, p.251.
55 Rothschild (East Central Europe), p.276.
56 On the expression of heterodox views, see Paul Shoup, 'Crisis and Reform in Yugoslavia', *Daedalus* 79, Spring 1989, pp.137–8. On general developments in Yugoslavia, see Denison Rusinow, *The Yugoslav Experiment 1948–1974*, Berkeley: University of California Press, 1977; April Carter, *Democratic Reform in Yugoslavia: The Changing Role of the Party*, Princeton: Princeton University Press, 1982.
57 Among the concessions granted by the tsar in the wake of the 1905 revolution was a parliamentary body in which this group was well placed to pursue its interests. On some elements of civil society at this time, see Harley D. Balzer (ed), *Russia's Missing Middle Class. The Professions in Russian History*, Armonk: M.E. Sharpe, 1996 and Thomas C. Owen, *Capitalism and Politics in Russia. A Social History of the Moscow Merchants*, Cambridge: Cambridge University Press, 1981.
58 This comment does not apply to the people of the Baltic republics.
59 This is what Geoffrey Hosking confuses with civil society when he argues that this existed in the USSR. Geoffrey Hosking, *The Awakening of the Soviet Union*, London: Heinemann, 1990, ch.4.
60 For a study of charities and self-help organisations which did maintain a presence in late Soviet times, see Anne White, *Democratization in Russia Under Gorbachev 1985–91. The Birth of a Voluntary Sector*, Basingstoke: Macmillan, 1999, esp. ch.3.
61 On the emergence of these organisations, and details on some of them, see *Spravochnik po neformal'nym obshchestvennym organizatsiiam i presse*, Moscow: SMOT Informatsionnoe agenstvo, 1989; *Neformal'naia Rossiia. O neformal'nykh politizirovannykh dvizheniiakh i gruppakh v RSFSR (opyt spravochnika)*, Moscow: Molodaia gvardiia, 1990; M.V. Maliutin, 'Neformaly v perestroike: opyt i perspektivy', Iu. Afanas'ev, *Inogo ne dano*, Moscow: Progress, 1988; Vera Tolz, *The USSR's Emerging Multiparty System*, New York: Praeger, 1990; M.Steven Fish, *Democracy from Scratch. Opposition and Regime in the New Russian Revolution*, Princeton: Princeton University Press, 1995; Vladimir Brovkin, 'Revolution from below: informal political associations in Russia 1988–1989', *Soviet Studies* 42, 2, April 1990, pp.233–57; Judith B. Sedaitis and Jim Butterfield (eds), *Perestroika from below*, Boulder: Westview Press, 1991; Stephen White, Graeme Gill and Darrell Slider, *The Politics of Transition: Shaping a Post-Soviet Future*, Cambridge: Cambridge University Press, 1993, ch.8; White (Democratization in Russia).
62 For a discussion of this see Stephen F. Cohen, 'The Friends and Foes of Change: Reformism and Conservatism in the Soviet Union', and comments by T.H. Rigby, S.Frederick Starr, Frederick Barghoorn and George Breslauer, *Slavic Review* 38, 2, June 1979, pp.187–223.
63 The émigré community was important in keeping this alive.
64 On Shelest, see Borys Lewytzkyi, *Politics and Society in Soviet Ukraine 1953–1980*, Edmonton: Canadian Institute of Ukrainian Studies, 1984, ch.4.
65 For a discussion of those organisations that did emerge, see Eugene Huskey, 'Kyrgyzstan: the fate of political liberalization', Dawisha and Parrott (Central Asia and the Caucasus), pp.250–4.
66 See Gill and Pitty.
67 Rothschild (East Central Europe), p.276.
68 Shoup, p.141. Also see Tomaz Mastnak, 'Civil Society in Slovenia: From Opposition to Power', *Studies in Comparative Communism* XXIII, 3/4, Autumn/Winter 1990, pp.305–17, and Adolf

Bibic, 'The Emergence of Pluralism in Slovenia', *Communist and Post-Communist Studies* 26, 4, December 1993, pp.367–86.
69 Rothschild (East Central Europe), p.276.
70 Formally an independent state had existed between March 1918 and January 1919, but this was recognised only by the German occupying forces. For a discussion of the weak and fitful attempts to foster a sense of national identity in the nineteenth century, see Jan Zaprudnik and Michael Urban, 'Belarus: from statehood to empire', Bremmer and Taras, pp.278–81.
71 On the Belorussian Soviet authorities attempting to build up a Belorussian political machine that excluded outsiders, see Michael E. Urban, *An Algebra of Soviet Power: Elite Circulation in the Belorussian Republic 1966–1986*, Cambridge: Cambridge University Press, 1989.
72 For the weakness of independent forces in Turkmenistan and Uzbekistan, see Michael Ochs, 'Turkmenistan: the quest for stability and control' and William Fierman, 'Political development in Uzbekistan: democratization?', Dawisha and Parrott (Central Asia and the Caucasus), 1997, pp.323–6 and 368–77. The development of an anti-nuclear movement in Kazakhstan reflects the problems of living in the republic which was the site of Soviet nuclear testing. For a list of 'informals' in Kazakhstan, see Spravochnik, pp.124–5.
73 In a reflection of its weakness, the Belorussian Popular Front was actually established in June 1989 in Vilnius, Lithuania.
74 Polonsky, p.175.
75 Rothschild (East Central Europe), p.321. More generally, Romanians constituted only 71.9% of the population in 1930. Rothschild (East Central Europe), p.284.
76 Rothschild (East Central Europe), p.285.
77 Rothschild (East Central Europe), p.295.
78 Rothschild (East Central Europe), p.321.
79 On the Ceausescu regime, see Edward Behr, *'Kiss the Hand You Cannot Bite.' The Rise and Fall of the Ceausescus*, Harmondsworth: Penguin, 1991 and Michael Shafir, *Romania. Politics, Economics and Society*, London: Frances Pinter, 1985, esp.ch.6.
80 On rural Serbia, see Michael Palairet, 'Rural Serbia in the Light of the Census of 1863', *The Journal of European Economic History* 24, 1, Spring 1995, pp.41–107.
81 Rothschild (East Central Europe), p.276. In Montenegro it was 33%.
82 Rothschild (East Central Europe), p.205.
83 The correlation is not exact. The strength of pre-communist civil society development cannot be measured in any precise fashion, but must rest upon historical, qualitative, analysis. The likelihood of imprecision is high.

4   Creating civil society?

1 According to a study by the European Bank for Reconstruction and Development, in 1998 the state possessed a 100% share in the dominant operator in Albania, Azerbaijan, Belarus, Bulgaria, Croatia, Macedonia, Georgia, Moldova, Poland, Romania, Slovakia, Turkmenistan, Ukraine and Uzbekistan, 95% in Tajikistan, 90% in the Kyrgyz Republic, 87% in Slovenia, 75% in Russia, and 51% in the Czech Republic, Estonia and Latvia. Only in Armenia (19%), Hungary (6%), Kazakhstan (45%) and Lithuania (40%) did the state have a minority share. European Bank for Reconstruction and Development, *Transition report 1998. Financial sector in transition*, London: EBRD, 1998, p.34.
2 Adrian Karatnycky, Alexander Motyl and Boris Shor (eds), *Nations in Transit 1997. Civil Society, Democracy and Markets in East Central Europe and the Newly Independent States*, New Brunswick: Transaction Publishers, 1997.
3 For a discussion of the situation in Poland, see Wojciech Sadurski, 'Freedom of the Press in Postcommunist Poland', *East European Politics and Societies* 10, 3, Fall 1996, pp.439–56.
4 For the argument that the Romanian media has been controlled by the state, with the few independent newspaper outlets being small and finding it difficult to survive, see Henry F.

Carey, 'From Big Lie to Small Lies: State Mass Media Dominance in Post-Communist Romania', *East European Politics and Societies* 10, 1, Winter 1996, pp.16–45.
5 EBRD (1998), p.34.
6 Even in the West many notionally autonomous bodies (especially charities) receive tax breaks from the state and are therefore at least in part financially reliant upon state largesse.
7 In purely structural terms, the so-called 'government organised non-government organisations' in Uzbekistan may be in a similar position to such bodies as quangos in the West, although their degree of independence is significantly less.
8 Although of course alone number is not sufficient. What is crucial is the nature of the interactions between the groups.
9 Karatnycky *et al*. Also see the discussions in Mary Kaldor and Ivan Vejvoda, 'Democratization in Central and East European Countries: An Overview', Mary Kaldor and Ivan Vejvoda (eds), *Democratization in Central and Eastern Europe*, London: Pinter, 1999.
10 The figures relate to different dates in some cases: Bulgaria 1994, Czech Republic and Georgia 1995, and Kazakhstan 1995–96. In the case of the Kyrgyz Republic the figures given actually range from 50–8000 and the average 11–1818. The former, lower, figures have been accepted as being more consistent with other sources.
11 It is also likely that the different investigators who produced the figures were working on different assumptions. The figures for Latvia compared with those for Estonia and Lithuania are difficult to understand otherwise.
12 Slovenia is an apparent exception according to the judgement given by Freedom House. But this judgement is at odds with those to be found in more qualitative discussions of Slovenian development. For example, see Danica Fink-Hafner, 'Organized Interests as Policy Actors in Slovenia', Attila Agh and Gabriella Ilonski (eds), *Parliaments and Organized Interests: The Second Steps*, Budapest: Hungarian Centre for Democracy Studies, 1996, pp.222–40, esp. p.234.
13 It is also above in the Kyrgyz Republic. However the report from there states that although there are as many as 8000 groups, only about 50 are actually operating. For an argument about the ambiguous status of the 'five supportive contexts' for civil society in the Kyrgyz Republic, see John Anderson, 'Creating a Framework for Civil Society in Kyrgyzstan', *Europe-Asia Studies* 52, 1, January 2000, pp.77–93.
14 For one discussion, see Douglas Saltmarshe, 'Civil society and sustainable development in Central Asia', *Central Asian Survey* 15, 3/4, December 1996, pp.387–98.
15 Although for the argument that most groups are created from the top and have little purpose other than getting financial support from NGOs, see Nora Dudwick, 'Political transformations in postcommunist Armenia: images and realities', Karen Dawisha and Bruce Parrott (eds), *Conflict, cleavage and change in Central Asia and the Caucasus*, Cambridge: Cambridge University Press, 1997, p.84.
16 A survey in Russia in December 1992 found that over the last three years (when public activity is commonly seen to be at a high level in 1990–91), 59.9% of the population took no part in the activities of any public organisation. Donna Bahry and Lucan Way, 'Citizen Activism in the Russian Transition', *Post-Soviet Affairs* 10, 4, October 1994, p.335. Another survey in the same year suggested that 53% of the population had engaged in one form of political participation (discussion with friends, attendance at meetings, participation in demonstrations, strikes, and party activities; voting was in addition to these activities). Ian McAllister and Stephen White, *Political Participation in Postcommunist Russia. Voting, Activism, and the Potential for Mass Protest*, Glasgow: University of Strathclyde, Centre for the Study of Public Policy, Studies in Public Policy No. 223, 1994, pp.12–13. For even lower figures, see Stephen Whitefield and Geoffrey Evans, 'Support for Democracy and Political Opposition in Russia, 1993–1995', *Post-Soviet Affairs* 12, 3, July 1996, pp.218–42. For a discussion of civil society, see Zinaida T. Golenkova, 'Civil Society in Russia', *Russian Social Science Review* 40, 1, January–February 1999, pp.4–18. Also Thomas F. Remington, 'Democratization and the new political order in Russia', Karen Dawisha and Bruce Parrott (eds*)*, *Democratic changes and authoritarian reactions in Russia, Ukraine, Belarus and Moldova*, Cambridge: Cambridge University Press, 1997, pp.88–9.

17 See discussions in Terry Cox and Laszlo Vass, 'Civil Society and Interest Representation in Hungarian Political Development', *The Journal of Communist Studies and Transition Politics* 10, 3, September 1994, pp.153–79; Ferenc Miszlivetz, 'Participation and Transition: Can the Civil Society Project Survive in Hungary?', and Bill Lomax, 'The Strange Death of 'Civil Society' in Post-Communist Hungary', both in *The Journal of Communist Studies and Transition Politics* 13, 1, March 1997, pp.27–40 and 41–63; Michael Bernhard, 'Civil Society After the First Transition: Dilemmas of Post-communist Democratization in Poland and Beyond', *Communist and Post-Communist Studies* 29, 3, September 1996, pp.309–330.
18 Put another way, according to one study citizens in Russia confine their political participation to elections. Donna Bahry and L. Way, 'Citizen activism in the Russian transition', *Post-Soviet Affairs* 10, 4, 1994, pp.330–66.
19 The main sources of figures are Richard Rose, Neil Munro and Tom Mackie, *Elections in Central and Eastern Europe*, Glasgow: Centre for the Study of Public Policy, University of Strathclyde, 1998, and Karen Henderson and Neil Robinson, *Post-Communist Politics. An Introduction*, London: Prentice-Hall, 1997. Also see Leslie Holmes, *Post-Communism. An Introduction*, Cambridge: Polity Press, 1997.
20 High levels of apathy were present under the communists in the 1980s. David J. Mason, Daniel N. Nelson and Bohdan M. Sklarski, 'Apathy and the Birth of Democracy: The Political Struggle', *East European Politics and Societies* 5, 2, Spring 1991, pp.205–33.
21 For an argument that support for political and economic liberalism is related to the economic opportunity structure available to people as a result of the changes accompanying the collapse of communism, see Judith S. Kullberg and William Zimmerman, 'Liberal Elites, Socialist Masses, and Problems of Russian Democracy', *World Politics* 51, 3, 1999, pp.323–58.
22 Most figures for 1992 are in response to the question: 'Here is a scale for ranking how our system of government works. Where on this scale would you put the present system with free elections and many parties? [our system of governing in five years time?]' Richard Rose and Christian Haerpfer, *New Democracies Between State and Market. A Baseline Report of Public Opinion*, Glasgow: University of Strathclyde, Centre for the Study of Public Policy, Studies in Public Policy No.204, 1992, p.99. All of the figures for Russia come from the 1996 Addendum to Richard Rose and Evgeny Tikhomirov, *Trends in the New Russia Barometer, 1992–1995*, Glasgow: University of Strathclyde, Centre for the Study of Public Policy, Studies in Public Policy No.256, 1995, in response to the question: 'Here is a scale for evaluating the political system. The top, plus 100, is the best; at the bottom, minus 100, is the worst. Where on this scale would you put our present system of governing/the system of governing we will have in five years?' The Russian figure for 1996 is for July, following the presidential election; the positive figure for January is about 10% points lower. Figures for 1993 (except for Russia) are from Richard Rose and Christian Haerpfer, *Adapting to Transformation in Eastern Europe. New Democracies Barometer II*, Glasgow: University of Strathclyde, Centre for the Study of Public Policy, Studies in Public Policy No.212., 1993, pp.24–5, for 1994 Richard Rose and Christian Haerpfer, *New Democracies Barometer III: Learning from What is Happening*, (Glasgow: University of Strathclyde, Centre for the Study of Public Policy, Studies in Public Policy No.230, 1994). For 1995 figures come from Richard Rose and Christian Haerpfer, *New Democracies Barometer IV: A 10-Nation Survey*, Glasgow: University of Strathclyde, Centre for the Study of Public Policy, Studies in Public Policy No.262, 1996. The question is the same as for 1992. The figures for the Baltic republics come from Richard Rose, *New Baltics Barometer II: A Survey Study*, Glasgow: University of Strathclyde, Centre for the Study of Public Policy, Studies in Public Policy No. 251,1995 pp.23–5 and Richard Rose, Vilmorus, Baltic Data House and Saar Poll, *New Baltic Barometer III: A Survey Study:* Glasgow: University of Strathclyde, Centre for the Study of Public Policy, Studies in Public Policy No.284, 1997, pp.20–1.
23 This has been computed by combining the movement in the positive and negative ratings over the period. This ignores fluctuations during the period.
24 For an argument based on opinion polling in 1992 about the extent and stability of popular support for democratic institutions and processes in Russia and Ukraine, see James L. Gibson, 'The Resilience of Mass Support for Democratic Institutions and Processes in the Nascent

Russian and Ukrainian Democracies', Vladimir Tismaneanu (ed), *Political Culture and Civil Society in Russia and the New States of Eurasia*, Armonk: M.E. Sharpe, 1995, pp.53–111.

25 Judgements about the former communist regime were also less negative among FSU countries than those in central Europe. For a discussion of this comparison between former, present and future regimes, see Richard Rose, William Mishler and Christian Haerpfer, *Democracy and Its Alternatives. Understanding Post-Communist Societies*, Cambridge: Polity Press, 1995, esp. ch.5.

26 Sources from which these figures were taken are: Richard Rose, Irina Boeva and Viacheslav Shironin, *How Russians Are Coping With Transition: New Russia Barometer II*, Glasgow: University of Strathclyde, Centre for the Study of Public Policy, Studies in Public Policy No.216, 1993; Richard Rose and Christian Haerpfer, *New Russia Barometer III: The Results*, Glasgow: University of Strathclyde, Centre for the Study of Public Policy, Studies in Public Policy No.228, 1994; Richard Rose, *New Russia Barometer V: Between Two Elections*, Glasgow: University of Strathclyde, Centre for the Study of Public Policy, Studies in Public Policy No.260, 1996; Richard Rose, *New Russia Barometer VI: After the Presidential Election*, Glasgow: University of Strathclyde, Centre for the Study of Public Policy, Studies in Public Policy No.272, 1996; and Studies in Public Policy Nos. 230, 262 and 284; New Democracies Barometer wysiwyg:// 78/http://rs2.tarki.hu:90/ndb/owa/ndb.choosevar The basic results are consistent with those reported in Matthew Wyman, *Public Opinion in Post-Communist Russia*, Basingstoke: Macmillan, 1997, esp. pp.96, 97 and 109, and William L. Miller, Stephen White and Paul Heywood, *Values and Political Change in Postcommunist Europe*, Basingstoke: Macmillan, 1998.

27 For an early discussion of the low levels of trust in the parliamentary bodies, see John R. Hibbing and Samuel C. Patterson, 'Public Trust in the New Parliaments of Central and Eastern Europe', *Political Studies* XLII, 4, 1994, pp.570–92.

28 For some details and discussion, see Pippa Norris (ed), *Critical Citizens. Global Support for Democratic Government*, Oxford: Oxford University Press, 1999, Hans-Dieter Klingemann and Dieter Fuchs (eds), *Beliefs in Government. Volume 1. Citizens and the State*, Oxford: Oxford University Press, 1995.

29 Rose, Boeva and Shironin (SiPP 216), p.42.

30 Rose (SiPP 250), p.40. This excludes a category described as 'Not very interested' which numbered 39%.

31 Rose (SiPP 260), pp.46–7. This excluded a category described as 'Little interest' which numbered 43%. For different figures for the period 1990–93, which suggests a higher level of interest (although even here the figure for little interest or none at all is given as 53% and 60% respectively in September and November 1993), see Wyman, p.260.

32 Miller, White and Heywood, p.97.

33 Richard Rose, *New Baltics Barometer II: A Survey Study*, Glasgow: University of Strathclyde, Centre for the Study of Public Policy, Studies in Public Policy No.251, 1995 p.21 and Rose *et al.* (SiPP 284), p.17.

34 Miller, White and Heywood, p.142.

35 Richard Rose, *Mobilizing Demobilized Voters in Post Communist Societies*, Glasgow: University of Strathclyde, Centre for the Study of Public Policy, Studies in Public Policy No.246, 1995, p.29. In Russia in 1993 and 1996 some 60% and 59%, respectively, believed that regular elections had no effect in making politicians do what ordinary people wanted. Miller, White and Heywood, p.379.

36 Even here one survey reported that in 1995 fewer than 10% of the population believed they could influence government decisions; 86% believed their representatives quickly lost touch with them. Andrew T. Green and Carol Skalnick Leff, 'The Quality of Democracy: Mass-Elite Linkages in the Czech Republic', *Democratization* 4, 4, Winter 1997, p.69.

37 For an argument which seeks to link the proliferation of independent groups following the collapse of the Czechoslovak regime with the legalisation of private property, see Sharon Wolchik, 'The Repluralization of Politics in Czechoslovakia', *Communist and Post-Communist Studies* 26, 4, December 1993, pp.412–31. For a discussion of this in relation to the former communist states, including some comments on electoral implications, see M. Steven Fish,

'The Determinants of Economic Reform in the Post-Communist World', *East European Politics and Societies* 12, 1, Winter 1998, pp.66–7.
38 For a stimulating discussion of some of the issues relating to this, see Claus Offe, 'Capitalism by Democratic Design? Democratic Theory Facing the Triple Transition in East Central Europe', *Social Research* 58, 4, 1991, pp.865–92. This is reprinted in Claus Offe, *Varieties of Transition. The East European and East German Experience*, Cambridge: Polity Press, 1996, pp.29–49.
39 These details come principally from the 'Transition assessments for each country' in EBRD, *Transition report 1998. Financial sector in transition*, London: EBRD, 1998, pp.148–99. The corresponding assessments in earlier volumes are also relevant. For one discussion of privatisation, see Ira W. Lieberman, Stilpon S. Nestor and Raj M. Desai (eds), *Between State and Market. Mass Privatization in Transition Economies*, Washington: World Bank, 1997.
40 See David Stark's discussion of 'recombinant property', in David Stark and Laszlo Bruszt, *Postsocialist Pathways. Transforming Politics and Property in East Central Europe*, Cambridge: Cambridge University Press, 1998, pp.143–9.
41 Yearly data are from EBRD, *Transition report 1995. Investment and enterprise development*, London: EBRD, 1995), p.11; EBRD, *Transition report 1996. Infrastructure and savings*, London: EBRD, 1996, p.11; EBRD, *Transition report 1997. Enterprise performance and growth*, London: EBRD, 1997, p.14; Transition report 1998, p.26; and EBRD, *Transition report 1999. Ten years of transition*, London: EBRD, 1999, p.24.
42 As for fn.41.
43 There is an enormous literature on privatisation. For some reviews, see Zoya Mladenova and James Angresano, 'Privatization in Bulgaria', *East European Quarterly* XXX, 4, January 1997, pp.495–516; Lavinia Stan, 'Romanian Privatization: Assessment of the First Five Years', *Communist and Post-Communist Studies* 28, 4, 1995, pp.427–35; Yudit Kiss, 'Privatization Paradoxes in East Central Europe', *East European Politics and Societies* 8, 1, Winter 1994, pp.122–52; Mehrdad Haghayeghi, 'Politics of Privatization in Kazakhstan', *Central Asian Survey* 16, 3, September 1997, pp.321–38; Michael Kaser, 'Privatization and agrarian reform in Caucasian economies', *Central Asian Survey* 16, 2, June 1997, pp.159–165; Michael Kaser, 'Economic transition in six Central Asian economies', *Central Asian Survey* 16, 1, March 1997, pp.5–26.
44 Another complicating factor has been the attempt by some regimes to restore at least some property to its pre-communist owners. Eg. Josef Burger, 'Politics of Restitution in Czechoslovakia, *East European Quarterly* XXVI, 4, January 1993, pp.485–98; Hilary Appel, 'Justice and the Reformulation of Property Rights in the Czech Republic', *East European Politics and Societies* 9, 1, Winter 1995, pp.22–40.
45 Defined by the EBRD as the 'most important' privatisation method. Transition report 1997, p.90. However in all cases there have been a variety of strategies of privatisation adopted.
46 eg. Jadwiga Staniszkis, 'Political Capitalism in Poland', *East European Politics and Societies* 5, 1, Winter 1991, pp.127–41; V. Zubek, 'The Polish Communist Elite and the Petty Entrepreneurs', *East European Quarterly* XXV, 3, September 1991, pp.339–62. For the argument that ex-cadres have the positions and skills (principally education) to enable them to play a prominent part in the emergence of new, non-farming, entrepreneurs, see Akos Rona-Tas, 'The First Shall Be Last? Entrepreneurship and Communist Cadres in the Transition from Socialism', *American Journal of Sociology* 100, 1, July 1994, pp.40–69.
47 It seems to have been more widespread in the FSU than in ECE. Judith S. Kullberg and William Zimmerman, 'Liberal Elites, Socialist Masses, and Problems of Russian Democracy', *World Politics* 51, 3, April, 1999, p.331. For one discussion of this, see David Lane and Cameron Ross, *The Transition from Communism to Capitalism. Ruling Elites from Gorbachev to Yeltsin*, Basingstoke: Macmillan, 1999, ch.9. Martha Brill Olcott said that privatisation in Kazakhstan 'put most of the nation's new wealth into a small group of Kazak (sic) hands' and implies that these had official connections. Martha Brill Olcott, 'The growth of political participation in Kazakhstan' (sic), Dawisha and Parrott (*Central Asia*), p.218.
48 They are also more likely to oppose further economic reform because of the implications this could have for their privileged position. Joel S. Hellman, 'Winners Take All: The Politics of

228 Notes

Partial Reform in Postcommunist Transitions', *World Politics* 50, 2, January 1998, pp.203–34. Also see Transition Report 1999, pp.108–10.

49 For example, Albania officially began the privatisation of large enterprises in 1995, and although the number of enterprises is small, 60% of GDP output came from the private sector by the middle of that year.

50 For a discussion of these and their role, see Leslie Holmes, *Politics in the Communist World*, Oxford: Oxford University Press, 1986, pp.209–16.

51 For some arguments along these lines, see Thomas Remington, 'Regime Change in Communist States', *Soviet Economy* 6, 1990, pp.160–90; and George Schopflin, 'The Road from Post-Communism', Stephen Whitefield (ed), *The New Institutional Architecture of Eastern Europe*, London: Macmillan, 1993, pp.183–200.

52 For a case study of the Polish situation which reaches this general conclusion, see Aleks Szczerbiak, 'Interests and Values: Polish Parties and Their Electorates', *Europe-Asia Studies* 51, 8, December 1999, pp.1401–32.

53 Valerie Bunce and Maria Csanadi, 'Uncertainty in the Transition: Post-Communism in Hungary', *East European Politics and Societies* 7, 2, Spring 1993, pp.240–75.

54 Attila Agh, *The Politics of Central Europe*, London: Sage, 1998, pp.103–4.

55 For one study of parties as parliamentary bodies, see Laszlo Szarvas, 'Parties and Party Factions in the Hungarian Parliament', *The Journal of Communist Studies and Transition Politics* 10, 3, September 1994, pp.120–36.

56 For a discussion of Hungarian parties chiefly in these terms, see Bill Lomax, 'Obstacles to the Development of Democratic Politics', *The Journal of Communist Studies and Transition Politics* 10, 3, September 1994, pp.81–100.

57 Agh (Central Europe) p.108. In some countries, nationalist parties have become prominent and pursued a divisive agenda, with different levels of success. For a list of nationalist parties, see Agh, pp.116 and 121.

58 See the discussion in Geoffrey Evans and Stephen Whitefield, 'Identifying the Bases of Party Competition in Eastern Europe', *British Journal of Political Science* 23, 4, October 1993, pp.521–48.

59 For example, Herbert Kitschelt, 'The Formation of Party Systems in East Central Europe', *Politics and Society* 20, 1, March, 1992, pp.7–50; Herbert Kitschelt, *Party Systems in East Central Europe. Consolidation or Fluidity?*, Glasgow, University of Strathclyde, Centre for the Study of Public Policy, Studies in Public Policy no. 241, 1995; Geoffrey Evans and Stephen Whitefield, (Identifying), pp.521–48; Geoffrey Evans and Stephen Whitefield, 'Social and Ideological Cleavage Formation in Post-Communist Hungary', *Europe-Asia Studies* 47, 7, 1995, pp.1177–204; Stephen Whitefield and Geoffrey Evans, 'The Emerging Structure of Partisan Divisions in Russian Politics', Matthew Wyman, Stephen White and Sarah Oates, *Elections and Voters in Post-communist Russia*, Cheltenham: Edward Elgar, 1998, pp.68–99. For an argument about the revival of class reflected in increased blue collar voting for communist successor parties in Hungary and Poland, see Ivan Szelenyi, Eva Fodor and Eric Hanley, 'Left Turn in Post-Communist Politics: Bringing Class Back In?', *East European Politics and Societies* 11, 1, Winter 1997, pp.190–224.

60 For one theory regarding stages of party development, see Jack Bielasiak, 'Substance and Process in the Development of Party Systems in East Central Europe', *Communist and Post-Communist Studies* 30, 1, March 1997, pp.23–44.

61 For example, Janos Simon, 'Electoral Systems and Democracy in Central Europe, 1990–1994' and Stanislaw Gebethner, 'Free Elections and Political Parties in Transition to Democracy in Central and Southeastern Europe', *International Political Science Review* 18, 4, October 1997, pp.361–79 and 381–99.

62 For a discussion which sees party competition developing primarily along a single major cleavage, pro-market liberal vs anti-market authoritarian, see Herbert Kitschelt, 'Formation of Party Cleavages in Post-Communist Democracies: Theoretical Propositions', *Party Politics* 1, 4, October 1995, pp.447–72.

Notes   229

63   Whitefield and Evans (Emerging). For a survey of the argument about some correspondence between social issue cleavage and voter choice, see Stephen Whitefield and Geoffrey Evans, 'Electoral Politics in Eastern Europe: Social and Ideological Influences on Partisanship in Post-Communist Societies', John Higley, Jan Pakulski and Wlodzimierz Wesolowski (eds), *Postcommunist Elites and Democracy in Eastern Europe*, Basingstoke: Macmillan, 1998, pp.226–50.
64   Kitschelt (Formation).
65   The 1996 election was surrounded by many claims of falsification.
66   The following parliamentary elections have been used for this and subsequent figures: Albania 1991, 1992, 1996, 1997; Armenia 1995, 1999; Bulgaria 1990, 1991, 1994, 1997; Croatia 1990, 1992, 1995, 2000; Czech Republic 1990, 1992, 1996, 1998; Estonia 1992, 1995, 1999; FRY Serbia 1990, 1992, 1993, 1997 Montenegro 1990, 1992, 1996, 1998; Georgia 1992, 1995, 1999; Hungary 1990, 1994, 1998; Latvia 1993, 1995, 1998; Lithuania 1992, 1996; Macedonia 1990, 1994; Moldova 1994, 1998; Poland 1991, 1993, 1997; Romania 1990, 1992, 1996; Russia 1993, 1995, 1999; Slovakia 1990, 1992, 1994, 1998; Slovenia 1990, 1992, 1996; Ukraine 1994, 1998.
67   The proportion is not exact because the data on parties in some countries is confused. In other words, looking at all the elections during this period, more than 94% of the parties saw their vote change by more than 10% from one election to the next.
68   Each party is counted once each time it participates in an election.
69   Data on elections from this part of the world are notoriously unreliable. Sources quote different figures, sometimes different parties are included in coalition arrangements, names change and are rendered in different ways, and some details do not appear to have been published. The data in this and the subsequent similar tables relate to lower house elections, and where there is a mixed party list and single member systems, voting figures are from the party list votes. Where there is more than one round of voting, figures relate to the first round. Where there is no threshold, 5% has been taken as the cut off. In the column headed 'Largest parties (in terms of votes)', parties are listed in order of the share of votes they received, and all parties exceeding the threshold have been listed. Independents, and in most cases those listed as 'others', have not been included in the figure for the number of parties in the parliament. Data are from Richard Rose, Neil Munro and Tom Mackie, *Elections in Central and Eastern Europe Since 1980*, Glasgow, University of Strathclyde, Centre for the Study of Public Policy, Studies in Public Policy no.300, 1998); Agh (Politics of Central Europe), pp.127–39; Open Society Archives, Central European University, Budapest.
70   Of the 460 seats in the Sejm, 391 were elected by PR in districts without a threshold, and 69 from national lists with a 5% threshold. Rose, Munro and Mackie, p.85. Electoral statistics are taken from this source, except for the Hungarian election in 1998.
71   There was actually a 5% national threshold for parties and 8% for coalitions; for national lists it was increased to 7%.
72   Freedom Union, Democratic Left Alliance, Homeland (began as Christian National Union), Centre Alliance, Polish Peasants' Party, Confederation for Independent Poland, Liberal Democratic Congress, Peasant Alliance, Solidarity.
73   Democratic Left Alliance, Polish Peasants' Party, Freedom Union, Union of Labour, Homeland, Confederation for Independent Poland, Non-Party Reform Bloc BBWR.
74   Solidarity Electoral Alliance (coalition uniting 40 parties and organisations from the centre and right, including from earlier elections H, CA, CIP, PA, S, NPRB; also the Christian Democrats and Movement for the Republic), Democratic Left Alliance, Freedom Union, Polish Peasants' Party, Movement for the Reconstruction of Poland. For a list of the bodies in AWS, see Aleks Szczerbiak, 'Electoral Politics in Poland: The Parliamentary Elections of 1997', *The Journal of Communist Studies and Transition Politics* 14, 3, September 1998, p.83.
75   The Hungarian system is a combination of 176 single member districts and 20 multi-member districts electing 120 deputies by PR with a 4% threshold; 90 are elected from a national list.
76   The numbers of seats elected by the different methods was changed: 176 SMC, 125 constituency list, 85 national list.

77 The numbers of seats elected by the different methods was changed: 176 SMC, 152 constituency list and 58 by national list.
78 Democratic Forum, Alliance of Free Democrats, Independent Smallholders, Hungarian Socialist Party, Alliance of Young Democrats (Fidesz), Christian Democratic People's Party.
79 Hungarian Socialist Party, Alliance of Free Democrats, Democratic Forum, Independent Smallholders, Christian Democratic People's Party, Alliance of Young Democrats.
80 Hungarian Socialist Party, Alliance of Young Democrats (actually became Hungarian Civic Party in April 1995), Independent Smallholders, Alliance of Free Democrats, Hungarian Justice and Life, Democratic Forum. DF did not exceed the threshold, but ran in a coalition and thereby gained representation.
81 On the basis of about a third of the votes, the HSP won 209 of the 386 seats (54.1%) and could have ruled alone. The coalition gave it a broader base of legitimacy and the two thirds necessary to change the constitution.
82 Although the HSP won most votes, a centre-right coalition led by AYD assumed office.
83 This was particularly the case given that many members of the former ruling PUWP did not transfer their membership to the new party. Frances Millard, 'The Shaping of the Polish Party System, 1989–93', *East European Politics and Societies* 8, 3, Fall 1994, p.473. Developments elsewhere in the region were also important for removing the apparent communist threat.
84 Solidarity had chosen not to transform itself into a party but instead to permit dual membership of Solidarity and political parties, with the result that a range of these began to shelter within its borders. Millard p.474. For a detailed study of the failure of Solidarity, with a good discussion of its structural problems, see Tomek Grabowski 'The Party That Never Was: The Rise and Fall of the Solidarity Citizens' Committees in Poland', *East European Politics and Societies* 10, 2, Spring 1996, pp.214–254.
85 The proliferation of parties was also encouraged by the Law on Political Parties which required only 15 adult supporters for registration. Stanislaw Gebethner, 'Parliamentary and Electoral Parties in Poland', Paul G. Lewis (ed), *Party Structure and Organization in East-Central Europe*, Cheltenham: Edward Elgar, 1996, p.121. In 1991 111 parties and groupings contested the election, with 29 having candidates in all seats. In 1997 the figures were 22 and 10 respectively. Szczerbiak (Electoral), p.59.
86 On the 1997 election Szczerbiak (Electoral), pp.58–83.
87 For a list of the bodies in AWS see Szczerbiak (Electoral), p.83.
88 On the rise of the Polish communist successor party, see Voytek Zubek, 'The Phoenix Out of the Ashes: The Rise to Power of Poland's Post-Communist SdRP', *Communist and Post-Communist Studies* 28. 3, 1995, pp.275–306. For a discussion of successor parties in Poland and Hungary, see Alison Mahr and John Nagle, 'Resurrection of the Successor Parties and Democratization in East-Central Europe', *Communist and Post-Communist Studies* 28, 4, 1995, pp.393–409. Mahr and Nagle argue that the key to their success was their moderate programs and images in comparison with the perceived failures of centre-right governments reflected most clearly in the hardship which stemmed from economic reform. On communist successor parties in general, see John T. Ishiyama, 'Communist Parties in Transition. Structures, Leaders, and Processes of Democratization in Eastern Europe', *Comparative Politics* 27, 2, January 1995, pp.147–66.
89 Miro Marody, 'Three Stages of Party System Emergence in Poland', *Communist and Post-Communist Studies* 28, 2, 1995, p.265.
90 These figures refer only to those which gained at least 1% electoral support.
91 See the comments in Evans and Whitefield (Identifying the Bases) and Whitefield and Evans, (Electoral Politics).
92 Szczerbiak (Electoral), pp.1415–26.
93 The figure for the 1989 election is 62%, and for the presidential elections in 1990 and 1995 61% and 65% respectively. Henderson and Robinson, p.345.
94 This is supported by the fact that, to the question 'Do you feel close to one political party or movement or not?', the following 'yes' response levels were achieved: 1991 20%, 1992 12%,

1993 15%, and 1995 19%. *New Democracy Barometer* wysiwyg://32:http://rs2.tarki.hu:90/ndb/owa/nd6.choosevar
95 For a discussion of both parties, see Lomax (Obstacles), pp.91–5.
96 For a discussion of Hungarian parties, see Bill Lomax, 'The Structure and Organization of Hungary's Political Parties', Lewis (Party Structure and Organization), pp.20–42. The governments formed in the first two elections in the Czech Republic also survived the respective electoral cycles.
97 See Robert G. Moser, 'Electoral Systems and the Number of Parties in Postcommunist States', *World Politics* 51, 3, April 1999, p.376.
98 For some examples, see the discussion in Henderson and Robinson, p.247. Also see Lomax (Obstacles).
99 Evans and Whitefield (Social and Ideological ... Hungary), p.1194.
100 Which is the argument of Evans and Whitefield (Social and Ideological ... Hungary). Figures for those saying they 'feel close' to one party or movement were 1991 16%, 1992 21%, 1993 21%, 1995 39%. New Democracies Barometer.
101 Half the deputies were elected in single member constituencies and half on the basis of party lists in constituencies through PR with a 4% threshold.
102 Bulgarian Socialist Party, Union of Democratic Forces, Bulgarian Agrarian National Union, Movement for Rights and Freedoms.
103 Union of Democratic Forces, Bulgarian Socialist Party, Movement for Rights and Freedoms.
104 Bulgarian Socialist Party, Union of Democratic Forces, Bulgarian Agrarian National Union, Movement for Rights and Freedoms, Bulgarian Business Bloc.
105 Union of Democratic Forces, Bulgarian Socialist Party, Union for National Salvation, Euroleft Coalition, Bulgarian Business Bloc. The UDF figure includes that for the People's Union.
106 The BSP won 211 of the 400 seats in the parliament (52.8%).
107 As a minority government, its position was unstable, and when it fell to a vote of no confidence in October 1992 it was succeeded by a non-party government of technocrats.
108 The BSP won 125 of the 240 seats (52%) in coalition with two small leftist splinters of other parties, the Political Club Ekoglasnost, and BANU-Aleksandr Stamboliiski.
109 100 seats were to be filled by SMC and 40 by PR with a 4% threshold.
110 115 seats were to be filled by SMC and 25 by PR with a 4% threshold.
111 The number of seats was increased to 155. 115 were filled by SMC and 40 by PR.
112 Socialist Party of Albania, Democratic Party of Albania.
113 Democratic Party of Albania, Socialist Party of Albania, Social Democratic Party.
114 Democratic Party of Albania, Socialist Party of Albania, Republican Party of Albania, National Front, Unity Party of Human Rights.
115 Socialist Party of Albania, Democratic Party of Albania.
116 The initial SPA government fell in June 1991 following popular protests, and was replaced by a new government led by the SPA but including members of the DPA. When it collapsed in December, a government of non-party experts was established.
117 The party won 99 of the 155 seats in coalition with the Social Democrats and Democratic Alliance.
118 For a list, see Rose, Munro and Mackie, p.11. For a study of the UDF, see Michael Waller and Georgi Karasimeonov, 'Party Organization in Post-communist Bulgaria', Lewis (Party Structure and Organization), pp.143–62.
119 Waller and Karasimeonov, p.138.
120 For a discussion of party programs, see Petar-Emil Mitev, 'The Party Manifestos for the Bulgarian 1994 Elections', *The Journal of Communist Studies and Transition Politics* 13, 1, March 1997, pp.64–90.
121 In 1990 when few parties had emerged, the wasted vote was negligible.
122 Now including the PU.
123 Although the following proportion of people answered that they did feel close to one political party or movement: 1991 62%, 1992 71%, 1993 55%, 1995 75%. New Democracies Barometer.

232   Notes

124 There were different thresholds for party alliances: 7% for two or three parties and 10% for four or more.
125 There were different thresholds for party alliances: 7% for two parties, 9% for three parties, and 11% for five or more parties.
126 Civic Forum, Communist Party of Bohemia and Moravia, Moravian Silesian Movement, Christian Democratic Union.
127 Civic Democratic Party, Communist Party of Bohemia and Moravia, Social Democratic Party, Liberal Social Union, Christian Democratic Union, Association for the Republic, Civic Democratic Alliance, Moravian Silesian Movement.
128 Civic Democratic Party, Social Democratic Party, Communist Party of Bohemia and Moravia, Christian Democratic Union, Association for the Republic, Civic Democratic Alliance.
129 Social Democratic Party, Civic Democratic Party, Freedom Union, Christian and Democratic Union-People's Party, Communist Party of Bohemia and Moravia.
130 Civic Forum gained 127 of the 200 seats (63.5%).
131 There were different thresholds for party alliances: 7% for two or three parties, and 10% for four or more.
132 Public Against Violence, Christian Democratic Movement, Slovak National Party, Party of the Democratic Left, Hungarian Coalition, Democratic Party, Green Party in Slovakia.
133 Movement for a Democratic Slovakia, Party of the Democratic Left, Christian Democratic Movement, Slovak National Party, Hungarian Coalition.
134 Movement for a Democratic Slovakia, Common Choice, Hungarian Coalition, Christian Democratic Movement, Democratic Union of Slovakia, Association of Workers of Slovakia, Slovak National Party.
135 Movement for a Democratic Slovakia, Slovak Democratic Coalition (a union of right and centrist parties), Party of the Democratic Left, Hungarian Coalition, Slovak National Party, Party of Civic Understanding.
136 This comprised PDL (communist successor party), the Democratic Union (formed by refugees from MDS and SNP) and CDM. It was a minority government, and relied on the support of HC.
137 Although MDS won most votes, the opposition coalition bloc clearly outpolled it and formed the government under SDC leadership.
138 Gabor Toka argues that voters in the Czech Republic were more likely to associate individual parties with issue choices than voters in Slovakia, Hungary and Poland. His data relate to 1992. Gabor Toka, *Political Parties and Democratic Consolidation in East Central Europe* Glasgow: University of Strathclyde, Centre for the Study of Public Policy, Studies in Public Policy No.279, 1997, pp.34–47. For the argument that the success of the SDs reflects the increased salience of class-based voting, see Petr Mateju and Blanka Rehakova, 'Turning Left or Class Realignment? Analysis of the Changing Relationship Between Class and Party in the Czech Republic, 1992–96', *East European Politics and Societies* 11, 3, Fall 1997, pp.501–42. On stabilisation along a left-right continuum, see Andrew T. Green and Carol Skalnik Leff, 'The Quality of Democracy: Mass-Elite Linkages in the Czech Republic', *Democratization* 4, 4, Winter 1997, pp.69–70. On changes within parties between 1992 and 1996, see David M. Olson, 'The experience of the Czech Republic', Karen Dawisha and Bruce Parrott (eds), *The Consolidation of Democracy in East-Central Europe*, Cambridge, Cambridge University Press, 1997, pp.178–83. Also Petr Kopecky, 'Parties in the Czech Parliament: From Transformative Towards Arena Type of Legislature', Paul G. Lewis (ed), *Party Structure and Organization in East Central Europe*, Cheltenham: Edward Elgar, 1996, pp.66–88.
139 Green and Leff, p.69.
140 Sharon L. Wolchik, 'Democratization and political participation in Slovakia', Dawisha and Parrott (*East Central Europe*), 1997, p.228. This is actually quite a high figure compared with much of the West. For some other figures, see Ales Kroupa and Tomas Kostelecky, 'Party Organization and Structure at National and Local Level in the Czech Republic Since 1989', Lewis (Party Structure and Organization), p.112. The figures for those saying they 'feel close' to a party or movement was: 1991 29%, 1992 36%, 1993 40% and 1995 30%. New Democracies Barometer.

141 Actually five participated in all elections, but by 1996 the vote for the Moravian Silesian Movement had fallen to 0.4%.
142 The vote for the CPBM and CDU was also reasonably consistent:

	1990	1992	1996
CPBM	13.2%	14.0%	10.3%
CDU	8.4%	6.3%	8.1%

143 In both republics the wasted vote was lower in the initial election than in the second one, reflecting the dominance of the political scene by the two movement parties, CF and PAV.
144 Wolchik argues for 'a good deal of fluctuation in both political parties and popular affiliation with particular parties.' Wolchik (Democratization), p.227.
145 In 1994 the PDL stood as part of the Common Choice coalition.
146 Wolchik (Democratization), p.228.
147 Latvia's Way Alliance, Latvian National Conservative, National Harmony Party, Latvian Farmers' Union, Equal Rights Movement, For Fatherland and Freedom, Latvian Christian Democratic, Authentic Democratic Party (DP (Saimnieks)).
148 Democratic Party (also called Saimnieks), Latvia's Way Alliance, National Movement for Latvia, For Fatherland and Freedom, Latvian Unity Party, United List, Latvian National Conservative, National Harmony Party, Latvian Socialist Party.
149 People's Party, Latvia's Way Alliance, National Harmony Party, For Fatherland and Freedom, Social Democratic Alliance, New Party.
150 This was a minority government with 48 of 100 seats. It relied on issue-based support from other parties.
151 LFU and LCD competed in the election under the UL banner; the Greens competed in association with LNC.
152 71 deputies were elected in single member constituencies and 70 at the national level by PR from closed party lists with a 4% threshold.
153 The same split in election methods as in 1992, but the threshold was increased by 1%.
154 Lithuanian Democratic Labour Party, Homeland Union, Christian Democratic Party, Social Democratic Party.
155 Homeland Union, Christian Democratic Party, Lithuanian Democratic Labour Party, Centre Movement, Social Democratic Party.
156 Social Democratic Coalition, New Union-Social Liberal, Liberal Union, Homeland Union-Lithuanian Conservative Party.
157 The LDLP won 73 seats in a parliament of 141. It was the successor to the reformist wing of the Lithuanian Communist Party that had broken with Moscow in December 1989.
158 Combined they had 86 seats in the 141 seat parliament.
159 Liberal Union, New Union-Social Liberal, Centre Union and Christian Democratic Union. The coalition was also supported by the Peasants Party and Polish Electoral Action.
160 Deputies are elected from multi-member constituencies on the basis of a quota. Unallocated seats are filled by parties meeting the quota and gaining at least 5% of the national vote. Any remaining unallocated seats are filled by PR at the national level.
161 Fatherland Union, Coalition Party and Rural Union, Estonian Centre Party, Moderates, Estonian National Independence Party, Fourth Power, Better Estonia.
162 Coalition Party and Rural Union (comprising the Estonian Coalition Party, Estonian Rural Union, Estonian Country People's Party, Estonian Pensioners and Families League, and Farmers' Assembly), Estonian Reform Party, Estonian Centre Party, Fatherland Union, Moderates, Our Home is Estonia (comprising the United People's Party and the Russian Party in Estonia), Right Wingers' Party (the Republican and Conservative People's Party).
163 Estonian Centre Party, Fatherland Union, Estonian Reform Party, Moderates, Coalition Party and Rural Union, Country People's Party, United People's Party (formerly part of OHE).
164 There were actually two coalitions prior to the next election. The first was led by Maat Laar of FU and comprised the three parties noted in the Table. The second, from October 1994, was led

234   *Notes*

by Andres Tarand of the Moderates and, as well as the above parties, included the Right Wingers' Party which split from the FU in June 1994.
165   The Estonian Centre Party was the movement party (PFE) successor.
166   Democratic Agrarian Party of Moldova, Socialist Party, Peasants and Intellectuals Bloc, Christian Democratic Popular Front Alliance.
167   Communist Party of Moldova, Democratic Convention of Moldova (an alliance of five groups including CDPFA), Bloc for a Democratic and Prosperous Moldova, Party of Democratic Forces.
168   Communist Party of Moldova, Electoral Bloc Braghis Alliance, Christian Democratic People's Party.
169   DAPM won 56 of 104 seats.
170   They had 61 and the CPM 40 of the 104 seats.
171   150 seats were to be filled by PR and there were 85 single member constituency seats.
172   PR 150 seats, SMC 85 seats.
173   Peace Bloc, 11 October Bloc, National Democratic Party of Georgia, Unity Bloc, Democratic Party, Green Party. These were the only parties to have 10 or more deputies elected. For details of the blocs, see Darrell Slider, 'Democratization in Georgia', Dawisha and Parrott (*Central Asia*), p.180.
174   Citizens Union of Georgia, National Democratic Party of Georgia, All-Georgian Union of Revival. AGUR was based overwhelmingly in the Ajar autonomous republic; of the 149,018 votes it received, 125,098 came from this region. Lincoln Allison, Alexander Kukhianidze, Malkhaz Matuberidze and Valeri Dolidze, 'Problems of Democratization in the Republic of Georgia', *Democratization* 3, 4, Winter 1996, p.528.
175   Citizens Union of Georgia, All-Georgian Union of Revival.
176   There were 40 seats filled by PR and 150 single member constituencies.
177   Republican Bloc, Shamiram Women's Party, Communist Party, National Democratic Union, Union for National Self-Determinaton.
178   Miasnutian (formerly RB), Communist Party, Rights and Unity, Armenian Revolutionary Federation, Country of Law, National Democratic Union.
179   RB won 119 of the 190 seats.
180   Miasnutian won 57 of the 131 seats; there were 32 independents.
181   Croatian Democratic Community, League of Communists of Croatia, which became the Party of Democratic Change.
182   Croatian Democratic Community, Croatian Social Liberal Party, Croatian Party of Rights, Croatian People's Party, Social Democratic Party, Croatian Farmers' Party, electoral bloc consisting of 3 groups: Dalmatian Action, Istrian Democratic Assembly and Rijeka Democratic Alliance, Serbian People's Party.
183   Croatian Democratic Community, Opposition Electoral Alliance, Croatian Social Liberal Party, Social Democratic Party, Croatian Party of Rights. The OEA comprised the Croatian People's Party, Croatian Peasants' Party, CSLP, CPR, Croatian Independent Democrats, Istrian Democratic Assembly and SDP.
184   Social Democratic Party-Croatian Social Liberal Party, Croatian Democratic Community, alliance of centrist parties (Croatian Peasants' Party, Istrian Democratic Assembly, Liberal Party, Croatian People's Party, and Croatian Social Democratic Action). The SDP-CSLP alliance included two smaller regional parties, the Primorian-Goranian Union and the Slavonian-Baranian Croatian Party.
185   The CDC actually won 209 of the 355 seats in the three chambers of the parliament.
186   The CDC won 85 of 138 seats.
187   The CDC won 75 seats.
188   Henderson and Robinson, p.326.
189   See the discussion in Terry D. Clark, 'The Lithuanian Political Party System: A Case Study in Democratic Consolidation', *East European Politics and Societies* 9, 1, Winter 1995, pp.41–62. Clark says there was a threshold of 5% and 5 parties exceeded it – the above and the Centre Union.
190   In addition, support for independents has been small – only 3% in 1996.

191 Although FU lost some members to two new parties, the Right Wingers Party and the Reformist Party, it combined in an electoral alliance with ENIP. The PFE turned into the Centre Party, while the Coalition and Rural People's Association was formed by the unification of the Secure Home electoral alliance and the Rural People's Party. On Estonian parties, see David Arter, 'Estonia After the March 1995 Riigikogu Election: Still an Anti-Party System?', *The Journal of Communist Studies and Transition Politics* 11, 3, September 1995, pp.249–71.
192 The Centre Party split, ENIP and FU merged, and the Moderate Party was formed.
193 Henderson and Robinson, p.322.
194 Reported in Arter, p.263.
195 William Crowther, 'The politics of democratization in postcommunist Moldova', Karen Dawisha and Bruce Parrott (eds), *Democratic changes and authoritarian reactions in Russia, Ukraine, Belarus and Moldova*, Cambridge: Cambridge University Press, 1997, p.309.
196 For some figures on the parties, see Allison *et al.*, p.525.
197 Nora Dudwick, 'Political transformation in postcommunist Armenia: images and realities', Karen Dawisha and Bruce Parrott (eds), *Conflict, Cleavage and Change in Central Asia and the Caucasus*, Cambridge: Cambridge University Press, 1997, pp.84–9.
198 Agh suggests a division between the historical rightist traditionalist CPR and CPP and the modernising CSLP and SDP. Agh (Politics of Central Europe), p.176. Although not many people 'feel close' to one party or movement: 1992 24%, 1993 35%, 1995 24%. New Democracies Barometer.
199 50% were elected by SMC and 50% by PR and national party lists.
200 Liberal Democratic Party of Russia, Russia's Choice, Communist Party of the Russian Federation, Women of Russia, Agrarian Party, Yabloko, Party of Russian Unity and Accord, Democratic Party of Russia.
201 Communist Party of the Russian Federation, Liberal Democratic Party of Russia, Our Home is Russia, Yabloko.
202 Communist Party of the Russian Federation, Unity, Fatherland-All Russia, Union of Rightist Forces, Yabloko, Zhirinovsky Bloc.
203 The first round occurred in March, the second in April and further rounds in July, August and November, after which 45 seats remained unfilled.
204 50% SMC, 50% PR.
205 Communist Party of Ukraine, Rukh, Peasants Party of Ukraine, Socialist Party of Ukraine.
206 Communist Party of Ukraine, Rukh, Socialist and Peasant Parties Bloc, Greens, People's Democratic Party, Hromada (All-Union Association), Progressive Socialist Party, Social Democratic Party.
207 Most deputies elected to the parliament were without party affiliation.
208 Three different systems applied for the three houses: a plurality system for the Chamber of Associated Labour, a majority system for the Chamber of Communes, and PR for the Socio-Political Chamber. For a discussion, see Franci Grad, 'The New Electoral System', Danica Fink-Hafner and John R. Robbins (eds), *Making a New Nation: The Formation of Slovenia*, Aldershot: Dartmouth, 1997, pp.172–81.
209 88 of the 90 seats are filled by PR from eight 11 member districts; unallocated seats are filled at the national level with a 2.5% threshold. The remaining two seats are for Italian and Hungarian ethnic minorities.
210 Party of Democratic Revival (communist party successor), Liberal Democracy, Christian Democratic Party, Slovenian People's Party, Democratic Party of Slovenia, Greens of Slovenia, Social Democratic Party, Socialist Party of Slovenia.
211 Liberal Democracy, Christian Democratic Party, United List of Social Democrats, Slovenian National Party, Slovenian People's Party, Democratic Party of Slovenia, Greens of Slovenia, Social Democratic Party.
212 Liberal Democracy, Slovenian People's Party, Social Democratic Party, Christian Democratic Party, United List of Social Democrats, Democratic Party of Pensioners, Slovenian National Party.

213 Liberal Democracy, Social Democratic Party, United List of Social Democrats, Slovenian People's Party, New Slovenia Christian People's Party, Democratic Party of Pensioners, Party of Slovenian Youth.
214 For the composition of the Demos bloc, see Rose, Munro and Mackie, p.109. Demos won 55% of the vote.
215 Liberal Democracy was actually the successor to the Federation of Socialist Youth of Slovenia, the communist era official youth organisation. ULSD was based on a successor to the former communists, the PDR which merged with ULSD in 1992. LD had 22 seats, CPD 15 and ULSD 14 in the 90 seat chamber.
216 Internal Macedonian Revolutionary Organisation-Democratic Party for Macedonian National Unity.
217 85 seats were elected by SMC and 35 by PR.
218 Internal Macedonian Revolutionary Organisation, League of Communists of Macedonia-Party of Democratic Reform, Party for Democratic Prosperity, Alliance of Reform Forces. IMRO won 31% of the seats, LCM 26%.
219 Social Democratic Union of Macedonia, Liberal Party, Party for Democratic Prosperity, Socialist Party of Macedonia.
220 Internal Macedonian Revolutionary Organisation, Social Democratic Union of Macedonia, Party for Democratic Prosperity, Democratic Alternative, Liberal Democratic Party (in alliance with the Democratic Party).
221 SDUM had 58 seats, LP 28 and SPM five. There were 120 seats.
222 IMRO had 59 seats, PDP 25.
223 On party proliferation, see Robert G. Moser, 'The Impact of Parliamentary Electoral Systems in Russia'; *Post-Soviet Affairs* 13, 3, July–September 1997, pp.284–302.
224 Richard Rose, Evgeny Tikhomirov and William Mishler, 'Understanding Multi-party Choice: The 1995 Duma Election', *Europe-Asia Studies* 49, 5, 1997, p.801.
225 Rose, Tikhomirov and Mishler, p.801.
226 On the weakness of party development in the regions, see Grigorii V. Golosov, 'From Adygeya to Yaroslavl: Factors of Party Development in the Regions of Russia, 1995–1998', *Europe-Asia Studies* 51, 8, December 1999, pp.1333–65.
227 Cf the comments of M. Steven Fish, 'The Advent of Multipartism in Russia, 1993–1995', *Post-Soviet Affairs* 11, 4, October–December 1995, pp.340–83. Also on parties see John Lowenhardt (ed), Party Politics in Post-Communist Russia, *The Journal of Communist Studies and Transition Politics* Special Issue, 14, 1–2, March–June 1998 and Michael Urban and Vladimir Gel'man, 'The development of political parties in Russia', Dawisha and Parrott (Russia ...), pp.175–219.
228 For the argument that between 1993 and 1995 the proportion of people willing to identify themselves as supporters of a particular party increased from 13.3% to 28.9%. Stephen Whitefield and Geoffrey Evans, 'Support for Democracy and Political Opposition in Russia, 1993–1995', *Post-Soviet Affairs* 12, 3, July–September 1996, pp.218–42. Without information relating to the parties individually, it is impossible to draw any firm conclusions from this about whether parties are being seen as representative of particular constituencies.
229 For example, William M. Reisinger, Arthur H. Miller and Vicki L. Hesli, 'Ideological Divisions and Party-building Prospects in Post-Soviet Russia', Matthew Wyman, Stephen White and Sarah Oates (eds), *Elections and Voters in Post-Communist Russia*, Cheltenham: Edward Elgar, 1998, pp.136–66. For the argument that there was a link between party platforms and voter attitudes in the 1993 election, see Matthew Wyman, Bill Miller, Stephen White and Paul Heywood, 'Parties and Voters in the Elections', Peter Lentini (ed), *Elections and Political Order in Russia. The implications of the 1993 elections to the Federal Assembly*, Budapest: Central European University Press, 1995, pp.124–42. Although on p.133 the authors say that after the campaign, only about a third of Russian voters said that there was a party that represented views like theirs. For the view that in 1995 parties generally failed to represent distinct constituencies, see Stephen White, Richard Rose and Ian McAllister, *How Russia Votes* (Chartham/NJ, Chatham House, 1997), pp.146–7 and 232–4. For the view that most of the electorate easily changes its

commitments, see Leonid Sedov, 'Consistency and Change among Russian Voters', Wyman, White and Oates, pp.228–39, esp. p.232.
230 For an argument that party programs were converging between 1993 and 1995, see Sarah Oates, 'Party Platforms: Towards a Definition of the Russian Political Spectrum', *The Journal of Communist Studies and Transition Politics* 14, 1 and 2, March–June 1998, pp.76–97. On the development of and changes in a left-right continuum in Russia, see Geoffrey Evans and Stephen Whitefield, 'The Evolution of Left and Right in Post-Soviet Russia', *Europe-Asia Studies* 50, 6, 1998, pp.1023–42.
231 Ian McAllister, Stephen White and Olga Kryshtanovskaya, 'Voting and Party Support in the December 1995 Duma Elections', *The Journal of Communist Studies and Transition Politics* 13, 1, March 1997, p.118.
232 Furthermore party identification levels have been low, with 78% professing no such identification in 1994. White, Rose and McAllister, p.135. The corresponding figure in the US and UK was, respectively, 13% and 8%.
233 Robert G. Moser, 'The Impact of Parliamentary Electoral Systems in Russia', *Post-Soviet Affairs* 13, 3, July–September 1997, p.297. The LDPR and CPRF were the only parties to run candidates in more than half the territorial seats.
234 Taras Kuzio, 'The 1994 Parliamentary Elections in Ukraine', *The Journal of Communist Studies and Transition Politics* 11, 4, December 1995, p.337. On the parties, see Andrew Wilson and Artur Bilous, 'Political Parties in Ukraine', *Europe-Asia Studies* 45, 4, 1993, pp.693–703.
235 John Higley, Jan Pakulski and Wlodzimierz Wesolowski, 'Introduction: Elite Change and Democratic Regimes in Eastern Europe', Higley, Pakulski and Wesolowski, 1998, p.30.
236 Sarah Birch, 'Nomenklatura Democratization: Electoral Clientelism in Post-Soviet Ukraine', *Democratization* 4, 4, Winter 1997, p.46. Ilya Prizel, 'Ukraine between proto-democracy and 'soft authoritarianism'', Dawisha and Parrott (Russia ...), p.355.
237 Birch pp.40–62.
238 The numbers acknowledging that they 'feel close' to one party or movement was as follows: 1991 20%, 1992 53%, 1995 22%. New Democracies Barometer.
239 Seats were allocated at the local constituency and national levels, with no threshold.
240 The threshold increased by 1% for every party which joined a coalition up to a maximum of 8%. There were multi-member local constituencies and a national constituency, both elected by PR. There were also special seats for ethnic minorities.
241 Plus 15 seats set aside for ethnic minorities.
242 Plus 19 seats set aside for ethnic minorities.
243 National Salvation Front, Hungarian Democratic Union, National Liberal Party. No other party won more than 2.6% of the vote.
244 Democratic National Salvation Front, Democratic Convention, Democratic Party (former NSF), Romanian National Unity Party, Hungarian Democratic Union, Greater Romania Party, Socialist Labour Party, Agrarian Democratic Party.
245 Democratic Convention, Social Democracy Party of Romania (formerly DNSF), Social Democratic Union, Hungarian Democratic Union, Greater Romania Party, Romanian National Unity Party.
246 Democratic Social Pole of Romania (including the Democratic Social Party, the Social Democratic Party, and the Humanist Party) Greater Romania Party, Democratic Party, National Liberal Party, Hungarian Democratic Union.
247 The NSF won 263 of the 396 seats.
248 DNSF had 117 of the 341 seats. The government relied on the support of GRP, RNUP and SLP. Initially the government was not formally a coalition, but such an arrangement was reached with the RNUP, the GRP and the communist successor SLP.
249 Together they won 175 seats in the 343 seat lower chamber.
250 This was to be a minority government which sought parliamentary support from the smaller parties, excluding the Greater Romania Party.
251 Founded in 1989, the SRM competed as part of Depos in 1992.

238 Notes

252 A combination of SMC and PR local constituencies.
253 Socialist Party of Serbia, Serbian Radical Party, Democratic Movement for Serbia. These were the only parties to win more than nine seats, winning respectively 101, 73 and 49 seats in the 250 seat parliament. Depos was an anti-Milosevic coalition formed in May 1992 by SRM, the Democratic Party of Serbia, Serbian Liberal Party, New Democracy-Movement for Serbia, and the Peasant Party.
254 Socialist Party of Serbia, Democratic Movement for Serbia (Depos), Serbian Radical Party, Democratic Party. These were the only parties to win more than nine seats.
255 Socialist Party of Serbia, Serbian Radical Party, Serbian Renewal Movement. Together these won 93% of the seats.
256 Democratic Opposition of Serbia, Socialist Party of Serbia, Serbian Radical Party, Party of Serbian Unity.
257 Democratic Party of Montenegrin Socialists, Peoples Party of Montenegro, Liberal Alliance of Montenegro, Serbian Radical Party. No other party won more than eight seats.
258 Democratic Party of Montenegrin Socialists, National Unity Coalition, Liberal Alliance of Montenegro. No other party won more than three seats.
259 For a Better Life (coalition of DPMS, PPM and Social Democratic Party), Socialist People's Party, Liberal Alliance of Montenegro, Democratic Alliance of Albanians, Democratic Union of Albanians.
260 SPS won 101 seats, SRP 73 seats and Depos 6 seats.
261 SPS won 123 of the 250 seats. ND is New Democracy, a member of Depos.
262 SPS won 44% of the seats, SRP 32%, SRM 18%.
263 The DOS consisted of 18 parties and was allied to new Yugoslav President Kostunica.
264 DPMS won 46 out of 85 seats.
265 The DPMS won 45 of 71 seats.
266 FBL coalition won 42 (Democratic Party of Montenegran Socialists 30, People's Party 7 and Social Democratic Party 5) seats in the 78 seat chamber; SPP won 29, LAM 5, and the other two one each.
267 The number of people saying they 'feel close' to one party or movement was: 1991 37%, 1992 34%, 1993 38%, 1995 41%. New Democracies Barometer.
268 On the fate of the communist parties, see John T. Ishiyama, 'Communist Parties in Transition. Structures, Leaders, and Processes of Democratization in Eastern Europe', *Comparative Politics* 27, 2, January 1995, pp.147–66, and Alison Mahr and John Nagle, (Resurrection), pp.393–409.
269 This typology comes from Fish (Determinants), p.64. He does not consider Serbia and Montenegro.
270 For one discussion of this, see Liah Greenfeld, *Nationalism. Five Roads to Modernity*, Cambridge: Harvard University Press, 1992, esp. pp.11–13.
271 More particularly by ethno-structural factors. For the argument that institutional power-sharing arrangements designed to ameliorate ethnic conflict actually exacerbate it by inserting ethnic considerations into all issues, by polarising policy preferences, and by multiplying the institutional weapons accessible to ethnic elites, see Philip G. Roeder, 'Peoples and States after 1989: The Political Costs of Incomplete National Revolutions', *Slavic Review* 58, 4, Winter 1999, pp.868–71. For arguments about the structuring effects of federalism on the fall of communism, see Valerie Bunce, *Subversive Institutions: The Design and the Destruction of Socialism and the State*, Cambridge: Cambridge University Press, 1999, and Carol Skalnik Leff, 'Democratization and Disintegration in Multinational States: The Breakup of the Communist Federations', *World Politics* 51, 2, January 1999, pp.205–35.
272 We should not assume that people of the same ethnic group will necessarily share the same values or outlooks, or will even acknowledge a common membership. Ukraine provides a striking case of this.
273 For an argument that where ethnic groups are most 'separated' (i.e. distinct in terms of regionalism, culture, religion, language and nationalism), democratisation can be facilitated because institutions must be pluralist and provide some room for the groups; otherwise the

state will either split or see the development of hegemony, see Raymond M. Basch, 'The Effects of Ethnic Separation on Democratization: A Comparative Study', *East European Quarterly* 32, 2, June 1998, pp.221–42. The argument rests on a comparison of Moldova, Ukraine and Belarus.
274 The figures have been taken from Karatnycky and checked with other sources. For the FSU, see Stephen K. Batalden and Sandra L. Batalden, *The Newly Independent States of Eurasia. Handbook of Former Soviet Republics*, Phoenix: Oryx Press, 1993. The figures are rounded.
275 Roeder (Peoples and States), pp.873–4.
276 For an analysis structured around what he calls nationalising states, national minorities and external national homelands, see Rogers Brubaker, *Nationalism Reframed. Nationhood and the National Question in the New Europe*, Cambridge: Cambridge University Press, 1996, ch.3. For an argument that in Bulgaria, Romania and Slovakia the weakness of opposition at the time of transition enabled former communists to retain power and use ethnic nationalism as a form of legitimation, see Milada Anna Vachudova and Tim Snyder, 'Are Transitions Transitory? Two Types of Political Change in Eastern Europe Since 1989', *East European Politics and Societies* 11, 1, Winter 1997, pp.1–35.
277 For a discussion of these which sees them as more important than suggested here, see John Nagle, 'Ethnos, Demos and Democratization: A Comparison of the Czech Republic, Hungary and Poland', *Democratization* 4, 2, Summer 1997, pp.28–56.
278 In 1989 the Gagauz constituted 4% of the population. For some opinion survey figures from the different national groups, see Crowther, pp.304–306.
279 For example, EECR 8, 1–2 Winter-Spring 1999, p.14.
280 Graham Smith and Andrew Wilson, 'Rethinking Russia's Post-Soviet Diaspora: The Potential for Political Mobilization in Eastern Ukraine and North-east Estonia', *Europe-Asia Studies* 49, 5, 1997, p.851.
281 Henderson and Robinson, p.206. For the view that this was less an attempt to secede than to place pressure on the citizenship policies of the government, see Graham S. Smith, *The Post-Soviet States. Mapping the Politics of Transition*, London: Arnold, 1999, pp.81–2.
282 Arter, p.261. On the weakness of Russian organisations, see Smith and Wilson, p.857.
283 Smith, Law et al., pp.114–15.
284 Russians have declined slightly as a proportion of the population from 30.3% in1989 to 28.7% in 1995. This, in part, reflects emigration. Toivo U. Raun, 'Democratization and political development in Estonia 1987–96' Dawisha and Parrott (East Central Europe), p.336.
285 For a discussion of the political orientations of the two communities, see Cynthia S. Kaplan, 'Political Culture in Estonia. The Impact of Two Traditions on Political Development', Tismaneanu, pp.227–67.
286 For a comparison with Estonia, see Pal Kosto and Boris Tsilevich, 'Patterns of Nation Building and Political Integration in a Bifurcated Postcommunist State: Ethnic Aspects of Parliamentary Elections in Latvia', *East European Politics and Societies* 11, 2, Spring 1997, pp.384–5.
287 Smith, Law et al., p.129.
288 Taras Kuzio, 'The 1994 Parliamentary Elections in Ukraine', *The Journal of Communist Studies and Transition Politics* 11, 4, December 1995, p.348.
289 See Dominique Arel, 'Ukraine. The Temptation of the Nationalizing State', Tismaneanu, pp.156–88.
290 On the inclusive nature of Rukh's early nationalism, see Alexander Motyl and Bohdan Krawchenko, 'Ukraine: from empire to statehood', Ian Bremmer and Ray Taras (eds), *New States, New Politics. Building the Post-Soviet Nations*, Cambridge: Cambridge University Press, 1997, pp.250–1.
291 See the discussion in Smith, Law et al., ch.6.
292 Smith and Wilson, p.850. For a regional breakdown of electoral results, see Andrew Wilson, 'Parties and Presidents in Ukraine and Crimea, 1994', *The Journal of Communist Studies and Transition Politics* 11, 4, December 1995, p. 369. For an argument which emphasises the importance of economic factors in the election, see Zenovia A. Sochor, 'Russocentrism, Regionalism, and the Political Culture of Ukraine', Tismaneanu, pp.189–226.

240 Notes

293 Andrew Wilson and Sarah Birch, 'Voting Stability, Political Gridlock: Ukraine's 1998 Parliamentary Elections', *Europe-Asia Studies* 51, 6, 1999, pp.1039–68. Also on the regional distribution of party support, see Peter R. Craumer and James I. Clem, 'Ukraine's Emerging Electoral Geography: A Regional Analysis of the 1998 Parliamentary Elections', *Post-Soviet Geography and Economics* 40, 1, 1999, pp.1–16 and Melvin J. Hinich, Valeri Khmelko and Peter C. Ordeshook, 'Ukraine's 1998 Parliamentary Election. A Spatial Analysis', *Post-Soviet Affairs* 15, 2, April–June 1999, pp.149–85.

294 This was actually instigated by the reaction of ethnic Serbs in Croatia to the nationalistic policies and symbols of the Tudjman regime. The Serbs took up arms in August 1990. The Jugoslav National Army supported the Krajina Serbs against the Croatian authorities between July and December 1991, Croat control was re-established militarily over part of this area in 1993 and other parts in 1995. In the interim a UN-brokered agreement had maintained the peace. Following the 1995 offensive, there was a mass exodus of Serbs from Krajina. For one discussion of the issue, see Brubaker pp.69–75.

295 Duncan M. Perry, 'The Republic of Macedonia: finding its way', Dawisha and Parrott (South-East Europe), p.253.

296 For the argument that these (along with patronage) were the central elements of the political tradition which the MDS represented, see Michael Carpenter, 'Slovakia and the Triumph of Nationalist Populism', *Communist and Post-Communist Studies* 30, 2, June 1997, pp.205–20.

297 For an analysis of the elite which dissects the clan, or zhuz, component, see Rustem Kadyrzhanov, 'The Ruling Elite of Kazakhstan in the Transitional Period', Vladimir Shlapentokh, Christopher Vanderpool and Boris Doktorov (eds), *The New Elite in Post-Communist Eastern Europe*, College Station: Texas A and M University Press, 1999, pp.144–61. For the argument, albeit based on a small sample, that there is little evidence of tribalism as a basis for identity, see Saulesh Esenova, '"Tribalism" and identity in contemporary circumstances: the case of Kazakhstan', *Central Asian Survey* 17, 3, September 1998, pp.443–62. On the structure of ethnic relations, Anatoly M. Khazanov, 'The ethnic problems of contemporary Kazakhstan', *Central Asian Survey* 14, 2, 1995, pp.243–64.

298 Smith, Law et al., chs 4, 7 and 9; Shahram Akbarzadeh, 'Nation-building in Uzbekistan', *Central Asian Survey* 15, 1, March 1996, pp.27–30.

299 For example, see Ian Bremmer and Cory Welt, 'The trouble with democracy in Kazakhstan', *Central Asian Survey* 15, 2, June 1996, pp.179–99. There has been neither widespread Russian emigration nor political mobilisation, the latter hindered by the provision that parties must be multi-ethnic and pan-republican in constituency. Olcott, pp.210–14.

300 Although in the conflicts in Tajikistan, the Russian and Uzbek minorities tended to support the old regime Nabiev/Rakhmonov forces. Muriel Atkin, 'Thwarted democratization in Tajikistan', Dawisha and Parrott (Central Asia and the Caucasus), pp.298–9.

301 See Graham Smith, Vivien Law, Andrew Wilson, Annette Bohr and Edward Allworth, *Nation-building in the Post-Soviet Borderlands. The Politics of National Identities*, Cambridge: Cambridge University Press, 1998, ch.2.

302 Karatnycky et al., pp.82–4.

303 Unfinished because two electoral cycles have not been completed. See Chapter 1.

5 Paths to democracy?

1 For an argument along these lines, see Adam Przeworski, *Democracy and the Market. Political and Economic Reforms in Eastern Europe and Latin America*, Cambridge: Cambridge University Press, 1991, esp. pp.183–7. Also Adam Przeworski, 'Economic reforms, public opinion, and political institutions: Poland in the Eastern European perspective', Luiz Carlos Bresser Pereira, Jose Maria Maravall and Adam Przeworski, *Economic Reforms in New Democracies. A Social Democratic Approach*, Cambridge: Cambridge University Press, 1993, pp.132–98.

2 By 1995, political regimes were established, so the impact economic change was to have on the establishment and early years of the regime's life should have been evident by this time. The ranking rests upon judgements made by the EBRD about progress made in reform in the

following areas: large and small-scale privatisation, enterprise restructuring, price liberalisation, trade and the foreign exchange system, competition policy, banking reform and interest rate liberalisation, and securities markets and non-bank financial institutions. European Bank for Reconstruction and Development, *Transition Report 1995. Investment and enterprise development*, London: EBRD, 1995, p.11. This ranking differs a little from that of Fish, principally because I have excluded the proportion of GDP provided by the private sector. This measure is different in kind to the evaluations provided by the EBRD on reform in the specific areas noted, and is also subject to influence by factors independent of the course of reform. M. Steven Fish, 'The Determinants of Economic Reform in the Post-Communist World', *East European Politics and Societies* 12, 1, Winter 1998, pp.34–5.

3   EBRD, *Transition report 1998. Financial sector in transition*, London: EBRD, 1998, pp.206–31. For some other figures on comparative performance, see Valerie Bunce, 'The Political Economy of Postsocialism', *Slavic Review* 58, 4, Winter 1999, pp.764–6.

4   These relate only to the period after major economic reform was introduced. Transition report 1998, pp.206–31.

5   Joel Hellman argues that those with the most radical reforms had the lowest overall output declines and the most rapid recoveries. Joel S. Hellman, 'Winners Take All: The Politics of Partial Reform in Postcommunist Transitions', *World Politics* 50, 2, 1998, p.209.

6   For Fish, the key is the identity of the rulers after the first post-communist election. He argues that the earliest and most radical reform occurred where new people not linked with the old regime came to power. Fish, p.60. For similar conclusions, see EBRD, *Transition report 1999. Ten years of transition*, London: EBRD, 1999, pp.106–14, Bunce (Political Economy), p.769, and M. Steven Fish, 'Postcommunist Subversion: Social Science and Democratization in East Europe and Eurasia', *Slavic Review* 58, 4, Winter 1999, pp.808–11. The problem with this argument is that in some cases major economic reform preceded the first post-communist election. Russia is a good example of this where economic liberalisation and privatisation both preceded the 1993 election. The argument can be rescued only by saying that the March 1990 Russian republican election is the relevant one, but this means that a post-communist election occurred before the communist system had fallen. The case of Hungary is even more difficult, given that economic liberalisation dates from the early 1960s. Nor can the argument be rescued by reference to the first 'non-leninist' or 'non-orthodox' communist election because of the institutional diversity that did exist among communist regimes.

7   For example, see this argument applied to Russia in A.M. Migranian, 'Dolgii put' k evropeiskomu domu', *Novyi mir* 7, 1989, pp.166–84. For arguments that political democracy is incompatible with a market economy in the FSU, see Michael Burawoy, 'The Soviet Descent into Capitalism', *American Journal of Sociology* 102, 5, March 1997, pp.1430–44 and Michael Burawoy and Pavel Krotov, 'The Soviet Transition from Socialism to Capitalism: Worker Control and Economic Bargaining in the Wood Industry', *American Sociological Review* 57, 1, February 1992, pp.16–38.

8   Przeworski.

9   Hellman, pp.212–14.

10 Hellman, pp.215–16.

11 For one discussion, see Judy Batt, 'The international dimension of democratisation in Czechoslovakia and Hungary', Geoffrey Pridham, Eric Herring and George Sanford (eds), *Building Democracy? The International Dimension of Democratisation in Eastern Europe*, Leicester: Leicester University Press, 1994, p.176.

12 Adrian G.V. Hyde-Price, 'Democratization in Eastern Europe. The external dimension', Geoffrey Pridham and Tatu Vanhanen (eds), *Democratization in Eastern Europe. Domestic and international perspectives*, London: Routledge, 1994, p.230. Also see John Pinder, 'The European Community and Democracy in Central and Eastern Europe', Pridham, Herring and Sanford, pp.124–5. For a discussion of the terms of 'democratic conditionality' and their application to Slovakia, see Geoffrey Pridham, 'Complying with the European Union's Democratic Conditionality: Transnational Party Linkages and Regime Change in Slovakia, 1993–1998', *Europe-Asia Studies* 51, 7, 1999, pp.1221–44.

13 These countries plus Slovakia and the Baltic states had signed European Agreements and thereby gained associate status earlier in the decade.
14 Graham Smith, Vivien Law, Andrew Wilson, Annette Bohr and Edward Allworth, *Nation-building in the Post-Soviet Borderlands. The Politics of National Identities*, Cambridge: Cambridge University Press, 1998, pp.108–9.
15 For example, see Arend Lijphart (ed), *Parliamentary versus Presidential Government*, Oxford: Oxford University Press, 1992; Juan J. Linz and Arturo Valenzuela (eds), *The Failure of Presidential Democracy: Comparative Perspectives*, Baltimore: The Johns Hopkins University Press, 1994; M. Shugart and J. Carey, *Presidents and Assemblies: Constitutional Design and Electoral Dynamics*, Cambridge: Cambridge University Press, 1992; Arend Lijphart and Carlos H. Waisman (eds), *Institutional Design in New Democracies. Eastern Europe and Latin America*, Boulder: Westview Press, 1996. The distinction between the two types follows that of Shugart and Carey, p.26. It concentrates on whether governmental survival is dependent on president or parliament, and which is the principal authority over the government.
16 For this argument set out explicitly, see Juan J. Linz, ' The Perils of Presidentialism', *The Journal of Democracy* 1, 1, Winter 1990, pp.51–69.
17 In addition to those works cited in fns 15 and 16, see Scott Mainwaring, 'Presidentialism, Multipartism and Democracy: The Difficult Combination', *Comparative Political Studies* 26, 2, July 1993, pp.198–228; Alfred Stepan and Cindy Skach, 'Constitutional Frameworks and Democratic Consolidation: Parliamentarism and Presidentialism', *World Politics* 46, 1, October 1993, pp.1–22.
18 Given the relative clarity of this division, it is not clear that the notion of 'super-executivism' used by Fish takes the analysis much further. It is also very difficult to operationalise. Fish (Post-Communist Subversion), pp.803–5.
19 Poland was not unambiguously parliamentary to begin with, because the president wielded significant power, but this was to become much more the case after 1992.
20 This follows Easter's argument, although it does not just rely upon the nature of old regime elites. Gerald M. Easter, 'Preference for Presidentialism: Postcommunist Regime Change in Russia and the NIS', *World Politics* 49, 2, January 1997, pp.184–211.
21 For one study of this in Poland, see Michael Bernhard, 'Civil Society After the First Transition: Dilemmas of Post-Communist Democratization in Poland and Beyond', *Communist and Post-Communist Studies* 29, 3, September 1996, pp.309–30. For a diagrammatic representation of the argument, see p.327.
22 Hellman, p.216.
23 Fish (Determinants), p.35.
24 For one discussion of this, see Michael Carpenter, 'Slovakia and the Triumph of Nationalist Populism', *Communist and Post-Communist Studies* 30, 2, June 1997, pp.205–20. Also see Milada Anna Vachudova and Tim Snyder, 'Are Transitions Transitory? Two Types of Political Change in Eastern Europe Since 1989', *East European Politics and Societies* 11, 1, Winter 1997, pp.24–6.
25 Fish (Determinants), p.35.
26 Hellman, p.216.
27 Although this was more because of the refusal of the ethnic minorities to participate than of their exclusion by representatives of the ethnic majority.
28 For a discussion of these regimes, see Philip G. Roeder, 'Varieties of Post-Soviet Authoritarian Regimes', *Post-Soviet Affairs* 10, 1, January–March 1994, pp.61–101.
29 Valerie Bunce, *Subversive Institutions. The Design and Destruction of Socialism and the State*, Cambridge: Cambridge University Press, 1999, pp.70–1.
30 It is not clear that it is. Action by Soviet troops in Latvia and Lithuania in January 1991, the refusal of East German security services to continue to break up demonstrations, the role of the 14th Soviet army in Moldova in 1992 and that of Georgian military figures in launching a coup against Gamsakhurdia and bringing back Shevardnadze are important cases where an argument may be made for independent action on the part of the military. It is also not clear how independently the military were acting in Yugoslavia.

6 Conclusion: democracy and post-communism

1 For a stimulating discussion which also reaches this conclusion, see Philip Roeder, 'Varieties of Post-Soviet Authoritarian Regimes', *Post-Soviet Affairs* 10, 1, Jan–March 1994, pp.61–101.
2 For the most systematic attempt to study this on a trans-national basis, see Juan J. Linz and Alfred Stepan, *The Breakdown of Democratic Regimes*, Baltimore: The Johns Hopkins University Press, 1978.
3 There is far too much to be summarised, but for one indication of the way in which thinking on this subject has developed, compare Guillermo O'Donnell, Philippe C. Schmitter and Laurence Whitehead (eds), *Transitions from Authoritarian Rule. Prospects for Democracy*, Baltimore: The Johns Hopkins University Press, 1986, and Juan J. Linz and Alfred Stepan, *Problems of Democratic Transition and Consolidation. Southern Europe, South America and Post-Communist Europe*, Baltimore: The Johns Hopkins University Press, 1996.
4 For a full discussion, see Graeme Gill, *The Dynamics of Democratization. Elites, Civil Society and the Transition Process*, Basingstoke: Macmillan, 2000.
5 The term seems to have been first used in Philippe C. Schmitter and Terry Lynn Karl, 'The Conceptual Travels of Transitologists and Consolidologists: How Far to the East Should They Attempt to Go?', *Slavic Review* 53, 1, Spring 1994, pp.173–85, but it has been taken up by others. For example, Valerie Bunce, 'Should Transitologists be Grounded?', *Slavic Review* 54, 1, Spring 1995, pp.111–27, and Roger D. Markwick, 'A Discipline in Transition?: From Sovietology to "Transitology"', *The Journal of Communist Studies and Transition Politics*, 12, 3, September 1996, pp.255–76.
6 Samuel P. Huntington, *The Third Wave. Democratization in the Late Twentieth Century*, Norman: University of Oklahoma Press, 1991.
7 This discussion relies heavily upon Sarah Meiklejohn Terry, 'Thinking About Post-communist Transitions: How Different Are They?', *Slavic Review* 52, 2, Summer 1993, pp.333–7; Schmitter and Karl (How Far); Bunce (Should Transitologists); Terry Lynn Karl and Philippe C. Schmitter, 'From an Iron Curtain to a Paper Curtain: Grounding Transitologists or Students of Postcommunism?', *Slavic Review* 54, 4, Winter 1995, pp.965–78; Valerie Bunce, 'Paper Curtains and Paper Tigers', *Slavic Review* 54, 4, Winter 1995, pp.979–87; Valerie Bunce, 'Can We Compare Democratization in the East Versus the South?', *Journal of Democracy* 6, 3, July 1995, pp.87–100; Valerie Bunce, 'Regional Differences in Democratization: The East Versus the South', *Post-Soviet Affairs* 14, 3, 1998, pp.187–211; and Valerie Bunce, *Subversive Institutions: The Design and Destruction of Socialism and the State*, Cambridge: Cambridge University Press, 1999. This issue is discussed in a somewhat different way in Gill (Dynamics of Democratization), ch 6.
8 The terms, and argument, come from Bunce (Regional Differences), pp.195–6 and 205.
9 Bunce (Regional Differences), p.206.
10 See Gill (Dynamics of Democratization), ch. 5.
11 For a fuller explication of this, see Gill (Dynamics of Democratization).
12 Huntington (Third Wave), p.166; also Gill (Dynamics of Democratization), pp.52–8.
13 For example, see the discussions in Laurence Whitehead (ed), *The International Dimensions of Democratization. Europe and the Americas*, Oxford: Oxford University Press, 1996, and Geoffrey Pridham (ed), *Encouraging Democracy: The International Context of Regime Transition in Southern Europe*, Leicester: Leicester University Press, 1991.
14 Bunce (Regional Differences), pp.194–5.
15 Bunce (Regional Differences), pp.199–202.
16 Leslie Holmes, *Post-Communism. An Introduction*, Cambridge: Polity Press, 1997, ch.1. For another stimulating analysis of the nature of post-communism, see Richard Sakwa, *Postcommunism* Buckingham: Open University Press, 1999. For a list of characteristics, see pp.5–6; also chs. 4–7. Also see Karen Henderson and Neil Robinson, *Post-Communist Politics. An Introduction*, London: Prentice Hall, 1997.
17 For example, see Stephen White, 'What is a Communist System?', *Studies in Comparative Communism* xvi, 4, 1983, pp.247–63, and the discussion in Leslie Holmes, *Politics in the Communist World*, Oxford: Clarendon Press, 1986.

Bibliography

Agh, Attila (1995), 'The permanent "constitutional crisis" in the democratic transition: the case of Hungary', Joachim Jens Hesse and Nevil Johnson (eds), *Constitutional Policy and Change in Europe*, Oxford: Oxford University Press.
Agh, Attila (1998), *The Politics of Central Europe*, London: Sage.
Agh, Attila and Sandor Kurtan (1995), 'The 1994 parliamentary elections in Hungary', *Democratisation and Europeanisation in Hungary: The First Parliament 1990–1994*, Budapest, Hungarian Center for Democracy Studies.
Aiyp, Naryn (1998), 'Kyrgyzstan: Askar Akayev's diminishing democracy', *Transitions*, 5, 10, October.
Akbarzadeh, Shahram (1996), 'Nation-building in Uzbekistan', *Central Asian Survey*, 15, 1, March.
Akbarzadeh, Shahram (1997), 'The political shape of Central Asia', *Central Asian Survey*, 16, 4, December.
'Albania' (1993), *East European Constitutional Review*, 2, 2, Spring.
Allison, Lincoln, Alexander Kukhianidze and Malkhaz Matsaberidze (1993), 'The Georgian election of 1992', *Electoral Studies*, 12, 2.
Allison, Lincoln, Alexander Kukhianidze and Malkhaz Matsaberidze (1996), 'The Georgian elections of 1995', *Electoral Studies*, 15, 2.
Allison, Lincoln, Alexander Kukhianidze, Malkhaz Matsaberidze and Valeri Dolidze (1996), 'Problems of democratization in the Republic of Georgia', *Democratization*, 3, 4, Winter.
Alstadt, Audrey L. (1997), 'Azerbaijan's struggle toward democracy', Karen Dawisha and Bruce Parrott (eds), *Conflict, Cleavage, and Change in Central Asia and the Caucasus*, Cambridge: Cambridge University Press.
Anderson, John (1995), 'Authoritarian political development in Central Asia: the case of Turkmenistan', *Central Asian Survey*, 14, 4, December.
Anderson, John (1997), 'Constitutional development in Central Asia', *Central Asian Survey*, 16, 3, September.
Anderson, John (2000), 'Creating a framework for civil society in Kyrgyzstan', *Europe-Asia Studies*, 52, 1, January.
Anderson, Perry (1974), *Lineages of the Absolutist State*, London: New Left Books.
Appel, Hilary (1995), 'Justice and the reformulation of property rights in the Czech Republic', *East European Politics and Societies*, 9, 1, Winter.
Arel, Dominique (1995), 'Ukraine. The temptation of the nationalizing state', Vladimir Tismaneanu (ed), *Political Culture and Civil Society in Russia and the New States of Eurasia*, Armonk: M.E. Sharpe.

Arter, David (1995), 'Estonia after the March 1995 Riigikogu election: still an anti-party system?', *The Journal of Communist Studies and Transition Politics*, 11, 3, September.
Ascherson, Neal (1981), *The Polish August. What Happened in Poland*, Harmondsworth: Penguin.
Atkin, Muriel (1997), 'Tajikistan: reform, reaction and civil war', Ian Bremmer and Ray Taras (eds), *New States New Politics. Building the Post-Soviet Nations*, Cambridge: Cambridge University Press.
Atkin, Muriel (1997), 'Thwarted democratization in Tajikistan', Karen Dawisha and Bruce Parrott (eds), *Conflict, Cleavage, and Change in Central Asia and the Caucasus*, Cambridge: Cambridge University Press.
Bach, Stanley (1996), From Soviet to parliament in Ukraine: the Verkhovna Rada during 1992–94', David M. Olson and Philip Norton (eds), *The New Parliaments of Central and Eastern Europe*, London: Frank Cass.
Bahry, Donna and Lucan Way (1994), 'Citizen activism in the Russian transition', *Post-Soviet Affairs*, 10, 4, October.
Balasz, Magdolna and Zsolt Enyedi (1996), 'Hungarian case studies: the Alliance of Free Democrats and the Alliance of Young Democrats', Paul G. Lewis (ed), *Party Structure and Organization in East Central Europe*, Cheltenham: Edward Elgar.
Balzer, Harley D. (ed) (1996), *Russia's Missing Middle Class. The Professions in Russian History*, Armonk: M.E. Sharpe.
Basch, Raymond M. (1998), 'The effects of ethnic separation on democratization: a comparative study', *East European Quarterly*, 32, 2, June.
Basom, Kenneth E. (1996), 'Prospects for democracy in Serbia and Croatia', *East European Quarterly*, xxix, 4, January.
Batalden, Stephen K. and Sandra L. Batalden (1993), *The Newly Independent States of Eurasia. Handbook of Former Soviet Republics*, Phoenix: Oryx Press.
Batt, Judy (1993), 'Czechoslovakia', Stephen Whitefield (ed), *The New Institutional Architecture of Eastern Europe*, London: Macmillan.
Batt, Judy (1994), 'The international dimension of democratisation in Czechoslovakia and Hungary', Geoffrey Pridham, Eric Herring and George Sanford (eds), *Building Democracy? The International Dimension of Democratisation in Eastern Europe*, Leicester: Leicester University Press.
Baylis, Thomas A. (1994), 'Plus ça change? Transformation and continuity among East European elites', *Communist and Post-Communist Studies* 27, 3, September.
Baylis, Thomas (1998), 'Elite change after communism: Eastern Germany, the Czech Republic and Slovakia', *East European Politics and Societies*, 12, 2, Spring.
Behr, Edward (1991), *'Kiss the Hand You Cannot Bite'. The Rise and Fall of the Ceausescus*, Harmondsworth: Penguin.
Bell, John D. (1997), 'Postcommunist Bulgaria', Karen Dawisha and Bruce Parrott (eds), *Politics, Power and the Struggle for Democracy in South-East Europe*, Cambridge: Cambridge University Press.
Berg-Schlosser, Dirk and Jeremy Mitchell (eds) (2000), *Conditions of Democracy in Europe, 1919–1939. Systematic Case Studies*, Basingstoke: Macmillan.
Bernhard, Michael (1993), 'Civil society and democratic transition in East Central Europe', *Political Science Quarterly*, 108, 2, Summer.
Bernhard, Michael (1993), *The Origins of Democratization in Poland: Workers, Intellectuals, and Oppositional Politics, 1976–1980*, New York: Columbia University Press.

Bernhard, Michael (1996), 'Civil society after the first transition: dilemmas of post-communist democratization in Poland and beyond', *Communist and Post-Communist Studies*, 29, 3, September.
Bernhard, Michael (1997), 'Semipresidentialism, charisma, and democratic institutions in Poland', Kurt von Mettenheim (ed), *Presidential Institutions and Democratic Politics. Comparing Regional and National Contests*, Baltimore: The Johns Hopkins University Press.
Bibic, Adolf (1993), 'The emergence of pluralism in Slovenia', *Communist and Post-Communist Studies*, 26, 4, December.
Bielasiak, Jack (1997), 'Substance and process in the development of party systems in East Central Europe', *Communist and Post-Communist Studies*, 30, 1, March.
Bilmanis, Alfred (1970), *A History of Latvia*, Westport: Greenwood Press.
Birch, Sarah (1997), 'Nomenklatura democratization: electoral clientelism in post-Soviet Ukraine', *Democratization*, 4, 4, Winter.
Bojcun, Marko (1995), 'The Ukrainian parliamentary elections in March–April 1994', *Europe-Asia Studies* 47, 2.
Bozoki, Andras (1993), 'Hungary's road to systematic change: the opposition roundtable', *East European Politics and Societies* 7, 2, Spring.
Bozoki, Andras (1994), 'Party formation and constitutional change in Hungary', *The Journal of Communist Studies and Transition Politics*, 10, 3, September.
Bremmer, Ian and Cory Welt (1996), 'The trouble with democracy in Kazakhstan', *Central Asian Survey*, 15, 2, June.
Brokl, Lubomir and Zdenka Mansfeldova (1998), 'Czech and Slovak political and parliamentary elites', John Higley, Jan Pakulski and Wlodzimierz Wesolowski (eds), *Postcommunist Elites and Democracy in Eastern Europe*, Basingstoke: Macmillan.
Brovkin, Vladimir (1990), 'Revolution from below: informal political associations in Russia 1988–1989', *Soviet Studies*, 42, 2, April.
Brubaker, Rogers (1996), *Nationalism Reframed. Nationhood and the National Question in the New Europe*, Cambridge: Cambridge University Press.
'Bulgaria' (1993), *East European Constitutional Review*, 2, 2, Spring.
Bunce, Valerie (1995), 'Can we compare democratization in the East versus the South?', *The Journal of Democracy*, 6, 3, July.
Bunce, Valerie (1995), 'Should transitologists be grounded?', *Slavic Review*, 54, 1, Spring.
Bunce, Valerie (1995), 'Paper curtains and paper tigers', *Slavic Review*, 54, 4, Winter.
Bunce, Valerie (1997), 'Presidents and the transition in Eastern Europe', Kurt von Mettenheim (ed), *Presidential Institutions and Democratic Politics. Comparing Regional and National Contests*, Baltimore: The Johns Hopkins University Press.
Bunce, Valerie (1998), 'Regional Differences in Democratization: The East Versus the South', *Post-Soviet Affairs*, 14, 3.
Bunce, Valerie (1999), 'The political economy of postsocialism', *Slavic Review*, 58, 4, Winter.
Bunce, Valerie (1999), *Subversive Institutions. The Design and the Destruction of Socialism and the State*, Cambridge: Cambridge University Press.
Bunce, Valerie and Maria Csanadi (1993), 'Uncertainty in the transition: post-Communism in Hungary', *East European Politics and Societies*, 7, 2, Spring.
Burawoy, Michael (1997), 'The Soviet descent into capitalism', *American Journal of Sociology*, 102, 5, March.
Burawoy, Michael and Pavel Krotov (1992), 'The Soviet transition from socialism to capitalism: worker control and economic bargaining in the wood industry', *American Sociological Review*, 57, 1, February.

Burger, Josef (1993), 'Politics of restitution in Czechoslovakia', *East European Quarterly*, XXVI, 4, January.
Butorova, Zora and Martin Butora (1995), 'Political parties, value orientations and Slovakia's road to independence', Gordon Wightman (ed), *Party Formation in East-Central Europe*, Aldershot: Edward Elgar.
Calda, Milos (1996), 'The roundtable talks in Czechoslovakia', Jon Elster (ed), *The Roundtable Talks and the Breakdown of Communism*, Chicago: University of Chicago Press.
Carey, Henry F. (1995), 'Irregularities or rigging: the 1992 Romanian parliamentary elections', *East European Quarterly*, xxix, 1, March.
Carey, Henry F. (1996), 'From big lie to small lies: state mass media dominance in post-communist Romania', *East European Politics and Societies*, 10, 1, Winter.
Carpenter, Michael (1997), 'Slovakia and the triumph of nationalist populism', *Communist and Post-Communist Studies*, 30, 2, June.
Carter, April (1982), *Democratic Reform in Yugoslavia: The Changing Role of the Party*, Princeton: Princeton University Press.
Casanova, Jose (1998), 'Ethno-linguistic and religious pluralism and democratic construction in Ukraine', Barnett R. Rubin and Jack Snyder (eds), *Post-Soviet Political Order. Conflict and State Building*, London: Routledge.
Clark, Terry D. (1995), 'The Lithuanian political party system: a case study of democratic consolidation', *East European Politics and Societies*, 9, 1, Winter.
Cohen, Lenard J. (1997), 'Embattled democracy: postcommunist Croatia in transition', Karen Dawisha and Bruce Parrott (eds), *Politics, Power and the Struggle for Democracy in South-East Europe*, Cambridge: Cambridge University Press.
Cohen, Stephen F. (1979), 'The friends and foes of change: reformism and conservatism in the Soviet Union', plus comments by T.H. Rigby, S.Frederick Starr, Frederick Barghoorn and George Breslauer, *Slavic Review* 38, 2, June.
Collier, David and Steven Levitsky (1997), 'Democracy with adjectives: conceptual innovation in comparative research', *World Politics* 49, 3, April.
Colomer, Joseph M. and Margot Pascual (1994), 'The Polish games of transition', *Communist and Post-Communist Studies*, 27, 3, September.
'Constitution Watch' (1992), *East European Constitutional Review*, 1, 1, Spring.
Corley, Felix (1998), 'Uzbekistan: Islam Karimov's everlasting first term', *Transitions*, 5, 10, October.
Corley, Felix (1999), 'Disputed Results', *Transitions*, 6, 2, February.
Cox, Terry and Laszlo Vass (1994), 'Civil society and interest representation in Hungarian political development', *The Journal of Communist Studies and Transition Politics*, 10, 3, September.
Crampton, Richard (1993), 'Bulgaria', Stephen Whitefield (ed), *The New Institutional Architecture of Eastern Europe*, London: Macmillan.
Craumer, Peter R. and James I. Clem (1999), 'Ukraine's emerging electoral geography: a regional analysis of the 1998 parliamentary elections', *Post-Soviet Geography and Economics*, 40, 1.
Crawford, Keith (1996), *East Central European Politics Today*, Manchester, Manchester University Press.
'Croatia' (1993), *East European Constitutional Review*, 2, 2, Spring.
Crowther, William (1997), 'The politics of democratization in postcommunist Moldova', Karen Dawisha and Bruce Parrott (eds), *Democratic Changes and Authoritarian Reactions in Russia, Ukraine, Belarus and Moldova*, Cambridge: Cambridge University Press.

Bibliography

Crowther, William (1997), 'Moldova: caught between nation and empire', Ian Bremmer and Ray Taras (eds), *New States New Politics. Building the Post-Soviet Nations*, Cambridge: Cambridge University Press.
Crowther, William and Steven D. Roper (1996), 'A comparative analysis of institutional development in the Romanian and Moldovan parliaments', David M. Olson and Philip Norton (eds), *The New Parliaments of Central and Eastern Europe*, London: Frank Cass.
'Czech Republic' (1993), *East European Constitutional Review*, 2, 1 and 2, Winter and Spring.
'Czech Republic' (1994), *East European Constitutional Review*, 3, 2, Spring.
Davies, Philip John and Andrejs Valdis Ozolins (1996), 'The Latvian parliamentary election of 1995', *Electoral Studies*, 15, 1.
Deletant, Dennis (1990), 'The Romanian elections of May 1990', *Representation*, 29, 108.
Dreifelds, Juris (1996), *Latvia in Transition*, Cambridge, Cambridge University Press.
Dudwick, Nora (1997), 'Armenia: paradise regained or lost?', Ian Bremmer and Ray Taras (eds), *New States New Politics. Building the Post-Soviet Nations*, Cambridge: Cambridge University Press.
Dudwick, Nora (1997), 'Political transformation in postcommunist Armenia: images and realities', Karen Dawisha and Bruce Parrott (eds), *Conflict, Cleavage, and Change in Central Asia and the Caucasus*, Cambridge: Cambridge University Press.
Dunlop, John B. (1993), *The Rise of Russia and the Fall of the Soviet Empire*, Princeton: Princeton University Press.
Easter, Gerald M. (1997), 'Preference for presidentialism: postcommunist regime change in Russia and the NIS', *World Politics*, 49, 2, January.
Edmunds, Timothy (1998), 'Power and powerlessness in Kazakhstani society: ethnic problems in perspective', *Central Asian Survey*, 17, 3, September.
Ekiert, Gregorz (1991), 'Democratization processes in East Central Europe: a theoretical reconsideration', *British Journal of Political Science* 21, 3.
Ekiert, Gregorz (1996), *The State Against Society*, Princeton: Princeton University Press.
Elster, Jon (1993–94), 'Bargaining over the presidency', *East European Constitutional Review*, 2, 4, and 3, 1, Fall–Winter.
Elster, Jon (1996), 'Introduction', Jon Elster (ed), *The Roundtable Talks and the Breakdown of Communism*, Chicago: University of Chicago Press.
Elster, Jon, Claus Offe and Ulrich K. Preuss (1998), *Institutional Design in Post-communist Societies. Rebuilding the Ship at Sea*, Cambridge: Cambridge University Press.
Esenov, Murad (1998), 'Turkmenistan: Saparmurat Niyazov's invincible rule', *Transitions*, 5, 10, October.
Esenova, Saulesh (1998), '"Tribalism" and identity in contemporary circumstances: the case of Kazakhstan', *Central Asian Survey*, 17, 3, September.
'Estonia' (1993–94), *East European Constitutional Review*, 2, 4 and 3, 1, Fall–Winter.
European Bank for Reconstruction and Development (1995), *Transition Report 1995. Investment and Enterprise Development*, London: EBRD.
European Bank for Reconstruction and Development (1996), *Transition Report 1996. Infrastructure and Savings*, London: EBRD.
European Bank for Reconstruction and Development (1997), *Transition Report 1997. Enterprise Performance and Growth*, London: EBRD.
European Bank for Reconstruction and Development (1998), *Transition Report 1998. Financial Sector in Transition*, London: EBRD.

European Bank for Reconstruction and Development (1999), *Transition Report 1999. Ten Years of Transition*, London: EBRD.
European Bank for Reconstruction and Development (2000), *Transition Report 2000. Employment, Skills and Transition*, London: EBRD.
Evans, Geoffrey and Stephen Whitefield (1993), 'Identifying the bases of party competition in Eastern Europe', *British Journal of Political Science*, 23, 4, October.
Evans, Geoffrey and Stephen Whitefield (1995), 'Social and ideological cleavage formation in post-communist Hungary', *Europe-Asia Studies*, 47, 7.
Evans, Geoffrey and Stephen Whitefield (1998), 'The evolution of left and right in post-Soviet Russia', *Europe-Asia Studies*, 50, 6.
Eyal, Jonathan (1993), 'Romania', Stephen Whitefield (ed), *The New Institutional Architecture of Eastern Europe*, London: Macmillan.
Fierman, William (1997), 'Political development in Uzbekistan: democratization?', Karen Dawisha and Bruce Parrott (eds), *Conflict, Cleavage and Change in Central Asia and the Caucasus*, Cambridge: Cambridge University Press.
Finer, S.E. (1974), *Comparative Government*, Harmondsworth: Penguin, first published 1970.
Fink-Hafner, Danica (1996), 'Organized interests as policy actors in Slovenia', Attila Agh and Gabriella Ilonski (eds), *Parliaments and Organized Interests: The Second Steps*, Budapest: Hungarian Centre for Democracy Studies.
Fish, M. Steven (1995), *Democracy from Scratch. Opposition and Regime in the New Russian Revolution*, Princeton: Princeton University Press.
Fish, M. Steven (1995), 'The advent of multipartism in Russia, 1993–1995', *Post-Soviet Affairs*, 11, 4, October–December.
Fish, M. Steven (1998), 'Democratization's requisites: the postcommunist experience', *Post-Soviet Affairs*, 14, 3, July–September.
Fish, M. Steven (1998), 'The determinants of economic reform in the post-communist world', *East European Politics and Societies* 12, 1, Winter.
Fish, M. Steven (1999), 'The end of Meciarism', *East European Constitutional Review*, 8, 1–2, Winter-Spring.
Fish, M. Steven (1999), 'Postcommunist subversion: social science and democratization in east Europe and Eurasia', *Slavic Review*, 58, 4, Winter.
Freedom House (1990), *Freedom in the World 1989–90. Political Rights and Civil Liberties*, New York: Freedom House.
Gaber, S. (1992), 'Elections in Slovenia – April 1990', *Representation* 31, 113.
Gebethner, Stanislaw (1996), 'Parliamentary and electoral parties in Poland', Paul G. Lewis (ed), *Party Structure and Organization in East-Central Europe*, Cheltenham: Edward Elgar.
Gebethner, Stanislaw (1997), 'Free elections and political parties in transition to democracy in central and southeastern Europe', *International Political Science Review*, 18, 4.
Gibson, James L. (1995), 'The resilience of mass support for democratic institutions and processes in the Nascent Russian and Ukrainian democracies', Vladimir Tismaneanu (ed), *Political Culture and Civil Society in Russia and the New States of Eurasia*, Armonk: M.E. Sharpe.
Gill, Graeme (1994), *The Collapse of a Single-Party System. The Disintegration of the Communist Party of the Soviet Union*, Cambridge: Cambridge University Press.
Gill, Graeme (1998), 'Elites and the Russian transition', Graeme Gill (ed), *Elites and Leadership in Russian Politics*, Basingstoke: Macmillan.

Gill, Graeme (2000), *The Dynamics of Democratization. Elites, Civil Society and the Transition Process*, Basingstoke: Macmillan.

Gill, Graeme and Roderic Pitty (1997), *Power in the Party. The Organization of Power and Central-Republican Relations in the CPSU*, Basingstoke: Macmillan.

Gill, Graeme and Roger D. Markwick (2000), *Russia's Stillborn Democracy? From Gorbachev to Yeltsin*, Oxford: Oxford University Press.

Gleason, Gregory (1997), 'Uzbekistan: the politics of national independence', Ian Bremmer and Ray Taras (eds), *New States New Politics. Building the Post-Soviet Nations*, Cambridge: Cambridge University Press.

Golenkova, Zinaida T. (1999), 'Civil society in Russia', *Russian Social Science Review*, 40, 1, January–February.

Golosov, Grigorii V. (1999), 'From Adygeya to Yaroslavl: factors of party development in the regions of Russia, 1995–1998', *Europe-Asia Studies*, 51, 8.

Grabowski, Tomek (1996), 'The party that never was: the rise and fall of the Solidarity Citizens' Committees in Poland', *East European Politics and Societies*, 10, 2, Spring.

Grad, Franci (1997), 'The new electoral system', Danica Fink-Hafner and John R. Robbins (eds), *Making a New Nation: The Formation of Slovenia*, Aldershot: Dartmouth.

Green, Andrew T. and Carol Skalnik Leff (1997), 'The quality of democracy: mass-elite linkages in the Czech Republic', *Democratization*, 4, 4, Winter.

Greenfield, Liah (1992), *Nationalism. Five Roads to Modernity*, Cambridge: Harvard University Press.

Haggard, Stephan and Robert R. Kaufmann (1995), *The Political Economy of Democratic Transitions*, Princeton: Princeton University Press.

Haghayeghi, Mehrdad (1997), 'Politics of privatization in Kazakhstan', *Central Asian Survey*, 16, 3, September.

Hague, Rod, Martin Harrop and Shaun Breslin (1992), *Comparative Government and Politics. An Introduction*, Basingstoke: Macmillan.

Hellman, Joel S. (1998), 'Winners take all: the politics of partial reform in postcommunist transitions, *World Politics*, 50, 2, January.

Henderson, Karen and Neil Robinson (1997), *Post-Communist Politics. An Introduction*, London: Prentice-Hall.

Hendryck, Dusan (1995), 'Constitutionalism and constitutional change in Czechoslovakia', Joachim Jens Hesse and Nevil Johnson (eds), *Constitutional Policy and Change in Europe*, Oxford: Oxford University Press.

Hibbing, John R. and Samuel C. Patterson (1994), 'Public trust in the new parliaments of central and eastern Europe', *Political Studies* XLII, 4.

Higley, John, Jan Pakulski and Wlodzimierz Wesolowski (1998), 'Introduction: elite change and democratic regimes in eastern Europe', John Higley, Jan Pakulski and Wlodzimierz Wesolowski (eds), *Postcommunist Elites and Democracy in Eastern Europe*, Basingstoke: Macmillan.

Hinich, Melvin J., Valeri Khmelko and Peter J. Ordeshook (1999), 'Ukraine's 1998 parliamentary elections. A spatial analysis', *Post-Soviet Affairs*, 15, 2, April–June.

Hodge, Nathan and Sharon Weinberger (1999), 'Azerbaijan's beleaguered opposition divides under pressure', *Transitions*, 6, 2, February.

Holmes, Leslie (1986), *Politics in the Communist World*, Oxford, Oxford University Press.

Holmes, Leslie (1997), *Post-Communism. An Introduction*, Cambridge: Polity Press.

Holmes, Stephen (1992), 'Conflict between executive and parliament intensifies in Lithuania', *East European Constitutional Review*, 1, 2, Summer.

Holmes, Stephen (1993–94), 'A forum on presidential powers', *East European Constitutional Review*, 2, 4 and 3, 1, Fall–Winter.
Hosking, Geoffrey (1990), *The Awakening of the Soviet Union*, London: Heinemann.
Hovannisian, Richard G. (1967), *Armenia on the Road to Independence 1918*, Berkeley: University of California Press.
Hruby, Suzanne (1982–83), 'The Church in Poland and its political influence', *Journal of International Affairs*, 36, 2.
Hunter, Shireen T. (1997), 'Azerbaijan: searching for new neighbours', Ian Bremmer and Ray Taras (eds), *New States New Politics. Building the Post-Soviet Nations*, Cambridge: Cambridge University Press.
Huntington, Samuel P. (1991), *The Third Wave. Democratization in the Late Twentieth Century*, Norman: University of Oklahoma Press.
Huskey, Eugene (1997), 'Kyrgyzstan: the fate of political liberalization', Karen Dawisha and Bruce Parrott (eds), *Conflict, Cleavage and Change in Central Asia and the Caucasus*, Cambridge: Cambridge University Press.
Huttenbach, Henry H. (1995), 'Post-Soviet crisis and disorder in Transcaucasia. The search for regional stability and security', Vladimir Tismaneanu (ed), *Political Culture and Civil Society in Russia and the New States of Eurasia*, Armonk: M.E. Sharpe.
Hyde-Price, Adrian G.V. (1994), 'Democratization in eastern Europe. The external dimension', Geoffrey Pridham and Tatu Vanhanen (eds), *Democratization in Eastern Europe. Domestic and International Perspectives*, London: Routledge.
Ilonski, Gabriella and Sandor Kurtan (1995), 'Hungary', *European Journal of Political Research* 28, 3/4.
Innes, Abby (1997), 'The breakup of Czechoslovakia: the impact of party development on the separation of the state', *East European Politics and Societies*, 11, 3, Fall.
Ishiyama, John T. (1993), Founding elections and the development of transitional parties: the cases of Estonia and Latvia, 1990–1992', *Communist and Post-Communist Studies*, 26, 3, September.
Ishiyama, John T. (1995), 'Communist parties in transition. Structures, leaders, and processes of democratization in Eastern Europe', *Comparative Politics*, 27, 2, January.
Ishiyama, John T. (1996), 'Electoral systems experimentation in the new eastern Europe: the single transferable vote and the additional member system in Estonia and Hungary', *East European Quarterly*, 29, 4.
Janos, Andrew C. (1989), 'The politics of backwardness in continental Europe, 1780–1945', *World Politics*, xli, 3, April.
Jasiewicz, Krysztof (1993), 'Polish parties on the eve of the 1993 elections: toward fragmentation or pluralism?', *Communist and Post-Communist Studies*, 26, 4, December.
Jones, Stephen F. (1997), 'Georgia: the trauma of statehood', Ian Bremmer and Ray Taras (eds), *New States New Politics. Building the Post-Soviet Nations*, Cambridge: Cambridge University Press.
Judah, Tim (1998), 'How Milosevic hangs on', *The New York Review of Books*, 16 July.
Kadyrzhanov, Rustem (1999), 'The ruling elite of Kazakhstan in the transitional period', Vladimir Shlapentokh, Christopher Vanderpool and Boris Doktorov (eds), *The New Elite in Post-Communist Eastern Europe*, College Station: Texas A and M University Press.
Kaldor, Mary and Ivan Vejvoda (1999), 'Democratization in central and east European countries: an overview', Mary Kaldor and Ivan Vejvoda (eds), *Democratization in Central and Eastern Europe*, London: Pinter.

Kaldor, Mary and Ivan Vejvoda (eds) (1999), *Democratization in Central and Eastern Europe*, London: Pinter.
Kaplan, Cynthia S. (1995), 'Political culture in Estonia. The impact of two traditions on political development', Vladimir Tismaneanu (ed), *Political Culture and Civil Society in Russia and the New States of Eurasia*, Armonk: M.E. Sharpe.
Karatnycky, Adrian, Alexander Motyl and Boris Shor (1997), *Nations in Transit 1997. Civil Society, Democracy and Markets in East Central Europe and the Newly Independent States*, New Brunswick: Transaction Publishers.
Karl, Terry Lynn and Philippe C. Schmitter (1995), 'From an iron curtain to a paper curtain: grounding transitologists or students of postcommunism?', *Slavic Review*, 54, 4, Winter.
Kaser, Michael (1997), 'Economic transition in six central Asian economies', *Central Asian Survey*, 16, 1, March.
Kaser, Michael (1997), 'Privatization and agrarian reform in Caucasian economies', *Central Asian Survey*, 16, 2, June.
Kask, Peet (1996), 'Institutional development of the parliament of Estonia', David M. Olson and Philip Norton (eds), *The New Parliaments of Central and Eastern Europe*, London: Frank Cass.
Khazanov, Anatoly M. (1995), 'The ethnic problems of contemporary Kazakhstan', *Central Asian Survey*, 14, 2.
Kiss, Yudit (1994), 'Privatization paradoxes in east central Europe', *East European Politics and Societies*, 8, 1, Winter.
Kitschelt, Herbert (1992), 'The formation of party systems in east central Europe', *Politics and Society*, 20, 1, March.
Kitschelt, Herbert (1995), 'Formation of party cleavages in post-communist democracies: theoretical propositions', *Party Politics*, 1, 4, October.
Kitschelt, Herbert (1995), *Party Systems in East Central Europe. Consolidation or Fluidity?*, Glasgow: University of Strathclyde, Centre for the Study of Public Policy, Studies in Public Policy No.241.
Klingemann, Hans-Dieter and Dieter Fuchs (eds) (1995), *Beliefs in Government. Volume 1. Citizens and the State*, Oxford: Oxford University Press.
Kolarova, Rumyana and Dimitr Dimitrov (1996), 'The roundtable talks in Bulgaria', Jon Elster (ed), *The Roundtable Talks and the Breakdown of Communism*, Chicago: University of Chicago Press.
Kopecky, Petr (1996), 'Parties in the Czech parliament: from transformative towards arena type of parliament', Paul G. Lewis (ed), *Party Structure and Organization in East Central Europe*, Cheltenham: Edward Elgar.
Korbonski, Andrzej (1984), 'Poland', Teresa Rakowska-Harmstone (ed), *Communism in Eastern Europe*, Manchester: Manchester University Press.
Kosto, Pal and Boris Tsilevich (1997), 'Patterns of nation-building and political integration in a bifurcated postcommunist state: ethnic aspects of parliamentary elections in Latvia', *East European Politics and Societies*, 11, 2, Spring.
Kovrig, Bennett (1984), 'Hungary', Teresa Rakowska-Harmstone (ed), *Communism in Eastern Europe*, Manchester: Manchester University Press.
Krickus, Richard J. (1997), 'Democratization in Lithuania', Karen Dawisha and Bruce Parrott (eds), *The Consolidation of Democracy in East Central Europe*, Cambridge: Cambridge University Press.

Kroupa, Ales and Tomas Kostelecky (1996), 'Party organization and structure at national and local level in the Czech Republic since 1989', Paul G. Lewis (ed), *Party Structure and Organization in East Central Europe*, Cheltenham: Edward Elgar.
Kullberg, Judith S. and William Zimmerman (1999), 'Liberal elites, socialist masses, and problems of Russian democracy', *World Politics*, 51, 3, April.
Kuusela, Kimmo (1994), 'The founding electoral systems in Eastern Europe, 1989–91', Geoffrey Pridham and Tatu Vanhanen (eds), *Democratization in Eastern Europe. Domestic and international perspectives*, London: Routledge.
Kuzio, Taras (1995), 'The 1994 parliamentary elections in Ukraine', *The Journal of Communist Studies and Transition Politics*, 11, 4, December.
Lane, David and Cameron Ross (1999), *The Transition from Communism to Capitalism. Ruling Elites from Gorbachev to Yeltsin*, Basingstoke: Macmillan.
Lang, David Marshall (1962), *A Modern History of Georgia*, London: Weidenfeld and Nicolson.
'Latvia' (1994), *East European Constitutional Review*, 3, 2, Spring.
Leff, Carol Skalnik (1999), 'Democratization and disintegration in multinational states: the breakup of the communist federations', *World Politics*, 51, 2, January.
Lewytzkyj, Borys (1984), *Politics and Society in Soviet Ukraine 1953–1980*, Edmonton: Canadian Institute of Ukrainian Studies.
Lieberman, Ira W., Stilpon S. Nestor and Raj M. Desai (1997), *Between State and Market. Mass Privatization in Transition Economies*, Washington: The World Bank.
Lijphart, Arend (1992), 'Democratization and constitutional choices in Czecho-Slovakia, Hungary and Poland 1989–91', *Journal of Theoretical Politics* 4, 2.
Lijphart, Arend (ed) (1992), *Parliamentary versus Presidential Government*, Oxford: Oxford University Press.
Lijphart, Arend and Carlos Waisman (eds) (1996), *Institutional Design in New Democracies. Eastern Europe and Latin America*, Boulder: Westview Press.
Linz, Juan J. (1975), 'Totalitarian and authoritarian regimes', Fred I. Greenstein and Nelson W. Polsby (eds), *Handbook of Political Science. Volume 3. Macropolitical Theory*, Reading/MA: Addison-Wesley Pub. Co.
Linz, Juan J. (1990), 'The perils of presidentialism', *The Journal of Democracy*, 1, 1, Winter.
Linz, Juan J. (1990), 'The virtues of parliamentarism', *The Journal of Democracy*, 1, 4, Fall.
Linz, Juan J. and Arturo Valenzuela (1994), *The Failure of Presidential Democracy: Comparative Perspectives*, Baltimore: The Johns Hopkins University Press.
Linz, Juan J. and Alfred Stepan (1978), *The Breakdown of Democratic Regimes*, Baltimore: The Johns Hopkins University Press.
Linz, Juan J. and Alfred Stepan (1996), *Problems of Democratic Transition and Consolidation. Southern Europe, South America, and Post-Communist Europe*, Baltimore: The Johns Hopkins University Press.
Lomax, Bill (1993), 'Hungary', Stephen Whitefield (ed), *The New Institutional Architecture of Eastern Europe*, Basingstoke: Macmillan.
Lomax, Bill (1994), 'Obstacles to the development of democratic politics', *The Journal of Communist Studies and Transition Politics*, 10, 3, September.
Lomax, Bill (1996), 'The structure and organization of Hungary's political parties', Paul G. Lewis (ed), *Party Structure and Organization in East Central Europe*, Cheltenham: Edward Elgar.

Lomax, Bill (1997), 'The strange death of 'civil society' in post-communist Hungary', *The Journal of Communist Studies and Transition Politics*, 13, 1, March.

Lomax, Bill (1999), 'The 1998 elections in Hungary: third time lucky for the Young Democrats', *The Journal of Communist Studies and Transition Politics*, 15, 2, June.

Lovenduski, Joni and Jean Woodall (1987), *Politics and Society in Eastern Europe*, London: Macmillan.

Lowenhardt, John (ed) (1998), 'Party politics in post-communist Russia, *The Journal of Communist Studies and Transition Politics*, Special Issue, 14, 1–2, March–June.

Luebbert, Gregory (1991), *Liberalism, Fascism or Social Democracy. Social Classes and the Political Origins of Regimes in Interwar Europe*, Oxford: Oxford University Press.

Lukashuk, Alexander (1993), 'The new draft constitution of Belarus: a shaky step toward the rule of law', *East European Constitutional Review*, 2, 1, Winter.

McAllister, Ian and Stephen White (1994), *Political Participation in Postcommunist Russia. Voting, Activism, and the Potential for Mass Protest*, Glasgow: University of Strathclyde, Centre for the Study of Public Policy, Studies in Public Policy No.223.

McAllister, Ian, Stephen White and Olga Kryshtanovskaia (1997), 'Voting and party support in the December 1995 Duma elections', *The Journal of Communist Studies and Transition Politics*, 13, 1, March.

MacFarlane, S. Neil (1998), 'Democratization, nationalism and regional security in the southern Caucasus', *Government and Opposition*, 32, 3.

McGregor, James P. (1996), 'Constitutional factors in politics in post-communist central and eastern Europe', *Communist and Post-Communist Studies*, 29, 2, June.

Mahr, Alison and John Nagle (1995), 'Resurrection of the successor parties and democratization in east central Europe', *Communist and Post-Communist Studies* 28, 4, December.

Mainwaring, Scott (1993), 'Presidentialism, multipartism and democracy: the difficult combination', *Comparative Political Studies*, 26, 2, July.

Maliutin, M.V. (1988), 'Neformaly v perestroike: opyt i perspektivy', Iu. Afanas'ev (ed), *Inogo ne dano*, Moscow: Progress.

Malova, Darina and Daniva Sivakova (1996), 'The National Council of the Slovak Republic: between democratic transition and national state-building', David M. Olson and Philip Norton (eds), *The New Parliaments of Central and Eastern Europe*, London: Frank Cass.

Markovich, Stephen S. (1998), 'Democracy in Croatia: views from the opposition', *East European Quarterly*, xxxii, 1, March.

Markwick, Roger D. (1996), 'A discipline in transition? From Sovietology to "transitology"', *The Journal of Communist Studies and Transition Politics*, 12, 3, September.

Marody, Mia (1995), 'Three stages of party system emergence in Poland', *Communist and Post-Communist Studies*, 28, 2, June.

Marples, David R. (1993), 'Belarus: the illusion of stability', *Post-Soviet Affairs*, 9, 3, July-September.

Mason, David J., Daniel N. Nelson and Bohdan M. Sklarski (1991), 'Apathy and the birth of democracy: the political struggle', *East European Politics and Societies* 5, 2, Spring.

Mastnak, Tomaz (1990), 'Civil society in Slovenia: from opposition to power', *Studies in Comparative Communism*, XXIII, 3/4, Autumn/Winter.

Mateju, Petr and Blanka Rehakova (1997), 'Turning left or class realignment? Analysis of the changing relationship between class and party in the Czech Republic, 1992–96', *East European Politics and Societies*, 11, 3, Fall.

Mathernova, Katarina (1993), 'Czecho?Slovakia: constitutional disappointments', A.E. Dick Howard (ed), *Constitution Making in Eastern Europe*, Washington: Woodrow Wilson Center Press.
Matlock, Jack E. Jr (2000), 'The nowhere nation', *The New York Review of Books*, 24 February.
Michta, Andrew A. (1997), 'Democratic consolidation in Poland after 1989', Karen Dawisha and Bruce Parrott (eds), *The Consolidation of Democracy in East-Central Europe*, Cambridge: Cambridge University Press.
Migranian, A.M. (1989), 'Dolgii put' k evropeiskomu domu', *Novyi mir*, 7.
Mihalisko, Kathleen J. (1997), 'Belarus: retreat to authoritarianism', Karen Dawisha and Bruce Parrott (eds), *Democratic Changes and Authoritarian Reactions in Russia, Ukraine, Belarus and Moldova*, Cambridge: Cambridge University Press.
Mihut, Liliana (1994), 'The emergence of political pluralism in Romania', *Communist and Post-Communist Studies*, 27, 4.
Millard, Frances (1994), 'The Polish parliamentary election of September 1993', *Communist and Post-Communist Studies*, 27, 3.
Millard, Frances (1994), 'The shaping of the Polish party system, 1989–93', *East European Politics and Societies*, 8, 3, Fall.
Miller, Nicholas J. (1997), 'A failed transition: the case of Serbia', Karen Dawisha and Bruce Parrott (eds), *Politics, Power and the Struggle for Democracy in South-East Europe*, Cambridge: Cambridge University Press.
Miller, William L., Stephen White and Paul Heywood (1998), *Values and Political Change in Postcommunist Europe*, Basingstoke: Macmillan.
Miszlivetz, Ferenc (1997), 'Participation and transition: can the civil society project survive in Hungary', *The Journal of Communist Studies and Transition Politics*, 13, 1, March.
Mitchell, B.R. (1976), *European Historical Statistics 1750–1970*, New York: Columbia University Press.
Mitev, Petar-Emil (1997), 'The party manifestos for the Bulgarian 1994 elections', *The Journal of Communist Studies and Transition Politics*, 13, 1, March.
Mladenova, Zoya and James Angresano (1997), 'Privatization in Bulgaria', *East European Quarterly*, XXX, 4, January.
Moser, Robert G. (1997), 'The Impact of Parliamentary Electoral Systems in Russia', *Post-Soviet Affairs* 13, 3, July–September.
Moser, Robert G. (1999), 'Electoral systems and the number of parties in postcommunist states', *World Politics*, 51, 3, April.
Motyl, Alexander and Bohdan Krawchenko (1997), 'Ukraine: from empire to statehood', Ian Bremmer and Ray Taras (eds), *New States New Politics. Building the Post-Soviet Nations*, Cambridge: Cambridge University Press.
Muiznicks, Nils (1997), 'Latvia: restoring a state, rebuilding a nation', Ian Bremmer and Ray Taras (eds), *New States New Politics. Building the Post-Soviet Nations*, Cambridge: Cambridge University Press.
Nagle, John (1997), 'Ethnos, demos and democratization: a comparison of the Czech Republic, Hungary and Poland', *Democratization*, 4, 2, Summer.
Neformal'naia Rossiia. O neformal'nykh politizirovannykh dvizheniiakh i gruppakh v RSFSR (opyt spravochnika), (1990), Moscow: Molodaia gvardiia.
Nelson, Daniel N. (1990), 'Romania', *Electoral Studies*, 9, 4.
Nissman, David (1997), 'Turkmenistan: just like old times', Ian Bremmer and Ray Taras (eds), *New States New Politics. Building the Post-Soviet Nations*, Cambridge: Cambridge University Press.

Bibliography

Nodel, Emmanuel (1963), *Estonia: Nation on the Anvil*, New York: Bookman Associates Inc.
Norris, Pippa (ed) (1999), *Critical Citizens. Global Support for Democratic Government*, Oxford: Oxford University Press.
Oates, Sarah (1998), 'Party platforms: towards a definition of the Russian political spectrum', *The Journal of Communist Studies and Transition Politics*, 14, 1 and 2, March–June.
Ochs, Michael (1997), 'Turkmenistan: the quest for stability and control', Karen Dawisha and Bruce Parrott (eds), *Conflict, Cleavage and Change in Central Asia and the Caucasus*, Cambridge: Cambridge University Press.
O'Donnell, Guillermo and Philippe C. Schmitter (1986), *Transitions from Authoritarian Rule. Tentative Conclusions about Uncertain Democracies*, Baltimore: The Johns Hopkins University Press.
O'Donnell, Guillermo, Philippe C. Schmitter and Laurence Whitehead (eds) (1986), *Transitions from Authoritarian Rule. Prospects for Democracy*, Baltimore: The John Hopkins University Press.
Offe, Claus (1991), 'Capitalism by democratic design? Democratic theory facing the triple transition in East Central Europe', *Social Research*, 58, 4.
Offe, Claus (1996), *Varieties of Transition. The East European and East German Experience*, Cambridge: Polity Press.
Olcott, Martha Brill (1997), 'The growth of political participation in Kazakstan' (sic), Karen Dawisha and Bruce Parrott (eds), *Conflict, Cleavage and Change in Central Asia and the Caucasus*, Cambridge: Cambridge University Press.
Olcott, Martha Brill (1997), 'Kazakhstan: pushing for Eurasia', Ian Bremmer and Ray Taras (eds), *New States New Politics. Building the Post-Soviet Nations*, Cambridge: Cambridge University Press.
Olson, David M. (1993), 'Dissolution of the state: political parties and the 1992 election in Czechoslovakia', *Communist and Post-Communist Studies*, 26, 3.
Olson, David M. (1993), 'Compartmentalized competition: the managed transitional election system of Poland', *Journal of Politics* 55, 2.
Olson, David M. (1997), 'The experience of the Czech Republic', Karen Dawisha and Bruce Parrott (eds), *The Consolidation of Democracy in East Central Europe*, Cambridge: Cambridge University Press.
OSCE, Office for Democratic Institutions and Human Rights, 'The Republic of Tajikistan. Elections to the Parliament 27 February 2000. Final report', Warsaw: OSCE, 17 May 2000.
Osiatynski, Wiktor (1996), 'The roundtable talks in Poland', Jon Elster (ed), *The Roundtable Talks and the Breakdown of Communism*, Chicago, University of Chicago Press.
Owen, Thomas C. (1981), *Capitalism and Politics in Russia. A Social History of the Moscow Merchants*, Cambridge: Cambridge University Press.
Palairet, Michael (1995), 'Rural Serbia in the light of the census of 1863', *The Journal of European Economic History*, 24, 1, Spring.
Paloczolay, Peter (1993), 'The new Hungarian constitutional state: challenges and perspectives', A.E. Dick Howard (ed), *Constitution Making in Eastern Europe*, Washington: Woodrow Wilson Center Press.
Pano, Nicholas (1997), 'The process of democratization in Albania', Karen Dawisha and Bruce Parrott (eds), *Politics, Power and the Struggle for Democracy in South-East Europe*, Cambridge: Cambridge University Press.

'Parliamentary and municipal elections in Montenegro', A report prepared by the staff of the Commission on Security and Cooperation in Europe, August 1998.

Perlmutter, Amos (1981), *Modern Authoritarianism. A Comparative Institutional Analysis*, New Haven: Yale University Press.

Perry, Duncan M. (1997), 'The Republic of Macedonia: finding its way', Karen Dawisha and Bruce Parrott (eds), *Politics, Power and the Struggle for Democracy in South-East Europe*, Cambridge: Cambridge University Press.

Pinder, John (1994), 'The European community and democracy in central and eastern Europe', Geoffrey Pridham, Eric Herring and George Sanford (eds), *Building Democracy? The International Dimension of Democratisation in Eastern Europe*, London: Leicester University Press.

Plakans, Andrejs (1997), 'Democratization and political participation in postcommunist societies: the case of Latvia', Karen Dawisha and Bruce Parrott (eds), *The Consolidation of Democracy in East Central Europe*, Cambridge: Cambridge University Press.

'Poland has a new constitution as conflict between two chambers of parliament continues' (1992), *East European Constitutional Review*, 1, 3, Fall.

Polonsky, Antony (1975), *The Little Dictators. The History of Eastern Europe Since 1918*, London: Routledge & Kegan Paul.

Pridham, Geoffrey (ed) (1991), *Encouraging Democracy: The International Context of Regime Transition in Southern Europe*, Leicester: Leicester University Press.

Pridham, Geoffrey (1999), 'Complying with the European Union's democratic conditionality: transnational party linkages and regime change in Slovakia, 1993–1998' *Europe-Asia Studies* 51, 7.

Prizel, Ilya (1997), 'Ukraine between proto-democracy and "soft" authoritarianism', Karen Dawisha and Bruce Parrott (eds), *Democratic Changes and Authoritarian Reactions in Russia, Ukraine, Belarus and Moldova*, Cambridge: Cambridge University Press.

Przeworski, Adam (1991), *Democracy and the Market. Political and Economic Reforms in Eastern Europe and Latin America*, Cambridge: Cambridge University Press.

Przeworski, Adam (1993), 'Economic reforms, public opinion, and political institutions: Poland in the Eastern European perspective', Luiz Carlos Bresser Pereira, Jose Maria Maravall and Adam Przeworski, *Economic Reforms in New Democracies. A Social Democratic Approach*, Cambridge: Cambridge University Press.

Przeworski, Adam, Michael Alvarez, Jose Antonio Cheibub and Fernando Limongi (1996), 'What makes democracies endure?', *The Journal of Democracy*, 7, 1, January.

Pusic, Verna (1994), 'Dictatorships with democratic legitimacy: democracy versus nation', *East European Politics and Societies*, 8, 3, Fall.

Rady, Martyn (1994), 'The 1994 Hungarian general election', *Representation* 32, 119.

Ramet, Sabrina Petra (1997), 'Democratization in Slovenia: the second stage', Karen Dawisha and Bruce Parrott (eds), *Politics, Power, and the Struggle for Democracy in South-East Europe*, Cambridge: Cambridge University Press.

Rapaczynski, Andrzej (1993), 'Constitutional politics in Poland: a report on the Constitutional Commission of the Polish Parliament', A.E. Dick Howard (ed), *Constitution Making in Eastern Europe*, Washington: Woodrow Wilson Center Press.

Raun, Toivo U. (1987), *Estonia and the Estonians*, Stanford: Hoover Institution Press.

Raun, Toivo U. (1997), 'Democratization and political development in Estonia, 1987–96', Karen Dawisha and Bruce Parrott (eds), *The Consolidation of Democracy in East Central Europe*, Cambridge: Cambridge University Press.

Raun, Toivo U. (1997), 'Estonia: independence redefined', Ian Bremmer and Ray Taras (eds), *New States New Politics. Building the Post-Soviet Nations*, Cambridge: Cambridge University Press.
Reisinger, William R. (1997), 'Choices facing the builders of a liberal democracy', Robert D. Grey (ed), *Democratic Theory and Post-Communist Change*, Upper Saddle River: Prentice Hall.
Reisinger, William M., Arthur H. Miller and Vicki L. Hesli (1998), 'Ideological divisions and party-building prospects in post-Soviet Russia', Matthew Wyman, Stephen White and Sarah Oates (eds), *Elections and Voters in Post-Communist Russia*, Cheltenham: Edward Elgar.
Reitz, John (1997), 'Progress in building institutions for the rule of law in Russia and Poland', Robert D. Grey (ed), *Democratic Theory and Post-Communist Change*, Upper Saddle River: Prentice Hall.
Remington, Thomas (1990), 'Regime change in communist states', *Soviet Economy*, 6, 1990.
Remington, Thomas F. (1997), 'Democratization and the new political order in Russia', Karen Dawisha and Bruce Parrott (eds), *Democratic Changes and Authoritarian Reactions in Russia, Ukraine, Belarus and Moldova*, Cambridge: Cambridge University Press.
Remmer, Karen L. (1985), 'Redemocratization and the impact of authoritarian rule in Latin America', *Comparative Politics*, 17, 3, April.
Remnick, David (1996), 'The war for the Kremlin', *The New Yorker*, 22 July.
Roeder, Philip G. (1994), 'Varieties of post-Soviet authoritarian regimes', *Post-Soviet Affairs* 10, 1, January–March.
Roeder, Philip G. (1999), 'Peoples and states after 1989: the political costs of incomplete national revolutions', *Slavic Review*, 58, 4, Winter.
Rona-Tas, Akos (1991), 'The selected and the elected: the making of the new parliamentary elite in Hungary', *East European Politics and Societies*, 5, 3, Fall.
Rona-Tas, Akos (1994), 'The first shall be last? Entrepreneurship and communist cadres in the transition from socialism', *American Journal of Sociology*, 100, 1, July.
Roper, Steven D. (1995), 'The Romanian party system and the catch-all party phenomenon', *East European Quarterly*, xxviii, 4, January.
Roper, Steven D. (1998), 'From opposition to government coalition: unity and fragmentation within the democratic convention of Romania', *East European Quarterly*, xxi, 4, January.
Rose, Richard and Christian Haerpfer (1992), *New Democracies Between State and Market. A Baseline Report on Public Opinion*, Glasgow: University of Strathclyde, Centre for the Study of Public Policy, Studies in Public Policy No.204.
Rose, Richard and Christian Haerpfer (1993), *Adapting to Transformation in Eastern Europe. New Democracies Barometer II*, Glasgow: University of Strathclyde, Centre for the Study of Public Policy, Studies in Public Policy No.212.
Rose, Richard, Irine Boeva and Viacheslav Shironin (1993), *How Russians Are Coping With Transition: New Russia Barometer II*, Glasgow: University of Strathclyde, Centre for the study of Public Policy, Studies in Public Policy No.216.
Rose, Richard and Christian Haerpfer (1994), *New Russia Barometer III: The Results*, Glasgow: University of Strathclyde, Centre for the Study of Public Policy, Studies in Public Policy No.228.

Rose, Richard and Christian Haerpfer (1994), *New Democracies Barometer III: Learning from What is Happening*, Glasgow: University of Strathclyde, Centre for the Study of Public Policy, Studies in Public Policy No.230.
Rose, Richard (1995), *Mobilizing Demobilized Voters in Post Communist Societies*, Glasgow: University of Strathclyde, Centre for the Study of Public Policy, Studies in Public Policy No.246.
Rose, Richard, William Mishler and Christian Haerpfer (1995), *Democracy and Its Alternatives. Understanding Post-Communist Societies*, Cambridge: Polity Press.
Rose, Richard (1995), *New Baltics Barometer II: A Survey Study*, Glasgow: University of Strathclyde, Centre for the Study of Public Policy, Studies in Public Policy No.251.
Rose, Richard and Evgeny Tikhomirov (1995), *Trends in the New Russia Barometer, 1992–1995*, Glasgow: University of Strathclyde, Centre for the Study of Public Policy, Studies in Public Policy No.256.
Rose, Richard (1996), *New Russia Barometer V: Between Two Elections*, Glasgow: University of Strathclyde, Centre for the Study of Public Policy, Studies in Public Policy No.260.
Rose, Richard (1996), *New Russia Barometer VI: After the Presidential Election*, Glasgow: University of Strathclyde, Centre for the Study of Public Policy, Studies in Public Policy No.272.
Rose, Richard and Christian Haerpfer (1996), *New Democracies Barometer IV: A 10-Nation Survey*, Glasgow: University of Strathclyde, Centre for the Study of Public Policy, Studies in Public Policy No.262.
Rose, Richard, Evgeny Tikhomirov and William Mishler (1997), 'Understanding multi-party choice: the 1995 Duma election', *Europe-Asia Studies*, 49, 5.
Rose, Richard, Vilmorus, Baltic Data House and Saar Poll (1997), *New Baltic Barometer III: A Survey Study*, Glasgow: University of Strathclyde, Centre for the Study of Public Policy, Studies in Public Policy No.284.
Rose, Richard, Neil Munro and Tom Mackie (1998), *Elections in Central and Eastern Europe Since 1990*, Glasgow: University of Strathclyde, Centre for the Study of Public Policy, Studies in Public Policy No.300.
Rothschild, Joseph (1974), *East Central Europe Between the Two World Wars*, Seattle: University of Washington Press.
Rothschild, Joseph (1993), *Return to Diversity. A Political History of East Central Europe Since World War II*, Oxford: Oxford University Press.
Rupnik, Jacques (1979), 'Dissent in Poland, 1968–78: the end of revisionism and the rebirth of civil society', Rudolf L. Tokes (ed), *Opposition in Eastern Europe*, London: Macmillan.
Rusinow, Denison (1977), *The Yugoslav Experiment 1948–1974*, Berkeley: University of California Press.
Sabaliunas, Leonas (1972), *Lithuania in Crisis. Nationalism to Communism 1939–1940*, Bloomington: Indiana University Press.
Sadurski, Wojciech (1996), 'Freedom of the press in postcommunist Poland', *East European Politics and Societies*, 10, 3, Fall.
Sajo, Andras (1996), 'The roundtable talks in Hungary', Jon Elster (ed), *The Roundtable Talks and the Breakdown of Communism*, Chicago: University of Chicago Press.
Sakwa, Richard (1999), *Postcommunism*, Buckingham: Open University Press.
Saltmarshe, Douglas (1996), 'Civil society and sustainable development in Central Asia', *Central Asian Survey* 15, 3/4, December.
Schmidt, Fabian (1996), 'Election fraud sparks protest', *Transition* 2, 13, 28 June.

Schmitter, Philippe C. and Terry Lynn Karl (1994), 'The conceptual travels of transitologists and consolidologists: how far to the east should they attempt to go?', *Slavic Review*, 53, 1, Spring.
Schopflin, George (1979), 'Opposition and para-opposition: critical currents in Hungary, 1968–1978', Rudolf L. Tokes (ed), *Opposition in Eastern Europe*, London: Macmillan.
Schopflin, George (1990), 'The political traditions of eastern Europe', *Daedalus*, 119, Winter.
Schopflin, George (1993), 'The road from post-communism', Stephen Whitefield (ed), *The New Institutional Architecture of Eastern Europe*, London: Macmillan.
Sedaitis, Judith B. and Jim Butterfield (eds) (1991), *Perestroika from below*, Boulder: Westview Press.
Sedov, Leonid (1998), 'Consistency and change among Russian voters', Matthew Wyman, Stephen White and Sarah Oates (eds), *Elections and Voters in Post-communist Russia*, Cheltenham: Edward Elgar.
Sekelj, Laszlo (2000), 'Parties and elections: the Federal Republic of Yugoslavia – change without transformation', *Europe-Asia Studies*, 52, 1, January.
Seleny, Anna (1999), 'Old political rationalities and new democracies. Compromise and confrontation: Hungary and Poland', *World Politics*, 51, 4, July.
Senn, Alfred Erich (1997), 'Lithuania: rights and responsibilities of independence', Ian Bremmer and Ray Taras (eds), *New States New Politics. Building the Post-Soviet Nations*, Cambridge: Cambridge University Press.
Seton-Watson, Hugh (1945), *Eastern Europe Between the Wars, 1918–1941*, London: Cambridge University Press.
Seton-Watson, Hugh (1967), *The Russian Empire 1801–1917*, Oxford: Oxford University Press.
Seton-Watson, Hugh (1970), 'The political system of eastern Europe between the wars', Stephen Fischer-Galati (ed), *Man, State, and Society in East European History*, New York: Praeger.
Shafir, Michael (1985), *Romania. Politics, Economics and Society*, London: Frances Pinter.
Sharpe, M.E. and Thomas C. Owen (1981), *Capitalism and Politics in Russia. A Social History of the Moscow Merchants*, Cambridge: Cambridge University Press.
Shoup, Paul (1989), 'Crisis and reform in Yugoslavia', *Daedalus*, 79, Spring.
Shugart, M. and J. Carey (1992), *Presidents and Assemblies: Constitutional Design and Electoral Dynamics*, Cambridge: Cambridge University Press.
Simechka, Milan (1984), *The Restoration of Order. The Normalization of Czechoslovakia 1969–1976*, London: Verso.
Simon, Janos (1997), 'Electoral systems and democracy in central Europe, 1990–1994', *International Political Science Review*, 18, 4, October.
Simon, Maurice D. (1996), 'Institutional development of Poland's post-communist Sejm: a comparative analysis', David M. Olson and Philip Norton (eds), *The New Parliaments of Central and Eastern Europe*, London: Frank Cass.
Skilling H.G. (1976), *Czechoslovakia's Interrupted Revolution*, Princeton: Princeton University Press.
Skilling, H.G. (1981), *Charter 77 and Human Rights in Czechoslovakia*, London: Allen and Unwin.
Skilling, H.G. (1985), 'Independent currents in Czechoslovakia', *Problems of Communism*, 34, 1, January–February.
Skilling, H.G. (1989), *Samizdat and an Independent Society in Central and Eastern Europe*, Columbus: Ohio State University Press.

Slider, Darrell (1997), 'Democratization in Georgia', Karen Dawisha and Bruce Parrott (eds), *Conflict, Cleavage and Change in Central Asia and the Caucasus*, Cambridge: Cambridge University Press.
'Slovakia' (1993–94), *East European Constitutional Review*, 2, 4 and 3, 1, Fall-Winter.
'Slovakia' (1994), *East European Constitutional Review*, 3, 2, Spring.
Smith, Graham S. (1999), *The Post-Soviet States. Mapping the Politics of Transition*, London: Arnold.
Smith, Graham and Andrew Wilson (1997), 'Rethinking Russia's post-Soviet diaspora: the potential for political mobilization in eastern Ukraine and north-east Estonia', *Europe-Asia Studies*, 49, 5.
Smith, Graham, Vivien Law, Andrew Wilson, Annette Bohr and Edward Allworth (1998), *Nation-building in the Post-Soviet Borderlands. The Politics of National Identities*, Cambridge: Cambridge University Press.
Sochor, Zenovia A. (1995), 'Russocentrism, regionalism, and the political culture of Ukraine', Vladimir Tismaneanu (ed), *Political Culture and Civil Society in Russia and the New States of Eurasia*, Armonk: M.E. Sharpe.
Sokolewicz, Wojciech (1995), 'The relevance of western models for constitution-building in Poland', Joachim Jens Hesse and Nevil Johnson (eds), *Constitutional Policy and Change in Europe*, Oxford: Oxford University Press.
Spravochnik po neformal'nym obshchestvennym organizatsiiam i presse (1989), Moscow: SMOT Informatsionnoe agenstvo.
Staar, Richard F. (1977), *The Communist Regimes in Eastern Europe*, Stanford: Hoover Institution Press.
Stan, Lavinia (1995), 'Romanian privatization: assessment of the first five years', *Communist and Post-Communist Studies*, 28, 4, December.
Staniszkis, Jadwiga (1984), *Poland's Self-Limiting Revolution*, Princeton: Princeton University Press.
Staniszkis, Jadwiga (1991), 'Political capitalism in Poland', *East European Politics and Societies*, 5, 1, Winter.
Stark, David and Laszlo Bruszt (1998), *Postsocialist Pathways. Transforming Politics and Property in East Central Europe*, Cambridge: Cambridge University Press.
'Statement of the National Democratic Institute (NDI) International Observer Delegation to Azerbaijan's November 5, 2000 Parliamentary Elections', Baku, November 7, 2000.
Stavljanin, Dragan (1999), 'Brothers at arm's length', *Transitions*, 6, 2, February.
Stepan, Alfred and Cindy Skach (1993), 'Constitutional frameworks and democratic consolidation: parliamentarianism and presidentialism', *World Politics*, 46, 1, October.
Stokes, Gale (1979), 'The social origins of east European politics', Daniel Chirot (ed), *The Origins of Backwardness in Eastern Europe. Economics and Politics from the Middle Ages Until the Early Twentieth Century*, Berkeley: University of California Press.
Suny, Ronald Grigor (1988), *The Making of the Georgian Nation*, Bloomington: Indiana University Press.
Szarvas, Laszlo (1994), 'Parties and party factions in the Hungarian parliament', *The Journal of Communist Studies and Transition Politics*, 10, 3, September.
Szczerbiak, Aleks (1998), 'Electoral politics in Poland: the parliamentary elections of 1997', *The Journal of Communist Studies and Transition Politics*, 14, 3, September.
Szczerbiak, Aleks (1999), 'Interests and values: Polish parties and their electorates', *Europe-Asia Studies*, 51, 8.

Szelenyi, Ivan, Eva Fodor and Eric Hanley (1997), 'Left turn in post-communist politics: bringing class back in?', *East European Politics and Societies*, 11, 1, Winter.

Taagepera, Rein (1990), 'The Baltic states', *Electoral Studies* 9, 4.

Terry, Sarah Meiklejohn (1993), 'Thinking about post-communist transitions: how different are they?', *Slavic Review*, 52, 2, Summer.

Toka, Gabor (1997), *Political Parties and Democratic Consolidation in East Central Europe*, Glasgow: University of Strathclyde, Centre for the Study of Public Policy, Studies in Public Policy No.279.

Tokes, Rudolf L. (1984), 'Hungarian reform imperatives', *Problems of Communism*, 33, 5, September–October.

Tokes, Rudolf L. (1996), *Hungary's Negotiated Revolution. Economic Reform, Social Change and Political Succession, 1957–1990*, Cambridge: Cambridge University Press.

Tokes, Rudolf L. (1997), 'Party politics and political participation in postcommunist Hungary', Karen Dawisha and Bruce Parrott (eds), *The Consolidation of Democracy in East-Central Europe*, Cambridge: Cambridge University Press.

Tolz, Vera (1990), *The USSR's Emerging Multiparty System*, New York: Praeger.

'Turkish party in Bulgaria allowed to Continue' (1992), *East European Constitutional Review*, 1, 2, Summer.

'Ukraine' (1993), *East European Constitutional Review*, 2, 2, Spring.

'Ukraine', (1993–94), *East European Constitutional Review* 2, 4, and 3, 1, Fall–Winter.

'Ukraine' (1995), *East European Constitutional Review*, 4, 1, Winter.

Urban, Michael E. (1989), *An Algebra of Soviet Power: Elite Circulation in the Belorussian Republic 1966–1986*, Cambridge: Cambridge University Press.

Urban, Michael E. (1992), 'Boris El'tsin, democratic Russia and the campaign for the Russian presidency', *Soviet Studies*, 44, 2.

Urban, Michael and Vladimir Gel'man (1997), 'The development of political parties in Russia', Karen Dawisha and Bruce Parrott (eds), *Democratic changes and authoritarian reactions in Russia, Ukraine, Belarus and Moldova*, Cambridge: Cambridge University Press.

Uzelak, Gordana (1998), 'Franjo Tudjman's nationalist ideology', *East European Quarterly*, xxxi, 4, January.

Vachudova Milada Anna and Tim Snyder (1997), 'Are transitions transitory? Two types of political change in Eastern Europe since 1989', *East European Politics and Societies*, 11, 1, Winter.

Varrak, Toomas (2000), 'Estonia: crisis and 'pre-emptive' authoritarianism', Dirk Berg-Schlosser and Jeremy Mitchell (eds) (2000), *Conditions of Democracy in Europe, 1919–1939. Systematic Case Studies*, Basingstoke: Macmillan.

Waller, Michael and Georgi Karasimeonov (1996), 'Party organization in post-communist Bulgaria', Paul G. Lewis (ed), *Party Structure and Organization in East Central Europe*, Cheltenham: Edward Elgar.

Weigle, Marcia A. and Jim Butterfield (1992), 'Civil society in reforming communist regimes. The logis of emergence', *Comparative Politics*, 25, 1, October.

Welsh, Helga A. (1994), 'Political transition processes in central and eastern Europe', *Comparative Politics*, 26, 4, July.

White, Anne (1999), *Democratization in Russia Under Gorbachev 1985–91. The Birth of a Voluntary Sector*, Basingstoke: Macmillan.

White, Stephen (1983), 'What is a communist system?', *Studies in Comparative Communism*, xvi, 4.

White Stephen, Graeme Gill and Darrell Slider (1993), *The Politics of Transition: Shaping a Post-Soviet Future, Cambridge:* Cambridge University Press.
White, Stephen, Richard Rose and Ian McAllister (1997), *How Russia Votes*, Chartham/ NJ: Chatham House.
Whitefield, Stephen and Geoffrey Evans (1996), 'Support for democracy and political opposition in Russia, 1993–1995', *Post-Soviet Affairs*, 12, 3, July.
Whitefield, Stephen and Geoffrey Evans (1998), 'Electoral politics in eastern Europe: social and ideological influences on partisanship in post-communist societies', John Higley, Jan Pakulski and Wlodzimierz Wesolowski (eds), *Postcommunist Elites and Democracy in Eastern Europe*, Basingstoke: Macmillan.
Whitefield, Stephen and Geoffrey Evans (1998), 'The emerging structure of partisan divisions in Russian politics', Matthew Wyman, Stephen White and Sarah Oates (eds), *Elections and Voters in Post-communist Russia*, Cheltenham: Edward Elgar.
Whitehead, Laurence (ed) (1996), *The International Dimensions of Democratization. Europe and the Americas*, Oxford: Oxford University Press.
Wightman, Gordon (1990), 'Czechoslovakia', *Electoral Studies*, 9, 4.
Wilder, Paul (1993), 'The Estonian elections of 1992: proportionality and party organization in a new democracy', *Representation* 31, 116.
Wilson, Andrew (1995), 'Parties and presidents in Ukraine and Crimea, 1994', *The Journal of Communist Studies and Transition Politics*, 11, 4, December.
Wilson, Andrew and Artur Bilous (1993), 'Political parties in Ukraine', *Europe-Asia Studies*, 45, 4.
Wilson, Andrew and Sarah Birch (1999), 'Voting stability, political gridlock: Ukraine's 1998 parliamentary elections', *Europe-Asia Studies*, 51, 6.
Wolchik, Sharon L. (1993), 'The Repluralization of Politics in Czechoslovakia', *Communist and Post-Communist Studies*, 26, 4, December.
Wolchik, Sharon L. (1997), 'Democratization and political participation in Slovakia', Karen Dawisha and Bruce Parrott (eds), *The Consolidation of Democracy in East-Central Europe*, Cambridge: Cambridge University Press.
Wyman, Matthew (1997), *Public Opinion in Post-Communist Russia*, Basingstoke: Macmillan.
Wyman, Matthew, Bill Miller, Stephen White and Paul Heywood (1995), 'Parties and voters in the elections', Peter Lentini (ed), *Elections and Political Order in Russia. The implications of the 1993 elections to the Federal Assembly*, Budapest: Central European University Press.
Zaprudnik, Jan and Michael Urban (1997), 'Belarus: from statehood to empire', Ian Bremmer and Ray Taras (eds), *New States New Politics. Building the Post-Soviet Nations*, Cambridge: Cambridge University Press.
Zifcak, Spencer (1995), 'The battle over presidential power in Slovakia', *East European Constitutional Review*, 4, 3, Summer.
Zubek, Voytek (1991), 'The Polish communist elite and the petty entrepreneurs', *East European Quarterly*, XXV, 3, September.
Zubek, Voytek (1993), 'The fragmentation of Poland's political party system', *Communist and Post-Communist Studies*, 26, 1, March.
Zubek, Voytek (1995), 'The phoenix out of the ashes: the rise to power of Poland's post-communist SdRP', *Communist and Post-Communist Studies* 28, 3, September.

Index

Abdullojonov, A. 78
Abkhazia 49, 50, 51, 168, 214
Adolet (Uzbekistan) 81
Agrarian Democratic Party (Romania) 157
Agrarian Party (Belarus) 74
Agrarian Party (Russia) 153, 155
Ahmeti, V. 34
Akaev, A. 61, 62, 63
Albania 2, 19, 20, 31, 34–5, 82, 95–6, 106, 113, 114, 115, 117, 124, 125, 126, 127, 160, 161, 162, 163, 170, 171, 175, 176, 180, 183–4, 190, 191, 192, 223
Albanian Party for Democratic Prosperity 65
Albanian Party of Labour 34
Alia, R. 34, 96
Aliev, H. 70–2
All-Georgian Union of Revival 147
Alliance of Free Democrats (Hungary) 28, 29, 134, 136, 137, 182
Alliance of Reform Forces (Macedonia) 154
Alliance of Young Democrats (Hungary) 28, 29, 30, 134, 136, 137, 182
Antall, J. 29, 30
Armenia 19, 20, 40, 51–3, 70, 82, 96, 98–9, 100, 104, 106, 107, 113, 114, 115, 117, 124, 125, 126, 127, 160, 161, 162, 167, 168, 172, 175, 176, 180, 185, 188, 223
Armenian Revolutionary Federation 52, 148, 168
Association for the Republic (Czech R.) 141
Association of Workers of Slovakia 142, 169

Authentic Democratic Party (Latvia) 145
Azat (Kazakhstan) 75
Azerbaijan 9, 19, 20, 51, 65, 82, 99, 103–4, 107, 111, 113, 114, 115, 117, 124, 125, 126, 127, 160, 161, 162, 167, 172, 173, 175, 176, 180, 188, 190, 192, 223
Azeri Popular Front 70–2, 217

Bafi, Y. 34
Barbalet, P. 48
Belarus 9, 11, 19, 55, 58, 65, 72–5, 82, 103, 104, 107, 111, 113, 114, 115, 117, 118, 119, 120, 121–2, 123, 124, 125, 126, 127, 161, 162, 169, 172, 173, 175, 176, 179, 180, 181, 190, 192, 194, 223
Berisha, S. 34, 35, 139
Better Estonia 146
Birkavs, V. 44
Birlik (Uzbekistan) 80
Bloc for a Democratic and Prosperous Moldova 147
Bosnia-Herzegovina 53, 63, 68, 114, 160, 161, 168, 187, 204
bourgeoisie 89, 91, 92, 93, 95, 98, 100, 102, 103
Braghis, D. 48
Brazauskas, A. 46
Brezhnev, L. 99, 101
Bulatovic, M. 69
Bulgaria 2, 19, 20, 31–4, 35, 64, 82, 95–6, 105, 106, 113, 114, 115, 117, 118, 119, 120, 121–2, 123, 124, 125, 126, 127, 161, 162, 163, 170, 171, 175, 176, 178, 180, 183–4, 192, 223
Bulgarian Agrarian National Union 138, 139

Index 265

Bulgarian Business Bloc 138, 139
Bulgarian Communist Party 31, 32
Bulgarian Socialist Party 31, 32, 33, 137, 138, 139, 140
Bunce, V. 11–13, 190–1, 198, 200–6

capitalism 11, 87–8
Ceausescu, N. 66, 104, 169, 190
Centre Alliance (Poland) 134
Centre Movement (Lithuania) 145
Centre Union (Lithuania) 46
Chechnya 57, 164
Chernomyrdin, V. 56, 152
Chornovil, V. 59
Christian Democratic Movement (Slovakia) 141, 142, 143
Christian Democratic National Peasants' Party (Romania) 66
Christian Democratic Party (Lithuania) 145, 149
Christian Democratic Party (Slovenia) 153, 154
Christian Democratic People's Party (Hungary) 28, 29, 134, 137
Christian Democratic People's Party (Moldova) 147
Christian Democratic Popular Front Alliance (Moldova) 47, 48, 146, 151
Christian Democratic Union (Czech R.) 141, 143, 233
Christian Democratic Union (Lithuania) 46
Christian Democratic Union-People's Party (Czech R.) 141
Citizens' Union of Georgia 50, 51, 147, 151
Civic Democratic Alliance (Czechoslovakia) 37
Civic Democratic Party (Czech R.) 37, 38, 140, 141, 143, 184, 185
Civic Democratic Union (Czechoslovakia) 37
Civic Forum (Czech R.) 36, 37, 141
civil society 13, 21–2, 27, 63, 83–110, 111–73, 181–93, 195, 196, 197–201
civil society forces 22–3, 24, 30, 31, 35, 40, 63, 64, 65–6, 81, 83–110, 111, 129, 133, 137, 181–93, 195, 196, 197–201
closed oligarchy 4–5, 40, 51–3, 69, 70–2, 72–5, 77–9, 82, 111, 172, 173, 192, 193
Club of Active Non-Partisans (Czechoslovakia) 37
Coalition Party and Rural Union (Estonia) 146, 150

Committee for the Defence of the Unjustly Prosecuted (Czechoslovakia) 94
Committee for National Salvation (Georgia) 49
Common Choice (Slovakia) 142
Commonwealth of Independent States 47, 48, 58, 72, 215
communism 1, 16, 88–9, 90–1, 91–2, 92–3, 93–4, 95–6, 97–8, 99, 100, 101, 102, 103, 104–5, 108–9, 202
Communist Party of Armenia 148
Communist Party of Bohemia and Moravia 141, 143, 233
Communist Party of Moldova 48, 49, 147
Communist Party of the Russian Federation 56–7, 152, 153, 155
Communist Party of Ukraine 57, 58, 59, 60, 153, 155, 167
Community of Sovereign Republics 74
Confederation for Independent Poland 134
Confederation of Trade Unions (Kazakhstan) 75
Constantinescu, E. 66, 67
constitution 13, 16, 19; Albania 34, 35; Armenia 51–2; Azerbaijan 71; Belarus 72–3; Bulgaria 31; Croatia 53, 54; Czech R. 38; Czechoslovakia 37; Estonia 42; FRY 68; Georgia 50; Hungary 19, 28–9; Kazakhstan 75–6; Kyrgyz R. 61, 62; Latvia 19, 44, 165; Lithuania 45, 46; Macedonia 65, 168; Moldova 47, 48; Poland 26, 27; Romania 66; Russia 55–6; Slovakia 37; Slovenia 64; Tajikistan 78, 79; Turkmenistan 79; Ukraine 60; Uzbekistan 80
Constitutional Assembly (Armenia) 52
Constitutional Court 29, 33, 48, 63, 73, 74, 76, 163
Country of Law (Armenia) 148
Country People's Party (Estonia) 146
Crimea 58, 167
Croatia 19, 20, 40, 53–4, 63, 82, 96, 100, 106, 107, 111, 113, 114, 115, 117, 118, 119, 120, 121–2, 125, 126, 127, 128, 160, 161, 162, 168, 170, 171, 172, 173, 175, 176, 178, 180, 185, 186–7, 188, 192, 196, 223
Croatian Democratic Community 53, 54, 148, 151, 186–7
Croatian Electoral Alliance 54
Croatian Farmers' Party 148

266 *Index*

Croatian Party of Rights 148
Croatian People's Party 148, 151
Croatian Social Liberal Party 148, 151
Czech Republic 2, 19, 35, 36, 38, 39, 40, 82, 113, 114, 115, 117, 118, 119, 120, 121–2, 123, 124, 125, 126, 127, 161, 162, 170, 171, 175, 176, 177, 178, 180, 184–5, 200, 223
Czechoslovakia 12, 21, 35–8, 90, 91, 93–4, 95, 96, 106, 108, 109, 128, 140, 175, 177, 184

Demirchian, K. 52
demobilisation 116–23, 200
democracy 1–6, 7, 11, 14, 17, 23–34, 35, 38, 40, 44–6, 63–4, 67, 82, 111, 114, 170–1, 173, 178–9, 180, 189, 191, 194
Democratic Agrarian Party of Moldova 48, 146, 151
Democratic Alliance of Albanians (Montenegro) 158
Democratic Alternative (Macedonia) 154
Democratic Bloc (Ukraine) 57
Democratic Convention (Romania) 66, 67, 157, 190
Democratic Convention of Moldova 147, 151
Democratic Forum (Hungary) 134
Democratic Left Alliance (Poland) 26, 27, 134, 135
Democratic Movement for Serbia 157, 158
Democratic National Salvation Front (Romania) 66, 67, 157
Democratic Opposition of Serbia 158
Democratic Opposition of Slovenia 63–4, 153, 155
Democratic Party (Georgia) 147
Democratic Party (Latvia) 145
Democratic Party (Poland) 25
Democratic Party (Romania) 67, 157
Democratic Party (Serbia) 68, 69, 158
Democratic Party (Slovakia) 141
Democratic Party (Tajikistan) 79
Democratic Party of Albania 34–5, 132, 138, 139, 140, 183
Democratic Party of Montenegrin Socialists 69, 158
Democratic Party of Pensioners (Slovenia) 154
Democratic Party of Russia 153
Democratic Party of Slovenia 153, 154
Democratic Party of Turkmenistan 79–80
Democratic Russia 55, 153

Democratic Russia's Choice 152
Democratic Social Party (Romania) 67
Democratic Social Pole of Romania 67, 157
Democratic Union (Slovakia) 39
Democratic Union of Albanians (Montenegro) 158
Democratic Union of Slovakia 142
democratisation 1–2, 13, 16, 197–9
Djukanovic, M. 69
Draskovic, V. 69
Druc, M. 47
Dubcek, A. 93

economic reform 12, 13, 14, 24, 37, 55, 174–9, 183, 184, 185, 186, 191, 201
Elchibey, A. 70, 71, 167–8
elections 2, 4, 5, 6, 8, 9, 10, 11–14, 19, 20, 23, 31, 131; Albania 8, 23, 34–5; Armenia 8, 10, 51–3; Azerbaijan 8, 10, 70–2; Belarus 8, 10, 72–5; Bulgaria 7, 23, 32, 33; Croatia 8, 53–4; Czech R. 7, 38; Czechoslovakia 23, 36; Estonia 8, 40–3; founding elections 11, 12–13, 23; FRY 8, 10; Georgia 8, 49–51; Hungary 7, 23; Kazakhstan 8, 10, 75–7; Kyrgyz R. 10, 61–3; Latvia 8, 43–4; Lithuania 7, 45–6; Macedonia 8, 64–5; Moldova 8, 99–100; Montenegro 8, 10, 69; Poland 7, 23, 24, 25; Romania 8, 66–7; Russia 8, 55–7; Serbia 10, 68–9; Slovakia 8, 38–40; Slovenia 7, 23, 63–4; Tajikistan 8, 10, 77–9; Turkmenistan 8, 10, 79–80; Ukraine 8, 57–61; Uzbekistan 8, 10, 80–1; Yugoslavia 23.
Electoral Action for Lithuania's Poles 163
Electoral Bloc Braghis Alliance (Moldova) 147
electoral fraud 6, 10, 19, 34, 51, 52, 54, 56, 57, 59, 60, 62, 63, 65, 67, 68, 69, 70, 71, 74, 76, 77, 78, 79, 80 81, 140, 190
electoral systems 17–18, 26, 28, 31, 73; PR 18, 19, 25–6, 28, 29, 31, 33, 34, 42, 43, 45, 48, 50, 52, 56, 59, 60, 64, 66, 71, 73, 134, 138, 141–2, 145, 146, 147, 154, 157, 158, 207; SMC 18, 19–20, 28, 29, 31, 45, 50, 52, 56, 59, 64, 71, 73, 75, 138, 148, 153, 154
11 October Bloc (Georgia) 147
elites 12, 15, 20, 21, 22, 23, 24, 28, 31, 38, 39, 55, 65, 99, 107, 129–30, 131, 172, 181–93, 195–201, 214

Equal Rights Movement (Latvia) 145
Erk (Uzbekistan) 80
Estonia 6, 7, 11, 19, 40–3, 82, 96–8, 106, 107, 108, 109, 113, 114, 115, 117, 118, 123, 124, 125, 126, 127, 161, 162, 164–6, 167, 170, 171, 175, 176, 178, 180, 185–6, 187, 188, 200, 223
Estonian Centre Party 146, 150
Estonian National Independence Party 42, 146
Estonian Reform Party 146, 150
ethnic democracy 4, 5, 6–7, 11, 14, 82, 111, 114–15, 171–2, 180, 191, 193, 194, 196
ethnic issue 31–3, 37–9, 41–4, 46–9, 51, 139, 140–4, 155, 160–70, 184, 187
European Union 178–9, 200
Euroleft Coalition (Bulgaria) 138

façade democracy 4, 5, 6–7, 11, 14, 82, 111, 114–15, 171–2, 180, 191, 192, 193, 194, 196
Farmers' Union (Latvia) 44, 149
Fatherland Progress (Uzbekistan) 81
Fatherland-All Russia 152
Fatherland Union (Estonia) 42, 146, 150
Fish, S. 13–14
Fokin, V. 58
For a Better Life (Montenegro) 158
For Fatherland and Freedom (Latvia) 145
Fourth Power (Estonia) 146
Free Democrats (Czech R.) 143
Free Estonia 41
Free Georgia 49
Freedom Union (Czech R.) 141
Freedom Union (Poland) 134, 135
FRY 9, 19, 20, 65, 67–9, 82, 107, 113, 114, 162, 168, 175, 190

Gaidar, E. 56
Gamsakhurdia, Z. 49, 50, 168, 192
Georgia 19, 20, 40, 49–51, 82, 96, 98–9, 100, 106, 107, 111, 113, 114, 115, 117, 124, 125, 126, 127, 160, 161, 162, 168, 172, 173, 175, 176, 179, 180, 185, 187, 188, 192, 223
Gheorgiu-Dej, G. 104
Gierek, E. 92
Gligorov, K. 65, 189
Godmanis, I. 43
Gomulka, W. 91, 92
Goncz, A. 29
Gorbachev, M. 41, 43, 45, 47, 55, 57, 61, 70, 75, 77, 99, 101, 102, 104, 164, 190, 197
Greater Romania Party 67, 156, 157, 169
Green Party (Georgia) 147
Green Party in Slovakia 141
Greens (Ukraine) 153
Greens of Slovenia 153, 154
Guseinov, P. 70
Guseinov, S. 70

Hajdari, A. 35
Havel, V. 21, 36, 38
Homeland (Poland) 134
Homeland Union (Lithuania) 46, 145, 146, 149, 150
Hoxha, E. 96
Hromada (Ukraine) 153
Hryb, M. 73
Humanist Party (Romania) 67
Hungarian Civic Party (Czechoslovakia) 37
Hungarian Coalition 39, 141, 142, 144
Hungarian Democratic Forum 28, 29, 30, 130, 136, 137, 182
Hungarian Democratic Union 132, 156, 157, 169
Hungarian Justice and Life 134
Hungarian Life and Way Party 163
Hungarian Socialist Party 29, 30, 134, 136, 137
Hungary 2, 12, 19, 20, 24, 27–31, 32, 33, 34, 36, 82, 90, 91, 92–3, 94, 95, 96, 100, 105–6, 108, 109, 113, 114, 115, 117, 118, 119, 120, 121–2, 123, 124, 125, 126, 128, 161, 162, 163, 170, 171, 175, 176, 178, 180, 182–3, 200, 202, 223
Husak, G. 94

Iliescu, I. 66–67
Independent Smallholders' Party (Hungary) 28, 29
intelligentsia 91, 92, 94, 97, 98–9, 101, 104
Internal Macedonian Revolutionary Organisation 64–5, 154, 156, 159
Iosseliani, D. 50, 51
Iskandarov, A. 77
Islamic Renaissance Party (Tajikistan) 79
Islamic Renaissance Party (Uzbekistan) 80
Ivashko, V. 57

Jaruzelski, W. 24
Joint Council of Workers' Deputies (Estonia) 41

Kadar, J. 94
Karimov, I. 80
Kazakhstan 19, 65, 75–7, 82, 103, 107, 113, 114, 115, 117, 124, 125, 126, 127, 161, 162, 169, 175, 176, 180, 190, 223
Kazhegeletin, A. 77
Kebich, V. 72, 73, 217
Khrushchev, N. 101
Klaus, V. 37, 38, 140, 177
Kocharian, R. 52
Kosovo 68, 160, 168, 184, 187
Kostunica, V. 69
Kovac, M. 39
Krajina 53, 54
Kravchuk, L. 55, 57, 58, 59, 60, 167
Kucan, M. 63, 64, 189
Kuchma, L. 58, 59, 60, 167
Kun, B. 92
Kwasniecki, A. 27
Kyrgyz Republic 19, 54, 61–3, 64, 65, 80, 82, 100, 102, 103, 104, 106, 107, 113, 114, 115, 117, 124, 125, 126, 127, 161, 162, 172, 175, 176, 180, 189, 223

Lali Badakhshan (Tajikistan) 79
Landsbergis, V. 45
Latin America 197–201
Latvia 6, 7, 11, 19, 40, 43–4, 82, 96–8, 106, 107, 108, 109, 113, 114, 115, 117, 124, 125, 126, 127, 161, 162, 165–6, 167, 170, 171, 175, 176, 178, 179, 180, 185–6, 187, 188, 200, 223
Latvian Christian Democratic Party 145
Latvian Farmers' Union 145
Latvian National Conservative Party 145
Latvian Socialist Party 145
Latvian Unity Party 145
Latvia's Way Alliance 44, 144, 145, 149
League of Communists of Croatia-Party of Democratic Change 148
League of Communists of Macedonia-Party of Democratic Reform 154, 156
League of Communists of Yugoslavia 63, 68
Liberal Alliance of Montenegro 158
Liberal Democracy (Slovenia) 153, 154, 155
Liberal Democratic Congress (Poland) 134
Liberal Democratic Party (Macedonia) 154
Liberal Democratic Party of Russia 56, 152, 153, 155, 163
Liberal Party (Macedonia) 154

Liberal Social Union (Czech R.) 141
Liberal Union (Lithuania) 46, 146
Lilov, A. 32
Lithuania 19, 20, 40, 44–6, 82, 96–8, 106, 107, 108, 109, 113, 114, 115, 117, 118, 124, 125, 126, 127, 161, 162, 163, 170, 171, 175, 176, 177, 178, 179, 180, 185, 186, 187, 188, 200, 223
Lithuanian Conservative Party 146
Lithuanian Democratic Labour Party 45–6, 145, 149–50, 186
Lucinschi, P. 46, 47, 48
Lukanov, A. 32
Lukashenka, A. 73–5, 169, 217
Luzhkov, Y. 152

Macedonia 19, 54, 64–5, 82, 100, 103, 106, 107, 113, 114, 115, 117, 125, 126, 127, 161, 162, 168, 172, 175, 176, 180, 189, 223
Makhkamov, K. 77
Majko, P. 35
Mamedov, Y. 70
Manukian, V. 52
Masaliev, A. 61, 62
Masol, V. 59, 60
Mazowiecki, T. 25, 133
Meciar, V. 7–8, 37, 38–40, 131, 140, 168–9, 171, 185
media 19, 29, 53, 54, 55, 61, 62, 68, 70, 71, 72, 73, 76, 77, 78, 79, 80–1, 108, 112–14, 121, 170–3, 184, 188, 191, 223
Meri, L. 42, 43
Miasnutian (Armenia) 53, 148
middle class 89, 91, 92, 93, 95, 97, 98, 100, 103, 104, 105
military 190–1, 192, 199–200
Milosevic, S. 53, 68–9, 131, 156, 159, 168
Mkhedrioni 50
Mladenov, P. 31, 32
Moderates (Estonia) 42, 146
Moghanu, A. 47
Moldavian Popular Front 46, 47, 164
Moldova 8, 19, 40, 46–9, 82, 96, 99–100, 106, 107, 113, 114, 115, 117, 124, 125, 126, 127, 160, 161, 162, 164, 171, 175, 176, 180, 185, 187–8, 223
Montenegro 9, 20, 65, 69, 105, 111, 114, 162
Moravian Silesian Movement 141
Moroz, O. 59, 60
Moslem Democratic Party (Azerbaijan) 71

Movement for a Democratic Slovakia 37, 38–9, 140, 142, 143, 144, 168–9, 184, 185
Movement for the Reconstruction of Poland 134
Movement for Rights and Freedoms (Bulgaria) 32, 33, 138, 139, 163, 210
Muravschi, V. 47
Mutalibov, A. 70, 167

Nabiev, R. 77–8
Nagorno-Karabakh 51, 52, 70, 99, 104, 167, 168, 188
Nakhichevan 70
Nano, F. 34, 35
National Democratic Party (Kazakhstan) 75
National Democratic Party (Macedonia) 168
National Democratic Party of Georgia 147
National Democratic Union (Armenia) 148
National Front (Albania) 138
National Harmony Party (Latvia) 44, 145
National Liberal Party (Romania) 157
National Movement for Latvia 44, 145
National Progress Party (Armenia) 52
National Salvation Front (Romania) 66, 67, 157
National Unity Coalition (Montenegro) 158
nationalism 38–44, 46–9, 53, 54, 67, 68–9, 96, 97, 99, 100, 101, 102, 103, 104, 105, 109, 156, 160–70, 183, 184, 185–8
Nazarbaev, N. 75–7
New Azerbaijan Party 71, 72
New Party (Latvia) 145
New Slovenia Christian People's Party 154
New Union-Social Liberal Party (Lithuania) 46, 146
Niyazov, S. 79–80
NGOs 69, 112, 114–15, 123, 127, 128, 161, 170–3, 182, 188, 190
nomenklatura 58, 72, 127
non-democracy 4, 5, 8–11, 14, 82, 111, 180, 191, 193, 194
Non-Party Reform Bloc (Poland) 134
Novotny, A. 93
Nuri, S. 79

Ochab, E. 91
Omonia (Albania) 163

open oligarchy 4–5, 31, 34–5, 38–40, 66–7, 82, 111, 172, 189, 192
Opposition Electoral Alliance (Croatia) 148, 151
Our Home is Estonia 146, 150, 165
Our Home is Russia 56, 152, 153

Panakhov, N. 70
Pan-Armenian National Movement 51, 52
parliament 4, 5, 12, 13, 16–17, 19, 20, 24, 25, 26, 28, 29, 34, 36, 42, 45, 47, 48, 49–50, 55–6, 60, 61, 62, 63–4, 66, 73–4, 75, 76, 121, 159, 179–81, 188–9, 194
Party of Civic Understanding (Slovakia) 142
Party of Democratic Forces (Moldova) 147
Party of the Democratic Left (Slovakia) 37, 39, 141, 142, 144
Party for Democratic Prosperity (Macedonia) 154, 168
Party of Democratic Revival 63, 153, 155
Party of Popular Unity and Justice (Tajikistan) 78
Party of Romanian National Unity 169
Party of Russian Unity and Accord 153
Party of Serbian Unity 158
Party of Slovenian Youth 154
Party of Social Progress (Moldova) 48
Patiashvili, D. 51
Peace Bloc (Georgia) 147
Peasant Alliance (Poland) 134
Peasants and Intellectuals Bloc (Moldova) 146
Peasant's Party of Ukraine 153
People's Democratic Party (Ukraine) 153
People's Democratic Party of Uzbekistan 80–1
People's Movement of Ukraine 57, 189
People's Party (Latvia) 145
People's Party of Montenegro 158
People's Party of Tajikistan 78
People's Unity Union (Kazakhstan) 75
Petkovski, T. 65
plebiscitary democracy 4, 5, 40, 49–51, 53–4, 54–7, 57–61, 61–3, 82, 111, 173, 187, 188, 192, 193
Pilsudski, J. 91
Poland 2, 12, 14, 19, 21, 24–7, 28, 30, 32, 33, 34, 36, 82, 91–2, 94, 95, 96, 100, 106, 108, 109, 113, 114, 115, 117, 118, 119, 120, 121–2, 123, 124, 125, 126, 127, 128, 161, 162, 163, 170,

171, 175, 176, 177, 178, 179, 180, 182–3, 200, 223
Polish United Worker's Party 24, 25
political parties 13, 18–19, 22, 84, 90, 91, 93, 95, 97, 98, 99, 101, 104, 108, 116, 121, 129–60, 170–3, 179, 182–93; Albania 34–5, 132, 138–40, 159; Armenia 51–3, 144, 148, 151, 159, 160; Azerbaijan 70–2, 133, 156; Belarus 72–5, 133, 156; Bulgaria 31–4, 129, 137–9, 140, 159, 160; Croatia 53–4, 144, 148, 151, 159, 160; Czech R. 36–40, 140–4, 159, 160; Czechoslovakia 36–8, 129; Estonia 40–3, 144, 146, 150, 159, 160; FRY 156–8; Georgia 49–51, 144, 174, 151, 159, 160; Hungary 28–31, 133–4, 136–7, 159, 160; Kazakhstan 75–7, 133, 156; Kyrgyz R. 61–3, 133, 151, 160; Latvia 44–5, 144–5, 149, 159, 160; Lithuania 45–6, 144, 145–6, 149–50, 159, 160; Macedonia 64–5, 156, 159, 160; Moldova 144, 146–7, 150–1, 154, 159; Montenegro 69, 156–9; Poland 24–7, 129, 133–6, 137, 159, 160; Romania 66–7, 132–3, 156, 159; Russia 54–7, 131, 151–2, 153, 155, 159; Serbia 68–9, 131, 156–8, 159; Slovakia 36–40, 131, 140–4, 159, 160; Slovenia 63–4, 153–4, 155–6, 159, 160; successor party 25, 26, 32, 33, 34, 35, 38, 40, 44, 45, 46, 48, 49, 56, 59, 60, 63, 65, 68, 74, 78, 79, 132, 137, 139, 144, 146, 147, 148, 156, 157, 158, 183, 184, 185, 187; Tajikistan 73–9, 133, 156; Turkmenistan 79–80, 133, 156; Ukraine 57–61, 153, 155, 159; Uzbekistan 80–1, 133, 156
Polish Peasants' Party 26–7, 134, 135
Popov, D. 32
Popular Front (Belarus) 72, 73.
Popular Front (Estonia) 40–1, 42, 43, 146, 150
Popular Front (Latvia) 43, 144, 165
Popular Union (Bulgaria) 139
post-communism 3, 4, 5, 9, 11–14, 201–3
Poszgay, I. 28
presidency 4, 12, 13, 16–17, 19, 20, 24, 25, 26, 28, 29, 32, 33, 34, 38, 39, 42, 45, 47, 48, 49–50, 54, 55–6, 57, 58, 60, 61, 62, 63–4, 65, 66, 68–9, 72, 73, 75, 76, 77, 78, 79, 80, 121, 159, 179–81, 188–9, 194

Primakov, E. 152
privatisation 123–8, 170–3, 174–9, 183, 184, 186
Progressive Socialist Party (Ukraine) 153
Public Against Violence (Slovakia) 36, 37, 141
Putin, V. 57, 152, 172

Rakhmonov, I. 77–8
Rastokhez (Tajikistan) 79
Rebirth and Consolidation (Moldova) 48
reform communists 11, 24, 28, 29, 30, 34, 41, 54–5, 64–5, 69, 98, 101, 155, 160, 182
religion 11, 98, 99, 194
Republican Bloc (Armenia) 52, 53, 148
Republican Party (Kazakhstan) 75
Republican Party of Albania 138
Republican People's Party (Kazakhstan) 77
Right Wingers' Party (Estonia) 146
rights 2–3, 5, 6, 7, 9, 10, 39, 40, 44, 47, 80
Rights and Unity (Armenia) 148
Roeder, P. 161–2, 206
Roman, P. 66
Romania 2, 8, 12, 19, 47, 65, 66–7, 82, 96, 99, 100, 103, 104–5, 107, 111, 113, 114, 115, 117, 118, 119, 120, 121–2, 123, 124, 125, 126, 127, 128, 161, 162, 164, 169, 170, 171, 172, 173, 175, 176, 178, 180, 181, 187, 190, 191, 192, 196, 223
Romanian National Unity Party 67, 157
Round Table 20, 23, 24, 25, 28, 29, 31, 32, 33, 36, 49, 63, 182, 183, 199, 200
Rubiks, A. 43, 44
Rukh 57, 58, 59, 153
Russia 14, 19, 20, 54–7, 58, 65, 73, 74, 75, 82, 88, 90, 91, 100–1, 102, 103, 106, 107, 113, 114, 115, 117, 118, 119, 120, 121–2, 123, 124, 125, 126, 127, 160, 161, 162, 163–4, 167, 169, 170, 171–2, 175, 176, 177, 179, 180, 189–90, 223
Russian Union (Lithuania) 163
Russia's Choice 56, 152, 153
Ruutel, A. 42

Sajudis 44–6, 145, 149, 186
Sakharov, A. 21
Sangheli, A. 47, 48
Savisaar, E. 41
Schuster, R. 39,

Serbia 19, 20, 63, 65, 68–9, 105, 114, 160, 161, 162, 163, 168, 170, 172, 192, 196
Serbian Civic Alliance 68
Serbian People's Party 148
Serbian Radical Party 157, 158
Serbian Renewal Movement 68, 69, 156
Shamiram Women's Party (Armenia) 148
Sharetsky, S. 74
Shelest, P. 102
Shevardnadze, E. 49, 50, 51, 99, 151, 192
Shoigu, S. 152
Shushkevich, S. 55, 58, 72, 73
Sigua, T. 49
Slovak Democratic Coalition 39, 142
Slovak National Party 39, 141, 142-3, 169
Slovakia 7, 19, 35, 36, 37, 38–40, 67, 82, 94, 111, 113, 114, 115, 117, 118, 119, 120, 121–2, 123, 124, 125, 126, 127, 128, 161, 162, 168–9, 170, 171, 172, 173, 175, 176, 177, 178, 180, 184–5, 192, 196, 223
Slovenia 19, 54, 63–4, 65, 82, 100, 103, 106, 107, 108, 109, 113, 114, 115, 117, 118, 119, 120, 121–2, 123, 125, 126, 127, 128, 161, 162, 163, 168, 170, 171, 175, 176, 178, 180, 189, 200, 223
Slovenian National Party 154
Slovenian People's Party 153, 154
Smallholders' Party (Hungary) 163
Snegur, M. 46, 47, 48, 164, 213
Social Democracy Party of Romania 67, 157
Social Democracy of the Polish Republic 25, 26, 27, 133, 135
Social Democratic Alliance (Latvia) 145
Social Democratic Coalition (Lithuania) 46, 146, 150
Social Democratic Party (Albania) 138
Social Democratic Party (Croatia) 54, 148
Social Democratic Party (Czech R.) 38, 140, 141, 143
Social Democratic Party (Lithuania) 145, 149
Social Democratic Party (Romania) 67
Social Democratic Party (Slovenia) 153, 154
Social Democratic Party (Ukraine) 153
Social Democratic Party (Uzbekistan) 81
Social Democratic Union (Romania) 157
Social Democratic Union of Macedonia 65, 154, 156
Social Liberal Party (Croatia) 54

Socialist Labour Party (Romania) 157
Socialist Party (Latvia) 44
Socialist Party (Moldova) 146
Socialist Party of Albania 34, 35, 132, 138, 140
Socialist Party of Macedonia 154
Socialist Party of Serbia 68, 69, 156, 157, 158
Socialist Party of Slovenia 153
Socialist Party of Ukraine 59, 153
Socialist and Peasant Parties Bloc (Ukraine) 153
Socialist People's Party (Montenegro) 158
Solidarity (Poland) 12, 24–7, 92, 133, 134, 135, 182
Solidarity Electoral Alliance (Poland) 134, 135
South Ossetia 49, 50, 51, 168, 214
Southern Europe 197–201
Stamboliskii, A. 95
state 173, 181–93
Stepashin, S. 57
Stolypin, P. 89
Stoyanov, P. 33
sultanism 4, 5, 75–7, 79–80, 80–1, 82, 111, 192, 193
Symonenko, P. 60

Tajikistan 19, 65, 77–9, 82, 103, 107, 112, 113, 114, 115, 117, 124, 125, 126, 127, 160, 161, 162, 175, 176, 179, 180, 190, 223
Ter-Petrossian, L. 51, 52, 168
trade unions 24, 31, 32–3, 74, 75, 76, 84, 91, 92, 93, 95, 100, 103, 108, 112
Trajkovski, B. 65
Transdnestr 47, 48, 49, 164, 187
transitology 197–201
Tudjman, F. 53, 54, 168, 171, 186–7
Tudor, C. 67
Turkmenistan 14, 19, 65, 79–80, 82, 103, 107, 112, 113, 114, 115, 117, 124, 125, 126, 127, 161, 162, 175, 176, 180, 190, 202, 223

Ukraine 8, 19, 54, 55, 57–61, 64, 65, 75, 82, 100, 102, 103, 106, 107, 113, 114, 115, 118, 119, 120, 121–2, 123, 124, 125, 126, 127, 161, 162, 167, 172, 175, 176, 180, 181, 189, 215, 223
Ulmanis, G. 44
Union of Democratic Forces (Bulgaria) 31, 32, 33, 137, 138, 140, 163

Union of Labour (Poland) 134
Union for National Salvation (Bulgaria) 138, 139
Union for National Self-Determination (Armenia) 148
Union of Rightist Forces (Russia) 153
United List (Croatia) 54
United List (Latvia) 145, 149
United List of Social Democrats (Slovenia) 154, 155
United Peasants' Party (Poland) 25, 129
United People's Party (Estonia) 146, 165
United Tajik Opposition 79
Unity (Russia) 57, 152, 153
Unity Bloc (Georgia) 147
Unity Party of Human Rights (Albania) 138, 163
urbanisation 87, 88, 95, 96, 104, 219
USSR 2, 11, 12, 14, 21, 43, 55, 57, 58, 70, 75, 77, 79, 80, 97, 98, 101, 102, 104, 108, 186, 188, 194, 195, 197, 198, 200
Uzbekistan 19, 65, 80–1, 82, 103, 107, 112, 113, 114, 115, 117, 124, 125, 126, 127, 161, 162, 175, 176, 180, 190, 223

Vagris, Ya. 43
Vahi, T. 42
Valyas, V. 41
Vicariou, N. 67
Voronin, V. 48

Walesa, L. 24, 25, 26, 27, 38, 133
Women of Russia 153, 155
Workers' Association of Slovakia 39
Workers' Defence Committee (Poland) 92

Yabloko 152, 153, 155
Yeltsin, B. 55, 56, 57, 58
Yugoslavia 53, 67, 68, 100, 103, 105, 160, 186, 190, 191, 194, 198

Zhelev, Z. 32, 33
Zhirinovsky, V. 131, 151
Zhirinovsky Bloc (Russia) 153
Zhivkov, T. 31, 96, 163
Ziuganov, G. 57